ACT

Math
Prep Course

JEFF KOLBY

DERRICK VAUGHN

Nova Press

Additional educational titles from Nova Press (available at novapress.net):

➤ **GRE Prep Course** (624 pages, includes software)

  GRE Math Bible (528 pages)

➤ **GMAT Prep Course** (624 pages, includes software)

  GMAT Math Prep Course (528 pages)

  GMAT Data Sufficiency Prep Course (422 pages)

➤ **Master The LSAT** (560 pages, includes software, and 2 official LSAT exams)

  Ace The LSAT Logic Games (504pages)

➤ **The MCAT Physics Book** (444 pages)

  The MCAT Biology Book (416 pages)

  The MCAT Chemistry Book (428 pages)

➤ **SAT Prep Course** (640 pages, includes software)

  SAT Math Bible (480 pages)

➤ **Speaking and Writing Strategies for the TOEFL® iBT:** (394 pages, includes audio CD)

➤ **Law School Basics:** A Preview of Law School and Legal Reasoning (224 pages)

➤ **Vocabulary 4000:** The 4000 Words Essential for an Educated Vocabulary (160 pages)

ISBN 1–889057–65–7

Nova Press
11659 Mayfield Avenue
Los Angeles, CA 90049

Phone: 1-800-949-6175
E-mail: info@novapress.net
Website: www.novapress.net

ABOUT THIS BOOK

If you don't have a pencil in your hand, get one now! Don't just read this book—write on it, study it, scrutinize it! In short, for the next four weeks, this book should be a part of your life. When you have finished the book, it should be marked-up, dog-eared, tattered and torn.

Although the ACT is a difficult test, it is a *very* learnable test. This is not to say that the ACT is "beatable." There is no bag of tricks that will show you how to master it overnight. You probably have already realized this. Some books, nevertheless, offer "inside stuff" or "tricks" which they claim will enable you to beat the test. These include declaring that answer-choices B, C, or D are more likely to be correct than choices A or E. This tactic, like most of its type, does not work. It is offered to give the student the feeling that he or she is getting the scoop on the test.

The ACT cannot be "beaten." But it can be mastered—through hard work, analytical thought, and by training yourself to think like a test writer. Many of the exercises in this book are designed to prompt you to think like a test writer. For example, you will find "Duals." These are pairs of similar problems in which only one property is different. They illustrate the process of creating ACT questions.

The ACT math section is not easy—nor is this book. To improve your ACT math score, you must be willing to work; if you study hard and master the techniques in this book, your score will improve—significantly.

This book will introduce you to numerous analytic techniques that will help you immensely, not only on the ACT but in college as well. For this reason, studying for the ACT can be a rewarding and satisfying experience.

To insure that you perform at your expected level on the actual ACT, you need to develop a level of mathematical skill that is greater than what is tested on the ACT. Hence, about 10% of the math problems in this book are harder than actual ACT math problems.

Although the quick-fix method is not offered in this book, about 15% of the material is dedicated to studying how the questions are constructed. Knowing how the problems are written and how the test writers think will give you useful insight into the problems and make them less mysterious. Moreover, familiarity with the ACT's structure will help reduce your anxiety. The more you know about this test, the less anxious you will be the day you take it.

CONTENTS

ORIENTATION

Format of the Math Section

The math section contains 60 multiple-choice questions and is 60 minutes long. The test measures mathematical skills typically obtained through grade 11 or 12, that is, through Trigonometry.

The questions are listed roughly in ascending order of difficulty. The section typically begins with Pre-Algebra questions, and progresses to Elementary Algebra, then to Intermediate Algebra, and then finally to Trigonometry. But there can be considerable overlap in these categories.

Section	Type	Time
Math	60 Multiple-choice Questions	60 minutes

Here are the approximate percentages of the content categories on the math section:

1) Pre-Algebra/Elementary Algebra (40%)
2) Intermediate Algebra/Coordinate Geometry (30%)
3) Trigonometry/Plane Geometry (23%)

The math section is always the second section of the test.

Scoring the ACT

There are four scores recorded:

1) Total score (based on all 60 questions)
2) Elementary Algebra (based on 24 questions)
3) Intermediate Algebra (based on 18 questions)
4) Trigonometry (based on 18 questions)

The total score is reported on a scale from 1 to 36, with 36 being the highest score possible. And the sub-scores are reported on a scale from 1 to 18, with 18 being the highest score possible. The average total score is about 21. Do not become discouraged if you "blow" a few questions. The average ACT student misses more than half of the questions on the math section.

In addition to the scaled score, you will be assigned a percentile ranking, which gives the percentage of students with scores below yours. For instance, if you score in the 80th percentile, then you will have scored better than 80 out of every 100 test takers. Both the total score and the sub-scores are given a percentile ranking.

Calculators

You may use a calculator on the test, but all problems can be solved without a calculator. Be careful not to overuse the calculator; it can slow you down. But if you are accustomed to using a calculator for even simple calculations, you should continue doing so.

You can use any standard scientific or graphing calculator. You cannot use advanced calculators, such as ones with built-in computer algebra systems (for example, TI-89). You also cannot use the calculator in a cell phone or any other electronic communication device.

Skipping and Guessing

Some questions on the ACT are rather hard, and it is a time-pressured test. So, you may not be able to finish the section.

Often students become obsessed with a particular problem and waste valuable time trying to solve it. To get a top score, learn to cut your losses and move on because all questions are worth the same number of points, regardless of difficulty level. So, often it is best to skip the hardest questions and concentrate on the easy and medium ones.

There is no guessing penalty on the ACT. So, if you skip a question or do not finish the section in time, be sure to mark an answer for every question.

The Structure of this Book

Because it can be rather dull to spend a lot of time reviewing basic math before tackling full-fledged ACT problems, the first few chapters present techniques that don't require much foundational knowledge of mathematics. Then, in latter chapters, review is introduced as needed.

Directions and Reference Material

Be sure you understand the directions below so that you do not need to read or interpret them during the test.

Directions

Solve each problem and decide which one of the choices given is best. Fill in the corresponding oval on your answer sheet.

Do not linger over problems that take too much time. Solve as many as you; then return to the others in the time you have left for this test.

You are permitted to use a calculator on this test. You may use your calculator for any problems you choose, but some problems may best be done without a calculator.

Notes

Unless otherwise stated, all of the following should be assumed.

1. Illustrative figures are NOT necessarily drawn to scale.

2. Geometric figures lie in a plane.

3. The word *line* indicates a straight line.

4. The word *average* indicates arithmetic mean.

Here is some reference material. You will not see this information on the actual test.

Reference Information

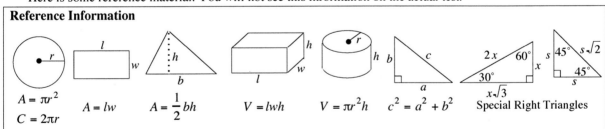

$A = \pi r^2$
$C = 2\pi r$ $A = lw$ $A = \dfrac{1}{2}bh$ $V = lwh$ $V = \pi r^2 h$ $c^2 = a^2 + b^2$ Special Right Triangles

The number of degrees of arc in a circle is 360.
The sum of the measures in degrees of the angles of a triangle is 180.

Part One
MATH

Substitution

Substitution is a very useful technique for solving ACT math problems. It often reduces hard problems to routine ones. In the substitution method, we choose numbers that have the properties given in the problem and plug them into the answer-choices. A few examples will illustrate.

Example 1:   If n is an odd integer, which one of the following is an even integer?

  (A) n^3
  (B) $n/4$
  (C) $2n + 3$
  (D) $n(n + 3)$
  (E) $\sqrt{n}$

We are told that n is an odd integer. So choose an odd integer for n, say, 1 and substitute it into each answer-choice. Now, n^3 becomes $1^3 = 1$, which is not an even integer. So eliminate (A). Next, $n/4 = 1/4$ is not an even integer—eliminate (B). Next, $2n + 3 = 2 \cdot 1 + 3 = 5$ is not an even integer—eliminate (C). Next, $n(n + 3) = 1(1 + 3) = 4$ is even and hence the answer is possibly (D). Finally, $\sqrt{n} = \sqrt{1} = 1$, which is not even—eliminate (E). The answer is (D).

➤   When using the substitution method, be sure to check every answer-choice because the number you choose may work for more than one answer-choice. If this does occur, then choose another number and plug it in, and so on, until you have eliminated all but the answer. This may sound like a lot of computing, but the calculations can usually be done in a few seconds.

Example 2:   If n is an integer, which of the following CANNOT be an even integer?

  (A) $2n + 2$
  (B) $n - 5$
  (C) $2n$
  (D) $2n + 3$
  (E) $5n + 2$

Choose n to be 1. Then $2n + 2 = 2(1) + 2 = 4$, which is even. So eliminate (A). Next, $n - 5 = 1 - 5 = -4$. Eliminate (B). Next, $2n = 2(1) = 2$. Eliminate (C). Next, $2n + 3 = 2(1) + 3 = 5$ is not even—it *may* be our answer. However, $5n + 2 = 5(1) + 2 = 7$ is not even as well. So we choose another number, say, 2. Then $5n + 2 = 5(2) + 2 = 12$ is even, which eliminates (E). Thus, choice (D), $2n + 3$, is the answer.

Example 3:   If $\dfrac{x}{y}$ is a fraction greater than 1, then which of the following must be less than 1?

(A) $\dfrac{3y}{x}$ (B) $\dfrac{x}{3y}$ (C) $\sqrt{\dfrac{x}{y}}$ (D) $\dfrac{y}{x}$ (E) y

We must choose x and y so that $\dfrac{x}{y} > 1$. So choose $x = 3$ and $y = 2$. Now, $\dfrac{3y}{x} = \dfrac{3 \cdot 2}{3} = 2$ is greater than 1, so eliminate (A). Next, $\dfrac{x}{3y} = \dfrac{3}{3 \cdot 2} = \dfrac{1}{2}$, which is less than 1—it may be our answer. Next, $\sqrt{\dfrac{x}{y}} = \sqrt{\dfrac{3}{2}} > 1$; eliminate (C). Now, $\dfrac{y}{x} = \dfrac{2}{3} < 1$. So it too may be our answer. Next, $y = 2 > 1$; eliminate (E). Hence, we must decide between answer-choices (B) and (D). Let $x = 6$ and $y = 2$. Then $\dfrac{x}{3y} = \dfrac{6}{3 \cdot 2} = 1$, which eliminates (B). Therefore, the answer is (D).

Problem Set A:

Solve the following problems by using substitution.

1.   If n is an odd integer, which of the following must be an even integer?

   (A) $n/2$
   (B) $4n + 3$
   (C) $2n$
   (D) n^4
   (E) $\sqrt{n}$

2.   If x and y are perfect squares, then which of the following is <u>not</u> necessarily a perfect square?

   (A) x^2
   (B) xy
   (C) $4x$
   (D) $x + y$
   (E) x^5

3.   If y is an even integer and x is an odd integer, which of the following expressions could be an even integer?

   (A) $3x + \dfrac{y}{2}$
   (B) $\dfrac{x + y}{2}$
   (C) $x + y$
   (D) $\dfrac{x}{4} - \dfrac{y}{2}$
   (E) $x^2 + y^2$

4.   If $0 < k < 1$, then which of the following must be less than k?

   (A) $\dfrac{3}{2}k$
   (B) $\dfrac{1}{k}$
   (C) $|k|$
   (D) $\sqrt{k}$
   (E) k^2

5. Suppose you begin reading a book on page h and end on page k. If you read each page completely and the pages are numbered and read consecutively, then how many pages have you read?

    (A) $h + k$
    (B) $h - k$
    (C) $k - h + 2$
    (D) $k - h - 1$
    (E) $k - h + 1$

6. If m is an even integer, then which of the following is the sum of the next two even integers greater than $4m + 1$?

    (A) $8m + 2$
    (B) $8m + 4$
    (C) $8m + 6$
    (D) $8m + 8$
    (E) $8m + 10$

7. If x^2 is even, which of the following must be true?

    I. x is odd.
    II. x is even.
    III. x^3 is odd.

    (A)   I only
    (B)   II only
    (C)   III only
    (D)   I and II only
    (E)   II and III only

8. Suppose x is divisible by 8 but not by 3. Then which of the following CANNOT be an integer?

    (A) $x/2$
    (B) $x/4$
    (C) $x/6$
    (D) $x/8$
    (E) x

9. If p and q are positive integers, how many integers are larger than pq and smaller than $p(q + 2)$?

    (A)   3
    (B) $p + 2$
    (C) $p - 2$
    (D) $2p - 1$
    (E) $2p + 1$

10. If x and y are prime numbers, then which one of the following cannot equal $x - y$?

    (A)   1
    (B)   2
    (C)   13
    (D)   14
    (E)   20

11. If x is an integer, then which of the following is the product of the next two integers greater than $2(x + 1)$?

    (A) $4x^2 + 14x + 12$
    (B) $4x^2 + 12$
    (C) $x^2 + 14x + 12$
    (D) $x^2 + x + 12$
    (E) $4x^2 + 14x$

12. If the integer x is divisible by 3 but not by 2, then which one of the following expressions is NEVER an integer?

    (A) $\dfrac{x+1}{2}$

    (B) $\dfrac{x}{7}$

    (C) $\dfrac{x^2}{3}$

    (D) $\dfrac{x^3}{3}$

    (E) $\dfrac{x}{24}$

13. If both x and y are positive even integers, then which of the following expressions must also be even?

    I. y^{x-1}

    II. $y-1$

    III. $x/2$

    (A)   I only
    (B)   II only
    (C)   III only
    (D)   I and III only
    (E)   I, II, and III

14. Which one of the following is a solution to the equation $x^4 - 2x^2 = -1$?

    (A)   0
    (B)   1
    (C)   2
    (D)   3
    (E)   4

15. If $x \neq 3/4$, which one of the following will equal -2 when multiplied by $\dfrac{3-4x}{5}$?

    (A) $\dfrac{5-4x}{4}$

    (B) $\dfrac{10}{3-4x}$

    (C) $\dfrac{10}{4x-3}$

    (D) $\dfrac{3-4x}{5}$

    (E) $\dfrac{4x-3}{10}$

Answers and Solutions to Problem Set A

1.   Choose $n = 1$. Then $n/2 = 1/2$, which is not even—eliminate (A). Next, $4n + 3 = 4 \cdot 1 + 3 = 7$, which is not even—eliminate (B). Next, $2n = 2 \cdot 1 = 2$ which is even and may therefore be the answer. Next, both (D) and (E) equal 1, which is not even. Hence, the answer is (C).

2.   Choose $x = 4$ and $y = 9$. Then $x^2 = 4^2 = 16$, which is a perfect square. (Note, we cannot eliminate x^2 because it may not be a perfect square for another choice of x.) Next, $xy = 4 \cdot 9 = 36$ which is a perfect square. Next, $4x = 4 \cdot 4 = 16$, which is a perfect square. Next, $x + y = 4 + 9 = 13$, which is <u>not</u> a perfect square. Hence, the answer is (D).

3.   Choose $x = 1$ and $y = 2$. Then $3x + \dfrac{y}{2} = 3 \cdot 1 + \dfrac{2}{2} = 4$, which is even. The answer is (A). Note: We don't need to check the other answer-choices because the problem asked for the expression that *could be* even. Thus, the first answer-choice that turns out even is the answer.

4.   Choose $k = \dfrac{1}{4}$. Then $\dfrac{3}{2}k = \dfrac{3}{2} \cdot \dfrac{1}{4} = \dfrac{3}{8} > \dfrac{1}{4}$; eliminate (A). Next, $\dfrac{1}{k} = \dfrac{1}{1/4} = 4 > \dfrac{1}{4}$; eliminate (B). Next, $|k| = \left|\dfrac{1}{4}\right| = \dfrac{1}{4}$; eliminate (C). Next, $\sqrt{k} = \sqrt{\dfrac{1}{4}} = \dfrac{1}{2} > \dfrac{1}{4}$; eliminate (D). Thus, by process of elimination, the answer is (E).

5.   Without substitution, this is a hard problem. With substitution, it's quite easy. Suppose you begin reading on page 1 and stop on page 2. Then you will have read 2 pages. Now, merely substitute $h = 1$ and $k = 2$ into the answer-choices to see which one(s) equal 2. Only $k - h + 1 = 2 - 1 + 1 = 2$ does. (Verify this.) The answer is (E).

6.   Suppose $m = 2$, an even integer. Then $4m + 1 = 9$, which is odd. Hence, the next even integer greater than 9 is 10. And the next even integer after 10 is 12. Now, $10 + 12 = 22$. So look for an answer-choice which equals 22 when $m = 2$.
     Begin with choice (A). Since $m = 2$, $8m + 2 = 18$—eliminate (A). Next, $8m + 4 = 20$—eliminate (B). Next, $8m + 6 = 22$. Hence, the answer is (C).

7.   Suppose $x^2 = 4$. Then $x = 2$ or $x = -2$. In either case, x is even. Hence, Statement I need not be true, which eliminates (A) and (D). Further, $x^3 = 8$ or $x^3 = -8$. In either case, x^3 is even. Hence, Statement III need not be true, which eliminates (C) and (E). Therefore, by process of elimination, the answer is (B).

8.   Suppose $x = 8$. Then x is divisible by 8 and is not divisible by 3. Now, $x/2 = 4$, $x/4 = 2$, $x/8 = 1$ and $x = 8$, which are all integers—eliminate (A), (B), (D), and (E). Hence, by process of elimination, the answer is (C).

9.   Let $p = 1$ and $q = 2$. Then $pq = 2$ and $p(q + 2) = 4$. This scenario has one integer, 3, greater than pq and less than $p(q + 2)$. Now, we plug $p = 1$ and $q = 2$ into the answer-choices until we find one that has the value 1. Look at choice (D): $2p - 1 = (2)(1) - 1 = 1$. Thus, the answer is (D).

10.   If $x = 3$ and $y = 2$, then $x - y = 3 - 2 = 1$. This eliminates (A). If $x = 5$ and $y = 3$, then $x - y = 5 - 3 = 2$. This eliminates (B). If $x = 17$ and $y = 3$, then $x - y = 17 - 3 = 14$. This eliminates (D). If $x = 23$ and $y = 3$, then $x - y = 23 - 3 = 20$. This eliminates (E). Hence, by process of elimination, the answer is (C).

Method II (without substitution): Suppose $x - y = 13$. Now, let x and y be distinct prime numbers, both greater than 2. Then both x and y are odd numbers since the only even prime is 2. Hence, $x = 2k + 1$, and $y = 2h + 1$, for some positive integers k and h. And $x - y = (2k + 1) - (2h + 1) = 2k - 2h = 2(k - h)$. Hence, $x - y$ is even. This contradicts the assumption that $x - y = 13$, an odd number. Hence, x and y cannot both be greater than 2. Next, suppose $y = 2$, then $x - y = 13$ becomes $x - 2 = 13$. Solving yields $x = 15$. But 15 is not prime. Hence, there does not exist prime numbers x and y such that $x - y = 13$. The answer is (C).

11. Suppose $x = 1$, an integer. Then $2(x + 1) = 2(1 + 1) = 4$. The next two integers greater than 4 are 5 and 6, and their product is 30. Now, check which of the answer-choices equal 30 when $x = 1$. Begin with (A): $4x^2 + 14x + 12 = 4(1)^2 + 14 \cdot 1 + 12 = 30$. No other answer-choice equals 30 when $x = 1$. Hence, the answer is (A).

12. The number 3 itself is divisible by 3 but not by 2. With this value for x, Choice (A) becomes $\frac{3+1}{2} = \frac{4}{2} = 2$, eliminate; Choice (C) becomes $\frac{3^2}{3} = \frac{9}{3} = 3$, eliminate; Choice (D) becomes $\frac{3^3}{3} = \frac{27}{3} = 9$, eliminate. Next, if $x = 21$, then Choice (B) becomes $\frac{21}{7} = 3$, eliminate. Hence, by process of elimination, the answer is (E).

13. If $x = y = 2$, then $y^{x-1} = 2^{2-1} = 2^1 = 2$, which is even. But $y - 1 = 2 - 1 = 1$ is odd, and $x/2 = 2/2 = 1$ is also odd. This eliminates choices (B), (C), (D), and (E). The answer is (A).

14. We could solve the equation, but it is much faster to just plug in the answer-choices. Begin with 0:

$$x^4 - 2x^2 = 0^4 - 2 \cdot 0^2 = 0 - 0 = 0$$

Hence, eliminate (A). Next, plug in 1:

$$x^4 - 2x^2 = 1^4 - 2 \cdot 1^2 = 1 - 2 = -1$$

Hence, the answer is (B).

15. If $x = 0$, then $\frac{3 - 4x}{5}$ becomes 3/5 and the answer-choices become

(A)   5/4
(B)   10/3
(C)   −10/3
(D)   3/5
(E)   −3/10

Multiplying Choice (C) by 3/5, gives $\left(\frac{3}{5}\right)\left(-\frac{10}{3}\right) = -2$. The answer is (C).

Substitution (Plugging In): Sometimes instead of making up numbers to substitute into the problem, we can use the actual answer-choices. This is called "Plugging In." It is a very effective technique, but not as common as Substitution.

Example 1:   The digits of a three-digit number add up to 18. If the ten's digit is twice the hundred's digit and the hundred's digit is 1/3 the unit's digit, what is the number?

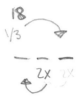

        (A)   246 = 12
        (B)   369 = 18
        (C)   531 = 9
        (D)   855 = 18
        (E)   893 = 20

First, check to see which of the answer-choices has a sum of digits equal to 18. For choice (A), $2 + 4 + 6 \neq 18$. Eliminate. For choice (B), $3 + 6 + 9 = 18$. This may be the answer. For choice (C), $5 + 3 + 1 \neq 18$. Eliminate. For choice (D), $8 + 5 + 5 = 18$. This too may be the answer. For choice (E), $8 + 9 + 3 \neq 18$. Eliminate. Now, in choice (D), the ten's digit is <u>not</u> twice the hundred's digit, $5 \neq 2 \cdot 8$. Eliminate. Hence, by process of elimination, the answer is (B). Note that we did not need the fact that the hundred's digit is 1/3 the unit's digit.

Problem Set B:

Use the method of Plugging In to solve the following problems.

1.   The ten's digit of a two-digit number is twice the unit's digit. Reversing the digits yields a new number that is 27 less than the original number. Which one of the following is the original number?

      (A)   12
      (B)   21
      (C)   43
      (D)   63
      (E)   83

2.   If $\dfrac{N+N}{N^2} = 1$, then $N =$

      (A)   1/6
      (B)   1/3
      (C)   1
      (D)   2
      (E)   3

3.   Suppose half the people on a bus exit at each stop and no additional passengers board the bus. If on the third stop the next to last person exits the bus, then how many people were on the bus?

      (A)   20
      (B)   16
      (C)   8
      (D)   6
      (E)   4

4.   The sum of the digits of a two-digit number is 12, and the ten's digit is one-third the unit's digit. What is the number?

      (A)   93 = 12
      (B)   54 = 9
      (C)   48 = 12
      (D)   39 = 12
      (E)   31

5.   If $\dfrac{x^6 - 5x^3 - 16}{8} = 1$, then x could be

      (A)   1
      (B)   2
      (C)   3
      (D)   5
      (E)   8

6.   Which one of the following is a solution to the equation $x^4 - 2x^2 = -1$?

      (A)   0
      (B)   1
      (C)   2
      (D)   3
      (E)   4

Answers and Solutions to Problem Set B

1.   The ten's digit must be twice the unit's digit. This eliminates (A), (C), and (E). Now reversing the digits in choice (B) yields 12. But $21 - 12 \neq 27$. This eliminates (B). Hence, by process of elimination, the answer is (D). $(63 - 36 = 27.)$

2.   Here we need only plug in answer-choices until we find the one that yields a result of 1. Start with 1, the easiest number to calculate with. $\frac{1+1}{1^2} = 2 \neq 1$. Eliminate (C). Next, choosing $N = 2$, we get $\frac{2+2}{2^2} = \frac{4}{4} = 1$. Hence, the answer is (D).

3.   Suppose there were 8 people on the bus—choice (C). Then after the first stop, there would be 4 people left on the bus. After the second stop, there would be 2 people left on the bus. After the third stop, there would be only one person left on the bus. Hence, on the third stop the next to last person would have exited the bus. The answer is (C).

4.   In choice (D), $3 + 9 = 12$ and $3 = \frac{1}{3} \cdot 9$. Hence, the answer is (D).

5.   We could solve the equation, but it is much faster to just plug in the answer-choices.

Begin with 1: $\frac{1^6 - 5(1)^3 - 16}{8} = \frac{1 - 5 - 16}{8} = \frac{-20}{8}$. Hence, eliminate (A).

Next, plug in 2: $\frac{2^6 - 5(2)^3 - 16}{8} = \frac{64 - 5(8) - 16}{8} = \frac{64 - 40 - 16}{8} = \frac{8}{8} = 1$. Hence, the answer is (B).

6.   Begin with 0: $x^4 - 2x^2 = 0^4 - 2 \cdot 0^2 = 0 - 0 = 0$. Hence, eliminate (A).

Next, plug in 1: $x^4 - 2x^2 = 1^4 - 2 \cdot 1^2 = 1 - 2 = -1$. Hence, the answer is (B).

Math Notes

We'll discuss many of the concepts in this chapter in depth later. But for now, we need a brief review of these concepts for many of the problems that follow.

1. **To compare two fractions, cross-multiply. The larger product will be on the same side as the larger fraction.**

   Example: Given $\dfrac{5}{6}$ vs. $\dfrac{6}{7}$. Cross-multiplying gives $5 \cdot 7$ vs. $6 \cdot 6$, or 35 vs. 36. Now 36 is larger than 35, so $\dfrac{6}{7}$ is larger than $\dfrac{5}{6}$.

2. **Taking the square root of a fraction between 0 and 1 makes it larger.**

   Example: $\sqrt{\dfrac{1}{4}} = \dfrac{1}{2}$ and $\dfrac{1}{2}$ is greater than $\dfrac{1}{4}$.

   Caution: This is not true for fractions greater than 1. For example, $\sqrt{\dfrac{9}{4}} = \dfrac{3}{2}$. But $\dfrac{3}{2} < \dfrac{9}{4}$.

3. **Squaring a fraction between 0 and 1 makes it smaller.**

   Example: $\left(\dfrac{1}{2}\right)^2 = \dfrac{1}{4}$ and $\dfrac{1}{4}$ is less than $\dfrac{1}{2}$.

4. $ax^2 \neq (ax)^2$. **In fact, $a^2 x^2 = (ax)^2$.**

   Example: $3 \cdot 2^2 = 3 \cdot 4 = 12$. But $(3 \cdot 2)^2 = 6^2 = 36$. This mistake is often seen in the following form: $-x^2 = (-x)^2$. To see more clearly why this is wrong, write $-x^2 = (-1)x^2$, which is negative. But $(-x)^2 = (-x)(-x) = x^2$, which is positive.

   Example: $-5^2 = (-1)5^2 = (-1)25 = -25$. But $(-5)^2 = (-5)(-5) = 5 \cdot 5 = 25$.

5. $\dfrac{\frac{1}{a}}{b} \neq \dfrac{1}{\frac{a}{b}}$. **In fact, $\dfrac{\frac{1}{a}}{b} = \dfrac{1}{ab}$ and $\dfrac{1}{\frac{a}{b}} = \dfrac{b}{a}$.**

   Example: $\dfrac{\frac{1}{2}}{3} = \dfrac{1}{2} \cdot \dfrac{1}{3} = \dfrac{1}{6}$. But $\dfrac{1}{\frac{2}{3}} = 1 \cdot \dfrac{3}{2} = \dfrac{3}{2}$.

6. $-(a + b) \neq -a + b$. **In fact, $-(a + b) = -a - b$.**
   Example: $-(2 + 3) = -5$. But $-2 + 3 = 1$.
   Example: $-(2 + x) = -2 - x$.

7. **Memorize the following factoring formulas—they occur frequently on the ACT.**
   A. $x^2 - y^2 = (x + y)(x - y)$
   B. $x^2 \pm 2xy + y^2 = (x \pm y)^2$
   C. $a(b + c) = ab + ac$

Problem Set C: Use the properties and techniques on the previous page to solve the following problems.

1. If $x \neq 0$, then which one of the following must be true?

   (A) $2x^2 = (2x)^2$

   (B) $2x^2 < (2x)^2$

   (C) $2x^2 \leq (2x)^2$

   (D) $2x^2 > (2x)^2$

   (E) $2x^2 \geq (2x)^2$

2. Which one of the following fractions is greatest?

   (A) 15/16
   (B) 7/9
   (C) 13/15
   (D) 8/9
   (E) 10/11

3. $1 + \dfrac{1}{1 - \dfrac{1}{2}} =$

   (A) 3
   (B) 5
   (C) 7
   (D) 9
   (E) 11

4. If the ratio of $\dfrac{1}{5}$ to $\dfrac{1}{4}$ is equal to the ratio of $\dfrac{1}{4}$ to x, then what is the value of x ?

   (A) 5/16
   (B) 4/11
   (C) 1
   (D) 4
   (E) 5

5. Which one of the following numbers is smallest?

   (A) $\left(\dfrac{7}{8}\right)^2$

   (B) $\sqrt{\dfrac{7}{8}}$

   (C) $\sqrt{\dfrac{8}{7}}$

   (D) $\left(\dfrac{8}{7}\right)^2$

   (E) $\dfrac{8}{7}$

6.   Let $a\#b$ be denoted by the expression $a\#b = -b^4$. Then $x\#(-y) =$

   (A) $-y^2$

   (B) y^4

   (C) $-y^4$

   (D) y^2

   (E) $|y|$

7. $\dfrac{1}{1-(.2)^2} =$

   (A) 25/24
   (B) 25/23
   (C) 24/15
   (D) 23/11
   (E) 21/9

8.   If $0 < x < 1$, which of the following expressions is greatest?

   (A) $\dfrac{1}{\sqrt{x}}$

   (B) $\sqrt{x}$

   (C) $\dfrac{1}{\pi}x$

   (D) x^3

   (E) x^4

9.   Which of the following are true?

I. $\dfrac{\sqrt{\frac{5}{6}}}{\left(\frac{5}{6}\right)^2} > 1$ II. $\dfrac{\sqrt{\frac{5}{6}}}{\left(\frac{6}{5}\right)^2} > 1$ III. $\sqrt{\dfrac{\sqrt{\frac{5}{6}}}{\sqrt{\frac{5}{6}}}} > 1$

   (A) I only
   (B) II only
   (C) I and II only
   (D) I and III only
   (E) I, II, and III

10.   If $x > y > 0$, which of the following are true?

I. $\dfrac{x+2}{y+2} > \dfrac{x}{y}$

II. $\dfrac{x+2}{y+2} = \dfrac{x}{y}$

III. $\dfrac{x+2}{y+2} > 1$

   (A) I only
   (B) II only
   (C) III only
   (D) I and III only
   (E) II and III only

Answers and Solutions to Problem Set C

1.   From the formula $a^2 x^2 = (ax)^2$, we see that $(2x)^2 = 2^2 \cdot x^2 = 4x^2$. Now, since $x \neq 0$, $4x^2$ is clearly larger than $2x^2$. Hence, the answer is (B).

2.   Begin by comparing 15/16 to each of the other answer-choices. Cross-multiplying 15/16 and 7/9 gives 135 vs. 112. Now, 135 is greater than 112, so 15/16 is greater than 7/9. Using this procedure to compare 15/16 to each of the remaining answer-choices shows that 15/16 is the greatest fraction listed. The answer is (A).

3. $1 + \dfrac{1}{1 - \dfrac{1}{2}} = 1 + \dfrac{1}{1/2} = 1 + 2 = 3$. The answer is (A).

4.   "The ratio of $\dfrac{1}{5}$ to $\dfrac{1}{4}$ is equal to the ratio of $\dfrac{1}{4}$ to x" means $\dfrac{1/5}{1/4} = \dfrac{1/4}{x}$, or $\dfrac{1}{5} \cdot \dfrac{4}{1} = \dfrac{1}{4} \cdot \dfrac{1}{x}$. This in turn reduces to $\dfrac{4}{5} = \dfrac{1}{4x}$. Cross-multiplying yields $16x = 5$, or $x = \dfrac{5}{16}$. The answer is (A).

5.   Squaring a fraction between 0 and 1 makes it smaller, and taking the square root of it makes it larger. Hence, Choice (A) is smaller than Choice (B). Choices (C), (D), (E) are all greater than one since 8/7 > 1. The answer is (A).

6. $x\#(-y) = -(-y)^4 = -y^4$. Note: The exponent applies only to the negative inside the parentheses. The answer is (C).

7. $\dfrac{1}{1-(.2)^2} = \dfrac{1}{1-.04} = \dfrac{1}{.96} = \dfrac{1}{96/100} = 1 \cdot \dfrac{100}{96} = \dfrac{100}{96} = \dfrac{25}{24}$. The answer is (A).

8.   Since x is a fraction between 0 and 1, $\sqrt{x}$ is greater than either x^3 or x^4. It's also greater than $\dfrac{1}{\pi}x$ since $\dfrac{1}{\pi}x$ is less than x. To tell which is greater between $\sqrt{x}$ and $\dfrac{1}{\sqrt{x}}$, let $x = \dfrac{1}{4}$ and plug it into each expression: $\sqrt{x} = \sqrt{\dfrac{1}{4}} = \dfrac{1}{2}$ and $\dfrac{1}{\sqrt{x}} = \dfrac{1}{\sqrt{1/4}} = \dfrac{1}{1/2} = 2$. Hence, $\dfrac{1}{\sqrt{x}}$ is greater than $\sqrt{x}$. The answer is (A).

9.   Squaring a fraction between 0 and 1 makes it smaller, and taking the square root of it makes it larger. Therefore, Statement I is true since the top part of the fraction is larger than the bottom. This eliminates (B). Next, Statement II is false. Squaring a fraction makes it smaller only if the fraction is between 0 and 1. This eliminates (C) and (E). Finally, Statement III is false. Since $\dfrac{5}{6} < \sqrt{\dfrac{5}{6}}$, we get

$$\dfrac{\dfrac{5}{6}}{\sqrt{\dfrac{5}{6}}} < 1$$

Although taking the square root of this expression will make it larger, it will still be less than 1. The answer is (A).

10. Statement I is not necessarily true. For example, if $x = 2$ and $y = 1$, then $\dfrac{x+2}{y+2} = \dfrac{2+2}{1+2} = \dfrac{4}{3} \not> 2 = \dfrac{2}{1} = \dfrac{x}{y}$. This is also a counterexample to Statement II. Hence, we can eliminate (A), (B), (D), and (E).

Thus, by process of elimination, the answer is (C).

However, it is instructive to prove that Statement III is true. From the expression $x > y > 0$, we get

$$x + 2 > y + 2$$

Since $y + 2 > 0$, dividing both sides of the above expression by $y + 2$ will not reverse the inequality:

$$\dfrac{x+2}{y+2} > 1$$

Hence, Statement III is necessarily true.

8. **Know these rules for radicals:**

A. $\sqrt{x}\sqrt{y} = \sqrt{xy}$

B. $\sqrt{\dfrac{x}{y}} = \dfrac{\sqrt{x}}{\sqrt{y}}$

9. **Pythagorean Theorem (For right triangles only):**

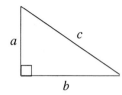

$c^2 = a^2 + b^2$

Example: What is the area of the triangle to the right?

(A)   6
(B)   7.5
(C)   8
(D)   11
(E)   15

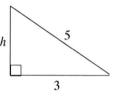

Since the triangle is a right triangle, the Pythagorean Theorem applies: $h^2 + 3^2 = 5^2$, where h is the height of the triangle. Solving for h yields $h = 4$. Hence, the area of the triangle is $\dfrac{1}{2}(base)(height) =$ $\dfrac{1}{2}(3)(4) = 6$. The answer is (A).

10. **When parallel lines are cut by a transversal, three important angle relationships are formed:**

Alternate interior angles are equal.

Corresponding angles are equal.

Interior angles on the same side of the transversal are supplementary.

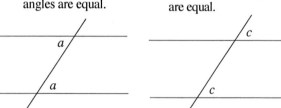

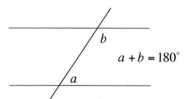

$a + b = 180°$

11. **In a triangle, an exterior angle is equal to the sum of its remote interior angles and therefore greater than either of them.**

$e = a + b$ and $e > a$ and $e > b$

12. **A central angle has by definition the same measure as its intercepted arc.**

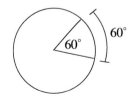

13.   **An inscribed angle has one-half the measure of its intercepted arc.**

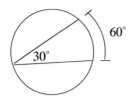

14.   **There are 180° in a straight angle.**

 $x + y = 180°$

15.   **The angle sum of a triangle is 180°.**

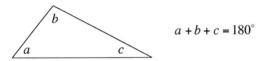 $a + b + c = 180°$

Example: In the triangle to the right, what is the degree measure of angle c ?

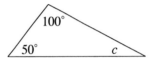

(A)   17
(B)   20
(C)   30
(D)   40
(E)   45

Since a triangle has $180°$, we get $100 + 50 + c = 180$. Solving for c yields $c = 30$. Hence, the answer is (C).

16.   **To find the percentage increase, find the absolute increase and divide by the original amount.**

Example: If a shirt selling for \$18 is marked up to \$20, then the absolute increase is $20 - 18 = 2$.

Thus, the percentage increase is $\dfrac{increase}{original\ amount} = \dfrac{2}{18} = \dfrac{1}{9} \approx 11\%$.

17.   **Systems of simultaneous equations can often be solved by merely adding or subtracting the equations.**

Example: If $4x + y = 14$ and $3x + 2y = 13$, then $x - y =$

Solution: Merely subtract the second equation from the first:

$$\begin{array}{r} 4x + y = 14 \\ (-)\quad 3x + 2y = 13 \\ \hline x - y = 1 \end{array}$$

18. **When counting elements that are in overlapping sets, the total number will equal the number in one group plus the number in the other group minus the number common to both groups. Venn diagrams are very helpful with these problems.**

     Example: If in a certain school 20 students are taking math and 10 are taking history and 7 are taking both, how many students are taking either math or history?

     Solution:

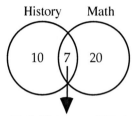

History   Math

Both History and Math

     By the principle stated above, we add 10 and 20 and then subtract 7 from the result. Thus, there are $(10 + 20) - 7 = 23$ students.

19. **The number of integers between two integers <u>inclusive</u> is one more than their difference.**

     For example: The number of integers between 49 and 101 inclusive is $(101 - 49) + 1 = 53$. To see this more clearly, choose smaller numbers, say, 9 and 11. The difference between 9 and 11 is 2. But there are three numbers between them inclusive—9, 10, and 11—one more than their difference.

20. **Rounding Off:** The convention used for rounding numbers is *"if the following digit is less than five, then the preceding digit is not changed. But if the following digit is greater than or equal to five, then the preceding digit is increased by one."*

     Example: 65,439 —> 65,000 (following digit is 4)
                   5.5671 —> 5.5700 (dropping the unnecessary zeros gives 5.57)

21. **Writing a number as a product of a power of 10 and a number $1 \le n < 10$ is called scientific notation. This notation has the following form: $n \times 10^c$, where $1 \le n < 10$ and c is an integer.**

     Example: $326,000,000 = 3.26 \times 10^8$
     Notice that the exponent is the number of significant places that the decimal is moved[*], not the number zeros. Students often use 6 as the exponent in the above example because there are 6 zeros.

     Example: $0.00007 = 7 \times 10^{-5}$
     Notice that for a small number the exponent is negative and for a large number the exponent is positive.

---

[*] Although no decimal is shown in the number 326,000,000, you can place a decimal at the end of the number and add as many trailing zeros as you like without changing the value of the number: $326,000,000 = 326,000,000.00 \ldots$.

Number Theory

This broad category is a popular source for ACT questions. At first, students often struggle with these problems since they have forgotten many of the basic properties of arithmetic. So, before we begin solving these problems, let's review some of these basic properties.

> *"The remainder is r when p is divided by q"* means $p = qz + r$; the integer z is called the quotient. For instance, *"The remainder is 1 when 7 is divided by 3"* means $7 = 3 \cdot 2 + 1$. Dividing both sides of $p = kq + r$ by k gives the following alternative form $p/k = q + r/k$.

Example 1: When the integer n is divided by 2, the quotient is u and the remainder is 1. When the integer n is divided by 5, the quotient is v and the remainder is 3. Which one of the following must be true?

(A) $2u + 5v = 4$
(B) $2u - 5v = 2$
(C) $4u + 5v = 2$
(D) $4u - 5v = 2$
(E) $3u - 5v = 2$

Translating *"When the integer n is divided by 2, the quotient is u and the remainder is 1"* into an equation gives

$$n = 2u + 1$$

Translating *"When the integer n is divided by 5, the quotient is v and the remainder is 3"* into an equation gives

$$n = 5v + 3$$

Since both expressions equal n, we can set them equal to each other:

$$2u + 1 = 5v + 3$$

Rearranging and then combining like terms yields

$$2u - 5v = 2$$

The answer is (B).

> A number n is even if the remainder is zero when n is divided by 2: $n = 2z + 0$, or $n = 2z$.

> A number n is odd if the remainder is one when n is divided by 2: $n = 2z + 1$.

➤ **The following properties for odd and even numbers are very useful—you should memorize them:**

$$even \times even = even$$
$$odd \times odd = odd$$
$$even \times odd = even$$

$$even + even = even$$
$$odd + odd = even$$
$$even + odd = odd$$

Example 2: Suppose p is even and q is odd. Then which of the following CANNOT be an integer?

  I. $\dfrac{p+q}{p}$

  II. $\dfrac{pq}{3}$

  III. $\dfrac{q}{p^2}$

  (A) I only   (B) II only   (C) III only   (D) I and II only   (E) I and III only

For a fractional expression to be an integer, the denominator must divide evenly into the numerator. Now, Statement I cannot be an integer. Since q is odd and p is even, $p + q$ is odd. Further, since $p + q$ is odd, it cannot be divided evenly by the even number p. Hence, $\dfrac{p+q}{p}$ cannot be an integer. Next, Statement II can be an integer. For example, if $p = 2$ and $q = 3$, then $\dfrac{pq}{3} = \dfrac{2 \cdot 3}{3} = 2$. Finally, Statement III cannot be an integer. $p^2 = p \cdot p$ is even since it is the product of two even numbers. Further, since q is odd, it cannot be divided evenly by the even integer p^2. The answer is (E).

➤ **Consecutive integers are written as $x, x + 1, x + 2, \ldots$**

➤ **Consecutive even or odd integers are written as $x, x + 2, x + 4, \ldots$**

➤ **The integer zero is neither positive nor negative, but it is even: $0 = 2 \times 0$.**

➤ **A *prime number* is an integer that is divisible only by itself and 1.**

   The prime numbers are 2, 3, 5, 7, 11, 13, 17, 19, 23, 29, 31, 37, 41, . . .

➤ **A number is divisible by 3 if the sum of its digits is divisible by 3.**

   For example, 135 is divisible by 3 because the sum of its digits (1 + 3 + 5 = 9) is divisible by 3.

➤ **A *common multiple* is a multiple of two or more integers.**

   For example, some common multiples of 2 and 5 are 0, 10, 20, 40, and 50.

➤ **The *least common multiple* (LCM) of two integers is the smallest positive integer that is a multiple of both.**

   For example, the LCM of 4 and 10 is 20. The standard method of calculating the LCM is to prime factor the numbers and then form a product by selecting each factor the greatest number of times it occurs. For 4 and 10, we get

$$4 = 2^2$$
$$10 = 2 \cdot 5$$

In this case, select 22 instead of 2 because it has the greater number of factors of 2, and select 5 by default since there are no other factors of 5. Hence, the LCM is $2^2 \cdot 5 = 4 \cdot 5 = 20$.

For another example, let's find the LCM of 8, 36, and 54. Prime factoring yields

$$8 = 2^3$$
$$36 = 2^2 \cdot 3^2$$
$$54 = 2 \cdot 3^3$$

In this case, select 23 because it has more factors of 2 than 22 or 2 itself, and select 33 because is has more factors of 3 than 32 does. Hence, the LCM is $2^3 \cdot 3^3 = 8 \cdot 27 = 216$.

A shortcut for finding the LCM is to just keep adding the largest number to itself until the other numbers divide into it evenly. For 4 and 10, we would add 10 to itself: $10 + 10 = 20$. Since 4 divides evenly in 20, the LCM is 20. For 8, 36, and 54, we would add 54 to itself: $54 + 54 + 54 + 54 = 216$. Since both 8 and 36 divide evenly into 216, the LCM is 216.

➤ **The absolute value of a number, | |, is always positive. In other words, the absolute value symbol eliminates negative signs.**

For example, $|-7| = 7$ and $|-\pi| = \pi$. Caution, the absolute value symbol acts only on what is inside the symbol, $|\;|$. For example, $-\left|-(7-\pi)\right| = -(7-\pi)$. Here, only the negative sign inside the absolute value symbol but outside the parentheses is eliminated.

➤ **The product (quotient) of positive numbers is positive.**

➤ **The product (quotient) of a positive number and a negative number is negative.**

For example, $-5(3) = -15$ and $\dfrac{6}{-3} = -2$.

➤ **The product (quotient) of an even number of negative numbers is positive.**

For example, $(-5)(-3)(-2)(-1) = 30$ is positive because there is an even number, 4, of positives. $\dfrac{-9}{-2} = \dfrac{9}{2}$ is positive because there is an even number, 2, of positives.

➤ **The product (quotient) of an odd number of negative numbers is negative.**

For example, $(-2)(-\pi)(-\sqrt{3}) = -2\pi\sqrt{3}$ is negative because there is an odd number, 3, of negatives. $\dfrac{(-2)(-9)(-6)}{(-12)\left(-18\!\big/_2\right)} = -1$ is negative because there is an odd number, 5, of negatives.

➤ **The sum of negative numbers is negative.**

For example, $-3 - 5 = -8$. Some students have trouble recognizing this structure as a sum because there is no plus symbol, +. But recall that subtraction is defined as negative addition. So $-3 - 5 = -3 + (-5)$.

➤ **A number raised to an even exponent is greater than or equal to zero.**

For example, $(-\pi)^4 = \pi^4 \geq 0$, and $x^2 \geq 0$, and $0^2 = 0 \cdot 0 = 0 \geq 0$.

Example 3: If a, b, and c are consecutive integers and $a < b < c$, which of the following must be true?

    I. $b - c = 1$

    II. $\dfrac{abc}{3}$ is an integer.

    III. $a + b + c$ is even.

    (A)   I only
    (B)   II only
    (C)   III only
    (D)   I and II only
    (E)   II and III only

Let x, $x + 1$, $x + 2$ stand for the consecutive integers a, b, and c, in that order. Plugging this into Statement I yields

$$b - c = (x + 1) - (x + 2) = -1$$

Hence, Statement I is false.

    As to Statement II, since a, b, and c are three consecutive integers, one of them must be divisible by 3. Hence, $\dfrac{abc}{3}$ is an integer, and Statement II is true.

    As to Statement III, suppose a is even, b is odd, and c is even. Then $a + b$ is odd since

$$even + odd = odd$$

Hence,

$$a + b + c = (a + b) + c = (odd) + even = odd$$

Thus, Statement III is not necessarily true. The answer is (B).

Example 4: If both x and y are prime numbers, which of the following CANNOT be the difference of x and y?

    (A) 1   (B) 3   (C) 9   (D) 15   (E) 23

Both 3 and 2 are prime, and $3 - 2 = 1$. This eliminates (A). Next, both 5 and 2 are prime, and $5 - 2 = 3$. This eliminates (B). Next, both 11 and 2 are prime, and $11 - 2 = 9$. This eliminates (C). Next, both 17 and 2 are prime, and $17 - 2 = 15$. This eliminates (D). Hence, by process of elimination, the answer is (E).

Example 5: If $-x = -\left|-(-2 + 5)\right|$, then $x =$

    (A) −7   (B) −3   (C) 3   (D) 7   (E) 9

Working from the innermost parentheses out, we get

$$-x = -\left|-(-2 + 5)\right|$$
$$-x = -\left|-(+3)\right|$$
$$-x = -\left|-3\right|$$
$$-x = -(+3)$$
$$-x = -3$$
$$x = 3$$

The answer is (C).

Problem Set D:

1. If the remainder is 1 when *m* is divided by 2 and the remainder is 3 when *n* is divided by 4, which of the following must be true?

    (A)   *m* is even.
    (B)   *n* is even.
    (C)   *m* + *n* is even.
    (D)   *mn* is even.
    (E)   *m/n* is even.

2. If *x* and *y* are both prime and greater than 2, then which of the following CANNOT be a divisor of *xy*?

    (A)   2
    (B)   3
    (C)   11
    (D)   15
    (E)   17

3. If 2 is the greatest number that will divide evenly into both *x* and *y*, what is the greatest number that will divide evenly into both 5*x* and 5*y*?

    (A)   2
    (B)   4
    (C)   6
    (D)   8
    (E)   10

4. If the average of the consecutive even integers *a*, *b*, and *c* is less than *a*/3, which of the following best describes the value of *a*?

    (A)   a is prime.
    (B)   a is odd.
    (C)   a is zero.
    (D)   a is positive.
    (E)   a is negative.

5. If $\dfrac{x+5}{y}$ is a prime integer, which of the following must be true?

    I. $y = 5x$
    II.   *y* is a prime integer.
    III. $\dfrac{x+5}{y}$ is odd.

    (A)   None
    (B)   I only
    (C)   II only
    (D)   I and II only
    (E)   II and III only

6. If *x* is both the cube and the square of an integer and *x* is between 2 and 200, what is the value of *x*?

    (A)   8
    (B)   16
    (C)   64
    (D)   125
    (E)   169

7.   In the two-digit number x, both the sum and the difference of its digits is 4. What is the value of x?

   (A)   13
   (B)   31
   (C)   40
   (D)   48
   (E)   59

8.   If p divided by 9 leaves a remainder of 1, which of the following must be true?

   I. p is even.
   II. p is odd.
   III. $p = 3 \cdot z + 1$ for some integer z.

   (A)   I only
   (B)   II only
   (C)   III only
   (D)   I and II only
   (E)   I and III only

9. p and q are integers. If p is divided by 2, the remainder is 1; and if q is divided by 6, the remainder is 1. Which of the following must be true.

   I. $pq + 1$ is even.

   II. $\dfrac{pq}{2}$ is an integer.

   III. pq is a multiple of 12.

   (A) I only   (B) II only   (C) III only   (D) I and II only   (E) I and III only

10. The smallest prime number greater than 53 is

   (A)   54
   (B)   55
   (C)   57
   (D)   59
   (E)   67

11. Which one of the following numbers is the greatest positive integer x such that 3^x is a factor of 27^5 ?

   (A)   5
   (B)   8
   (C)   10
   (D)   15
   (E)   19

12. If x, y, and z are consecutive integers in that order, which of the following must be true?

   I. xy is even.
   II. $x - z$ is even.
   III. x^z is even.

   (A)   I only
   (B)   II only
   (C)   III only
   (D)   I and II only
   (E)   I and III only

13. If $-x - 2 = -\left|-(6 - 2)\right|$, then $x =$

    (A) −5
    (B) −2
    (C) 0
    (D) 2
    (E) 5

14. If the sum of two prime numbers x and y is odd, then the product of x and y must be divisible by

    (A) 2
    (B) 3
    (C) 4
    (D) 5
    (E) 8

15. If $\dfrac{x + y}{x - y} = 3$ and x and y are integers, then which one of the following must be true?

    (A) x is divisible by 4
    (B) y is an odd number
    (C) y is an even integer
    (D) x is an even number
    (E) x is an irreducible fraction

16. A two-digit even number is such that reversing its digits creates an odd number greater than the original number. Which one of the following cannot be the first digit of the original number?

    (A) 1
    (B) 3
    (C) 5
    (D) 7
    (E) 9

17. Let a, b, and c be three integers, and let a be a perfect square. If $a/b = b/c$, then which one of the following statements must be true?

    (A) c must be an even number
    (B) c must be an odd number
    (C) c must be a perfect square
    (D) c must not be a perfect square
    (E) c must be a prime number

18. If $n > 2$, then the sum, S, of the integers from 1 through n can be calculated by the following formula: $S = n(n + 1)/2$. Which one of the following statements about S must be true?

    (A) S is always odd.
    (B) S is always even.
    (C) S must be a prime number.
    (D) S must not be a prime number.
    (E) S must be a perfect square.

19. If n is an odd number greater than 5 and a multiple of 5, then what is the remainder when n is divided by 10?

    (A) 1
    (B) 3
    (C) 5
    (D) 7
    (E) 9

20. Which one of the following could be the difference between two numbers both of which are divisible by 2, 3 and 4?

(A) 71
(B) 72
(C) 73
(D) 74
(E) 75

21. A number, when divided by 12, gives a remainder of 7. If the same number is divided by 6, then the remainder must be
(A) 1
(B) 2
(C) 3
(D) 4
(E) 5

22. Let x be a two-digit number. If the sum of the digits of x is 9, then the sum of the digits of the number $(x + 10)$ is

(A) 1
(B) 8
(C) 10
(D) either 8 or 10
(E) either 1 or 10

23. $\dfrac{39693}{3} =$

(A) 33231
(B) 13231
(C) 12331
(D) 23123
(E) 12321

24. The number of positive integers less than 1000 that are divisible by 3 is

(A) 332
(B) 333
(C) 334
(D) 335
(E) 336

25. If n^3 is an odd integer, which one of the following expressions is an even integer?

(A) $2n^2 + 1$
(B) n^4
(C) $n^2 + 1$
(D) $n(n + 2)$
(E) n

26. If the product of two integers is odd, then the sum of those two integers must be

(A) odd
(B) even
(C) prime
(D) divisible by the difference of the two numbers
(E) a perfect square

27. If the sum of three consecutive integers is odd, then the first and the last integers must be

    (A) odd, even
    (B) odd, odd
    (C) even, odd
    (D) even, even
    (E) none of the above

28. If l, m, and n are positive integers such that $l < m < n$ and $n < 4$, then $m =$

    (A) 0
    (B) 1
    (C) 2
    (D) 3
    (E) 4

29. If two non-zero positive integers p and q are such that $p = 4q$ and $p < 8$, then $q =$

    (A) 1
    (B) 2
    (C) 3
    (D) 4
    (E) 5

30. If n is an integer, then which one of the following expressions must be even?

    (A) $n^2 + 1$
    (B) $n(n + 2)$
    (C) $n(n + 1)$
    (D) $n(n + 4)$
    (E) $(n + 1)(n + 3)$

31. If p and q are different prime numbers and $pq/2$ is also a prime number, then $p + q$ is

    (A) an odd number
    (B) an even number
    (C) a prime number
    (D) a negative number
    (E) not a prime number

32. The sum of three consecutive positive integers must be divisible by which of the following?

    (A) 2
    (B) 3
    (C) 4
    (D) 5
    (E) 6

Answers and Solutions to Problem Set D

1.   The statement *"the remainder is 1 when m is divided by 2"* translates into

$$m = 2u + 1$$

The statement *"the remainder is 3 when n is divided by 4"* translates into

$$n = 4v + 3$$

Forming the sum of m and n gives

$$m + n = 2u + 1 + 4v + 3 = 2u + 4v + 4 = 2(u + 2v + 2)$$

Since we have written $m + n$ as a multiple of 2, it is even. The answer is (C).

Method II (Substitution)
Let $m = 3$ and $n = 7$. Then

$$3 = 2 \cdot 1 + 1$$

and

$$7 = 4 \cdot 1 + 3$$

Now, both 3 and 7 are odd, which eliminates (A) and (B). Further, $3 \cdot 7 = 21$ is odd, which eliminates (D). Finally, 3/7 is not an integer, which eliminates (E). Hence, by process of elimination, the answer is (C).

2.   Since x and y are prime and greater than 2, xy is the product of two odd numbers and is therefore odd. Hence, 2 cannot be a divisor of xy. The answer is (A).

3.   Since 2 divides evenly into x, we get $x = 2z$. Hence, $5x = 5(2z) = 10z$. In other words, $5x$ is divisible by 10. A similar analysis shows that $5y$ is also divisible by 10. Since 10 is the greatest number listed, the answer is (E).

4.   Let a, $a + 2$, $a + 4$ stand for the consecutive even integers a, b, and c, in that order. Forming the average of a, b, and c yields

$$\frac{a+b+c}{3} = \frac{a+a+2+a+4}{3} = \frac{3a+6}{3} = a + 2$$

Setting this less than $a/3$ gives $a + 2 < \dfrac{1}{3}a$

Multiplying by 3 yields $3a + 6 < a$

Subtracting 6 and a from both sides yields $2a < -6$

Dividing by 2 yields $a < -3$

Hence, a is negative, and the best answer is (E).

5.   If $x = 1$ and $y = 3$, then

$$y \neq 5x$$

and

$$\frac{x+5}{y} = \frac{1+5}{3} = \frac{6}{3} = 2,$$

which is prime and not odd. Hence, Statements I and III are not necessarily true. Next, let $x = 3$ and $y = 4$. Then y is not prime and

$$\frac{x+5}{y} = \frac{3+5}{4} = \frac{8}{4} = 2,$$

which is prime. Hence, Statement II is not necessarily true. The answer is (A).

6.   Since x is both a cube and between 2 and 200, we are looking at the integers:

$$2^3, 3^3, 4^3, 5^3$$

which reduce to

$$8, 27, 64, 125$$

There is only one perfect square, $64 = 8^2$, in this set. The answer is (C).

7.   Since the sum of the digits is 4, x must be 13, 22, 31, or 40. Further, since the difference of the digits is 4, x must be 40, 51, 15, 62, 26, 73, 37, 84, 48, 95, or 59. We see that 40 and only 40 is common to the two sets of choices for x. Hence, x must be 40. The answer is (C).

8.   First, let's briefly review the concept of division. "Seven divided by 3 leaves a remainder of 1" means that $7 = 3 \cdot 2 + 1$. By analogy, "x divided by y leaves a remainder of 1" means that $x = y \cdot q + 1$, where q is an integer.

     Hence, *"p divided by 9 leaves a remainder of 1"* translates into $p = 9 \cdot q + 1$. If $q = 1$, then $p = 10$ which is even. But if $q = 2$, then $p = 19$ which is odd. Hence, neither Statement I nor Statement II need be true. This eliminates (A), (B), (D), and (E). Hence, the answer is (C).

     Let's verify that Statement III is true. $p = 9 \cdot q + 1 = 3(3q) + 1 = 3z + 1$, where $z = 3q$.

9.   Statement I is true: From *"If p is divided by 2, the remainder is 1,"* $p = 2u + 1$; and from *"if q is divided by 6, the remainder is 1,"* $q = 6v + 1$. Hence, $pq + 1 =$

$$(2u + 1)(6v + 1) + 1 =$$

$$12uv + 2u + 6v + 1 + 1 =$$

$$12uv + 2u + 6v + 2 =$$

$$2(6uv + u + 3v + 1)$$

Since we have written $pq + 1$ as a multiple of 2, it is even.

Method II

Since p and q each leave a remainder of 1 when divided by an even number, both are odd. Now, the product of two odd numbers is another odd number. Hence, pq is odd, and therefore $pq + 1$ is even.

Now, since $pq + 1$ is even, pq is odd. Hence, $pq/2$ is not an integer, and Statement II is not necessarily true. Next, Statement III is not necessarily true. For example, if $p = 3$ and $q = 7$, then $pq = 21$, which is not a multiple of 12. The answer is (A).

10. Since the question asks for the *smallest* prime greater than 53, we start with the smallest answer-choice. 54 is not prime since $54 = 2(27)$. 55 is not prime since $55 = 5(11)$. 57 is not prime since $57 = 3(19)$. Now, 59 *is* prime. Hence, the answer is (D).

11. $27^5 = \left(3^3\right)^5 = 3^{15}$. Hence, $x = 15$ and the answer is (D).

12. Since x and y are consecutive integers, one of them must be even. Hence, the product xy is even and Statement I is true. As to Statement II, suppose z is odd, then x must be odd as well. Now, the difference of two odd numbers is an even number. Next, suppose z is even, then x must be even as well. Now, the difference of two even numbers is again an even number. Hence, Statement II is true. As to Statement III, let $x = 1$, then $z = 3$ and $x^z = 1^3 = 1$, which is odd. Thus, Statement III is not necessarily true. The answer is (D).

13. Working from the innermost parentheses out, we get

$$-x - 2 = -\left|-(6 - 2)\right|$$
$$-x - 2 = -\left|-4\right|$$
$$-x - 2 = -(+4)$$
$$-x - 2 = -4$$
$$-x = -2$$
$$x = 2$$

The answer is (D).

14.   We are told that the sum of the prime numbers x and y is odd. For a sum of two numbers to be odd, one number must be odd and another even. There is only one even prime number—2; all others are odd. Hence, either x or y must be 2. Thus, the product of x and y is a multiple of 2 and therefore is divisible by 2. The answer is (A).

15.   Solution: $\dfrac{x + y}{x - y} = 3$. Multiplying both sides of this equation by $(x - y)$ yields

$$x + y = 3(x - y)$$
$$x + y = 3x - 3y$$
$$-2x = -4y$$
$$x = 2y$$

Since we have expressed x as 2 times an integer, it is even. The answer is (D).

16.   Let the original number be represented by *xy*. (Note: here *xy* does not denote multiplication, but merely the position of the digits: *x* first, then *y*.). Reversing the digits of *xy* gives *yx*. We are told that *yx* > *xy*. This implies that *y* > *x*. (For example, 73 > 69 because 7 > 6.) If *x* = 9, then the condition *y* > *x* cannot be satisfied. Hence, *x* cannot equal 9. The answer is (E).

Method II:
Let the original number be represented by *xy*. In expanded form, *xy* can be written as $10x + y$. For example, $53 = 5(10) + 3$. Similarly, $yx = 10y + x$. Since *yx* > *xy*, we get $10y + x > 10x + y$. Subtracting *x* and *y* from both sides of this equation yields $9y > 9x$. Dividing this equation by 9 yields *y* > *x*. Now, if *x* = 9, then the inequality *y* > *x* cannot be satisfied. The answer is (E).

17.   Cross multiplying the equation $a/b = b/c$ yields

$$ac = b^2$$

Dividing by *a* yields $$c = b^2/a$$

We are given that *a* is a perfect square. Hence, $a = k^2$, for some number *k*. Replacing *a* in the bottom equation with k^2, we get $c = b^2/k^2 = (b/k)^2$. Since we have written *c* as the square of a number, it is a perfect square. The answer is (C).

18.   Observe that *n* and $(n + 1)$ are consecutive integers. Hence, one of the numbers is even. Therefore, the 2 in the denominator divides evenly into either *n* or $(n + 1)$, eliminating 2 from the denominator. Thus, *S* can be reduced to a product of two integers. Remember, a prime number cannot be written as the product of two integers (other than itself and 1). Hence, *S* is not a prime number, and the answer is (D).

19.   The set of numbers greater than 5 and divisible by 5 is {10, 15, 20, 25, 30, 35, . . .}. Since *n* is odd, the possible values for *n* are 15, 25, 35, ... Any number in this list, when divided by 10, leaves a remainder of 5. The answer is (C).

20.   A number divisible by all three numbers 2, 3, and 4 is also divisible by 12. Hence, each number can be written as a multiple of 12. Let the first number be represented as $12a$ and the second number as $12b$. Assuming *a* > *b*, the difference between the two numbers is $12a - 12b = 12(a - b)$. Observe that this number is also a multiple of 12. Hence, the answer must also be divisible by 12. Since 72 is the only answer-choice divisible by 12, the answer is (B).

21.   We are told that the remainder is 7 when the number is divided by 12. Hence, we can represent the number as $12x + 7$. Now, 7 can be written as 6 + 1. Plugging this into the expression yields

$$12x + (6 + 1) =$$
$$(12x + 6) + 1 = \quad \text{by regrouping}$$
$$6(2x + 1) + 1 \quad \text{by factoring 6 out of the first two terms}$$

This shows that the remainder is 1 when the expression $12x + 7$ is divided by 6. The answer is (A).

Method II (Substitution):

Choose the number 19, which gives a remainder of 7 when divided by 12. Now, divide 19 by 6:

$$\frac{19}{6} = 3\frac{1}{6}$$

This shows that 6 divides into 19 with a remainder of 1. The answer is (A).

22.   Let's take a two-digit number whose digits add up to 9, say, 72. Adding 10 to this number gives 82. The sum of the digits of this number is 10. Now, let's choose another two-digit number whose digits add up to 9, say, 90. Then $x + 10 = 90 + 10 = 100$. The sum of the digits of this number is 1. Hence, the sum of the numbers is either 1 or 10. The answer is (E).

23.   Observe that all the digits of the dividend 39693 are divisible by 3. So 3 will divide the dividend into such a number that each of its digits will be 1/3 the corresponding digit in the dividend (i.e., 39693). For example, the third digit in the dividend is 6, and hence the third digit in the quotient will be 2, which is 1/3 of 6. Applying the same process to all digits gives the quotient 13231. The answer is (B).

24.   In the ordered set of integers from 1 through 999, every third integer is a multiple of 3. Hence, the number of integers in this set of 999 integers that are multiples of 3 is 999/3 = 333. The answer is (B).

25.   Suppose $n = 1$. Then $n^3 = 1^3 = 1$, which is odd. Now, we plug this value for n into each of the answer-choices to see which ones are even. Thus, $2n^2 + 1$ becomes $2(1)^2 + 1 = 3$, which is not even. So eliminate (A). Next, $n^4 = 1^4 = 1$ is not even—eliminate (B). Next, $n^2 + 1 = 1^2 + 1 = 2$ is even, so the answer is possibly (C). Next, $n(n + 2) = 1(1 + 2) = 3$ is not even—eliminate (D). Finally, $n = 1$, which is not even—eliminate (E). Hence, by the process of elimination, the answer is (C).

26.   If the product of the two numbers is odd, then each number in the product must be odd. Recall that the sum of two odd numbers is an even number. The answer is (B).

27.   Let the three consecutive integers be x, $x + 1$, and $x + 2$. The sum of these integers is $3x + 3$. According to the question, this sum is odd. Hence $3x + 3$ is odd. Recall that if the sum of two integers is odd, then one of the integers is odd and the other one is even. Since 3 in the expression $3x + 3$ is odd, $3x$ must be even. Now, recall that the product of two numbers is odd only when one of the numbers is odd and the other is even. So x must be even. If x is an even number, then $x + 2$ is also even. Thus, the first and the last integers must both be even. The answer is (D).

28.   We are given that l, m, and n are three positive integers such that $l < m < n$. This implies that l, m, and n are each greater than zero and not equal to each other. Since n is less than 4, the numbers l, m, and n must have the values 1, 2, and 3, respectively. Hence, the answer is (C).

29.   Dividing both sides of the equation $p = 4q$ by 4, we get $q = p/4$. We are also given that $p < 8$. Dividing both sides of this inequality by 4 yields, $p/4 < 8/4$. Simplifying it, we get $p/4 < 2$. But $q = p/4$. Hence, $q < 2$. The only non-zero positive integer less than 2 is 1. Hence, $q = 1$. The answer is (A).

30.   Answer-choice (C) consists of the product of two consecutive integers. Now, of any two consecutive integers, one of the integers must be even. Hence, their product must be even. The answer is (C).

31.   Since $pq/2$ is prime, it is an integer. Hence, either p or q must be even; otherwise, the 2 would not cancel and $pq/2$ would be a fraction. The only even prime number is 2. Hence, either p or q, but not both, must be 2. The other one is an odd prime number. Now, the sum of an even number and an odd number is an odd number. The answer is (A).

32.   Let the three consecutive positive integers be n, $n + 1$, and $n + 2$. The sum of these three positive integers is

$$n + (n + 1) + (n + 2) =$$
$$3n + 3 =$$
$$3(n + 1)$$

Since we have written the sum as a multiple of 3, it is divisible by 3. The answer is (B).

Geometry

About one-third of the math problems on the ACT involve geometry. (There are no proofs.) Fortunately, the figures on the ACT **are drawn to scale** (even though the official direction say that figures are not necessarily drawn to scale). Hence, you can check your work and in some cases even solve a problem by "eyeballing" the drawing. We'll discuss this technique in detail later.

Following is a discussion of the basic properties of geometry. You probably know many of these properties. Memorize any that you do not know.

Lines & Angles

When two straight lines meet at a point, they form an angle. The point is called the vertex of the angle, and the lines are called the sides of the angle.

The angle to the right can be identified in three ways:

1. $\angle x$
2. $\angle B$
3. $\angle ABC$ or $\angle CBA$

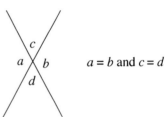

When two straight lines meet at a point, they form four angles. The angles opposite each other are called vertical angles, and they are congruent (equal). In the figure to the right, $a = b$, and $c = d$.

$a = b$ and $c = d$

Angles are measured in degrees, °. By definition, a circle has 360°. So, an angle can be measured by its fractional part of a circle. For example, an angle that is $\dfrac{1}{360}$ of the arc of a circle is 1°. And an angle that is $\dfrac{1}{4}$ of the arc of a circle is $\dfrac{1}{4} \times 360 = 90°$.

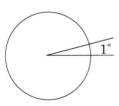

1/360 of an arc
of a circle

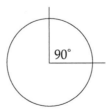

1/4 of an arc
of a circle

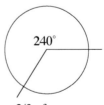

2/3 of an arc
of a circle

There are four major types of angle measures:

An **acute angle** has measure less than 90°:

A **right angle** has measure 90°:

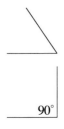

45

An **obtuse angle** has measure greater than 90°:

A **straight angle** has measure 180°:  $x + y = 180°$

Example: In the figure to the right, if the quotient of a
and b is 7/2, then $b =$

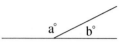

(A) 30   (B) 35   (C) 40   (D) 46   (E) 50

Since a and b form a straight angle, $a + b = 180$. Now, translating "the quotient of a and b is 7/2" into an
equation gives $\dfrac{a}{b} = \dfrac{7}{2}$. Solving for a yields $a = \dfrac{7}{2}b$. Plugging this into the equation $a + b = 180$ yields

$$\frac{7}{2}b + b = 180$$
$$7b + 2b = 360$$
$$9b = 360$$
$$b = 40$$

The answer is (C).

Example: In the figure to the right, what is the measure
of angle y ?

(A)   80
(B)   84
(C)   85
(D)   87
(E)   90

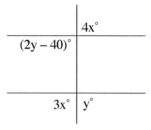

Since $4x$ and $2y - 40$ represent vertical angles, $4x = 2y - 40$. Since $3x$ and y form a straight angle, $3x + y = 180$. This yields the following system:

$$4x = 2y - 40$$
$$3x + y = 180$$

Solving this system for y yields $y = 84$. Hence, the answer is (B).

Two angles are **supplementary** if their angle sum is 180°:

45°   135°

45 + 135 = 180

Two angles are **complementary** if their angle sum is 90°:

60°

30°

30 + 60 = 90

Perpendicular lines meet at right angles: 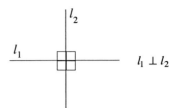 $l_1 \perp l_2$

Two lines in the same plane are parallel if they never intersect. Parallel lines have the same slope.

When parallel lines are cut by a transversal, three important angle relationships exist:

Alternate interior angles are equal.

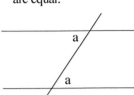

Corresponding angles are equal.

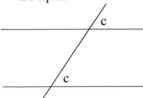

Interior angles on the same side of the transversal are supplementary.

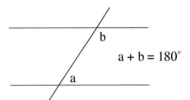

$a + b = 180°$

The shortest distance from a point to a line is along a new line that passes through the point and is perpendicular to the original line.

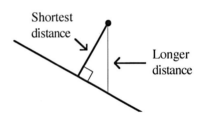

Triangles

A triangle containing a right angle is called a *right triangle*. The right angle is denoted by a small square:

A triangle with two equal sides is called *isosceles*. The angles opposite the equal sides are called the base angles, and they are congruent (equal). A triangle with all three sides equal is called *equilateral*, and each angle is 60°. A triangle with no equal sides (and therefore no equal angles) is called *scalene*:

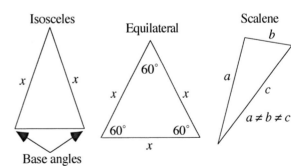

Isosceles

Equilateral

Scalene

Base angles

The altitude to the base of an isosceles or equilateral triangle bisects the base and bisects the vertex angle:

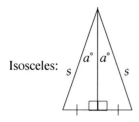

Isosceles:

Equilateral:

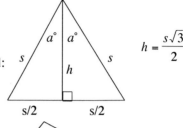

$h = \dfrac{s\sqrt{3}}{2}$

The angle sum of a triangle is 180°:

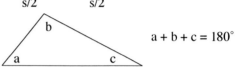

$a + b + c = 180°$

Example: In the figure to the right, $w =$
(A) 30   (B) 32   (C) 40   (D) 52   (E) 60

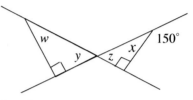

$x + 150 = 180$	since x and 150 form a straight angle
$x = 30$	solving for x
$z + x + 90 = 180$	since the angle sum of a triangle is 180°
$z + 30 + 90 = 180$	replacing x with 30
$z = 60$	solving for z
$z = y = 60$	since y and z are vertical angles
$w + y + 90 = 180$	since the angle sum of a triangle is 180°
$w + 60 + 90 = 180$	replacing y with 60
$w = 30$	solving for w

The answer is (A).

The area of a triangle is $\dfrac{1}{2}bh$, where b is the base and h is the height. Sometimes the base must be extended in order to draw the altitude, as in the third drawing directly below:

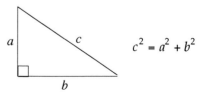

$A = \dfrac{1}{2}bh$

In a triangle, the longer side is opposite the larger angle, and vice versa:

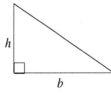

50° is larger than 30°, so side b is longer than side a.

Pythagorean Theorem (right triangles only): The square of the hypotenuse is equal to the sum of the squares of the legs.

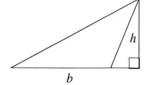

$c^2 = a^2 + b^2$

Pythagorean triples: The numbers 3, 4, and 5 can always represent the sides of a right triangle and they appear very often: $5^2 = 3^2 + 4^2$. Another, but less common, Pythagorean Triple is 5, 12, 13: $13^2 = 5^2 + 12^2$.

Two triangles are similar (same shape and usually different sizes) if their corresponding angles are equal. If two triangles are similar, their corresponding sides are proportional:

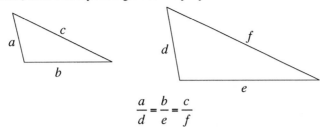

$$\frac{a}{d} = \frac{b}{e} = \frac{c}{f}$$

If two angles of a triangle are congruent to two angles of another triangle, the triangles are similar.

In the figure to the right, the large and small triangles are similar because both contain a right angle and they share $\angle A$..

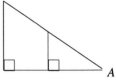

Two triangles are congruent (identical) if they have the same size and shape.

In a triangle, an exterior angle is equal to the sum of its remote interior angles and is therefore greater than either of them:

$e = a + b$ and $e > a$ and $e > b$

In a triangle, the sum of the lengths of any two sides is greater than the length of the remaining side:

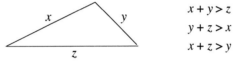

$x + y > z$
$y + z > x$
$x + z > y$

Example: In the figure to the right, what is the value of x ?

    (A)   30
    (B)   32
    (C)   35
    (D)   40
    (E)   47

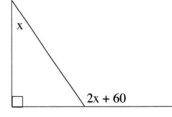

Since $2x + 60$ is an exterior angle, it is equal to the sum of the remote interior angles. That is, $2x + 60 = x + 90$. Solving for x gives $x = 30$. The answer is (A).

In a 30°–60°–90° triangle, the sides have the following relationships:

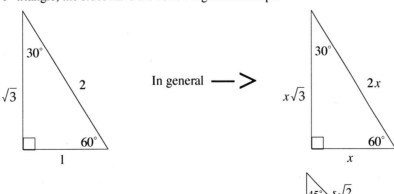

In general $\longrightarrow$

In a 45°–45°–90° triangle, the sides have the following relationships:

Quadrilaterals

A *quadrilateral* is a four-sided closed figure, where each side is a straight line.

The angle sum of a quadrilateral is 360°. You can view a quadrilateral as being composed of two 180-degree triangles:

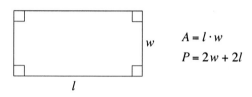

A *parallelogram* is a quadrilateral in which the opposite sides are both parallel and congruent. Its area is *base × height*:

$A = bh$

The diagonals of a parallelogram bisect each other:

A parallelogram with four right angles is a *rectangle*. If w is the width and l is the length of a rectangle, then its area is $A = l \cdot w$ and its perimeter is $P = 2w + 2l$.

$A = l \cdot w$

$P = 2w + 2l$

Example: In the figure to the right, what is the perimeter of the pentagon?

    (A)   12
    (B)   13
    (C)   17
    (D)   20
    (E)   25

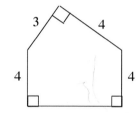

Add the following line to the figure:

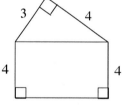

Since the legs of the right triangle formed are of lengths 3 and 4, the triangle must be a 3-4-5 right triangle. Hence, the added line has length 5. Since the bottom figure is a rectangle, the length of the base of the figure is also 5. Hence, the perimeter of the pentagon is 3 + 4 + 4 + 5 + 4 = 20. The answer is (D).

If the opposite sides of a rectangle are equal, it is a square and its area is $A = s^2$ and its perimeter is $P = 4s$, where s is the length of a side:

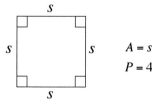

$A = s^2$

$P = 4s$

The diagonals of a square bisect each other and are perpendicular to each other:

A quadrilateral with only one pair of parallel sides is a *trapezoid*. The parallel sides are called *bases*, and the non-parallel sides are called *legs*:

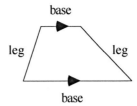

The area of a trapezoid is the average of the two bases times the height:

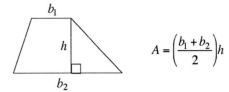

$$A = \left(\frac{b_1 + b_2}{2}\right)h$$

Volume

The volume of a rectangular solid (a box) is the product of the length, width, and height. The surface area is the sum of the area of the six faces:

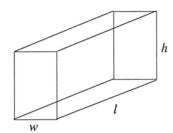

$$V = l \cdot w \cdot h$$
$$S = 2wl + 2hl + 2wh$$

If the length, width, and height of a rectangular solid (a box) are the same, it is a cube. Its volume is the cube of one of its sides, and its surface area is the sum of the areas of the six faces:

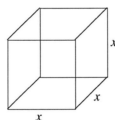

$$V = x^3$$
$$S = 6x^2$$

Example: The volume of the cube to the right is *x* and its surface area is *x*. What is the length of an edge of the cube?

(A)   6
(B)   10
(C)   18
(D)   36
(E)   48

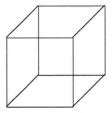

Let *e* be the length of an edge of the cube. Recall that the volume of a cube is e^3 and its surface area is $6e^2$. Since we are given that both the volume and the surface area are *x*, these expressions are equal:

$$e^3 = 6e^2$$
$$e^3 - 6e^2 = 0$$
$$e^2(e - 6) = 0$$
$$e^2 = 0 \ \text{ or } \ e - 6 = 0$$
$$e = 0 \ \text{ or } \ e = 6$$

We reject $e = 0$ since in that case no cube would exist. Hence, $e = 6$ and the answer is (A).

The volume of a cylinder is $V = \pi r^2 h$, and the lateral surface (excluding the top and bottom) is $S = 2\pi rh$, where r is the radius and h is the height:

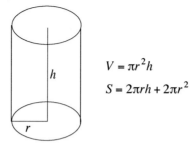

$$V = \pi r^2 h$$
$$S = 2\pi rh + 2\pi r^2$$

Circles

A circle is a set of points in a plane equidistant from a fixed point (the center of the circle). The perimeter of a circle is called the *circumference*.

A line segment from a circle to its center is a *radius*.

A line segment with both end points on a circle is a *chord*.

A chord passing though the center of a circle is a *diameter*.

A diameter can be viewed as two radii, and hence a diameter's length is twice that of a radius.

A line passing through two points on a circle is a *secant*.

A piece of the circumference is an *arc*.

The area bounded by the circumference and an angle with vertex at the center of the circle is a *sector*.

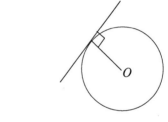

A tangent line to a circle intersects the circle at only one point. The radius of the circle is perpendicular to the tangent line at the point of tangency:

Two tangents to a circle from a common exterior point of the circle are congruent:

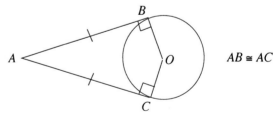

$$AB \cong AC$$

An angle inscribed in a semicircle is a right angle:

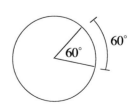

A central angle has by definition the same measure as its intercepted arc:

An inscribed angle has one-half the measure of its intercepted arc:

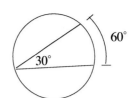

The area of a circle is πr^2, and its circumference (perimeter) is $2\pi r$, where r is the radius:

$A = \pi r^2$

$C = 2\pi r$

On the ACT, $\pi \approx 3$ is a sufficient approximation for π. You don't need $\pi \approx 3.14$.

Example: In the figure to the right, the circle has center O and its radius is 2. What is the length of arc ACB ?

(A) $\dfrac{\pi}{3}$ (B) $\dfrac{2\pi}{3}$ (C) π (D) $\dfrac{4\pi}{3}$ (E) $\dfrac{7\pi}{3}$

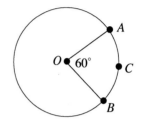

The circumference of the circle is $2\pi r = 2\pi(2) = 4\pi$. A central angle has by definition the same degree measure as its intercepted arc. Hence, arc ACB is also 60°. Now, the circumference of the circle has 360°. So arc ACB is $\dfrac{1}{6}$ (= 60/360) of the circle's circumference. Hence, arc $ACB = \dfrac{1}{6}(4\pi) = \dfrac{2}{3}\pi$. The answer is (B).

Shaded Regions

To find the area of the shaded region of a figure, subtract the area of the unshaded region from the area of the entire figure.

Example: What is the area of the shaded region formed by the circle and the rectangle in the figure to the right?

(A) $15 - 2\pi$
(B) $15 - \pi$
(C) 14
(D) $16 - \pi$
(E) 15π

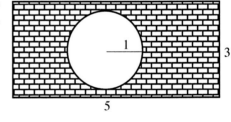

To find the area of the shaded region subtract the area of the circle from the area of the rectangle:

area of rectangle	–	area of circle
$3 \cdot 5$	–	$\pi \cdot 1^2$
15	–	π

The answer is (B).

Example: In the figure to the right, the radius of the larger circle is three times that of the smaller circle. If the circles are concentric, what is the ratio of the shaded region's area to the area of the smaller circle?

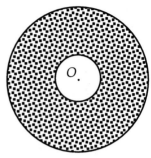

(A)   10:1
(B)   9:1
(C)   8:1
(D)   3:1
(E)   5:2

Since we are not given the radii of the circles, we can choose any two positive numbers such that one is three times the other. Let the outer radius be 3 and the inner radius be 1. Then the area of the outer circle is $\pi 3^2 = 9\pi$, and the area of the inner circle is $\pi 1^2 = \pi$. So the area of the shaded region is $9\pi - \pi = 8\pi$. Hence, the ratio of the area of the shaded region to the area of the smaller circle is $\dfrac{8\pi}{\pi} = \dfrac{8}{1}$. Therefore, the answer is (C).

"Birds-Eye" View

Most geometry problems on the ACT require straightforward calculations. However, some problems measure your insight into the basic rules of geometry. For this type of problem, you should step back and take a "birds-eye" view of the problem. The following example will illustrate.

Example: In the figure to the right, O is both the center of the circle with radius 2 and a vertex of the square *OPRS*. What is the length of diagonal *PS* ?

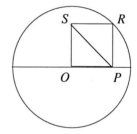

(A)   1/2   (B) $\dfrac{\sqrt{2}}{2}$ (C)   4   (D)   2   (E) $2\sqrt{5}$

The diagonals of a square are equal. Hence, line segment OR (not shown) is equal to SP. Now, OR is a radius of the circle and therefore OR = 2. Hence, SP = 2 as well, and the answer is (D).

Problem Set E:

1.   In the figure to the right, what is the value of *y* ?

(A) $\sqrt{23}$
(B) $\sqrt{27}$
(C) $\sqrt{29}$
(D) $\sqrt{33}$
(E) $\sqrt{35}$

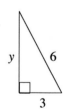

2.   In the figure to the right, circle P has diameter 2 and circle Q has diameter 1. What is the area of the shaded region?

(A) $3\pi/4$
(B) 3π
(C) $7\pi/2$
(D) 5π
(E) 6π

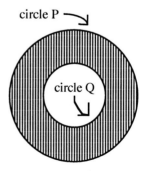

3. In the figure to the right, *QRST* is a square. If the shaded region is bounded by arcs of circles with centers at *Q*, *R*, *S*, and *T*, then the area of the shaded region is

(A) 9
(B) 36
(C) $36 - 9\pi$
(D) $36 - \pi$
(E) $9 - 3\pi$

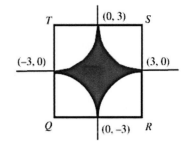

4. In the figure to the right, *QRST* is a square. If the area of each circle is 2π, then the area of square *QRST* is

(A) $\sqrt{2}$
(B) 4
(C) $\sqrt{2}\pi$
(D) $4\sqrt{2}$
(E) 32

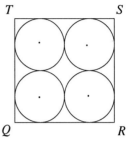

5. In the figure to the right, if *O* is the center of the circle, then *y* =

(A) 75
(B) 76
(C) 77
(D) 78
(E) 79

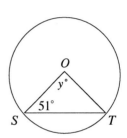

6. In the figure to the right, the value of $a + b$ is

(A) 118
(B) 119
(C) 120
(D) 121
(E) 122

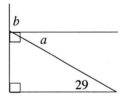

7. If $l_1 \| l_2$ in the figure to the right, what is the value of x?

(A) 30
(B) 45
(C) 60
(D) 72
(E) 90

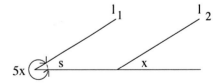

8. In the figure to the right, *O* is the center of the circle. Which one of the following must be true?

(A) $PQ > OQ$
(B) $OP \geq OQ$
(C) $PQ = OQ$
(D) $OQ < OP$
(E) $PQ \leq OP$

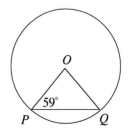

9. In the figure to the right, x is both the radius of the larger circle and the diameter of the smaller circle. The area of the shaded region is

    (A) $\dfrac{3}{4}\pi x^2$

    (B) $\dfrac{\pi}{3}$

    (C) $\dfrac{4}{3}\pi x^2$

    (D) $\dfrac{3}{5}\pi x^2$

    (E) πx^2

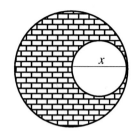

10. In the figure to the right, the circle with center O is inscribed in the square $PQRS$. The combined area of the shaded regions is

    (A) $36 - 9\pi$

    (B) $36 - \dfrac{9}{2}\pi$

    (C) $\dfrac{36 - 9\pi}{2}$

    (D) $18 - 9\pi$

    (E) $9 - \dfrac{9}{4}\pi$

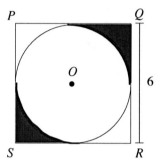

11. In the figure to the right, the length of QS is

    (A) $\sqrt{51}$
    (B) $\sqrt{61}$
    (C) $\sqrt{69}$
    (D) $\sqrt{77}$
    (E) $\sqrt{89}$

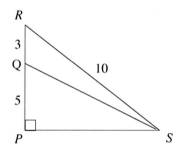

12. In the figure to the right, which one of the following must be true about y ?

    (A) $y > 37$
    (B) $y < 35$
    (C) $y > 40$
    (D) $y > 42$
    (E) $y > 45$

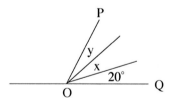

$\angle\,POQ = 70°$ and x > 15

13. In the figure to the right, if $l \| k$, then what is the value of y ?

    (A) 20
    (B) 45
    (C) 55
    (D) 75
    (E) 110

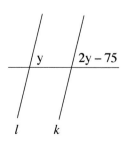

14. In the figure to the right, both triangles are right triangles. The area of the shaded region is

    (A)   1/2
    (B)   2/3
    (C)   7/8
    (D)   3/2
    (E)   5/2

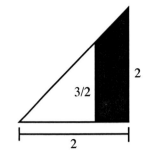

15. In the figure to the right, the radius of the larger circle is twice that of the smaller circle. If the circles are concentric, what is the ratio of the shaded region's area to the area of the smaller circle?

    (A)   10:1
    (B)   9:1
    (C)   3:1
    (D)   2:1
    (E)   1:1

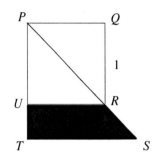

16. In the figure to the right, $\triangle PST$ is an isosceles right triangle, and $PS = 2$. What is the area of the shaded region *URST* ?

    (A)   4
    (B)   2
    (C)   5/4
    (D)   5/6
    (E)   1/2

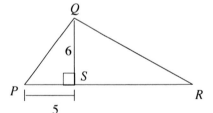

17. In the figure to the right, the area of $\triangle PQR$ is 40. What is the area of $\triangle QRS$?

    (A)   10
    (B)   15
    (C)   20
    (D)   25
    (E)   45

18. In the figure to the right, *PQRS* is a square and *M* and *N* are midpoints of their respective sides. What is the area of quadrilateral *PMRN* ?

    (A)   8
    (B)   10
    (C)   12
    (D)   14
    (E)   16

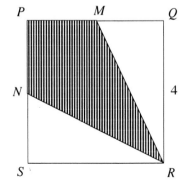

19. In the figure to the right, O is the center of the circle. If the area of the circle is 9π, then the perimeter of the sector *PRQO* is

(A) $\dfrac{\pi}{2} - 6$

(B) $\dfrac{\pi}{2} + 6$

(C) $\dfrac{3}{4}\pi + 6$

(D) $\dfrac{\pi}{2} + 18$

(E) $\dfrac{3}{4}\pi + 18$

20. Let A denote the area of a circular region. Which of the following denotes the circumference of that circular region?

(A) $\sqrt{\dfrac{A}{\pi}}$

(B) $2\dfrac{A}{\sqrt{\pi}}$

(C) $2\pi\sqrt{A}$

(D) $2\sqrt{\dfrac{A}{\pi}}$

(E) $2\pi\sqrt{\dfrac{A}{\pi}}$

21. Ship X and ship Y are 5 miles apart and are on a collision course. Ship X is sailing directly north, and ship Y is sailing directly east. If the point of impact is 1 mile closer to the current position of ship X than to the current position of ship Y, how many miles away from the point of impact is ship Y at this time?

(A) 1
(B) 2
(C) 3
(D) 4
(E) 5

22. The figure to the right represents a square with sides of length 4 surmounted by a circle with center O. What is the outer perimeter of the figure?

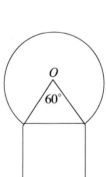

(A) $\dfrac{5}{6}\pi + 12$

(B) $\pi + 12$

(C) $\dfrac{49}{9}\pi + 12$

(D) $\dfrac{20}{3}\pi + 12$

(E) $9\pi + 12$

23. In $\triangle ABC$ to the right, $AB = AC$ and $x = 30$.
    What is the value of y ?
    (A)   30
    (B)   40
    (C)   50
    (D)   65
    (E)   75

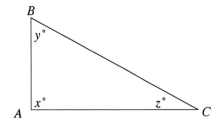

Note, figure not drawn to scale.

24. In the figure to the right, $c^2 = 6^2 + 8^2$. What is the
    area of the triangle?

    (A)   12
    (B)   18
    (C)   24
    (D)   30
    (E)   36

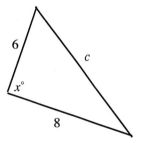

25. If the total surface area of cube S is 22, what is the volume of S ?

    (A) $\dfrac{1}{3}\sqrt{\dfrac{11}{3}}$

    (B) $\dfrac{\sqrt{11}}{3}$

    (C) $11/3$

    (D) $\dfrac{11}{3}\sqrt{\dfrac{11}{3}}$

    (E) $121/9$

26. In the figure to the right, what is the area of the
    triangle?

    (A)   5
    (B)   9
    (C)   10
    (D)   15
    (E)   It cannot be determined from the information
           given

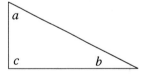

$a = x$, $b = 2x$, and $c = 3x$.

27. In the figure to the right, $\triangle ABC$ is inscribed in the circle
    and AB is a diameter of the circle. What is the radius of
    the circle?

    (A)   3/2
    (B)   2
    (C)   5/2
    (D)   5
    (E)   6

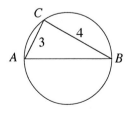

Duals

28. In the figure to the right, the circle is inscribed in the square. If the area of the square is 16 square feet, what is the area of the shaded region?

    (A) $16 - 16\pi$
    (B) $16 - 4.4\pi$
    (C) $16 - 4\pi$
    (D) 2π
    (E) 4π

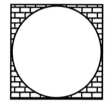

29. In the figure to the right, the circle is inscribed in the square. If the area of the circle is 1.21π square feet, what is the area of the shaded region?

    (A) $14 - 14.4\pi$
    (B) $4.84 - 1.21\pi$
    (C) $8 - 3\pi$
    (D) 1.21π
    (E) $11\pi/2$

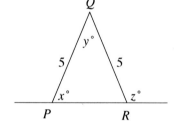

Duals

30. In $\triangle PQR$ to the right, $x = 60$. What is the value of y?

    (A)   60
    (B)   55
    (C)   50
    (D)   45
    (E)   40

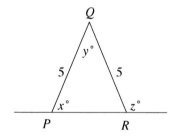

31. In $\triangle PQR$ to the right, $y + z = 150$. What is the value of y?

    (A)   60
    (B)   55
    (C)   50
    (D)   45
    (E)   40

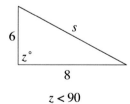

32. In the figure to the right, what is the area of the triangle?

    (A)   5
    (B)   9
    (C)   10
    (D)   15
    (E)   It cannot be determined from the information given

33. If point *P* in the figure to the right makes one complete revolution around the triangle which has height 4, what is the length of the path traveled by *P*?

    (A) $\sqrt{150}$
    (B) 14
    (C) $\sqrt{200}$
    (D) 15
    (E) 16

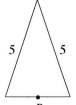

34. The opposite sides of quadrilateral *Q* are parallel and one of the four angles of *Q* is 90 degrees. If θ is an angle of quadrilateral *Q*, which one of the following must be true?

    (A) $\theta = 80°$
    (B) $\theta = 88°$
    (C) $\theta = 90°$
    (D) $\theta = 91°$
    (E) It cannot be determined from the information given

35. In the figure to the right, the coordinates of *A* are $(\sqrt{3}, 3)$. If $\triangle ABO$ is equilateral, what is the area of $\triangle ABO$?

    (A) $\frac{1}{2}\sqrt{3}$
    (B) $\frac{3}{2}\sqrt{3}$
    (C) $3\sqrt{3}$
    (D) $6\sqrt{3}$
    (E) $9\sqrt{3}$

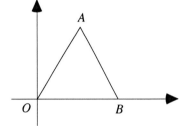

36. In the figure to the right, *E* is the midpoint of *AD*. What is the length of *EB*?

    (A) 1
    (B) 2
    (C) 11/5
    (D) 5/2
    (E) 3

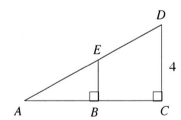

37. If the sides *x* of the rectangle to the right are increased by 3 units, the resulting figure is a square with area 20. What was the original area?

    (A) $20 - 3\sqrt{20}$
    (B) $20 - 2\sqrt{20}$
    (C) $20 - \sqrt{20}$
    (D) $20 - \sqrt{2}$
    (E) 19

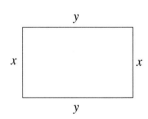

Duals

38. In the figure to the right, h denotes the height and b the base of the triangle. If $2b + h = 6$, what is the area of the triangle?

(A)   1
(B)   2
(C)   3
(D)   4
(E)   Not enough information

39. In the figure to the right, h denotes the height and b the base of the triangle. If $(bh)^2 = 16$, what is the area of the triangle?

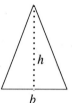

(A)   1
(B)   2
(C)   3
(D)   4
(E)   Not enough information

Duals

40. If the ratio of an edge of cube S and the greatest distance between two points on the cube is $1 : \sqrt{3}$, then the volume of cube S must be

(A)   greater than 8
(B)   less than 8
(C)   equal to 8
(D)   greater than or equal to 8
(E)   Not enough information to decide

41. If the length of a diagonal across a face of cube S is 2, then the volume of cube S must be

(A)   greater than 8
(B)   less than 8
(C)   equal to 8
(D)   greater than or equal to 8
(E)   Not enough information to decide

42. In the parallelogram to the right, $\angle BAD + \angle BCD = 140$. What is the measure of $\angle ABC$?

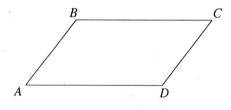

(A)   100
(B)   110
(C)   120
(D)   125
(E)   142

43. An equilateral triangle is inscribed in a circle, as shown to the right. If the radius of the circle is 2, what is the area of the triangle?

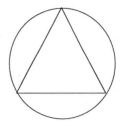

   (A) $\dfrac{\sqrt{2}}{2}$

   (B) $\sqrt{2}$
   (C) $\sqrt{3}$
   (D) $3\sqrt{3}$
   (E) $10\sqrt{3}$

44. The triangle to the right has side DC of the square as its base. If $DM = 5$ and M is the midpoint of side AB, what is the area of the shaded region?

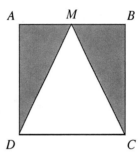

   (A) 5/2
   (B) $\sqrt{10}$
   (C) $\sqrt{15}$
   (D) 4
   (E) 10

45. A square with sides of length 3 is intersected by a line at S and T. What is the maximum possible distance between S and T?

   (A) $\sqrt{6}$ (B) $2\sqrt{3}$ (C) $3\sqrt{2}$ (D) $2\sqrt{5}$ (E) 9

46. In the triangle to the right, what is the value of $\dfrac{x+y+z}{15}$?

 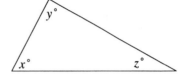

   (A) 9
   (B) 10
   (C) 11
   (D) 12
   (E) 13

47. If a square has an area of a^2 and a right-angled isosceles triangle also has area is a^2, then which one of the following must be true?

   (A) The perimeter of the square is greater than the perimeter of the triangle.
   (B) The perimeter of the square is less than the perimeter of the triangle.
   (C) The perimeter of the square is equal to the perimeter of the triangle.
   (D) The perimeter of the square is greater than or equal to the perimeter of the triangle.
   (E) It cannot be determined which perimeter is greater from the information given

48. The perimeter of a square is equal to the perimeter of a rectangle whose length and width are $6m$ and $4m$, respectively. The side of the square is

   (A) $3m$
   (B) $4m$
   (C) $5m$
   (D) $6m$
   (E) $7m$

49. If the circumference of a circle is $4m$, then the ratio of circumference of the circle to the diameter of the circle is

(A) π
(B) 4
(C) 2π
(D) 4π
(E) 16

50. In Triangle ABC, $\angle A$ is 10 degrees greater than $\angle B$, and $\angle B$ is 10 degrees greater than $\angle C$. The value of Angle B is

(A) 30
(B) 40
(C) 50
(D) 60
(E) 70

51. Two squares each with sides of length s are joined to form a rectangle. The area of the rectangle is

(A) s^2
(B) $2s^2$
(C) $4s^2$
(D) $8s^2$
(E) $16s^2$

52. A person travels 16 miles due north and then 12 miles due east. How far is the person from his initial location?

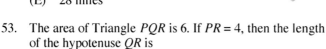

(A) 4 miles
(B) 8 miles
(C) 14 miles
(D) 20 miles
(E) 28 miles

53. The area of Triangle PQR is 6. If $PR = 4$, then the length of the hypotenuse QR is

(A) 1
(B) 2
(C) 3
(D) 4
(E) 5

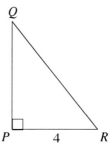

54. In the figure, the equation of line AB is $y = -\dfrac{5}{3}x + 10$.

The area of the shaded portion is

(A) 12
(B) 30
(C) 100/3
(D) 60
(E) 100

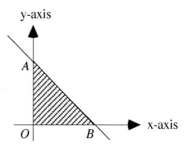

55. In the figure to the right, which one of the following must be true about the angle θ ?

   (A) $\theta = 60°$
   (B) $\theta < 60°$
   (C) $\theta > 60°$
   (D) $\theta > 70°$
   (E) It cannot be determined from the information given

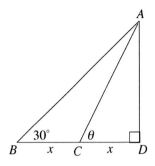

56. In the figure, if $x = 54°$ and $y = 72°$, then $z =$

   (A) $54°$
   (B) $56°$
   (C) $72°$
   (D) $76°$
   (E) $98°$

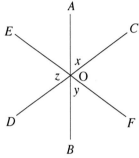

O is the point of intersection of the three lines in the figure.

57. If one of the sides of the rectangle shown in the figure has a length of 3, then the area of the rectangle is
   (A) 9
   (B) 13.5
   (C) 18
   (D) 27
   (E) 54

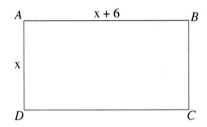

58. The value of $x + y + z =$

   (A) 120°
   (B) 160°
   (C) 180°
   (D) 270°
   (E) 360°

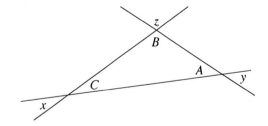

59. In the figure, what is the area of Triangle *ABC* ?

   (A) 25
   (B) 50
   (C) $100/\sqrt{2}$
   (D) 100
   (E) $100\sqrt{2}$

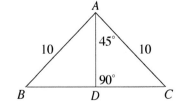

60. In the triangle to the right, $y/x = 3$. Which one of the following must be true?

    (A) $4x > z$
    (B) $4x < z$
    (C) $4x \leq z$
    (D) $4x = z$
    (E) It cannot be determined from the information given

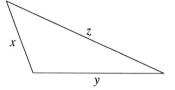

61. In the figure to the right, which one of the following statements about the circumference C of the circle and the perimeter P of Square $PQRS$ must be true?

    (A) $C > P$
    (B) $C < P$
    (C) $C \leq P$
    (D) $C = P$
    (E) It cannot be determined from the information given

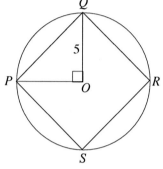

O is the center of the circle, and the radius of the circle is 5.

62. In the figure, what is the value of x?

    (A) $20°$
    (B) $30°$
    (C) $40°$
    (D) $50°$
    (E) $60°$

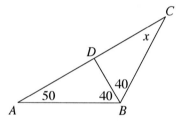

63. The area of the Triangle ABC shown in the figure is 30. The area of Triangle ADC is

    (A) 5
    (B) 10
    (C) 15
    (D) 20
    (E) 25

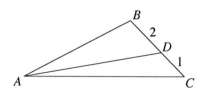

64. In the figure, what is the value of y ?

    (A) 7.5
    (B) 15
    (C) 30
    (D) 40
    (E) 45

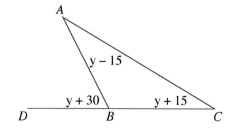

65. A circle is depicted in the rectangular coordinate system as shown. The value of *x* is

    (A) 4
    (B) 6
    (C) 8
    (D) 10
    (E) 12

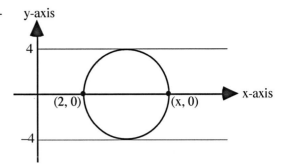

66. In the figure, the ratio of *x* to *y* is 2. What is the value of *y*?

    (A) 108
    (B) 90
    (C) 68
    (D) 45
    (E) 36

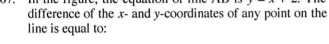

67. In the figure, the equation of line AB is $y = x + 2$. The difference of the *x*- and *y*-coordinates of any point on the line is equal to:

    (A) −4
    (B) −2
    (C) 0
    (D) 2
    (E) 4

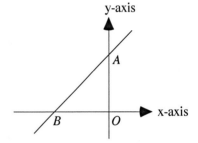

Answers and Solutions to Problem Set E

1.   In the figure to the right, what is the value of y ?

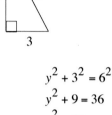

    (A) $\sqrt{23}$
    (B) $\sqrt{27}$
    (C) $\sqrt{29}$
    (D) $\sqrt{33}$
    (E) $\sqrt{35}$

Since we have a right triangle, the Pythagorean Theorem yields $y^2 + 3^2 = 6^2$

Simplifying yields $y^2 + 9 = 36$

Subtracting 9 from both sides yields $y^2 = 27$

Taking the square root of both sides yields $y = \sqrt{27}$

The answer is (B).

2.   In the figure to the right, circle P has diameter 2 and circle Q has diameter 1. What is the area of the shaded region?

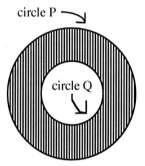

    (A) $\dfrac{3}{4}\pi$
    (B) 3π
    (C) $\dfrac{7}{2}\pi$
    (D) 5π
    (E) 6π

Since the diameter of circle P is 2, its radius is 1. So the area of circle P is $\pi(1)^2 = \pi$. Since the diameter of circle Q is 1, its radius is $\dfrac{1}{2}$. So the area of circle Q is $\pi\left(\dfrac{1}{2}\right)^2 = \dfrac{1}{4}\pi$. The area of the shaded region is the difference between the area of circle P and the area of circle Q: $\pi - \dfrac{1}{4}\pi = \dfrac{3}{4}\pi$. The answer is (A).

3.   In the figure to the right, *QRST* is a square. If the shaded region is bounded by arcs of circles with centers at Q, R, S, and T, then the area of the shaded region is

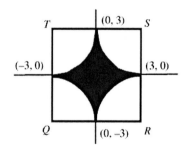

    (A)   9
    (B)   36
    (C) $36 - 9\pi$
    (D) $36 - \pi$
    (E) $9 - 3\pi$

Each arc forms a quarter of a circle. Taken together the four arcs constitute one whole circle. From the drawing, we see that the radii of the arcs are each length 3, so the area of the four arcs together is $\pi(3)^2 = 9\pi$. Since the square has sides of length 6, its area is 36. Hence, the area of the shaded region is $36 - 9\pi$. The answer is (C).

4.   In the figure to the right, *QRST* is a square. If the area of
      each circle is 2π, then the area of square *QRST* is

      (A) $\sqrt{2}$
      (B)   4
      (C) $\sqrt{2}\pi$
      (D) $4\sqrt{2}$
      (E)   32

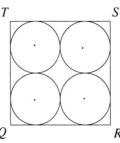

Setting the area of a circle equal to 2π gives $\pi r^2 = 2\pi$

Dividing both sides of this equation by π gives $r^2 = 2$

Taking the square root of both sides gives $r = \sqrt{2}$

Hence, the diameter of each circle is $d = 2r = 2\sqrt{2}$

Adding the diameters to the diagram gives

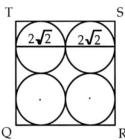

Clearly, in this diagram, the sides of the square are length $2\sqrt{2} + 2\sqrt{2} = 4\sqrt{2}$. Hence, the area of the
square is $4\sqrt{2} \cdot 4\sqrt{2} = 16 \cdot 2 = 32$. The answer is (E).

5.   In the figure to the right, if *O* is the center of the circle,
      then *y* =

      (A)   75
      (B)   76
      (C)   77
      (D)   78
      (E)   79

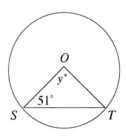

OS and *OT* are equal since they are radii of the circle. Hence, ΔSOT is isosceles. Therefore, $S = T = 51°$.
Recalling that the angle sum of a triangle is $180°$, we get $S + T + y = 51° + 51° + y = 180°$. Solving for *y*
gives $y = 78°$. The answer is (D).

6.   In the figure to the right, the value of $a + b$ is

      (A)   118
      (B)   119
      (C)   120
      (D)   121
      (E)   122

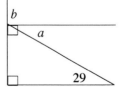

Since the two horizontal lines are parallel (Why?), angle *a* and the angle with measure 29 are alternate
interior angles and therefore are equal. Further, from the drawing, angle *b* is $90°$. Hence, $a + b = 29 + 90 =$
119. The answer is (B).

7.   If $l_1 \| l_2$ in the figure to the right, what is the value of x?

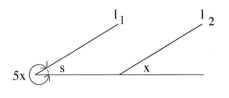

    (A)   30
    (B)   45
    (C)   60
    (D)   72
    (E)   90

Since $l_1 \| l_2$, s and x are corresponding angles and therefore are congruent.

Now, about any point there are 360°. Hence,	$5x + s = 360$
Substituting x for s in this equation gives	$5x + x = 360$
Combining like terms gives	$6x = 360$
Dividing by 6 gives	$x = 60$

The answer is (C).

8.   In the figure to the right, O is the center of the circle. Which one of the following must be true?

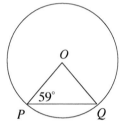

    (A) $PQ > OQ$
    (B) $OP \geq OQ$
    (C) $PQ = OQ$
    (D) $OQ < OP$
    (E) $PQ \leq OP$

ΔOPQ is isosceles. (Why?). Hence, $P = Q = 59°$. Now, the angle sum of a triangle is 180. So

$$O + P + Q = 180.$$

Substituting $P = Q = 59°$ into this equation gives $O + 59 + 59 = 180.$

Solving for O gives $O = 62.$

Now, since O is the largest angle in ΔOPQ, the side opposite it, PQ, is the longest side of the triangle. The answer is (A).

9.   In the figure to the right, x is both the radius of the larger circle and the diameter of the smaller circle. The area of the shaded region is

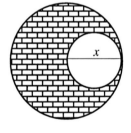

    (A) $\dfrac{3}{4}\pi x^2$

    (B) $\dfrac{\pi}{3}$

    (C) $\dfrac{4}{3}\pi x^2$

    (D) $\dfrac{3}{5}\pi x^2$

    (E) πx^2

Since x is the radius of the larger circle, the area of the larger circle is πx^2. Since x is the diameter of the smaller circle, the radius of the smaller circle is $\dfrac{x}{2}$. Therefore, the area of the smaller circle is

$\pi\left(\dfrac{x}{2}\right)^2 = \pi\dfrac{x^2}{4}$. Subtracting the area of the smaller circle from the area of the larger circle gives

$\pi x^2 - \pi\dfrac{x^2}{4} = \dfrac{4}{4}\pi x^2 - \pi\dfrac{x^2}{4} = \dfrac{4\pi x^2 - \pi x^2}{4} = \dfrac{3\pi x^2}{4}$. The answer is (A).

10. In the figure to the right, the circle with center O is inscribed in the square $PQRS$. The combined area of the shaded regions is

(A) $36 - 9\pi$

(B) $36 - \dfrac{9}{2}\pi$

(C) $\dfrac{36 - 9\pi}{2}$

(D) $18 - 9\pi$

(E) $9 - \dfrac{9}{4}\pi$

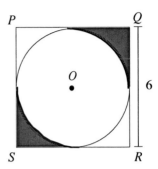

The area of square $PQRS$ is $6^2 = 36$. Now, the radius of the circle is 3. (Why?) So the area of the circle is $\pi(3)^2 = 9\pi$. Subtracting the area of the circle from the area of the square yields $36 - 9\pi$. This is the combined area of the regions outside the circle and inside the square. Dividing this quantity by 2 gives $\dfrac{36 - 9\pi}{2}$. The answer is (C).

11. In the figure to the right, the length of QS is

(A) $\sqrt{51}$

(B) $\sqrt{61}$

(C) $\sqrt{69}$

(D) $\sqrt{77}$

(E) $\sqrt{89}$

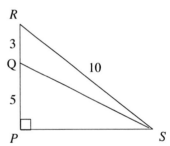

The length of PR is $PR = 3 + 5 = 8$. Applying the Pythagorean Theorem to triangle PRS yields

$$8^2 + (PS)^2 = 10^2$$

Squaring yields $\qquad\qquad 64 + (PS)^2 = 100$

Subtracting 64 from both sides yields $\qquad (PS)^2 = 36$

Taking the square root of both sides yields $\qquad PS = \sqrt{36} = 6$

Now, applying the Pythagorean Theorem to triangle PQS yields $\qquad (QS)^2 = 5^2 + 6^2$

Squaring and adding yields $\qquad (QS)^2 = 61$

Taking the square root of both sides yields $\qquad QS = \sqrt{61}$

The answer is (B).

12. In the figure to the right, which one of the following must be true about y ?

    (A) $y > 37$
    (B) $y < 35$
    (C) $y > 40$
    (D) $y > 42$
    (E) $y > 45$

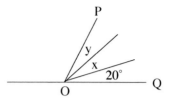

$\angle POQ = 70°$ and $x > 15$

Since $\angle POQ = 70°$, we get $x + y + 20 = 70$. Solving this equation for y yields $y = 50 - x$. Now, we are given that $x > 15$. Hence, the expression $50 - x$ must be less than 35:

$$x > 15$$
$$-x < -15$$
$$50 - x < 50 - 15$$
$$50 - x < 35$$

The answer is (B).

13. In the figure to the right, if $l \| k$, then what is the value of y ?

    (A) 20
    (B) 45
    (C) 55
    (D) 75
    (E) 110

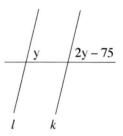

Since lines l and k are parallel, we know that the corresponding angles are equal. Hence, $y = 2y - 75$. Solving this equation for y gives $y = 75$. The answer is (D).

14. In the figure to the right, both triangles are right triangles. The area of the shaded region is

    (A) 1/2
    (B) 2/3
    (C) 7/8
    (D) 3/2
    (E) 5/2

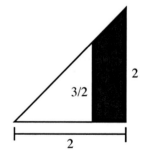

Since the height and base of the larger triangle are the same, the slope of the hypotenuse is 45°. Hence, the base of the smaller triangle is the same as its height, 3/2. Thus, the area of the shaded region = (area of the larger triangle) – (area of the smaller triangle) = $\left(\frac{1}{2} \cdot 2 \cdot 2\right) - \left(\frac{1}{2} \cdot \frac{3}{2} \cdot \frac{3}{2}\right) = 2 - \frac{9}{8} = \frac{7}{8}$. The answer is (C).

15. In the figure to the right, the radius of the larger circle is twice that of the smaller circle. If the circles are concentric, what is the ratio of the shaded region's area to the area of the smaller circle?

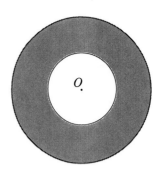

(A) 10:1
(B) 9:1
(C) 3:1
(D) 2:1
(E) 1:1

Suppose the radius of the larger circle is 2 and the radius of the smaller circle is 1. Then the area of the larger circle is $\pi r^2 = \pi(2)^2 = 4\pi$, and the area of the smaller circle is $\pi r^2 = \pi(1)^2 = \pi$. Hence, the area of the shaded region is $4\pi - \pi = 3\pi$. Now, $\dfrac{area\ of\ shaded\ region}{area\ of\ smaller\ circle} = \dfrac{3\pi}{\pi} = \dfrac{3}{1}$. The answer is (C).

16. In the figure to the right, $\triangle PST$ is an isosceles right triangle, and $PS = 2$. What is the area of the shaded region $URST$?

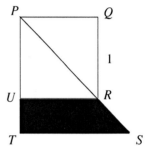

(A) 4
(B) 2
(C) 5/4
(D) 5/6
(E) 1/2

Let x stand for the distances TP and TS. Applying The Pythagorean Theorem to the right triangle PST gives

$$TP^2 + TS^2 = PS^2$$

Substituting x for TP and TS and substituting 2 for PS gives

$$x^2 + x^2 = 2^2$$

Squaring and combining like terms gives

$$2x^2 = 4$$

Dividing by 2 gives

$$x^2 = 2$$

Finally, taking the square root gives

$$x = \sqrt{2}$$

Adding this information to the diagram gives

Now, the area of the shaded region equals

$$(\text{area of triangle PST}) - (\text{area of triangle PRU}) =$$

$$\left(\frac{1}{2}\cdot\sqrt{2}\cdot\sqrt{2}\right)-\left(\frac{1}{2}\cdot1\cdot1\right)=\left(\frac{1}{2}\cdot2\right)-\left(\frac{1}{2}\right)=1-\frac{1}{2}=\frac{1}{2}$$

The answer is (E).

17.   In the figure to the right, the area of ΔPQR is 40. What is the area of ΔQRS ?

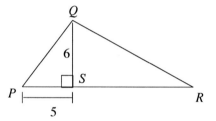

    (A)   10
    (B)   15
    (C)   20
    (D)   25
    (E)   45

The area of triangle PQS is $\frac{1}{2}\cdot5\cdot6=15$. Now, (the area of ΔQRS) = (the area of ΔPQR) − (the area of ΔPQS) = 40 − 15 = 25. The answer is (D).

18.   In the figure to the right, *PQRS* is a square and *M* and *N* are midpoints of their respective sides. What is the area of quadrilateral *PMRN* ?

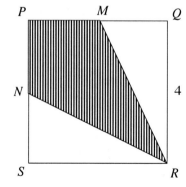

    (A)   8
    (B)   10
    (C)   12
    (D)   14
    (E)   16

Since M is the midpoint of side PQ, the length of MQ is 2. Hence, the area of triangle MQR is $\frac{1}{2}\cdot2\cdot4=4$.

A similar analysis shows that the area of triangle NSR is 4. Thus, the unshaded area of the figure is 4 + 4 = 8. Subtracting this from the area of the square gives 16 − 8 = 8. The answer is (A).

19. In the figure to the right, O is the center of the circle. If the area of the circle is 9π, then the perimeter of the sector *PRQO* is

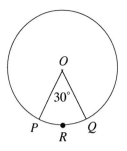

(A) $\dfrac{\pi}{2} - 6$

(B) $\dfrac{\pi}{2} + 6$

(C) $\dfrac{3}{4}\pi + 6$

(D) $\dfrac{\pi}{2} + 18$

(E) $\dfrac{3}{4}\pi + 18$

Since the area of the circle is 9π, we get

$$\pi r^2 = 9\pi$$
$$r^2 = 9$$
$$r = 3$$

Now, the circumference of the circle is

$$C = 2\pi r = 2\pi 3 = 6\pi$$

Since the central angle is $30°$, the length of arc *PRQ* is

$$\frac{30}{360}C = \frac{1}{12} \cdot 6\pi = \frac{1}{2}\pi$$

Hence, the perimeter of the sector is

$$\frac{1}{2}\pi + 3 + 3 = \frac{1}{2}\pi + 6$$

The answer is (B).

20. Let A denote the area of a circular region. Which of the following denotes the circumference of that circular region?

(A) $\sqrt{\dfrac{A}{\pi}}$

(B) $2\dfrac{A}{\sqrt{\pi}}$

(C) $2\pi\sqrt{A}$

(D) $2\sqrt{\dfrac{A}{\pi}}$

(E) $2\pi\sqrt{\dfrac{A}{\pi}}$

Since A denotes the area of the circular region, we get

$$A = \pi r^2$$
$$\frac{A}{\pi} = r^2$$
$$\sqrt{\frac{A}{\pi}} = r$$

Hence, the circumference is $C = 2\pi r = 2\pi\sqrt{\dfrac{A}{\pi}}$

The answer is (E).

21.   Ship X and ship Y are 5 miles apart and are on a collision course. Ship X is sailing directly north, and ship Y is sailing directly east. If the point of impact is 1 mile closer to the current position of ship X than to the current position of ship Y, how many miles away from the point of impact is ship Y at this time?

(A)   1
(B)   2
(C)   3
(D)   4
(E)   5

Let d be the distance ship Y is from the point of collision. Then the distance ship X is from the point of collision is d – 1. The following diagram depicts the situation:

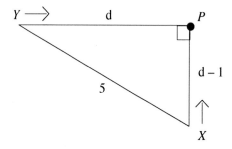

Applying the Pythagorean Theorem to the diagram yields

$$d^2 + (d-1)^2 = 5^2$$

$$d^2 + d^2 - 2d + 1 = 25$$

$$2d^2 - 2d - 24 = 0$$

$$d^2 - d - 12 = 0$$

$$(d-4)(d+3) = 0$$

$$d = 4 \quad \text{or} \quad d = -3$$

Since *d* denotes distance, we reject *d* = –3. Hence, *d* = 4 and the answer is (D).

22.   The figure to the right represents a square with sides of length 4 surmounted by a circle with center *O*. What is the outer perimeter of the figure?

(A) $\frac{5}{6}\pi + 12$

(B) $\pi + 12$

(C) $\frac{49}{9}\pi + 12$

(D) $\frac{20}{3}\pi + 12$

(E) $9\pi + 12$

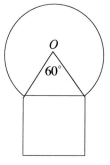

Since two sides of the triangle are radii of the circle, they are equal. Hence, the triangle is isosceles, and the base angles are equal:

Since the angle sum of a triangle is 180, we get

$$x + x + 60 = 180$$

$$2x = 120$$

$$x = 60$$

Hence, the triangle is equilateral. Therefore, the radius of the circle is 4, and the circumference is $C = 2\pi r = 2\pi 4 = 8\pi$. Now, the portion of the perimeter formed by the circle has length $\dfrac{360 - 60}{360} \cdot C = \dfrac{5}{6} \cdot 8\pi = \dfrac{20}{3}\pi$.

Adding the three sides of the square to this expression gives $\dfrac{20}{3}\pi + 12$. The answer is (D).

23. In $\triangle ABC$ to the right, $AB = AC$ and $x = 30$.
     What is the value of y ?
     (A) 30
     (B) 40
     (C) 50
     (D) 65
     (E) 75

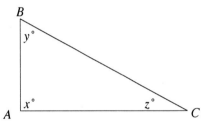

Note, figure not drawn to scale.

Since $AB = AC$, $\triangle ABC$ is isosceles. Hence, its base angles are equal: $y = z$. Since the angle sum of a triangle is 180°, we get $x + y + z = 180$. Replacing z with y and x with 30 in this equation and then simplifying yields

$$30 + y + y = 180$$
$$30 + 2y = 180$$
$$2y = 150$$
$$y = 75$$

The answer is (E).

24. In the figure to the right, $c^2 = 6^2 + 8^2$. What is the
     area of the triangle?

     (A) 12
     (B) 18
     (C) 24
     (D) 30
     (E) 36

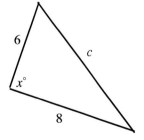

Recall that a triangle is a right triangle if and only if the square of the longest side is equal to the sum of the squares of the shorter sides (Pythagorean Theorem). Hence, $c^2 = 6^2 + 8^2$ implies that the triangle is a right triangle. So the area of the triangle is $\dfrac{1}{2} \cdot 6 \cdot 8 = 24$. The answer is (C).

25.   If the total surface area of cube S is 22, what is the volume of S?

(A) $\dfrac{1}{3}\sqrt{\dfrac{11}{3}}$

(B) $\dfrac{\sqrt{11}}{3}$

(C)   11/3

(D) $\dfrac{11}{3}\sqrt{\dfrac{11}{3}}$

(E)   121/9

Since the total surface area of the cube is 22 and each of the cube's six faces has the same area, the area of each face is $\dfrac{22}{6}$, or $\dfrac{11}{3}$. Now, each face of the cube is a square with area $\dfrac{11}{3}$, so the length of a side of the cube is $\sqrt{\dfrac{11}{3}}$. Hence, the volume of the cube is $\sqrt{\dfrac{11}{3}}\cdot\sqrt{\dfrac{11}{3}}\cdot\sqrt{\dfrac{11}{3}}=\dfrac{11}{3}\cdot\sqrt{\dfrac{11}{3}}$. The answer is (D).

26.   In the figure to the right, what is the area of the triangle?

(A)   5
(B)   9
(C)   10
(D)   15
(E)   It cannot be determined from the information given

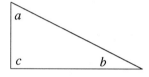

$a = x$, $b = 2x$, and $c = 3x$.

From the information given, we can determine the measures of the angles:

$$a + b + c = x + 2x + 3x = 6x = 180$$

Dividing the last equation by 6 gives

$$x = 30$$

Hence, $a = 30$, $b = 60$, and $c = 90$. However, different size triangles can have these angle measures, as the diagram below illustrates:

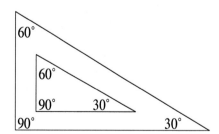

Hence, the information given is not sufficient to determine the area of the triangle. The answer is (E).

27. In the figure to the right, $\triangle ABC$ is inscribed in the circle and *AB* is a diameter of the circle. What is the radius of the circle?

    (A) 3/2
    (B) 2
    (C) 5/2
    (D) 5
    (E) 6

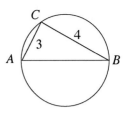

Recall from geometry that a triangle inscribed in a semicircle is a right triangle. Hence, we can use the Pythagorean Theorem to calculate the length of *AB*:

$$AC^2 + BC^2 = AB^2$$

or

$$3^2 + 4^2 = AB^2$$

or

$$25 = AB^2$$

or

$$5 = AB$$

Hence, the radius of the circle is $\dfrac{diameter}{2} = \dfrac{5}{2}$. The answer is (C).

28. In the figure to the right, the circle is inscribed in the square. If the area of the square is 16 square feet, what is the area of the shaded region?

    (A) $16 - 16\pi$
    (B) $16 - 4.4\pi$
    (C) $16 - 4\pi$
    (D) 2π
    (E) 4π

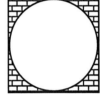

Since the area of the square is 16, the length of a side is

$$\sqrt{16} = 4$$

Since the circle is inscribed in the square, a diameter of the circle has the same length as a side of the square. Hence, the radius of the circle is

$$\frac{diameter}{2} = \frac{4}{2} = 2$$

Therefore, the area of the circle is

$$\pi \cdot 2^2 = 4\pi$$

and the area of the shaded region is

$$16 - 4\pi$$

The answer is (C).

29. In the figure to the right, the circle is inscribed in the square. If the area of the circle is 1.21π square feet, what is the area of the shaded region?

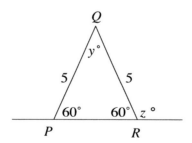

(A) $14 - 14.4\pi$
(B) $4.84 - 1.21\pi$
(C) $8 - 3\pi$
(D) 1.21π
(E) $11\pi/2$

Since the area of the circle is 1.21π, we get

$$\pi r^2 = 1.21\pi$$

Dividing by π yields

$$r^2 = 1.21$$

Taking the square root of both sides gives

$$r = 1.1$$

So the diameter of the circle is

$$d = 2r = 2(1.1) = 2.2$$

Hence, a side of the square has length 2.2, and the area of the square is

$$(2.2)^2 = 4.84$$

Therefore, the area of the shaded region is

$$4.84 - 1.21\pi$$

The answer is (B).

30. In ΔPQR to the right, $x = 60$. What is the value of y?

(A)   60
(B)   55
(C)   50
(D)   45
(E)   40

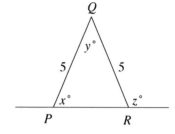

Since ΔPQR is isosceles, its base angles are equal:

Remembering that the angle sum of a triangle is $180°$, we see y is also $60°$. The answer is (A).

31.   In $\triangle PQR$ to the right, $y + z = 150$. What is the
value of y?

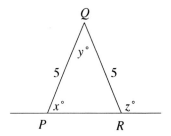

(A)   60
(B)   55
(C)   50
(D)   45
(E)   40

Again, since the base angles of an isosceles triangle are equal, the diagram becomes

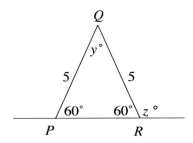

Since x and z form a straight angle, $x + z = 180$. Hence, we have the system:

$$x + z = 180$$
$$y + z = 150$$

Subtracting these equations yields $x - y = 30$. Since there are two variables and only one equation, we need another equation in order to determine y. However, since the angle sum of a triangle is $180°$, $x + x + y = 180$, or $2x + y = 180$. This yields the system:

$$x - y = 30$$
$$2x + y = 180$$

Adding the equations gives $3x = 210$. Hence, $x = 70$. Plugging this value for x back into either equation gives $y = 40$. The answer is (E).

32.   In the figure to the right, what is the area of the
triangle?

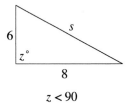

(A)   5
(B)   9
(C)   10
(D)   15
(E)   It cannot be determined from the information
given

Since we do not know the value of z, the triangle can vary in size. Each of the triangles illustrated below satisfies the given information, yet one has an area greater than the other:

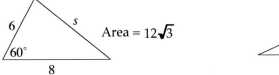

The answer is (E).

33. If point *P* in the figure to the right makes one complete revolution around the triangle which has height 4, what is the length of the path traveled by *P*?

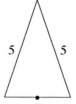

(A) $\sqrt{150}$
(B) 14
(C) $\sqrt{200}$
(D) 15
(E) 16

Add the height to the diagram:

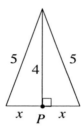

Applying the Pythagorean Theorem to either of the right triangles formed above yields

$$x^2 + 4^2 = 5^2$$

Solving for *x* yields

$$x = 3$$

Hence, the base of the triangle is $2x = 2(3) = 6$, and therefore the perimeter is $5 + 5 + 6 = 16$. The answer is (E).

34. The opposite sides of quadrilateral *Q* are parallel and one of the four angles of *Q* is 90 degrees. If θ is an angle of quadrilateral Q, which one of the following must be true?

(A) $\theta = 80°$
(B) $\theta = 88°$
(C) $\theta = 90°$
(D) $\theta = 91°$
(E) It cannot be determined from the information given

Note, a quadrilateral is a closed figure formed by four straight lines. Now, the given information generates the following diagram:

Here, our goal is to show that the other three angles are also 90 degrees. It will help to extend the sides as follows:

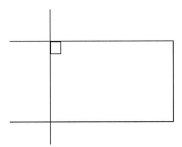

Since corresponding angles are congruent, we get

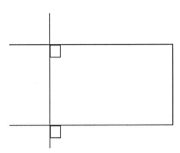

Or

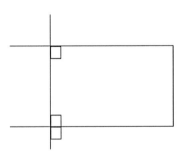

Continuing in this manner will show that the other two angles are also 90 degrees. Hence, θ is 90°. The answer is (C).

35.   In the figure to the right, the coordinates of *A* are $(\sqrt{3}, 3)$. If $\triangle ABO$ is equilateral, what is the area of $\triangle ABO$?

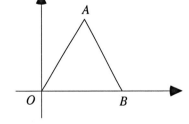

(A) $\frac{1}{2}\sqrt{3}$

(B) $\frac{3}{2}\sqrt{3}$

(C) $3\sqrt{3}$

(D) $6\sqrt{3}$

(E) $9\sqrt{3}$

Since the coordinates of *A* are $(\sqrt{3}, 3)$, the diagram becomes

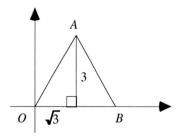

Further, since $\triangle ABO$ is equilateral, the diagram becomes

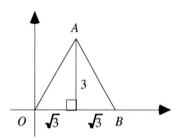

Hence, the area is $\frac{1}{2} \cdot b \cdot h = \frac{1}{2} \cdot 2\sqrt{3} \cdot 3 = 3\sqrt{3}$. The answer is (C).

36. In the figure to the right, E is the midpoint of AD.
     What is the length of EB?

     (A)   1
     (B)   2
     (C)   11/5
     (D)   5/2
     (E)   3

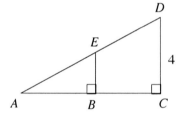

Recall from geometry that if two angles of one triangle are equal to two angles of another triangle then the triangles are similar. Hence, $\triangle ACD$ is similar to $\triangle ABE$ since they share angle A and both are right triangles.

   Since E is the midpoint of AD, the diagram becomes

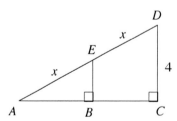

Since $\triangle ABE$ and $\triangle ACD$ are similar, their corresponding sides are proportional:

$$\frac{EB}{EA} = \frac{DC}{DA}$$

or

$$\frac{EB}{x} = \frac{4}{2x}$$

Solving for EB yields

$$EB = 2$$

The answer is (B).

37. If the sides x of the rectangle to the right are increased by 3 units, the resulting figure is a square with area 20. What was the original area?

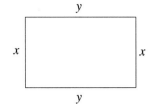

    (A) $20 - 3\sqrt{20}$
    (B) $20 - 2\sqrt{20}$
    (C) $20 - \sqrt{20}$
    (D) $20 - \sqrt{2}$
    (E)   19

The area of the original rectangle is $A = xy$. So the goal in this problem is to find the values of x and y.

Lengthening side x of the original figure by 3 units yields

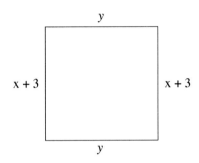

The area of this figure is $y(x + 3) = 20$. Since the resulting figure is a square, $y = x + 3$. Hence, we have the system:

$$y(x + 3) = 20$$
$$y = x + 3$$

Solving this system gives $x = \sqrt{20} - 3$ and $y = \sqrt{20}$. Hence, the area is $A = xy = \left(\sqrt{20} - 3\right)\left(\sqrt{20}\right) = 20 - 3\sqrt{20}$. The answer is (A).

38. In the figure to the right, h denotes the height and b the base of the triangle. If $2b + h = 6$, what is the area of the triangle?

    (A)   1
    (B)   2
    (C)   3
    (D)   4
    (E)   Not enough information

The area of a triangle is $\frac{1}{2} \, base \times height$. For the given triangle, this becomes

$$Area = \frac{1}{2} b \times h$$

Solving the equation $2b + h = 6$ for h gives $h = 6 - 2b$. Plugging this into the area formula gives

$$Area = \frac{1}{2} b(6 - 2b)$$

Since the value of b is not given, we cannot determine the area. Hence, there is not enough information, and the answer is (E).

39. In the figure to the right, h denotes the height and b the base of the triangle. If $(bh)^2 = 16$, what is the area of the triangle?

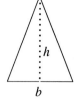

(A)   1
(B)   2
(C)   3
(D)   4
(E)   Not enough information

Taking the square root of both sides of the equation $(bh)^2 = 16$ gives

$$bh = 4$$

Plugging this into the area formula gives

$$Area = \frac{1}{2} \cdot b \cdot h = \frac{1}{2} \cdot 4 = 2$$

Hence, the answer is (B).

40. If the ratio of an edge of cube S and the greatest distance between two points on the cube is $1 : \sqrt{3}$, then the volume of cube S must be

(A)   greater than 8
(B)   less than 8
(C)   equal to 8
(D)   greater than or equal to 8
(E)   Not enough information

There is not enough information to decide since different size cubes can have the ratio $1 : \sqrt{3}$:

Ratio: $\dfrac{2}{2\sqrt{3}} = \dfrac{1}{\sqrt{3}}$

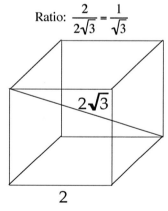

Volume: 8

Ratio: $\dfrac{1}{\sqrt{3}}$

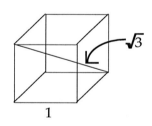

Volume: 1

The answer is (E).

41. If the length of a diagonal across a face of cube *S* is 2, then the volume of cube *S* must be

    (A) greater than 8
    (B) less than 8
    (C) equal to 8
    (D) greater than or equal to 8
    (E) Not enough information to decide

A diagram illustrating the situation is shown below:

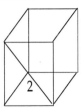

Looking at the face in isolation gives

Applying the Pythagorean Theorem to this diagram gives

$$x^2 + x^2 = 2^2$$

$$2x^2 = 4$$

$$x^2 = 2$$

$$x = \sqrt{2}$$

Hence, the volume of the cube is $V = x^3 = \left(\sqrt{2}\right)^3 < 8$. The answer is (B).

42. In the parallelogram to the right, $\angle BAD + \angle BCD = 140$. What is the measure of $\angle ABC$?

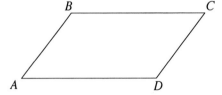

    (A) 100
    (B) 110
    (C) 120
    (D) 125
    (E) 142

Since opposite angles of a parallelogram are equal, $\angle ABC = \angle ADC$. Further, since there are 360° in a parallelogram,

$$\angle ABC + \angle ADC + \angle BAD + \angle BCD = 360$$

$$\angle ABC + \angle ADC + 140 = 360$$

$$\angle ABC + \angle ABC = 220$$

$$2\angle ABC = 220$$

$$\angle ABC = 110$$

The answer is (B).

43. An equilateral triangle is inscribed in a circle, as
     shown to the right. If the radius of the circle is **2**,
     what is the area of the triangle?

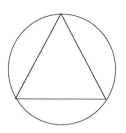

(A) $\dfrac{\sqrt{2}}{2}$

(B) $\sqrt{2}$

(C) $\sqrt{3}$

(D) $3\sqrt{3}$

(E) $10\sqrt{3}$

Adding radii to the diagram yields

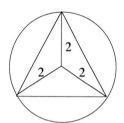

Now, viewing the bottom triangle in isolation yields

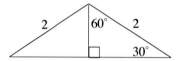

Recall, in a 30°–60°–90° triangle, the side opposite the 30° angle is 1/2 the length of the hypotenuse, and

the side opposite the 60° angle is $\dfrac{\sqrt{3}}{2}$ times the length of the hypotenuse. Hence, the altitude of the above

triangle is 1, and the base is $\sqrt{3}+\sqrt{3}=2\sqrt{3}$. Thus, the area of the triangle is $A=\dfrac{1}{2}\cdot 2\sqrt{3}\cdot 1=\sqrt{3}$. By

symmetry, the area of the inscribed triangle is $3A = 3\sqrt{3}$. The answer is (D).

44. The triangle to the right has side *DC* of the square
     as its base. If *DM* = 5 and *M* is the midpoint of
     side *AB*, what is the area of the shaded region?

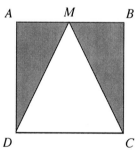

(A)   5/2

(B) $\sqrt{10}$

(C) $\sqrt{15}$

(D)   4

(E)   10

Adding the given information to the diagram gives

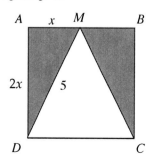

Applying The Pythagorean Theorem yields

$$x^2 + (2x)^2 = 5^2$$
$$x^2 + 4x^2 = 5^2$$
$$5x^2 = 5^2$$
$$x^2 = 5$$
$$x = \sqrt{5}$$

Hence, the area of the square is $2x \cdot 2x = 2\sqrt{5} \cdot 2\sqrt{5} = 20$. Since the height of the unshaded triangle is the same as the length of a side of the square, the area of the triangle is

$$A = \frac{1}{2}\left(2\sqrt{5}\right)\left(2\sqrt{5}\right) = 10$$

Subtracting this from the area of the square gives

$$20 - 10 = 10$$

The answer is (E).

45. A square with sides of length 3 is intersected by a line at S and T. What is the maximum possible distance between S and T?

   (A) $\sqrt{6}$ (B) $2\sqrt{3}$ (C) $3\sqrt{2}$ (D) $2\sqrt{5}$ (E) 9

The maximum possible distance between S and T will occur when the line intersects the square at opposite vertices:

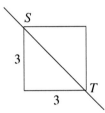

Hence, the maximum distance is the length of the diagonal of the square. Applying the Pythagorean Theorem yields

$$ST^2 = 3^2 + 3^2$$
$$ST^2 = 18$$
$$ST = \sqrt{18} = 3\sqrt{2}$$

The answer is (C).

46. In the triangle to the right, what is the value of
$\dfrac{x+y+z}{15}$?

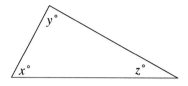

(A)   9
(B)   10
(C)   11
(D)   12
(E)   13

Since the angle sum of a triangle is 180°, $x + y + z = 180$. Plugging this into the expression $\dfrac{x+y+z}{15}$ yields

$$\frac{x+y+z}{15} = \frac{180}{15} = 12$$

The answer is (D).

47. If a square has an area of a^2 and a right-angled isosceles triangle also has area is a^2, then which one of the following must be true?

(A)   The perimeter of the square is greater than the perimeter of the triangle.
(B)   The perimeter of the square is less than the perimeter of the triangle.
(C)   The perimeter of the square is equal to the perimeter of the triangle.
(D)   The perimeter of the square is greater than or equal to the perimeter of the triangle.
(E)   It cannot be determined which perimeter is greater from the information given

Remember that the area of a square is equal to the length of its side squared. Since the area of the square is a^2, the side of the square is a. Hence, the perimeter of the square is $P = a + a + a + a = 4a$.

Now, let b represent the length of the equal sides of the right-angled isosceles triangle, and let c represent the length of the hypotenuse:

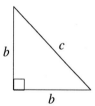

Since the hypotenuse of a right triangle is opposite the right angle, the sides labeled b are the base and height of the triangle. The area of the triangle is $\frac{1}{2}$ base × height = $\frac{1}{2}bb = \frac{1}{2}b^2$. We are given that the area of the triangle is a^2. Hence, $\frac{1}{2}b^2 = a^2$. Solving this equation for b yields $b = \sqrt{2}a$. To calculate the hypotenuse, c, of the triangle we apply the Pythagorean Theorem:

$$c^2 = b^2 + b^2$$
$$c^2 = 2b^2$$
$$c = \sqrt{2b^2}$$
$$c = \sqrt{2}b$$
$$c = \sqrt{2}\sqrt{2}a \qquad \text{(since } b = \sqrt{2}a\text{)}$$
$$c = 2a$$

The perimeter of the triangle is $P = b + b + c = 2b + c = 2\sqrt{2}a + 2a = a(2\sqrt{2} + 2)$. Recall that $\sqrt{2} \approx 1.4$. Hence, $a(2\sqrt{2} + 2) \approx a(2.8 + 2) = 4.48a > 4a$. Hence, the perimeter of the triangle is greater than the perimeter of the square, and the answer is (B).

48. The perimeter of a square is equal to the perimeter of a rectangle whose length and width are *6m* and *4m*, respectively. The side of the square is

   (A) *3m*
   (B) *4m*
   (C) *5m*
   (D) *6m*
   (E) *7m*

The length of the rectangle is *6m* and the width of the rectangle is *4m*. From the standard formula for the perimeter of a rectangle, we get

$$P = 2L + 2W = 2(6m) + 2(4m) = 20m$$

Now, the formula for the perimeter of a square is $4x$, where x represents the length of a side of the square. Since we are given that the perimeter of the square is equal to that of the rectangle, we write

$$4x = 20m$$

$$x = \frac{20m}{4} = 5m$$

The answer is (C).

49. If the circumference of a circle is *4m*, then the ratio of circumference of the circle to the diameter of the circle is

   (A) π
   (B) 4
   (C) 2π
   (D) 4π
   (E) 16

The formula for the circumference of a circle with diameter d is $C = 2\pi r = \pi(2r) = \pi d$ (since the diameter is twice the radius, $d = 2r$). Hence, the ratio of the circumference of the circle to its diameter is

$$\frac{C}{d} =$$

$$\frac{\pi d}{d} =$$

$$\pi$$

The answer is (A).

Note: The fact that the circumference of the circle is *4m* was not used in solving the problem. Thus, the answer is independent of the size of the circle. In other words, the ratio of the circumference of a circle to its diameter is always π.

50. In Triangle *ABC*, $\angle A$ is 10 degrees greater than $\angle B$, and $\angle B$ is 10 degrees greater than $\angle C$. The value of angle B is

   (A) 30   (B) 40   (C) 50   (D) 60   (E) 70

We are given that $\angle A$ is 10 degrees greater than $\angle B$. Expressing this as an equation gives

$$\angle A = \angle B + 10$$

We are also given that $\angle B$ is 10 degrees greater than $\angle C$. Expressing this as an equation gives

$$\angle B = \angle C + 10$$

In a triangle, the sum of the three angles is 180 degrees. Expressing this as an equation gives

$$\angle A + \angle B + \angle C = 180$$

Solving these three equations for $\angle B$, we get $\angle B = 60$ degrees. The answer is (D).

51. Two squares each with sides of length *s* are joined to form a rectangle. The area of the rectangle is

   (A) s^2
   (B) $2s^2$
   (C) $4s^2$
   (D) $8s^2$
   (E) $16s^2$

The area of a square with side *s* is s^2. On joining two such squares, the resulting area will be twice the area of either square: $2s^2$. The answer is (B).

52. A person travels 16 miles due north and then 12 miles due east. How far is the person from his initial location?

   (A) 4 miles
   (B) 8 miles
   (C) 14 miles
   (D) 20 miles
   (E) 28 miles

Solution:

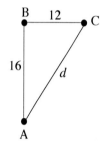

A: Initial position
B: Second position
C: Final position

The path taken by the person can be represented diagrammatically as shown. Let *d* be the distance between his initial location and his final location. Since a person traveling due north has to turn 90 degrees to travel due east, the Angle ABC is a right angle. Hence, we can apply the Pythagorean Theorem to the triangle, which yields

$$d^2 = 12^2 + 16^2$$
$$d^2 = 400$$
$$d = \sqrt{400}$$
$$d = 20$$

The answer is (D).

53. The area of Triangle *PQR* is 6. If *PR* = 4, then the length of the hypotenuse *QR* is

   (A) 1
   (B) 2
   (C) 3
   (D) 4
   (E) 5

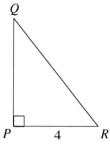

Triangle *PQR* is a right triangle with the base *PR* equal to 4 and height *PQ*. The area of Triangle *PQR* is $\frac{1}{2}bh = 6$. Substituting the known quantities into this formula yields $\frac{1}{2}(4)(PQ) = 6$. Solving this equation for *PQ* yields *PQ* = 3. Applying the Pythagorean Theorem to the triangle yields

$$\left(PQ\right)^2 + \left(PR\right)^2 = \left(QR\right)^2$$
$$3^2 + 4^2 = \left(QR\right)^2 \qquad \text{by substitution}$$
$$25 = \left(QR\right)^2$$
$$5 = QR \qquad \text{by taking the square root of both sides}$$

The answer is (E).

54. In the figure, the equation of line AB is $y = -\dfrac{5}{3}x + 10$.

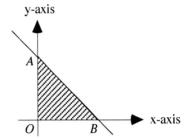

The area of the shaded portion is

(A) 12
(B) 30
(C) 100/3
(D) 60
(E) 100

To find the y-intercept of a line, we set $x = 0$: $y = -\dfrac{5}{3}(0) + 10 = 10$. Hence, the height of the triangle is 10.

To find the x-intercept of a line, we set $y = 0$: $-\dfrac{5}{3}x + 10 = 0$. Solving this equation for x yields $x = 6$.

Hence, the base of the triangle is 6. Therefore, the area of shaded portion (which is a triangle) is $\dfrac{1}{2} \cdot 6 \cdot 10 = 30$. The answer is (B).

55. In the figure to the right, which one of the following must be true about the angle θ ?

(A) $\theta = 60°$
(B) $\theta < 60°$
(C) $\theta > 60°$
(D) $\theta > 70°$
(E) It cannot be determined from the information given

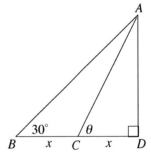

In the figure, $CD = x$ and AC is the hypotenuse of the right triangle ADC. Recall that in a right triangle the hypotenuse is the longest side. Hence, $AC > x$. Now, consider triangle ABC. Observe that $\angle B$ is opposite side AC and $\angle BAC$ is opposite side BC. Since, $BC = x$ and $AC > x$, we can write that $AC > BC$. Recall that in a triangle, the angle opposite the greater side is the greater angle. Hence, $\angle B > \angle BAC$. Since $\angle B = 30°$, $\angle BAC$ must be less than 30°. From the exterior angle theorem, $\theta = \angle B + \angle BAC = 30 + \angle BAC$. We have already derived that $\angle BAC < 30°$. Adding 30 to both sides of this inequality yields $30 + \angle BAC < 60$. Replacing $30 + \angle BAC$ with θ, we get $\theta < 60$. The answer is (B).

56. In the figure, if $x = 54°$ and $y = 72°$, then $z =$

(A) 54°
(B) 56°
(C) 72°
(D) 76°
(E) 98°

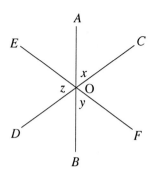

O is the point of intersection
of the three lines in the figure.

From the figure, observe that $\angle AOC$ and $\angle BOD$ are vertical angles between the lines AB and CD. Hence, $\angle AOC = \angle BOD = x$. Since a straight angle has 180°, we get the following equation:

$\angle EOD + \angle BOD + \angle BOF = 180$
$z + x + y = 180$ since $\angle EOD = z$, $\angle BOD = x$, $\angle BOF = y$
$z + 54 + 72 = 180$ since $x = 54°$ and $y = 72°$
$z = 180 - 54 - 72 = 54$

The answer is (A)

57. If one of the sides of the rectangle shown in the figure has a length of 3, then the area of the rectangle is
(A) 9
(B) 13.5
(C) 18
(D) 27
(E) 54

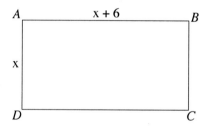

We are given that one of the sides of the rectangle has length 3. This implies that either x or $x + 6$ equals 3. If $x + 6$ equals 3, then x must be –3, which is impossible since a length cannot be negative. Hence, $x = 3$ and $x + 6 = 3 + 6 = 9$. The area of the rectangle, being the product of two adjacent sides of the rectangle, is $x(x + 6) = 3(9) = 27$. The answer is (D).

58. The value of $x + y + z =$

(A) 120°
(B) 160°
(C) 180°
(D) 270°
(E) 360°

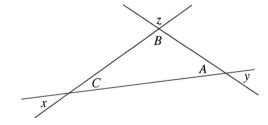

Since angles A, B, and C are the interior angles of the triangle, their angle sum is 180°. Hence, $A + B + C = 180$. Since A and y are vertical angles, they are equal. This is also true for angles B and z and angles C and x. Substituting these values into the equation yields $y + z + x = 180$. The answer is (C).

59. In the figure, what is the area of Triangle *ABC* ?

    (A) 25
    (B) 50
    (C) $100/\sqrt{2}$
    (D) 100
    (E) $100\sqrt{2}$

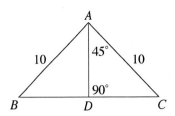

In a triangle, the sum of the interior angles is 180 degrees. Applying this to Triangle *ADC* yields

$$\angle DAC + \angle C + \angle CDA = 180$$
$$45 + \angle C + 90 = 180 \qquad \text{since } \angle DAC = 45° \text{ and } \angle CDA = 90°$$
$$\angle C = 180 - 90 - 45 = 45$$

In Triangle *ABC*, *AB* = *AC*. Recall that angles opposite equal sides of a triangle are equal. Hence, $\angle B = \angle C$. We have already derived that $\angle C = 45°$. Hence, $\angle B = \angle C = 45°$. Again, the sum of the interior angles of a triangle is 180 degrees. Applying this to Triangle *ABC* yields

$$\angle A + \angle B + \angle C = 180$$
$$\angle A + 45 + 45 = 180$$
$$\angle A = 90$$

This implies that Triangle *ABC* is a right triangle with right angle at *A*. Hence, the area of the triangle is

$$\frac{1}{2}(\text{the product of the sides containing the right angle}) =$$

$$\frac{1}{2}AB \cdot AC =$$

$$\frac{1}{2}10 \cdot 10 =$$

$$50$$

The answer is (B).

60. In the triangle to the right, $y/x = 3$. Which one of the following must be true?

    (A) $4x > z$
    (B) $4x < z$
    (C) $4x \leq z$
    (D) $4x = z$
    (E) It cannot be determined from the information given

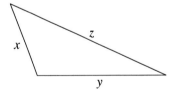

In a triangle, the sum of any two sides is greater than the third side. Hence, $x + y > z$. We are given $y/x = 3$. Multiplying both sides of this equation by *x* yields $y = 3x$. Substituting this into the inequality $x + y > z$, we get $x + 3x > z$, or $4x > z$. Hence, the answer is (A).

61. In the figure to the right, which one of the following statements about the circumference *C* of the circle and the perimeter *P* of Square *PQRS* must be true?

    (A) $C > P$
    (B) $C < P$
    (C) $C \leq P$
    (D) $C = P$
    (E) It cannot be determined from the information given

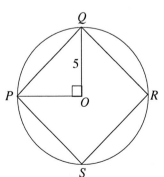

O is the center of the circle, and the radius of the circle is 5.

The shortest distance between two points is along the line joining them. So, the lengths of the arcs *PQ*, *QR*, *RS*, and *SP* are greater than the lengths of the sides *PQ*, *QR*, *RS*, and *SP*, respectively. The circumference of the circle is the sum of lengths of the arcs *PQ*, *QR*, *RS*, and *SP*, and the perimeter of the square is the sum of the sides *PQ*, *QR*, *RS*, and *SP*. Since each arc is greater than the corresponding side, the circumference of the circle must be greater than the perimeter of the square. Hence, the answer is (A).

62.   In the figure, what is the value of *x*?

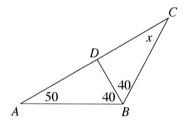

(A)   20°
(B)   30°
(C)   40°
(D)   50°
(E)   60°

In the figure, ∠*B* is the sum of ∠*ABD* and ∠*DBC*. So, ∠*B* = ∠*ABD* + ∠*DBC* = 40 + 40 = 80. Now, recall that the sum of the angles in a triangle is 180°. Hence,

$$∠A + ∠B + ∠C = 180$$
$$50 + 80 + x = 180 \qquad \text{since } ∠A = 50 \text{ and } ∠B = 80$$
$$130 + x = 180$$
$$x = 50$$

The answer is (D).

63.   The area of the Triangle *ABC* shown in the figure is 30. The area of Triangle *ADC* is

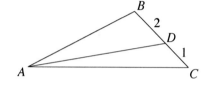

(A)   5
(B)   10
(C)   15
(D)   20
(E)   25

Let's add an altitude to Triangle *ABC* by extending side *BC* as shown in the figure below.

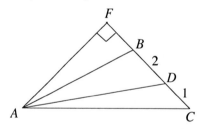

The formula for the area of a triangle is *A* = (1/2)(base)(height). Hence, the area of Triangle *ABC* = (1/2)(*BC*)(*AF*) = (1/2)(2 + 1)(*AF*) = (3/2)(*AF*) = 30 (the area of Triangle *ABC* is given to be 30). Solving this equation for *AF* yields *AF* = 20. Now, the area of Triangle *ADC* = (1/2)(*DC*)(*AF*) = (1/2)(1)(20) = 10. The answer is (B).

64.   In the figure, what is the value of *y* ?

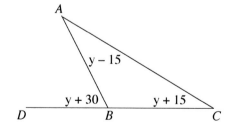

(A)   7.5
(B)   15
(C)   30
(D)   40
(E)   45

Observe that ∠*DBA* is an exterior angle of Triangle *ABC*. Applying the exterior angle theorem yields

$$∠DBA = ∠A + ∠C$$
$$y + 30 = (y - 15) + (y + 15)$$
$$y + 30 = 2y \qquad \text{by adding like terms}$$
$$30 = y \qquad \text{by subtracting } y \text{ from both sides}$$

The answer is (C).

65. A circle is depicted in the rectangular coordinate system as shown. The value of *x* is

(A) 4
(B) 6
(C) 8
(D) 10
(E) 12

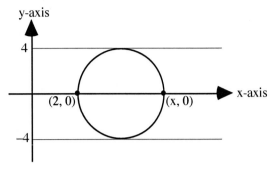

The figure shows that the circle is located between the lines *y* = 4 and *y* = –4 and that the circle is symmetric to *x*-axis. From this, we make two observations: 1) The center of the circle is on the *x*-axis. 2) The diameter of the circle is 8. Since the center of the circle is on the *x*-axis, the points (2, 0) and (*x*, 0) must be diametrically opposite points of the circle. That is, they are end points of a diameter of the circle. Hence, the distance between the two points, *x* – 2, must equal the length of the diameter. Hence, *x* – 2 = 8. Adding 2 to both sides of this equation, we get *x* = 10. The answer is (D).

66. In the figure, the ratio of *x* to *y* is 2. What is the value of *y* ?

(A) 108
(B) 90
(C) 68
(D) 45
(E) 36

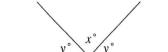

Since the ratio of *x* to *y* is 2, we get *x/y* = 2. Solving this equation for *x* yields *x* = 2*y*. Since the sum of the angles made by a line is 180°, *y* + *x* + *y* = 180. Substituting 2*y* for *x* in this equation yields

$$y + 2y + y = 180$$
$$4y = 180$$
$$y = 45$$

The answer is (D).

67. In the figure, the equation of line AB is *y* = *x* + 2. The difference of the *x*- and *y*-coordinates of any point on the line is equal to:

(A) –4
(B) –2
(C) 0
(D) 2
(E) 4

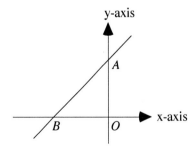

Since the coordinates *x* and *y* are on the line, we know that *y* = *x* + 2. Hence, the difference of *x* and *y* is

$$x - y = x - (x + 2) = -2$$

The answer is (B).

When Drawing a Geometric Figure or Checking a Given One, Be Sure to Include Drawings of Extreme Cases As Well As Ordinary Ones.

Tip!

Example 1:   In the figure to the right, what is the value of angle *x*?

(A) $x > 45°$
(B) $x < 45°$
(C) $x = 45°$
(D) $x \geq 45°$
(E)   It cannot be determined from the information given

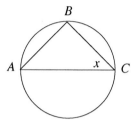

AC is a chord.
B is a point on the circle.

Although in the drawing *AC* looks to be a diameter, that cannot be assumed. All we know is that *AC* is a chord. Hence, numerous cases are possible, three of which are illustrated below:

Case I   Case II   Case III

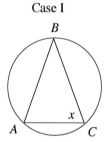   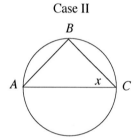   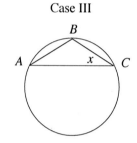

In Case I, *x* is greater than 45°; in Case II, *x* equals 45°; in Case III, *x* is less than 45°. Hence, the answer is (E).

Example 2:   Three rays emanate from a common point and form three angles with measures *p, q, r*. Which one of the following is the measure of angle *q + r*?

(A) $q + r > 180°$
(B) $q + r < 180°$
(C) $q + r = 180°$
(D) $q + r \leq 180°$
(E)   It cannot be determined from the information given

It is natural to make the drawing symmetric as follows:

In this case, $p = q = r = 120°$, so $q + r = 240°$. However, there are other drawings possible. For example:

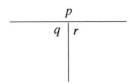

In this case, $q + r = 180°$ and therefore it cannot be determined from the information given. The answer is (E).

Problem Set F:

1. In triangle ABC, $AB = 5$ and $AC = 3$. Which one of the following is the measure of the length of side BC ?

    (A) $BC < 7$
    (B) $BC = 7$
    (C) $BC > 7$
    (D) $BC \le 7$
    (E) It cannot be determined from the information given

2. In the figure to the right, what is the area of $\triangle ABC$?

    (A) 6
    (B) 7
    (C) 8
    (D) 9
    (E) It cannot be determined from the information given

    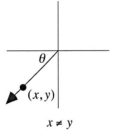

3. In the figure to the right, which one of the following is the measure of angle θ ?

    (A) $\theta < 45°$
    (B) $\theta > 45°$
    (C) $\theta = 45°$
    (D) $\theta \le 45°$
    (E) It cannot be determined from the information given

    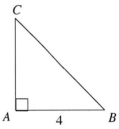

4. In isosceles triangle ABC, $CA = CB = 4$. Which one of the following is the area of triangle ABC ?

    (A) 7
    (B) 8
    (C) 9
    (D) 10
    (E) It cannot be determined from the information given

Answers and Solutions to Problem Set F

1.   In triangle ABC, $AB = 5$ and $AC = 3$. Which one of the following is the measure of the length of side BC ?

    (A) $BC < 7$
    (B) $BC = 7$
    (C) $BC > 7$
    (D) $BC \leq 7$
    (E) It cannot be determined from the information given

The most natural drawing is the following:

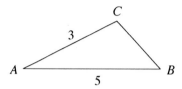

In this case, the length of side BC is less than 7. However, there is another drawing possible, as follows:

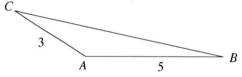

In this case, the length of side BC is greater than 7. Hence, there is not enough information to decide, and the answer is (E).

2.   In the figure to the right, what is the area of $\triangle ABC$?

    (A) 6
    (B) 7
    (C) 8
    (D) 9
    (E) It cannot be determined from the information given

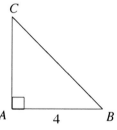

Although the drawing looks to be an isosceles triangle, that cannot be assumed. We are not given the length of side AC: it could be 4 units long or 100 units long, we don't know. Hence, the answer is (E).

3.   In the figure to the right, which one of the following is the measure of angle θ ?

    (A) $\theta < 45°$
    (B) $\theta > 45°$
    (C) $\theta = 45°$
    (D) $\theta \leq 45°$
    (E) It cannot be determined from the information given

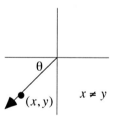

There are two possible drawings:

In Case I, $\theta < 45°$. Whereas, in Case II, $\theta > 45°$. This is a double case, and the answer therefore is (E).

4.   In isosceles triangle *ABC*, *CA* = *CB* = 4. Which one of the following is the area of triangle *ABC* ?

   (A) 7
   (B) 8
   (C) 9
   (D) 10
   (E) It cannot be determined from the information given

There are many possible drawings for the triangle, two of which are listed below:

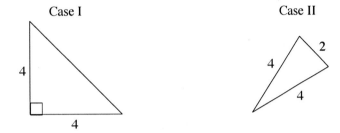

In Case I, the area is 8. In Case II, the area is $\sqrt{15}$ This is a double case and therefore the answer is (E).

Eye-Balling

Surprisingly, on the ACT you can often solve geometry problems by merely "eye-balling" the given drawing. Even on problems whose answers you can't get directly by looking, you often can eliminate a couple of the answer-choices.

- All figures are drawn to scale (even though the official direction say that figures are not necessarily drawn to scale). Hence, if an angle looks like it's about 90°, it is; if one figure looks like it's about twice as large as another figure, it is.

All the problems in this section were solved before. Now, we will solve them by eye-balling the drawings.

Example 1:   In the figure to the right, if $l \parallel k$, then what is the value of y ?

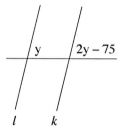

        (A)   20
        (B)   45
        (C)   55
        (D)   75
        (E)   110

By eye-balling the drawing, we can see that y is less than 90°. It appears to be somewhere between 65° and 85°. But 75° is the only answer-choice in that range. Hence, the answer is (D).

Example 2:   In the figure to the right, the area of the shaded region is

        (A)   1/2
        (B)   2/3
        (C)   7/8
        (D)   3/2
        (E)   5/2

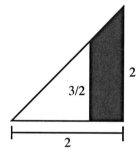

The area of the larger triangle is $A = \dfrac{1}{2}bh = \dfrac{1}{2} \cdot 2 \cdot 2 = 2$. Now, by eye-balling the drawing, the area of the shaded region looks to be about half that of the larger triangle. Therefore, the answer should be about $\dfrac{1}{2} \cdot 2 = 1$. The closest answer-choice to 1 is 7/8. The answer is (C).

    Note: On the ACT, answer-choices are listed in order of size: usually from smallest to largest (unless the question asks for the smallest or largest). Hence, in the previous example, 2/3 is smaller than 7/8 because it comes before 7/8.

Problem Set G:

The following problems have been solved before. Now, solve them by eye-balling the figures.

1. In the figure to the right, the radius of the larger circle is twice that of the smaller circle. If the circles are concentric, what is the ratio of the shaded region's area to the area of the smaller circle?

(A) 10:1
(B) 9:1
(C) 3:1
(D) 2:1
(E) 1:1

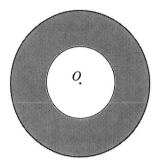

2. In the figure to the right, $\triangle PST$ is an isosceles right triangle, and $PS = 2$. What is the area of the shaded region *URST*?

(A) 4
(B) 2
(C) 5/4
(D) 5/6
(E) 1/2

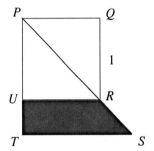

3. In the figure to the right, the area of $\triangle PQR$ is 40. What is the area of $\triangle QRS$?

(A) 10
(B) 15
(C) 20
(D) 25
(E) 45

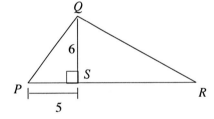

4. In the figure to the right, *PQRS* is a square and *M* and *N* are midpoints of their respective sides. What is the area of quadrilateral *PMRN*?

(A) 8
(B) 10
(C) 12
(D) 14
(E) 16

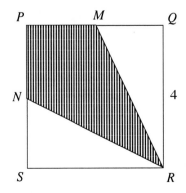

Answers and Solutions to Problem Set G

1. In the figure to the right, the radius of the larger circle is twice that of the smaller circle. If the circles are concentric, what is the ratio of the shaded region's area to the area of the smaller circle?

    (A)   10:1
    (B)   9:1
    (C)   3:1
    (D)   2:1
    (E)   1:1

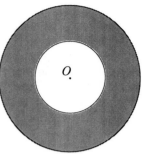

The area of the shaded region appears to be about three times the area of the smaller circle, so the answer should be (C). Let's verify this. Suppose the radius of the larger circle is 2 and the radius of the smaller circle is 1. Then the area of the larger circle is $\pi r^2 = \pi(2)^2 = 4\pi$, and the area of the smaller circle is $\pi r^2 = \pi(1)^2 = \pi$. Hence, the area of the shaded region is $4\pi - \pi = 3\pi$. Now, $\dfrac{area\ of\ shaded\ region}{area\ of\ smaller\ circle} = \dfrac{3\pi}{\pi} = \dfrac{3}{1}$. The answer is (C).

2. In the figure to the right, ΔPST is an isosceles right triangle, and $PS = 2$. What is the area of the shaded region $URST$?

    (A)   4
    (B)   2
    (C)   5/4
    (D)   5/6
    (E)   1/2

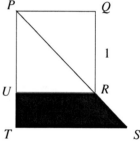

The area of the square is $1^2 = 1$. Now, the area of the shaded region appears to be about half that of the square. Hence, the area of the shaded region is about 1/2. The answer is (E).

3. In the figure to the right, the area of ΔPQR is 40. What is the area of ΔQRS?

    (A)   10
    (B)   15
    (C)   20
    (D)   25
    (E)   45

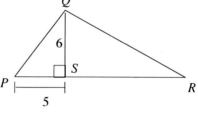

Clearly from the drawing, the area of ΔQRS is greater than half the area of ΔPQR. This eliminates (A), (B), and (C). Now, the area of ΔQRS cannot be greater than the area of ΔPQR. This eliminates (E). The answer is (D).

4. In the figure to the right, $PQRS$ is a square and M and N are midpoints of their respective sides. What is the area of quadrilateral $PMRN$?

    (A)   8
    (B)   10
    (C)   12
    (D)   14
    (E)   16

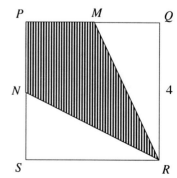

Since the square has sides of length 4, its area is 16. Now, the area of the shaded region appears to be half that of the square. Hence, its area is 8. The answer is (A).

Coordinate Geometry

On a number line, the numbers increase in size to the right and decrease to the left:

If we draw a line through the point 0 perpendicular to the number line, we will form a grid:

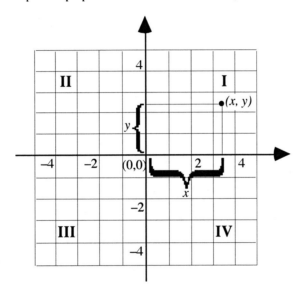

The thick horizontal line in the above diagram is called the x-axis, and the thick vertical line is called the y-axis. The point at which the axes meet, $(0, 0)$, is called the origin. On the x-axis, positive numbers are to the right of the origin and increase in size to the right; further, negative numbers are to the left of the origin and decrease in size to the left. On the y-axis, positive numbers are above the origin and ascend in size; further, negative numbers are below the origin and descend in size. As shown in the diagram, the point represented by the ordered pair (x, y) is reached by moving x units along the x-axis from the origin and then moving y units vertically. In the ordered pair (x, y), x is called the *abscissa* and y is called the *ordinate*; collectively they are called coordinates. The x and y axes divide the plane into four quadrants, numbered I, II, III, and IV counterclockwise. Note, if $x \neq y$, then (x, y) and (y, x) represent different points on the coordinate system. The points $(2, 3)$, $(-3, 1)$, $(-4, -4)$, and $(4, -2)$ are plotted in the following coordinate system:

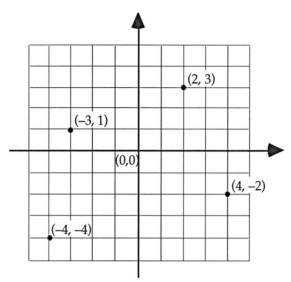

Example: In the figure to the right, polygon *ABCO* is a square. If the coordinates of *B* are $(h, 4)$, what is the value of *h* ?

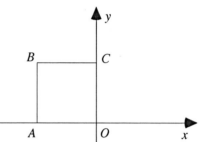

(A)   4
(B) $4\sqrt{2}$
(C) $-4\sqrt{2}$
(D) -4
(E)   not enough information

Since the *y*-coordinate of point *B* is 4, line segment *CO* has length 4. Since figure *ABCO* is a square, line segment *AO* also has length 4. Since point *B* is in the second quadrant, the *x*-coordinate of *B* is –4. The answer is (D). Be careful not to choose 4. *h* is the *x*-coordinate of point *B*, not the length of the square's side.

Distance Formula:

The distance formula is derived by using the Pythagorean Theorem. Notice in the figure below that the distance between the points (x, y) and (a, b) is the hypotenuse of a right triangle. The difference $y - b$ is the measure of the height of the triangle, and the difference $x - a$ is the length of base of the triangle. Applying the Pythagorean Theorem yields

$$d^2 = (x - a)^2 + (y - b)^2$$

Taking the square root of both sides this equation yields

$$\boxed{d = \sqrt{(x - a)^2 + (y - b)^2}}$$

Example: In the figure to the right, the circle is centered at the origin and passes through point *P*. Which of the following points does it also pass through?

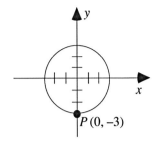

(A)   (3, 3)
(B) $(-2\sqrt{2}, -1)$
(C)   (2, 6)
(D) $(-\sqrt{3}, \sqrt{3})$
(E)   (−3, 4)

Since the circle is centered at the origin and passes through the point (0, −3), the radius of the circle is 3. Now, if any other point is on the circle, the distance from that point to the center of the circle (the radius) must also be 3. Look at choice (B). Using the distance formula to calculate the distance between $\left(-2\sqrt{2}, -1\right)$ and (0, 0) (the origin) yields

$$d = \sqrt{\left(-2\sqrt{2} - 0\right)^2 + \left(-1 - 0\right)^2} = \sqrt{\left(-2\sqrt{2}\right)^2 + \left(-1\right)^2} = \sqrt{8 + 1} = \sqrt{9} = 3$$

Hence, $\left(-2\sqrt{2}, -1\right)$ is on the circle, and the answer is (B).

Midpoint Formula:

The midpoint M between points (*x*, *y*) and (*a*, *b*) is given by

$$M = \left(\frac{x + a}{2}, \frac{y + b}{2}\right)$$

In other words, to find the midpoint, simply average the corresponding coordinates of the two points.

Example: In the figure to the right, polygon *PQRO* is a square and *T* is the midpoint of side *QR*. What are the coordinates of *T* ?

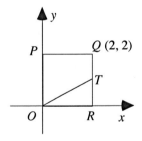

(A)   (1, 1)
(B)   (1, 2)
(C)   (1.5, 1.5)
(D)   (2, 1)
(E)   (2, 3)

Since point *R* is on the *x*-axis, its *y*-coordinate is 0. Further, since *PQRO* is a square and the *x*-coordinate of *Q* is 2, the *x*-coordinate of *R* is also 2. Since *T* is the midpoint of side *QR*, the midpoint formula yields

$$T = \left(\frac{2 + 2}{2}, \frac{2 + 0}{2}\right) = \left(\frac{4}{2}, \frac{2}{2}\right) = (2, 1)$$

The answer is (D).

Slope Formula:

The slope of a line measures the inclination of the line. By definition, it is the ratio of the vertical change to the horizontal change (see figure below). The vertical change is called the *rise*, and the horizontal change is called the *run*. Thus, the slope is the *rise over the run*.

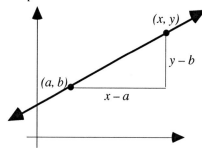

Forming the *rise over the run* in the above figure yields

$$m = \frac{y - b}{x - a}$$

Example: In the figure to the right, what is the slope of line passing through the two points?

(A) 1/4
(B) 1
(C) 1/2
(D) 3/2
(E) 2

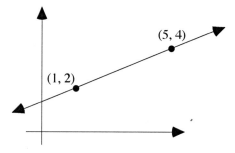

The slope formula yields $m = \dfrac{4-2}{5-1} = \dfrac{2}{4} = \dfrac{1}{2}$. The answer is (C).

Slope-Intercept Form:

Multiplying both sides of the equation $m = \dfrac{y-b}{x-a}$ by $x - a$ yields

$$y - b = m(x - a)$$

Now, if the line passes through the y-axis at $(0, b)$, then the equation becomes

$$y - b = m(x - 0)$$

or

$$y - b = mx$$

or

$$y = mx + b$$

This is called the slope-intercept form of the equation of a line, where m is the slope and b is the y-intercept. This form is convenient because it displays the two most important bits of information about a line: its slope and its y-intercept.

Example: In the figure to the right, the equation of the line is $y = \frac{9}{10}x + k$. Which one of the following must be true about line segments AO and BO?

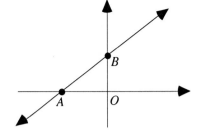

(A) $AO > BO$
(B) $AO < BO$
(C) $AO \leq BO$
(D) $AO = BO$
(E) $AO = BO/2$

Since $y = \frac{9}{10}x + k$ is in slope-intercept form, we know the slope of the line is $\frac{9}{10}$. Now, the ratio of BO to AO is the slope of the line (rise over run). Hence, $\frac{BO}{AO} = \frac{9}{10}$. Multiplying both sides of this equation by AO yields $BO = \frac{9}{10}AO$. In other words, BO is $\frac{9}{10}$ the length of AO. Hence, AO is longer. The answer is (A).

Intercepts:

The *x*-intercept is the point where the line crosses the *x*-axis. It is found by setting $y = 0$ and solving the resulting equation. The *y*-intercept is the point where the line crosses the *y*-axis. It is found by setting $x = 0$ and solving the resulting equation.

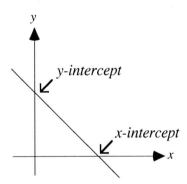

Example: Graph the equation $x - 2y = 4$.

Solution: To find the *x*-intercept, set $y = 0$. This yields $x - 2 \cdot 0 = 4$, or $x = 4$. So the *x*-intercept is $(4, 0)$. To find the *y*-intercept, set $x = 0$. This yields $0 - 2y = 4$, or $y = -2$. So the *y*-intercept is $(0, -2)$. Plotting these two points and connecting them with a straight line yields

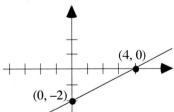

Areas and Perimeters:

Often, you will be given a geometric figure drawn on a coordinate system and will be asked to find its area or perimeter. In these problems, use the properties of the coordinate system to deduce the dimensions of the figure and then calculate the area or perimeter. For complicated figures, you may need to divide the figure into simpler forms, such as squares and triangles. A couple examples will illustrate:

Example: What is the area of the quadrilateral in the coordinate system to the right?

(A)   2
(B)   4
(C)   6
(D)   8
(E)   11

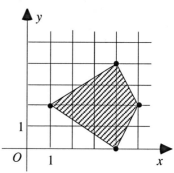

If the quadrilateral is divided horizontally through the line $y = 2$, two congruent triangles are formed. As the figure to the right shows, the top triangle has height 2 and base 4. Hence, its area is

$$A = \frac{1}{2}bh = \frac{1}{2}\cdot 4\cdot 2 = 4$$

The area of the bottom triangle is the same, so the area of the quadrilateral is $4 + 4 = 8$. The answer is (D).

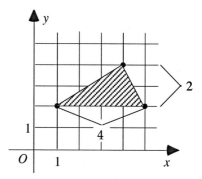

Example: What is the perimeter of Triangle *ABC* in the figure to the right?

(A) $5 + \sqrt{5} + \sqrt{34}$
(B) $10 + \sqrt{34}$
(C) $5 + \sqrt{5} + \sqrt{28}$
(D) $2\sqrt{5} + \sqrt{34}$
(E) $\sqrt{5} + \sqrt{28}$

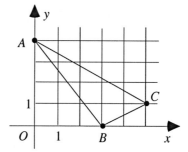

Point *A* has coordinates $(0, 4)$, point *B* has coordinates $(3, 0)$, and point *C* has coordinates $(5, 1)$. Using the distance formula to calculate the distances between points *A* and *B*, *A* and *C*, and *B* and *C* yields

$$\overline{AB} = \sqrt{(0-3)^2 + (4-0)^2} = \sqrt{9+16} = \sqrt{25} = 5$$

$$\overline{AC} = \sqrt{(0-5)^2 + (4-1)^2} = \sqrt{25+9} = \sqrt{34}$$

$$\overline{BC} = \sqrt{(5-3)^2 + (1-0)^2} = \sqrt{4+1} = \sqrt{5}$$

Adding these lengths gives the perimeter of Triangle *ABC*:

$$\overline{AB} + \overline{AC} + \overline{BC} = 5 + \sqrt{34} + \sqrt{5}$$

The answer is (A).

Problem Set H:

1. In the figure to the right, O is the center of the circle. What is the area of the circle?

    (A) 2π
    (B) 3π
    (C) 5.5π
    (D) 7π
    (E) 9π

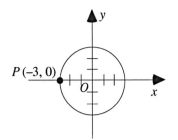

2. In the figure to the right, which one of the following must be true about the value of the y-coordinate of point P?

    (A) $y < 6$
    (B) $y > 6$
    (C) $y > 5$
    (D) $y = 6$
    (E) $y < 5$

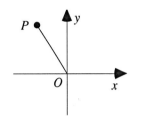

P is a point in the coordinate system and $OP = 6$.

3. In the figure to the right, the equation of the line is $y = px + a$. Which one of the following is the value of p?

    (A) $p = \dfrac{-1}{2}$

    (B) $p = \dfrac{a}{b}$

    (C) $p = \dfrac{-a}{b}$

    (D) $p = \dfrac{b}{a}$

    (E) $p = \dfrac{-b}{a}$

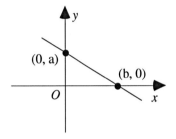

4. In the figure to the right, which one of the following must be true?

    (A) $y < x$
    (B) $y > x$
    (C) $y < 4$
    (D) $y = x$
    (E) $y > 5$

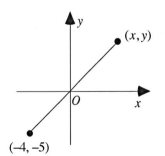

5. In the figure to the right, a is the x-coordinate of point P and b is the y-coordinate of point Q. In which quadrant is the point (a, b)?

    (A) I
    (B) II
    (C) III
    (D) IV
    (E) cannot be determined from the information given

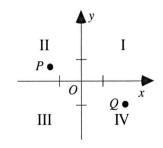

6.   In the figure to the right, if *x* = 4, then *y* =

    (A)   1
    (B)   2
    (C)   3
    (D)   4
    (E)   5.1

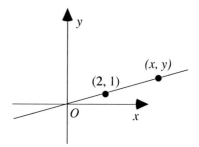

7.   In the figure to the right, which of the following could be the coordinates of a point in the shaded region?

    (A)   (1, 2)
    (B)   (−2, 3)
    (C)   (3, −5)
    (D)   (−5, 1)
    (E)   (−1, −6)

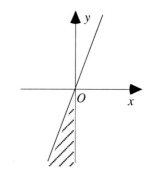

8.   In the figure to the right, which of the following points lies within the circle?

    (A)   (3.5, 9.5)
    (B)   (−7, 7)
    (C)   (−10, 1)
    (D)   (0, 11)
    (E)   (5.5, 8.5)

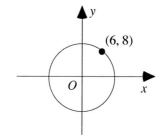

9.   In the figure to the right, the grid consists of unit squares. What is the area of the polygon?

    (A)   7
    (B)   9
    (C)   10
    (D)   12
    (E)   15

10.   In the figure to the right, which of the following points is three times as far from *P* as from *Q* ?

    (A)   (0, 3)
    (B)   (1, 1)
    (C)   (4, 5)
    (D)   (2, 3)
    (E)   (4, 1)

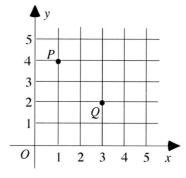

11. In the figure to the right, what is the area of quadrilateral *ABCO* ?

    (A)   3
    (B)   5
    (C)   6.5
    (D)   8
    (E)   13

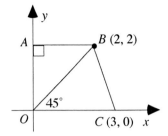

12. In the figure to the right, which quadrants contain points (x,y) such that $xy = -2$?

    (A)   I only
    (B)   II only
    (C)   III and IV only
    (D)   II and IV only
    (E)   II, III, and IV

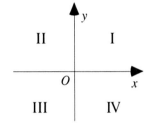

13. If the square in the figure to the right is rotated clockwise about the origin until vertex *V* is on the negative *y*-axis, then the new *y*-coordinate of *V* is

    (A)   -2
    (B) $-2\sqrt{2}$
    (C)   -4
    (D) $-3\sqrt{2}$
    (E)   -8

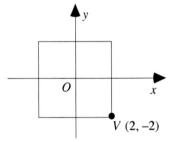

14. In the standard coordinate system, which of the following points is the greatest distance from the origin:

    (A) $(-4, -1)$
    (B) $(-3, 3)$
    (C) $(4, 0)$
    (D) $(2, 3)$
    (E) $(0, 4)$

15. What is the perimeter of Triangle *ABC* in the figure to the right?

    (A) $5 + \sqrt{2} + \sqrt{29}$
    (B) $5 + 2\sqrt{2} + \sqrt{29}$
    (C) $5 + 4\sqrt{2} + \sqrt{29}$
    (D) $3\sqrt{2} + \sqrt{34}$
    (E) $4\sqrt{2} + \sqrt{34}$

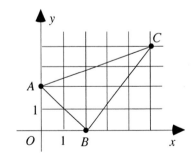

Answers and Solutions to Problem Set H

1. In the figure to the right, O is the center of the circle.
    What is the area of the circle?

    (A) 2π
    (B) 3π
    (C) 5.5π
    (D) 7π
    (E) 9π

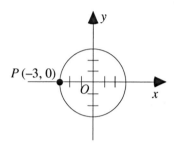

Since the circle is centered at the origin and passes through the point $(-3,0)$, the radius of the circle is 3.
Hence, the area is $A = \pi r^2 = \pi 3^2 = 9\pi$. The answer is (E).

2. In the figure to the right, which one of the following
    must be true about the value of the y-coordinate of
    point P ?

    (A) $y < 6$
    (B) $y > 6$
    (C) $y > 5$
    (D) $y = 6$
    (E) $y < 5$

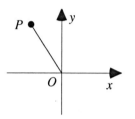

P is a point in the coordinate
system and $OP = 6$.

Whatever the coordinates of P are, the line OP is the hypotenuse of a right triangle with sides being the
absolute value of the x and y coordinates. Hence, OP is greater than the y-coordinate of point P. The
answer is (A).

This problem brings up the issue of how much you can assume when viewing a diagram. We are told
that P is a point in the coordinate system and that it appears in the second quadrant. Could P be on one of
the axes or in another quadrant? No. Although P could be anywhere in Quadrant II (not necessarily where
it is displayed), P could not be on the y-axis because the "position of points, angles, regions, etc. can be
assumed to be in the order shown." If P were on the y-axis, then it would not be to the left of the y-axis, as
it is in the diagram. That is, the order would be different.

3. In the figure to the right, the equation of the line is
    $y = px + a$. Which one of the following is the value of
    p ?

    (A) $p = \dfrac{-1}{2}$

    (B) $p = \dfrac{a}{b}$

    (C) $p = \dfrac{-a}{b}$

    (D) $p = \dfrac{b}{a}$

    (E) $p = \dfrac{-b}{a}$

Since $(b, 0)$ is the x-intercept of the line, it must satisfy the equation: $0 = pb + a$

Subtracting a from both sides yields $-a = pb$

Dividing both sides by b yields $\dfrac{-a}{b} = p$

The answer is (C).

4. In the figure to the right, which one of the following must be true?

    (A) $y < x$
    (B) $y > x$
    (C) $y < 4$
    (D) $y = x$
    (E) $y > 5$

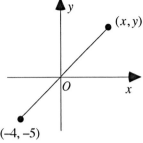

Since the line passes through $(-4, -5)$ and $(0, 0)$, its slope is $m = \dfrac{rise}{run} = \dfrac{-5-0}{-4-0} = \dfrac{5}{4}$. Notice that the rise, 5, is larger than the run, 4. Hence, the y-coordinate will always be larger in absolute value than the x-coordinate. The answer is (B).

5. In the figure to the right, a is the x-coordinate of point P and b is the y-coordinate of point Q. In which quadrant is the point (a, b) ?

    (A) I
    (B) II
    (C) III
    (D) IV
    (E) cannot be determined from the information given

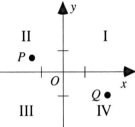

Since P is in Quadrant II, its x-coordinate is negative. That is, a is negative. Since Q is in Quadrant IV, its y-coordinate is negative. That is, b is negative. Hence, (a, b) is in Quadrant III. The answer is (C).

6. In the figure to the right, if $x = 4$, then $y =$

    (A) 1
    (B) 2
    (C) 3
    (D) 4
    (E) 5.1

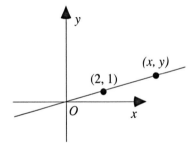

Let's write the equation of the line, using the slope-intercept form, $y = mx + b$. Since the line passes through the origin, $b = 0$. This reduces the equation to $y = mx$. Calculating the slope between $(2, 1)$ and $(0, 0)$ yields $m = \dfrac{1-0}{2-0} = \dfrac{1}{2}$. Plugging this into the equation yields $y = \dfrac{1}{2}x$. Since $x = 4$, we get $y = \dfrac{1}{2} \cdot 4 = 2$. The answer is (B).

7. In the figure to the right, which of the following could be the coordinates of a point in the shaded region?

    (A) $(1, 2)$
    (B) $(-2, 3)$
    (C) $(3, -5)$
    (D) $(-5, 1)$
    (E) $(-1, -6)$

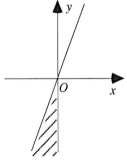

The shaded region is entirely within the third quadrant. Now, both coordinates of any point in Quadrant III are negative. The only point listed with both coordinates negative is $(-1, -6)$. The answer is (E).

8.   In the figure to the right, which of the following points lies within the circle?

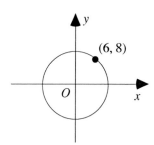

(A)   (3.5, 9.5)
(B)   (−7, 7)
(C)   (−10, 1)
(D)   (0, 11)
(E)   (5.5, 8.5)

For a point to be within a circle, its distance from the center of the circle must be less than the radius of the circle. The distance from (6, 8) to (0, 0) is the radius of the circle: $R = \sqrt{(6-0)^2 + (8-0)^2} = \sqrt{36+64} = \sqrt{100} = 10$. Now, let's calculate the distance between (−7, 7) and (0, 0) $R = \sqrt{(-7-0)^2 + (7-0)^2} = \sqrt{49+49} = \sqrt{98} < 10$. The answer is (B).

9.   In the figure to the right, the grid consists of unit squares. What is the area of the polygon?

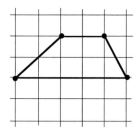

(A)   7
(B)   9
(C)   10
(D)   12
(E)   15

Dividing the polygon into triangles and squares yields

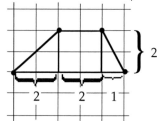

The triangle furthest to the left has area $A = \frac{1}{2}bh = \frac{1}{2} \cdot 2 \cdot 2 = 2$. The square has area $A = s^2 = 2^2 = 4$. The triangle furthest to the right has area $A = \frac{1}{2} \cdot 1 \cdot 2 = 1$. The sum of the areas of these three figures is $2 + 4 + 1 = 7$. The answer is (A).

10.   In the figure to the right, which of the following points is three times as far from P as from Q?

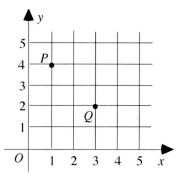

(A)   (0, 3)
(B)   (1, 1)
(C)   (4, 5)
(D)   (2, 3)
(E)   (4, 1)

From the distance formula, the distance between (4,1) and Q is $\sqrt{2}$, and the distance between (4,1) and P is $\sqrt{(4-1)^2 + (1-4)^2} = \sqrt{3^2 + (-3)^2} = \sqrt{2 \cdot 3^2} = 3\sqrt{2}$. The answer is (E).

11.   In the figure to the right, what is the area of quadrilateral
      ABCO ?

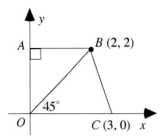

    (A)   3
    (B)   5
    (C)   6.5
    (D)   8
    (E)   13

Dropping a vertical line from point *B* perpendicular to the *x*-axis will form a square and a triangle:

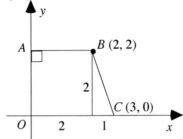

From the figure, we see that the square has area $s^2 = 2^2 = 4$, and the triangle has area $\frac{1}{2}bh = \frac{1}{2} \cdot 1 \cdot 2 = 1$.

Hence, the area of the quadrilateral is $4 + 1 = 5$. The answer is (B). Note, with this particular solution, we did not need to use the properties of the diagonal line in the original diagram.

12.   In the figure to the right, which quadrants contain points
      (x,y) such that $xy = -2$?

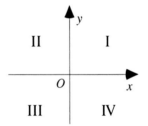

    (A)   I only
    (B)   II only
    (C)   III and IV only
    (D)   II and IV only
    (E)   II, III, and IV

If the product of two numbers is negative, the numbers must have opposite signs. Now, only the coordinates of points in quadrants II and IV have opposite signs. The diagram below illustrates the sign pattern of points for all four quadrants. The answer is (D).

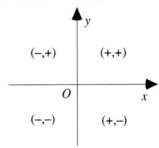

13. If the square in the figure to the right is rotated clockwise about the origin until vertex *V* is on the negative *y*-axis, then the new *y*-coordinate of *V* is

(A)   –2
(B) $-2\sqrt{2}$
(C)   –4
(D) $-3\sqrt{2}$
(E)   –8

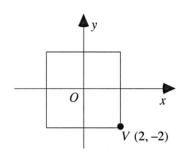

Calculating the distance between *V* and the origin yields $\sqrt{(2-0)^2 + (-2-0)^2} = \sqrt{4+4} = \sqrt{8} = 2\sqrt{2}$. Since the square is rotated about the origin, the distance between the origin and *V* is fix. Hence, the new *y*-coordinate of *V* is $-2\sqrt{2}$. The diagram below illustrates the position of *V* after the rotation. The answer is (B).

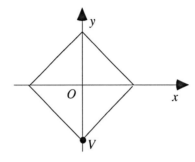

14. In the standard coordinate system, which of the following points is the greatest distance from the origin:

(A)   (–4, –1)
(B)   (–3, 3)
(C)   (4, 0)
(D)   (2, 3)
(E)   (0, 4)

Using the distance formula to calculate the distance of each point from the origin yields

$$d = \sqrt{(-4)^2 + (-1)^2} = \sqrt{17}$$
$$d = \sqrt{(-3)^2 + (3)^2} = \sqrt{18}$$
$$d = \sqrt{(4)^2 + (0)^2} = \sqrt{16}$$
$$d = \sqrt{(2)^2 + (3)^2} = \sqrt{13}$$
$$d = \sqrt{(0)^2 + (4)^2} = \sqrt{16}$$

The answer is (B).

15. What is the perimeter of Triangle *ABC* in the figure to the right?

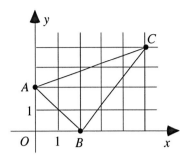

(A) $5 + \sqrt{2} + \sqrt{29}$
(B) $5 + 2\sqrt{2} + \sqrt{29}$
(C) $5 + 4\sqrt{2} + \sqrt{29}$
(D) $3\sqrt{2} + \sqrt{34}$
(E) $4\sqrt{2} + \sqrt{34}$

Point *A* has coordinates (0, 2), point *B* has coordinates (2, 0), and point *C* has coordinates (5, 4). Using the distance formula to calculate the distances between points *A* and *B*, *A* and *C*, and *B* and *C* yields

$$\overline{AB} = \sqrt{(0-2)^2 + (2-0)^2} = \sqrt{4+4} = \sqrt{8} = 2\sqrt{2}$$
$$\overline{AC} = \sqrt{(0-5)^2 + (2-4)^2} = \sqrt{25+4} = \sqrt{29}$$
$$\overline{BC} = \sqrt{(2-5)^2 + (0-4)^2} = \sqrt{9+16} = 5$$

Adding these lengths gives the perimeter of Triangle *ABC*:

$$\overline{AB} + \overline{AC} + \overline{BC} = 2\sqrt{2} + \sqrt{29} + 5$$

The answer is (B).

Elimination Strategies

On hard problems, if you are asked to find the least (or greatest) number, then eliminate the least (or greatest) answer-choice.

This rule also applies to easy and medium problems. When people guess on these types of problems, they most often choose either the least or the greatest number. But if the least or the greatest number were the answer, most people would answer the problem correctly, and it therefore would not be a hard problem.

Example: What is the maximum number of points common to the intersection of a square and a triangle if no two sides coincide?

   (A)   4
   (B)   5
   (C)   6
   (D)   8
   (E)   9

By the above rule, we eliminate answer-choice (E).

On hard problems, eliminate the answer-choice "not enough information."

When people cannot solve a problem, they most often choose the answer-choice "not enough information." But if this were the answer, then it would not be a "hard" problem.

On hard problems, eliminate answer-choices that <u>merely</u> repeat numbers from the problem.

Example: If the sum of x and 20 is 8 more than the difference of 10 and y, what is the value of $x + y$?

   (A)   −2
   (B)   8
   (C)   9
   (D)   28
   (E)   not enough information

By the above rule, we eliminate choice (B) since it merely repeats the number 8 from the problem. By Strategy 2, we would also eliminate choice (E). **Caution:** If choice (B) contained more than the number 8, say, $8 + \sqrt{2}$, then it would not be eliminated by the above rule.

On hard problems, eliminate answer-choices that can be derived from elementary operations.

Strategy

Example: In the figure to the right, what is the perimeter of parallelogram ABCD?

(A) 12
(B) $10 + 6\sqrt{2}$
(C) $20 + \sqrt{2}$
(D) 24
(E) not enough information

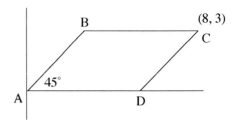

Using the above rule, we eliminate choice (D) since $24 = 8 \cdot 3$. Further, using Strategy 2, eliminate choice (E). Note, 12 was offered as an answer-choice because some people will interpret the drawing as a rectangle tilted halfway on its side and therefore expect it to have one-half its original area.

After you have eliminated as many answer-choices as you can, choose from the more complicated or more unusual answer-choices remaining.

Strategy

Example: Suppose you were offered the following answer-choices:

(A) $4 + \sqrt{3}$
(B) $4 + 2\sqrt{3}$
(C) 8
(D) 10
(E) 12

Then you would choose either (A) or (B).

Problem Set I:

1. What is the maximum number of 3x3 squares that can be formed from the squares in the 6x6 checker board to the right?

    (A)   4
    (B)   6
    (C)   12
    (D)   16
    (E)   24

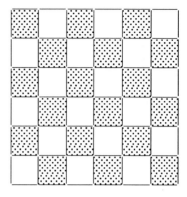

2. Let *P* stand for the product of the first 5 positive integers. What is the greatest possible value of *m* if $\frac{P}{10^m}$ is an integer?

    (A)   1
    (B)   2
    (C)   3
    (D)   5
    (E)   10

3. After being marked down 20 percent, a calculator sells for $10. The original selling price was

    (A) $20   (B) $12.5   (C) $12   (D) $9   (E) $7

4. The distance between cities A and B is 120 miles. A car travels from A to B at 60 miles per hour and returns from B to A along the same route at 40 miles per hour. What is the average speed for the round trip?

    (A) 48   (B) 50   (C) 52   (D) 56   (E) 58

5. If **w** is 10 percent less than **x,** and **y** is 30 percent less than **z,** then **wy** is what percent less than **xz**?

    (A) 10%   (B) 20%   (C) 37%   (D) 40%   (E) 100%

6. In the game of chess, the Knight can make any of the moves displayed in the diagram to the right. If a Knight is the only piece on the board, what is the greatest number of spaces from which not all 8 moves are possible?

    (A)   8
    (B)   24
    (C)   38
    (D)   48
    (E)   56

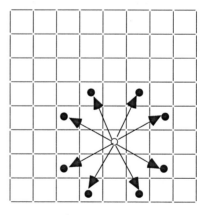

7. How many different ways can 3 cubes be painted if each cube is painted one color and only the 3 colors red, blue, and green are available? (Order is not considered, for example, green, green, blue is considered the same as green, blue, green.)

    (A)   2
    (B)   3
    (C)   9
    (D)   10
    (E)   27

8. What is the greatest prime factor of $\left(2^4\right)^2 - 1$?

    (A)   3
    (B)   5
    (C)   11
    (D)   17
    (E)   19

9. Suppose five circles, each 4 inches in diameter, are cut from a rectangular strip of paper 12 inches long. If the least amount of paper is to be wasted, what is the width of the paper strip?

    (A)   5
    (B) $4 + 2\sqrt{3}$
    (C)   8
    (D) $4\left(1 + \sqrt{3}\right)$
    (E)   not enough information

10. Let C and K be constants. If $x^2 + Kx + 5$ factors into $(x + 1)(x + C)$, the value of K is

    (A)   0
    (B)   5
    (C)   6
    (D)   8
    (E)   not enough information

Answers and Solutions to Problem Set I

1.   What is the maximum number of 3x3 squares
      that can be formed from the squares in the
      6x6 checker board to the right?

      (A)   4
      (B)   6
      (C)   12
      (D)   16
      (E)   24

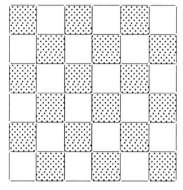

Clearly, there are more than four 3x3 squares in the checker board—eliminate (A). Next, eliminate (B) since it merely repeats a number from the problem. Further, eliminate (E) since it is the greatest. This leaves choices (C) and (D). If you count carefully, you will find sixteen 3x3 squares in the checker board. The answer is (D).

2.   Let *P* stand for the product of the first 5 positive integers. What is the greatest possible value of *m* if $\dfrac{P}{10^m}$ is an integer?

      (A)   1
      (B)   2
      (C)   3
      (D)   5
      (E)   10

Since we are to find the greatest value of *m*, we eliminate (E)—the greatest. Also, eliminate 5 because it is repeated from the problem. Now, since we are looking for the largest number, start with the greatest number remaining and work toward the smallest number. The first number that works will be the answer. To this end, let $m = 3$. Then $\dfrac{P}{10^m} = \dfrac{1 \cdot 2 \cdot 3 \cdot 4 \cdot 5}{10^3} = \dfrac{120}{1000} = \dfrac{3}{25}$. This is not an integer, so eliminate (C). Next, let $m = 2$. Then $\dfrac{P}{10^m} = \dfrac{1 \cdot 2 \cdot 3 \cdot 4 \cdot 5}{10^2} = \dfrac{120}{100} = \dfrac{6}{5}$. This still is not an integer, so eliminate (B). Hence, by process of elimination, the answer is (A).

3.   After being marked down 20 percent, a calculator sells for $10. The original selling price was

      (A) $20
      (B) $12.5
      (C) $12
      (D) $9
      (E) $7

Twenty dollars is too large. The discount was only 20 percent—eliminate (A). Both (D) and (E) are impossible since they are less than the selling price—eliminate. 12 is the eye-catcher: 20% of 10 is 2 and 10 + 2 = 12. This is too easy for a hard problem—eliminate. Thus, by process of elimination, the answer is (B).

4.   The distance between cities A and B is 120 miles. A car travels from A to B at 60 miles per hour and returns from B to A along the same route at 40 miles per hour. What is the average speed for the round trip?

   (A)   48
   (B)   50
   (C)   52
   (D)   56
   (E)   58

We can eliminate 50 (the mere average of 40 and 60) since that would be too elementary. Now, the average must be closer to 40 than to 60 because the car travels for a longer time at 40 mph. But 48 is the only number given that is closer to 40 than to 60. The answer is (A).

It's instructive to also calculate the answer. $Average\ Speed = \dfrac{Total\ Distance}{Total\ Time}$. Now, a car traveling at 40 mph will cover 120 miles in 3 hours. And a car traveling at 60 mph will cover the same 120 miles in 2 hours. So the total traveling time is 5 hours. Hence, for the round trip, the average speed is $\dfrac{120+120}{5} = 48$.

5.   If **w** is 10 percent less than **x**, and **y** is 30 percent less than **z**, then **wy** is what percent less than **xz**?

   (A)   10%
   (B)   20%
   (C)   37%
   (D)   40%
   (E)   100%

We eliminate (A) since it repeats the number 10 from the problem. We can also eliminate choices (B), (D), and (E) since they are derivable from elementary operations:

$$20 = 30 - 10$$
$$40 = 30 + 10$$
$$100 = 10 \cdot 10$$

This leaves choice (C) as the answer.

   Let's also solve this problem directly. The clause

   w is 10 percent less than x

translates into

$$w = x - .10x$$

Simplifying yields

   1) $w = .9x$

Next, the clause

   y is 30 percent less than **z**

translates into

$$y = z - .30z$$

Simplifying yields

   2) $y = .7z$

Multiplying 1) and 2) gives

$$wy = (.9x)(.7z) = .63xz = xz - .37xz$$

Hence, **wy** is 37 percent less than **xz**. The answer is (C).

6.   In the game of chess, the Knight can make any of the moves displayed in the diagram to the right. If a Knight is the only piece on the board, what is the greatest number of spaces from which not all 8 moves are possible?

(A)   8
(B)   24
(C)   38
(D)   48
(E)   56

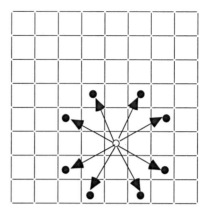

Since we are looking for the <u>greatest</u> number of spaces from which not all 8 moves are possible, we can eliminate the greatest number, 56. Now, clearly not all 8 moves are possible from the outer squares, and there are 28 outer squares—not 32. Also, not all 8 moves are possible from the next to outer squares, and there are 20 of them—not 24. All 8 moves are possible from the remaining squares. Hence, the answer is 28 + 20 = 48. The answer is (D). Notice that 56, (32 + 24), is given as an answer-choice to catch those who don't add carefully.

7.   How many different ways can 3 cubes be painted if each cube is painted one color and only the 3 colors red, blue, and green are available? (Order is not considered, for example, green, green, blue is considered the same as green, blue, green.)

(A)   2
(B)   3
(C)   9
(D)   10
(E)   27

Clearly, there are more than 3 color combinations possible. This eliminates (A) and (B). We can also eliminate (C) and (E) because they are both multiples of 3, and that would be too ordinary, too easy, to be the answer. Hence, by process of elimination, the answer is (D).

Let's also solve this problem directly. The following list displays all 27 ($= 3 \cdot 3 \cdot 3$) color combinations possible (without restriction):

RRR	BBB	GGG
RRB	BBR	GGR
RRG	BBG	GGB
RBR	BRB	GRG
RBB	BRR	GRR
RBG	BRG	GRB
RGR	BGB	GBG
RGB	BGR	GBR
RGG	BGG	GBB

If order is not considered, then there are 10 distinct color combinations in this list. You should count them.

8.   What is the greatest prime factor of $\left(2^4\right)^2 - 1$?

   (A)   3
   (B)   5
   (C)   11
   (D)   17
   (E)   19

$\left(2^4\right)^2 - 1 = (16)^2 - 1 = 256 - 1 = 255$. Since the question asks for the <u>greatest</u> prime factor, we eliminate 19, the greatest number. Now, we start with the next largest number and work our way up the list; the first number that divides into 255 evenly will be the answer. Dividing 17 into 255 gives

$$17\overline{)255} = 15$$

Hence, 17 is the largest prime factor of $\left(2^4\right)^2 - 1$. The answer is (D).

9.   Suppose five circles, each 4 inches in diameter, are cut from a rectangular strip of paper 12 inches long. If the least amount of paper is to be wasted, what is the width of the paper strip?

   (A)   5
   (B) $4 + 2\sqrt{3}$
   (C)   8
   (D) $4\left(1 + \sqrt{3}\right)$
   (E)   not enough information

Since this is a hard problem, we can eliminate (E), "not enough information." And because it is too easily derived, we can eliminate (C), (8 = 4 + 4). Further, we can eliminate (A), 5, because answer-choices (B) and (D) form a more complicated set. At this stage we cannot apply any more elimination rules; so if we could not solve the problem, we would guess either (B) or (D).

   Let's solve the problem directly. The drawing below shows the position of the circles so that the paper width is a minimum.

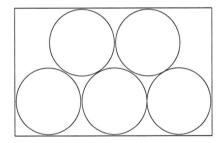

Now, take three of the circles in isolation, and connect the centers of these circles to form a triangle:

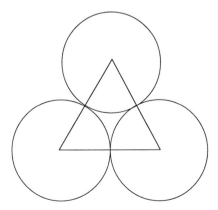

Since the triangle connects the centers of circles of diameter 4, the triangle is equilateral with sides of length 4.

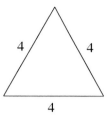

Drawing an altitude gives

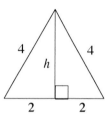

Applying the Pythagorean Theorem to either right triangle gives	$h^2 + 2^2 = 4^2$
Squaring yields	$h^2 + 4 = 16$
Subtracting 4 from both sides of this equation yields	$h^2 = 12$
Taking the square root of both sides yields	$h = \sqrt{12} = \sqrt{4 \cdot 3}$
Removing the perfect square 4 from the radical yields	$h = 2\sqrt{3}$
Summarizing gives	

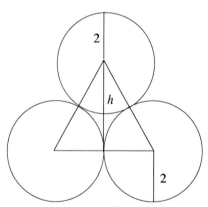

Adding to the height, $h = 2\sqrt{3}$, the distance above the triangle and the distance below the triangle to the edges of the paper strip gives

$$width = (2 + 2) + 2\sqrt{3} = 4 + 2\sqrt{3}$$

The answer is (B).

10. Let C and K be constants. If $x^2 + Kx + 5$ factors into $(x + 1)(x + C)$, the value of K is

 (A) 0
 (B) 5
 (C) 6
 (D) 8
 (E) not enough information

Since the number 5 is merely repeated from the problem, we eliminate (B). Further, since this is a hard problem, we eliminate (E), "not enough information."

Now, since 5 is prime, its only factors are 1 and 5. So, the constant C in the expression $(x + 1)(x + C)$ must be 5:

$$(x + 1)(x + 5)$$

Multiplying out this expression yields

$$\left(x + 1\right)\left(x + 5\right) = x^2 + 5x + x + 5$$

Combining like terms yields

$$\left(x + 1\right)\left(x + 5\right) = x^2 + 6x + 5$$

Hence, $K = 6$, and the answer is (C).

Inequalities

Inequalities are manipulated algebraically the same way as equations with one exception:

Multiplying or dividing both sides of an inequality by a negative number reverses the inequality. That is, if $x > y$ and $c < 0$, then $cx < cy$.

Example: For which values of x is $4x + 3 > 6x - 8$?

As with equations, our goal is to isolate x on one side:

Subtracting 6x from both sides yields	$-2x + 3 > -8$
Subtracting 3 from both sides yields	$-2x > -11$
Dividing both sides by –2 and reversing the inequality yields	$x < 11/2$

Positive & Negative Numbers

A number greater than 0 is positive. On the number line, positive numbers are to the right of 0. A number less than 0 is negative. On the number line, negative numbers are to the left of 0. Zero is the only number that is neither positive nor negative; it divides the two sets of numbers. On the number line, numbers increase to the right and decrease to the left.

The expression $x > y$ means that x is greater than y. In other words, x is to the right of y on the number line:

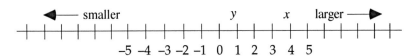

We usually have no trouble determining which of two numbers is larger when both are positive or one is positive and the other negative (e.g., $5 > 2$ and $3.1 > -2$). However, we sometimes hesitate when both numbers are negative (e.g., $-2 > -4.5$). When in doubt, think of the number line: if one number is to the right of the number, then it is larger. As the number line below illustrates, –2 is to the right of –4.5. Hence, –2 is larger than –4.5.

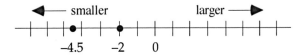

Miscellaneous Properties of Positive and Negative Numbers

1. The product (quotient) of positive numbers is positive.

2. The product (quotient) of a positive number and a negative number is negative.

3. The product (quotient) of an even number of negative numbers is positive.

4. The product (quotient) of an odd number of negative numbers is negative.

5. The sum of negative numbers is negative.

6. A number raised to an even exponent is greater than or equal to zero.

Example: If $xy^2z < 0$, then which one of the following statements must also be true?

> I. $xz < 0$
>
> II. $z < 0$
>
> III. $xyz < 0$

(A) None   (B) I only   (C) III only   (D) I and II   (E) II and III

Since a number raised to an even exponent is greater than or equal to zero, we know that y^2 is positive (it cannot be zero because the product xy^2z would then be zero). Hence, we can divide both sides of the inequality $xy^2z < 0$ by y^2:

$$\frac{xy^2 z}{y^2} < \frac{0}{y^2}$$

Simplifying yields $xz < 0$

Therefore, I is true, which eliminates (A), (C), and (E). Now, the following illustrates that $z < 0$ is not necessarily true:

$$-1 \cdot 2^2 \cdot 3 = -12 < 0$$

This eliminates (D). Hence, the answer is (B).

Absolute Value

The absolute value of a number is its distance on the number line from 0. Since distance is a positive number, absolute value of a number is positive. Two vertical bars denote the absolute value of a number: $|x|$. For example, $|3| = 3$ and $|-3| = 3$. This can be illustrated on the number line:

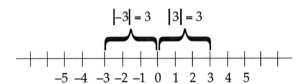

Students rarely struggle with the absolute value of numbers: if the number is negative, simply make it positive; and if it is already positive, leave it as is. For example, since –2.4 is negative, $|-2.4| = 2.4$ and since 5.01 is positive $|5.01| = 5.01$.

Further, students rarely struggle with the absolute value of positive variables: if the variable is positive, simply drop the absolute value symbol. For example, if $x > 0$, then $|x| = x$.

However, negative variables can cause students much consternation. If x is negative, then $|x| = -x$. This often confuses students because the absolute value is positive but the $-x$ appears to be negative. It is actually positive—it is the negative of a negative number, which is positive. To see this more clearly let $x = -k$, where k is a <u>positive</u> number. Then x is a negative number. So $|x| = -x = -(-k) = k$. Since k is positive so is $-x$. Another way to view this is $|x| = -x = (-1) \cdot x = (-1)$(a negative number) = a positive number.

Example: If $x = -|x|$, then which one of the following statements could be true?

   I. $x = 0$

   II. $x < 0$

   III. $x > 0$

   (A) None   (B) I only   (C) III only   (D) I and II   (E) II and III

Statement I could be true because $-|0| = -(+0) = -(0) = 0$. Statement II could be true because the right side of the equation is always negative $[-|x| = -(\text{a positive number}) = \text{a negative number}]$. Now, if one side of an equation is always negative, then the other side must always be negative, otherwise the opposite sides of the equation would not be equal. Since Statement III is the opposite of Statement II, it must be false. But let's show this explicitly: Suppose x were positive. Then $|x| = x$, and the equation $x = -|x|$ becomes $x = -x$. Dividing both sides of this equation by x yields $1 = -1$. This is contradiction. Hence, x cannot be positive. The answer is (D).

Higher Order Inequalities

These inequalities have variables whose exponents are greater than 1. For example, $x^2 + 4 < 2$ and $x^3 - 9 > 0$. The number line is often helpful in solving these types of inequalities.

Example: For which values of x is $x^2 > -6x - 5$?

First, replace the inequality symbol with an equal symbol: $x^2 = -6x - 5$

Adding $6x$ and 5 to both sides yields $x^2 + 6x + 5 = 0$

Factoring yields (see General Trinomials in the chapter Factoring) $(x + 5)(x + 1) = 0$

Setting each factor to 0 yields $x + 5 = 0$ and $x + 1 = 0$

Or $x = -5$ and $x = -1$

Now, the only numbers at which the expression can change sign are –5 and –1. So –5 and –1 divide the number line into three intervals. Let's set up a number line and choose test points in each interval:

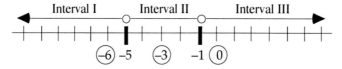

When $x = -6$, $x^2 > -6x - 5$ becomes $36 > 31$. This is true. Hence, all numbers in Interval I satisfy the inequality. That is, $x < -5$. When $x = -3$, $x^2 > -6x - 5$ becomes $9 > 13$. This is false. Hence, no numbers in Interval II satisfy the inequality. When $x = 0$, $x^2 > -6x - 5$ becomes $0 > -5$. This is true. Hence, all numbers in Interval III satisfy the inequality. That is, $x > -1$. The graph of the solution follows:

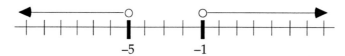

Note, if the original inequality had included the greater-than-or-equal symbol, $\geq$, the solution set would have included both –5 and –1. On the graph, this would have been indicated by filling in the circles above –5 and –1. The open circles indicate that –5 and –1 are not part of the solution.

Summary of steps for solving higher order inequalities:

1. Replace the inequality symbol with an equal symbol.
2. Move all terms to one side of the equation (usually the left side).
3. Factor the equation.
4. Set the factors equal to 0 to find zeros.
5. Choose test points on either side of the zeros.
6. If a test point satisfies the original inequality, then all numbers in that interval satisfy the inequality. Similarly, if a test point does not satisfy the inequality, then no numbers in that interval satisfy the inequality.

Transitive Property

$$\boxed{\text{If } x < y \text{ and } y < z, \text{ then } x < z}$$

Example: If $\dfrac{1}{Q} > 1$, which of the following must be true?

(A) $1 < Q^2$ (B) $\dfrac{1}{Q^2} > 2$ (C) $1 > Q^2$ (D) $\dfrac{1}{Q^2} < 1$ (E) $Q < Q^2$

Since $\dfrac{1}{Q} > 1$ and $1 > 0$, we know from the transitive property that $\dfrac{1}{Q}$ is positive. Hence, Q is positive.

Therefore, we can multiply both sides of $\dfrac{1}{Q} > 1$ by Q without reversing the inequality:

$$Q \cdot \frac{1}{Q} > 1 \cdot Q$$

Reducing yields $1 > Q$

Multiplying both sides again by Q yields $Q > Q^2$

Using the transitive property to combine the last two inequalities yields $1 > Q^2$

The answer is (C).

Like Inequalities Can Be Added

$$\boxed{\text{If } x < y \text{ and } w < z, \text{ then } x + w < y + z}$$

Example: If $2 < x < 5$ and $3 < y < 5$, which of the following best describes $x - y$?

(A) $-3 < x - y < 2$
(B) $-3 < x - y < 5$
(C) $0 < x - y < 2$
(D) $3 < x - y < 5$
(E) $2 < x - y < 5$

Multiplying both sides of $3 < y < 5$ by -1 yields $-3 > -y > -5$. Now, we usually write the smaller number on the left side of the inequality. So $-3 > -y > -5$ becomes $-5 < -y < -3$. Add this inequality to the like inequality $2 < x < 5$:

$$
\begin{array}{r}
2 < x < 5 \\
(+) \quad -5 < -y < -3 \\
\hline
-3 < x - y < 2
\end{array}
$$

The answer is (A).

Problem Set J:

1. If $1 < x < y$, which of the following must be true?

   (A) $-x^2 < -y^2$ (B) $\dfrac{x}{y} < \dfrac{y}{x}$ (C) $\dfrac{y}{x} < \dfrac{x}{y}$ (D) $\dfrac{-x}{y} < \dfrac{-y}{x}$ (E) $x^2 > y^2$

2. If $-3 < x < -1$ and $3 < y < 7$, which of the following best describes $\dfrac{x-y}{2}$?

   (A) $-5 < \dfrac{x-y}{2} < -2$

   (B) $-3 < \dfrac{x-y}{2} < -1$

   (C) $-2 < \dfrac{x-y}{2} < 0$

   (D) $2 < \dfrac{x-y}{2} < 5$

   (E) $3 < \dfrac{x-y}{2} < 7$

3. If x is an integer and $y = -2x - 8$, what is the least value of x for which y is less than 9?

   (A) -9 (B) -8 (C) -7 (D) -6 (E) -5

4. Which one of the following could be the graph of $3 - 6x \le \dfrac{4x+2}{-2}$?

5. If line segment AD has midpoint M_1 and line segment M_1D has midpoint M_2, what is the value of $\dfrac{M_1D}{AM_2}$?

   (A) 1/2 (B) 2/3 (C) 3/4 (D) 4/5 (E) 5/6

6. If $x < y < -1$, which of the following must be true?

   (A) $\dfrac{x}{y} > xy$ (B) $\dfrac{y}{x} > x + y$ (C) $\dfrac{y}{x} > xy$ (D) $\dfrac{y}{x} < x + y$ (E) $\dfrac{y}{x} > \dfrac{x}{y}$

7. Which of the following represents all solutions of the inequality $x^2 < 2x$?

   (A) $-1 < x < 1$ (B) $0 < x < 2$ (C) $1 < x < 3$ (D) $2 < x < 4$ (E) $4 < x < 6$

●────────●────────●
x   0   y

8. Given the positions of numbers x and y on the number line above, which of the following must be true?

   I. $xy > 0$

   II. $\dfrac{x}{y} < 0$

   III. $x - y > 0$

   (A) I only
   (B) II only
   (C) III only
   (D) I and II only
   (E) I, II, and III

9. If $\begin{array}{c} x^4 y < 0 \\ xy^4 > 0 \end{array}$, which of the following must be true?

   (A) $x > y$ (B) $y > x$ (C) $x = y$ (D) $x < 0$ (E) $y > 0$

10. If n is an integer, what is the least value of n such that $\dfrac{1}{3^n} < 0.01$?

   (A) 2
   (B) 3
   (C) 4
   (D) 5
   (E) 6

11. If the average of 10, 14, and n is greater than or equal to 8 and less than or equal to 12, what is the least possible value of n ?

   (A) –12   (B) –6   (C) 0   (D) 6   (E) 12

12. If $\begin{array}{c} 3x + y < 4 \\ x > 3 \end{array}$, which of the following must be true?

   (A) $y < -5$ (B) $y < -10$ (C) $x = y$ (D) $x < 3$ (E) $y > 0$

$$2 - 3x \ ? \ 5$$

13. Of the following symbols, which one can be substituted for the question mark in the above expression to make a true statement for all values of x such that $-1 < x \le 2$?

   (A) =   (B) <   (C) ≥   (D) >   (E) ≤

14. Let x, y, z be three different positive integers each less than 20. What is the smallest possible value of expression $\dfrac{x - y}{-z}$?

   (A) –18   (B) –17   (C) –14   (D) –11   (E) –9

15. If $x > 0$ and $|x| = \dfrac{1}{x}$, then $x =$

   (A) –1   (B) 0   (C) 1   (D) 2   (E) 3

16. Four letters—a, b, c, and d—represent one number each from one through four. No two letters represent the same number. It is known that $c > a$ and $a > d$. If b = 2, then $a =$

    (A)   1
    (B)   2
    (C)   3
    (D)   4
    (E)   Not enough information to decide.

17. If $r > t$ and $r < 1$ and $rt = 1$, then which one of the following must be true?

    (A) $r > 0$ and $t < -1$
    (B) $r > -1$ and $t < -1$
    (C) $r < -1$ and $t > -1$
    (D) $r < 1$ and $t > 1$
    (E) $r > 1$ and $t < 0$

18. If $x > y > 0$ and $p > q > 0$, then which one of the following expressions must be greater than 1?

    (A) $\dfrac{x + p}{y + q}$

    (B) $\dfrac{x + q}{y + p}$

    (C) $\dfrac{x}{p}$

    (D) $\dfrac{xq}{yp}$

    (E) $\dfrac{yq}{xp}$

19. If $2x + y > m$ and $2y + x < n$, then $x - y$ must be greater than

    (A) $m + n$
    (B) $m - n$
    (C) mn
    (D) $2m + n$
    (E) $n - m$

20. If $p > 2$, then which one of the following inequalities must be false?

    (A) $2p > 7$
    (B) $3p < 7$
    (C) $p < 3$
    (D) $p > 4$
    (E) $3p < 6$

Answers and Solutions to Problem Set J

1.   If $1 < x < y$, which one of the following must be true?

   (A) $-x^2 < -y^2$ (B) $\dfrac{x}{y} < \dfrac{y}{x}$ (C) $\dfrac{y}{x} < \dfrac{x}{y}$ (D) $\dfrac{-x}{y} < \dfrac{-y}{x}$ (E) $x^2 > y^2$

From $1 < x < y$, we know that both x and y are positive. So dividing both sides of $x < y$ by x yields $1 < \dfrac{y}{x}$; and dividing both sides of $x < y$ by y yields $\dfrac{x}{y} < 1$. Hence, $\dfrac{x}{y} < 1 < \dfrac{y}{x}$. By the transitive property of inequalities, $\dfrac{x}{y} < \dfrac{y}{x}$. The answer is (B).

2.   If $-3 < x < -1$ and $3 < y < 7$, which of the following best describes $\dfrac{x-y}{2}$?

   (A) $-5 < \dfrac{x-y}{2} < -2$

   (B) $-3 < \dfrac{x-y}{2} < -1$

   (C) $-2 < \dfrac{x-y}{2} < 0$

   (D) $2 < \dfrac{x-y}{2} < 5$

   (E) $3 < \dfrac{x-y}{2} < 7$

Multiplying both sides of $3 < y < 7$ by -1 yields $-3 > -y > -7$. Now, we usually write the smaller number on the left side of an inequality. So $-3 > -y > -7$ becomes $-7 < -y < -3$. Add this inequality to the like inequality $-3 < x < -1$:

$$\begin{array}{r} -3 < x < -1 \\ (+)\qquad \underline{-7 < -y < -3} \\ -10 < x - y < -4 \end{array}$$

Dividing $-10 < x - y < -4$ by 2 yields $\dfrac{-10}{2} < \dfrac{x-y}{2} < \dfrac{-4}{2}$, or $-5 < \dfrac{x-y}{2} < -2$. The answer is (A).

3.   If x is an integer and $y = -2x - 8$, what is the least value of x for which y is less than 9?

   (A) -9 (B) -8 (C) -7 (D) -6 (E) -5

Since y is less than 9 and $y = -2x - 8$, we get	$-2x - 8 < 9$
Adding 8 to both sides of this inequality yields	$-2x < 17$
Dividing by -2 and reversing the inequality yields	$x > -\dfrac{17}{2} = -8.5$
Since x is an integer and is to be as small as possible,	$x = -8$
The answer is (B).	

4. Which one of the following could be the graph of $3 - 6x \le \dfrac{4x + 2}{-2}$?

(A) ◄━━━━━━━●━━━━━━━━━━━━━━━━
             ┬
             0

(B) ━━━━━━━●━━━━●━━━━━━━━━━━━
            ┬
            0

(C) ◄━━━━━━●━━━━━●━━━━━━━━━━►
             ┬
             0

(D) ━━━━━━━━━━●━━━━━━━━━━━━━►
             ┬
             0

(E) ━━━━━━━●━━━━━━━►━━━━━━━━━
             ┬
             0

Multiplying both sides of the inequality by –2 yields	$-2(3 - 6x) \ge 4x + 2$
Distributing the –2 yields	$-6 + 12x \ge 4x + 2$
Subtracting $4x$ and adding 6 to both sides yields	$8x \ge 8$
Dividing both sides of the inequality by 8 yields	$x \ge 1$

The answer is (D).

5. If line segment AD has midpoint M_1 and line segment M_1D has midpoint M_2, what is the value of $\dfrac{M_1D}{AM_2}$?

(A) $\dfrac{1}{2}$ (B) $\dfrac{2}{3}$ (C) $\dfrac{3}{4}$ (D) $\dfrac{4}{5}$ (E) $\dfrac{5}{6}$

Let 4 be the length of line segment AD. Since M_1 is the midpoint of AD, this yields

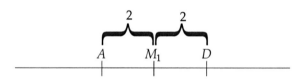

Now, since M_2 is the midpoint of M_1D, this yields

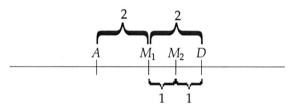

From the diagram, we see that $M_1D = 2$ and $AM_2 = 3$. Hence, $\dfrac{M_1D}{AM_2} = \dfrac{2}{3}$. The answer is (B).

6. If $x < y < -1$, which of the following must be true?

(A) $\dfrac{x}{y} > xy$ (B) $\dfrac{y}{x} > x + y$ (C) $\dfrac{y}{x} > xy$ (D) $\dfrac{y}{x} < x + y$ (E) $\dfrac{y}{x} > \dfrac{x}{y}$

Since the sum of negative numbers is negative, $x + y$ is negative. Since the quotient of an even number of negative numbers is positive, $\dfrac{y}{x}$ is positive. Hence, $\dfrac{y}{x} > x + y$. The answer is (B).

7. Which of the following represents all solutions of the inequality $x^2 < 2x$?

    (A) $-1 < x < 1$ (B) $0 < x < 2$ (C) $1 < x < 3$ (D) $2 < x < 4$ (E) $4 < x < 6$

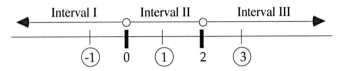

Forming an equation from $x^2 < 2x$ yields $x^2 = 2x$
Subtracting $2x$ from both sides yields $x^2 - 2x = 0$
Factoring yields $x(x - 2) = 0$
Setting each factor to zero yields $x = 0$ and $x - 2 = 0$
Solving yields $x = 0$ and $x = 2$
Setting up a number line and choosing test points (the circled numbers on the number line below) yields

Now, if $x = -1$, the inequality $x^2 < 2x$ becomes $(-1)^2 < 2(-1)$, or $1 < -2$. This is false. Hence, Interval I is not a solution. If $x = 1$, the inequality $x^2 < 2x$ becomes $1^2 < 2(1)$, or $1 < 2$. This is true. Hence, Interval II is a solution. If $x = 3$, the inequality $x^2 < 2x$ becomes $3^2 < 2(3)$, or $9 < 6$. This is false. Hence, Interval III is not a solution. Thus, only Interval II is a solution:

The answer is (B).

8. Given the positions of numbers x and y on the number line above, which of the following must be true?

    I. $xy > 0$

    II. $\dfrac{x}{y} < 0$

    III. $x - y > 0$

    (A) I only
    (B) II only
    (C) III only
    (D) I and II only
    (E) I, II, and III

Since x is to the left of zero on the number line, it's negative. Since y is to the right of zero, it's positive. Now, the product or quotient of a positive number and a negative number is negative. Hence, Statement I is false and Statement II is true. Regarding Statement III, since x is to the left of y on the number line, $x < y$. Subtracting y from both sides of this inequality yields $x - y < 0$. Hence, Statement III is false. Therefore, the answer is (B).

9.   If $\begin{array}{l} x^4 y < 0 \\ xy^4 > 0 \end{array}$, which of the following must be true?

(A) $x > y$ (B) $y > x$ (C) $x = y$ (D) $x < 0$ (E) $y > 0$

Since x is raised to an even exponent, it is greater than or equal to zero. Further, since $x^4 y \neq 0$, we know that neither x nor y is zero (otherwise $x^4 y = 0$). Hence, we may divide $x^4 y < 0$ by x^4 without reversing the inequality:

$$\frac{x^4 y}{x^4} < \frac{0}{x^4}$$

Simplifying yields $y < 0$

A similar analysis of the inequality $xy^4 > 0$ shows that $x > 0$. Hence, $x > y$. The answer is (A).

10.   If n is an integer, what is the least value of n such that $\dfrac{1}{3^n} < 0.01$?

(A)   2
(B)   3
(C)   4
(D)   5
(E)   6

Replacing 0.01 with its fractional equivalent, $\dfrac{1}{100}$, yields $\dfrac{1}{3^n} < \dfrac{1}{100}$

Multiplying both sides by 3^n and 100 and then simplifying yields $100 < 3^n$

Beginning with $n = 2$, we plug in larger and larger values of n until we reach one that makes $100 < 3^n$ true. The table below summarizes the results:

n	$100 < 3^n$	
2	$100 < 3^2 = 9$	False
3	$100 < 3^3 = 27$	False
4	$100 < 3^4 = 81$	False
5	$100 < 3^5 = 243$	True

Since 5 is the first integer to work, the answer is (D).

11.   If the average of 10, 14, and n is greater than or equal to 8 and less than or equal to 12, what is the least possible value of n ?

(A)   −12
(B)   −6
(C)   0
(D)   6
(E)   12

Translating the clause "the average of 10, 14, and n is greater than or equal to 8 and less than or equal to 12" into an inequality yields

$$8 \leq \frac{10 + 14 + n}{3} \leq 12$$

Adding 10 and 14 yields $8 \leq \dfrac{24 + n}{3} \leq 12$

Multiplying <u>each</u> term by 3 yields $24 \leq 24 + n \leq 36$

Subtracting 24 from each term yields $0 \leq n \leq 12$

Hence, the least possible value of n is 0. The answer is (C).

12.   If $\begin{array}{c}3x + y < 4 \\ x > 3\end{array}$, which of the following must be true?

(A) $y < -5$ (B) $y < -10$ (C) $x = y$ (D) $x < 3$ (E) $y > 0$

Subtracting $3x$ from both sides of $3x + y < 4$ yields $y < 4 - 3x$. Now, multiplying both sides of $x > 3$ by -3 yields $-3x < -9$. Adding 4 to both sides yields $4 - 3x < -5$. Now, using the transitive property to combine $y < 4 - 3x$ and $4 - 3x < -5$ yields $y < 4 - 3x < -5$. Hence, $y < -5$. The answer is (A).

$$2 - 3x \; ? \; 5$$

13.   Of the following symbols, which one can be substituted for the question mark in the above expression to make a true statement for all values of x such that $-1 < x \le 2$?

(A) $=$ (B) $<$ (C) $\ge$ (D) $>$ (E) $\le$

Multiply each term of the inequality $-1 < x \le 2$ by -3 (this is done because the original expression involves $-3x$):

$$3 > -3x \ge -6$$

Add 2 to each term of this inequality (this is done because the original expression adds 2 and $-3x$):

$$5 > 2 - 3x \ge -4$$

Rewrite the inequality in standard form (with the smaller number on the left and the larger number on the right):

$$-4 \le 2 - 3x < 5$$

The answer is (B).

14.   Let x, y, z be three different positive integers each less than 20. What is the smallest possible value of expression $\dfrac{x - y}{-z}$ is

(A) -18 (B) -17 (C) -14 (D) -11 (E) -9

First, bring the negative symbol in the expression $\dfrac{x - y}{-z}$ to the top:

$$\frac{-(x - y)}{z}$$

Then distribute the negative symbol:

$$\frac{y - x}{z}$$

To make this expression as small as possible, we need to make both the $y - x$ and z as small as possible. To make $y - x$ as small as possible, let $y = 1$ and $x = 19$. Then $y - x = 1 - 19 = -18$. With these choices for y and x, the smallest remaining value for z is 2. This gives

$$\frac{y - x}{z} = \frac{1 - 19}{2} = \frac{-18}{2} = -9$$

In this case, we made the numerator as small as possible. Now, let's make the denominator as small as possible. To that end, chose $z = 1$ and $y = 2$ and $x = 19$. This gives

$$\frac{y - x}{z} = \frac{2 - 19}{1} = \frac{-17}{1} = -17$$

The answer is (B).

15. If $x > 0$ and $|x| = \dfrac{1}{x}$, then $x =$

    (A) −1   (B) 0   (C) 1   (D) 2   (E) 3

Since $x > 0$, $|x| = x$. And the equation $|x| = \dfrac{1}{x}$ becomes $x = \dfrac{1}{x}$. Multiplying both sides of this equation by x yields $x^2 = 1$. Taking the square root of both sides gives $x = \pm 1$. Since we are given that $x > 0$, x must equal 1. The answer is (C).

16. Four letters—a, b, c, and d—represent one number each from one through four. No two letters represent the same number. It is known that $c > a$ and $a > d$. If b = 2, then $a =$

    (A)   1
    (B)   2
    (C)   3
    (D)   4
    (E)   Not enough information to decide.

Combining the inequalities $c > a$ and $a > d$ gives $c > a > d$. Since $b = 2$, a, c, and d must represent the remaining numbers 1, 3, and 4—not necessarily in that order. In order to satisfy the condition $c > a > d$, c must be 4, a must be 3, and d must be 1. The answer is (C).

17. If $r > t$ and $r < 1$ and $rt = 1$, then which one of the following must be true?

    (A) $r > 0$ and $t < -1$
    (B) $r > -1$ and $t < -1$
    (C) $r < -1$ and $t > -1$
    (D) $r < 1$ and $t > 1$
    (E) $r > 1$ and $t < 0$

Note that the product of r and t is 1. The product of two numbers is positive only if both numbers are positive or both numbers are negative. Since $rt = 1$ and $r > t$, there are two possibilities:

$$\text{Case I (both negative): } -1 < r < 0 \text{ and } t < -1$$
$$\text{Case II (both positive): } 0 < t < 1 \text{ and } r > 1$$

The second case violates the condition $r < 1$. Hence, Case I is true, and the answer is (B).

18. If $x > y > 0$ and $p > q > 0$, then which one of the following expressions must be greater than 1?

    (A) $\dfrac{x+p}{y+q}$

    (B) $\dfrac{x+q}{y+p}$

    (C) $\dfrac{x}{p}$

    (D) $\dfrac{xq}{yp}$

    (E) $\dfrac{yq}{xp}$

Adding the given inequalities $x > y > 0$ and $p > q > 0$ yields

$$x + p > y + q > 0$$

Since $y + q$ is positive, dividing the inequality by $y + q$ will not reverse the inequality:

$$\frac{x+p}{y+q} > \frac{y+q}{y+q}$$

$$\frac{x+p}{y+q} > 1$$

Hence, the answer is (A).

19.   If $2x + y > m$ and $2y + x < n$, then $x - y$ must be greater than

   (A) $m + n$
   (B) $m - n$
   (C) mn
   (D) $2m + n$
   (E) $n - m$

Aligning the system of inequalities vertically yields

$$2x + y > m$$
$$2y + x < n$$

Multiplying both sides of the bottom inequality by -1 and flipping the direction of the inequality yields

$$-2y - x > -n$$

Adding this inequality to the top inequality yields

$$(2x + y) + (-2y - x) > m - n$$
$$(2x - x) + (-2y + y) > m - n$$
$$x - y > m - n$$

The answer is (B).

20.   If $p > 2$, then which one of the following inequalities must be false?

   (A) $2p > 7$
   (B) $3p < 7$
   (C) $p < 3$
   (D) $p > 4$
   (E) $3p < 6$

We are given that $p > 2$. Multiplying both sides of this inequality by 3 yields $3p > 6$. The answer is (E).

Fractions & Decimals

Fractions

A fraction consists of two parts: a numerator and a denominator.

$$\frac{numerator}{denominator}$$

If the numerator is smaller than the denominator, the fraction is called *proper* and is less than one. For example: $\frac{1}{2}$, $\frac{4}{5}$, and $\frac{3}{\pi}$ are all proper fractions and therefore less than 1.

If the numerator is larger than the denominator, the fraction is called *improper* and is greater than 1. For example: $\frac{3}{2}$, $\frac{5}{4}$, and $\frac{\pi}{3}$ are all improper fractions and therefore greater than 1.

An improper fraction can be converted into a *mixed fraction* by dividing its denominator into its numerator. For example, since 2 divides into 7 three times with a remainder of 1, we get

$$\frac{7}{2} = 3\frac{1}{2}$$

To convert a mixed fraction into an improper fraction, multiply the denominator and the integer and then add the numerator. Then, write the result over the denominator. For example, $5\frac{2}{3} = \frac{3 \cdot 5 + 2}{3} = \frac{17}{3}$.

In a negative fraction, the negative symbol can be written on the top, in the middle, or on the bottom; however, when a negative symbol appears on the bottom, it is usually moved to the top or the middle: $\frac{5}{-3} = \frac{-5}{3} = -\frac{5}{3}$. If both terms in the denominator of a fraction are negative, the negative symbol is often factored out and moved to the top or middle of the fraction: $\frac{1}{-x-2} = \frac{1}{-(x+2)} = -\frac{1}{x+2}$ or $\frac{-1}{x+2}$.

 To compare two fractions, cross-multiply. The larger number will be on the same side as the larger fraction.

Strategy

Example: Which of the following fractions is larger?

$$\frac{9}{10} \qquad\qquad \frac{10}{11}$$

Cross-multiplying gives $9 \cdot 11$ versus $10 \cdot 10$, which reduces to 99 versus 100. Now, 100 is greater than 99. Hence, $\frac{10}{11}$ is greater than $\frac{9}{10}$.

Always reduce a fraction to its lowest terms.

Example: If $x \neq -1$, then $\dfrac{2x^2 + 4x + 2}{(x+1)^2} =$

    (A) 0   (B) 1   (C) 2   (D) 4   (E) 6

Factor out the 2 in the expression:

$$\frac{2\left(x^2 + 2x + 1\right)}{(x+1)^2}$$

Factor the quadratic expressions:

$$\frac{2(x+1)(x+1)}{(x+1)(x+1)}$$

Finally, canceling the $(x+1)$'s gives 2. The answer is (C).

To solve a fractional equation, multiply both sides by the LCD (lowest common denominator) to clear fractions.

Example: If $\dfrac{x+3}{x-3} = y$, what is the value of x in terms of y?

  (A) $3-y$ (B) $\dfrac{3}{y}$ (C) $\sqrt{y+12}$ (D) $\dfrac{-3y-3}{1-y}$ (E) $3y^2$

First, multiply both sides of the equation by $x-3$: $(x-3)\dfrac{x+3}{x-3} = (x-3)y$

Cancel the $(x-3)$'s on the left side of the equation: $x+3 = (x-3)y$
Distribute the y: $x+3 = xy - 3y$
Subtract xy and 3 from both sides: $x - xy = -3y - 3$
Factor out the x on the left side of the equation: $x(1-y) = -3y - 3$

Finally, divide both sides of the equation by $1-y$: $x = \dfrac{-3y-3}{1-y}$

Hence, the answer is (D).

Complex Fractions: When dividing a fraction by a whole number (or vice versa), you must keep track of the main division bar:

$$\frac{\dfrac{a}{b}}{c} = a \cdot \frac{c}{b} = \frac{ac}{b}. \text{ But } \frac{a}{\dfrac{b}{c}} = \frac{a}{b} \cdot \frac{1}{c} = \frac{a}{bc}.$$

Example: $\dfrac{1 - \dfrac{1}{2}}{3} =$

    (A) 6   (B) 3   (C) 1/3   (D) 1/6   (E) 1/8

Solution: $\dfrac{1-\dfrac{1}{2}}{3} = \dfrac{\dfrac{2}{2}-\dfrac{1}{2}}{3} = \dfrac{\dfrac{2-1}{2}}{3} = \dfrac{\dfrac{1}{2}}{3} = \dfrac{1}{2} \cdot \dfrac{1}{3} = \dfrac{1}{6}.$ The answer is (D).

Example: If $z \neq 0$ and $yz \neq 1$, then $\dfrac{1}{y - \dfrac{1}{z}} =$

(A) $\dfrac{yz}{zy - 1}$ (B) $\dfrac{y - z}{z}$ (C) $\dfrac{yz - z}{z - 1}$ (D) $\dfrac{z}{zy - 1}$ (E) $\dfrac{y - z}{zy - 1}$

Solution: $\dfrac{1}{y - \dfrac{1}{z}} = \dfrac{1}{\dfrac{z}{z}y - \dfrac{1}{z}} = \dfrac{1}{\dfrac{zy - 1}{z}} = 1 \cdot \dfrac{z}{zy - 1} = \dfrac{z}{zy - 1}$. The answer is (D).

 Note!   **Multiplying fractions is routine: merely multiply the numerators and multiply the denominators:** $\dfrac{a}{b} \cdot \dfrac{c}{d} = \dfrac{ac}{bd}$. **For example,** $\dfrac{1}{2} \cdot \dfrac{3}{4} = \dfrac{1 \cdot 3}{2 \cdot 4} = \dfrac{3}{8}$.

 Note!   **Two fractions can be added quickly by cross-multiplying:** $\dfrac{a}{b} \pm \dfrac{c}{d} = \dfrac{ad \pm bc}{bd}$

Example: $\dfrac{1}{2} - \dfrac{3}{4} =$

(A) $-5/4$ (B) $-2/3$ (C) $-1/4$ (D) $-1/2$ (E) $-2/3$

Cross-multiplying the expression $\dfrac{1}{2} - \dfrac{3}{4}$ yields $\dfrac{1 \cdot 4 - 2 \cdot 3}{2 \cdot 4} = \dfrac{4 - 6}{8} = \dfrac{-2}{8} = -\dfrac{1}{4}$. Hence, the answer is (C).

Example: Which of the following equals the average of x and $\dfrac{1}{x}$?

(A) $\dfrac{x + 2}{x}$ (B) $\dfrac{x^2 + 1}{2x}$ (C) $\dfrac{x + 1}{x^2}$ (D) $\dfrac{2x^2 + 1}{x}$ (E) $\dfrac{x + 1}{x}$

The average of x and $\dfrac{1}{x}$ is $\dfrac{x + \dfrac{1}{x}}{2} = \dfrac{\dfrac{x^2 + 1}{x}}{2} = \dfrac{x^2 + 1}{x} \cdot \dfrac{1}{2} = \dfrac{x^2 + 1}{2x}$. Thus, the answer is (B).

 Note!   **To add three or more fractions with different denominators, you need to form a common denominator of all the fractions.**

For example, to add the fractions in the expression $\dfrac{1}{3} + \dfrac{1}{4} + \dfrac{1}{18}$, we have to change the denominator of each fraction into the common denominator 36 (note, 36 is a common denominator because 3, 4, and 18 all divide into it evenly). This is done by multiply the top and bottom of each fraction by an appropriate number (this does not change the value of the expression because any number divided by itself equals 1):

$$\dfrac{1}{3}\left(\dfrac{12}{12}\right) + \dfrac{1}{4}\left(\dfrac{9}{9}\right) + \dfrac{1}{18}\left(\dfrac{2}{2}\right) = \dfrac{12}{36} + \dfrac{9}{36} + \dfrac{2}{36} = \dfrac{12 + 9 + 2}{36} = \dfrac{23}{36}$$

You may remember from algebra that to find a common denominator of a set of fractions, you prime factor the denominators and then select each factor the greatest number of times it occurs in any of the factorizations. That is too cumbersome, however. A better way is to simply add the largest denominator to itself until all the other denominators divide into it evenly. In the above example, we just add 18 to itself to get the common denominator 36.

To find a common denominator of a set of fractions, simply add the largest denominator to itself until all the other denominators divide into it evenly.

Fractions often behave in unusual ways: **Squaring a fraction makes it smaller, and taking the square root of a fraction makes it larger.** (**Caution:** This is true only for proper fractions, that is, fractions between 0 and 1.)

Example: $\left(\frac{1}{3}\right)^2 = \frac{1}{9}$ and $\frac{1}{9}$ is less than $\frac{1}{3}$. Also $\sqrt{\frac{1}{4}} = \frac{1}{2}$ and $\frac{1}{2}$ is greater than $\frac{1}{4}$.

You can cancel only over multiplication, not over addition or subtraction.

For example, the c's in the expression $\dfrac{c + x}{c}$ cannot be canceled. However, the c's in the expression $\dfrac{cx + c}{c}$ can be canceled as follows: $\dfrac{cx + c}{c} = \dfrac{\cancel{c}(x + 1)}{\cancel{c}} = x + 1$.

Decimals

If a fraction's denominator is a power of 10, it can be written in a special form called a *decimal fraction*. Some common decimals are $\frac{1}{10} = .1$, $\frac{2}{100} = .02$, $\frac{3}{1000} = .003$. Notice that the number of decimal places corresponds to the number of zeros in the denominator of the fraction. Also note that the value of the decimal place decreases to the right of the decimal point:

$$\underset{.1}{\ulcorner}\text{tenths} \quad \underset{2}{\ulcorner}\text{hundredths} \quad \underset{3}{\ulcorner}\text{thousandths} \quad \underset{4}{\ulcorner}\text{ten-thousandths}$$

This decimal can be written in expanded form as follows:

$$.1234 = \frac{1}{10} + \frac{2}{100} + \frac{3}{1000} + \frac{4}{10000}$$

Sometimes a zero is placed before the decimal point to prevent misreading the decimal as a whole number. The zero has no affect on the value of the decimal. For example, $.2 = 0.2$.

Fractions can be converted to decimals by dividing the denominator into the numerator. For example, to convert $\frac{5}{8}$ to a decimal, divide 8 into 5 (note, a decimal point and as many zeros as necessary are added after the 5):

$$
\begin{array}{r}
.625 \\
8\overline{)5.000} \\
\underline{48} \\
20 \\
\underline{16} \\
40 \\
\underline{40} \\
0
\end{array}
$$

The procedures for adding, subtracting, multiplying, and dividing decimals are the same as for whole numbers, except for a few small adjustments.

- **Adding and Subtracting Decimals:** To add or subtract decimals, merely align the decimal points and then add or subtract as you would with whole numbers.

$$
\begin{array}{r}
1.369 \\
+\quad 9.7 \\
\hline
11.069
\end{array}
\qquad
\begin{array}{r}
12.45 \\
-\quad 6.367 \\
\hline
6.083
\end{array}
$$

- **Multiplying Decimals:** Multiply decimals as you would with whole numbers. The answer will have as many decimal places as the sum of the number of decimal places in the numbers being multiplied.

$$
\begin{array}{rl}
1.23 & \text{2 decimal places} \\
\times\quad 2.4 & \text{1 decimal place} \\
\hline
492 & \\
246\quad & \\
\hline
2.952 & \text{3 decimal places}
\end{array}
$$

- **Dividing Decimals:** Before dividing decimals, move the decimal point of the divisor all the way to the right and move the decimal point of the dividend the same number of spaces to the right (adding zeros if necessary). Then divide as you would with whole numbers.

$$
.24\overline{)\,.6\,} = 24\overline{)\,60.0\,}
$$

$$
\begin{array}{r}
2.5 \\
24\overline{)60.0} \\
48 \\
\hline
120 \\
120 \\
\hline
0
\end{array}
$$

Example: $\dfrac{1}{5}$ of .1 percent equals:

(A) 2   (B) .2   (C) .02   (D) .002   (E) .0002

Recall that percent means to divide by 100. So .1 percent equals $\dfrac{.1}{100} = .001$. To convert $\dfrac{1}{5}$ to a decimal, divide 5 into 1:

$$
\begin{array}{r}
.2 \\
5\overline{)1.0} \\
10 \\
\hline
0
\end{array}
$$

In percent problems, "of" means multiplication. So multiplying .2 and .001 yields

$$
\begin{array}{r}
.001 \\
\times\quad .2 \\
\hline
.0002
\end{array}
$$

Hence, the answer is (E). Note, you may be surprised to learn that the ACT would consider this to be a hard problem.

Example: The decimal .1 is how many times greater than the decimal $(.001)^3$?

        (A)   10
        (B) 10^2
        (C) 10^5
        (D) 10^8
        (E) 10^{10}

Converting .001 to a fraction gives $\dfrac{1}{1000}$. This fraction, in turn, can be written as $\dfrac{1}{10^3}$, or 10^{-3}. Cubing this expression yields $(.001)^3 = \left(10^{-3}\right)^3 = 10^{-9}$. Now, dividing the larger number, .1, by the smaller number, $(.001)^3$, yields

$$\frac{.1}{(.001)^3} = \frac{10^{-1}}{10^{-9}} = 10^{-1-(-9)} = 10^{-1+9} = 10^8$$

Hence, .1 is 10^8 times as large as $(.001)^3$. The answer is (D).

Example: Let $x = .99$, $y = \sqrt{.99}$, and $z = (.99)^2$. Then which of the following is true?

        (A) $x < z < y$
        (B) $z < y < x$
        (C) $z < x < y$
        (D) $y < x < z$
        (E) $y < z < x$

Converting .99 into a fraction gives $\dfrac{99}{100}$. Since $\dfrac{99}{100}$ is between 0 and 1, squaring it will make it smaller and taking its square root will make it larger. Hence, $(.99)^2 < .99 < \sqrt{.99}$. The answer is (C). Note, this property holds for all proper decimals (decimals between 0 and 1) just as it does for all proper fractions.

Problem Set K:
=======

1. $\dfrac{\dfrac{2}{4}}{3} =$

    (A) 1/6   (B) 3/8   (C) 3/2   (D) 8/3   (E) 6

2.   Which one of the following fractions is greatest?

    (A) 5/6   (B) 4/5   (C) 1/2   (D) 2/3   (E) 3/4

3.   If $x \ne \pm 3$, then $\dfrac{x^2 + 6x + 9}{x + 3} \cdot \dfrac{x^2 - 9}{x - 3} =$

    (A) $\dfrac{x+3}{x-3}$ (B) -1 (C) $(x+3)^2$ (D) $\left(\dfrac{x+3}{x-3}\right)^2$ (E) 1

4. $\dfrac{1}{\dfrac{4}{3}-1}=$

    (A) $-1/3$ (B) $-1/4$ (C) $3/4$ (D) 3 (E) $9/2$

5. If $0 < x < 1$, which of the following must be true?

    I. $x^2 < x$ II. $x < \dfrac{1}{x^2}$ III. $\sqrt{x} < x$

    (A) I only   (B) II only   (C) III only   (D) I and II only   (E) I, II, and III

6. In the following pairs of numbers, which are reciprocals of each other?

    I. 1 and 1   II. $\dfrac{1}{11}$ and -11 III. $\sqrt{5}$ and $\dfrac{\sqrt{5}}{5}$

    (A) I only   (B) II only   (C) I and II only   (D) I and III only   (E) II and III only

7. $\dfrac{6^4 - 6^3}{5} =$

    (A) $1/5$ (B) 6^3 (C) $6/5$ (D) 6^4 (E) $\dfrac{6^3}{5}$

8. $\dfrac{1}{1-\dfrac{1}{1-\dfrac{1}{2}}}=$

    (A) -2 (B) -1 (C) $3/2$ (D) 2 (E) 4

9. $\dfrac{1}{10^9} - \dfrac{1}{10^{10}} =$

    (A) $-\dfrac{1}{10}$ (B) $-\dfrac{1}{10^9}$ (C) $-\dfrac{1}{10^{19}}$ (D) $\dfrac{9}{10^{10}}$ (E) $\dfrac{9}{10}$

10. If $x \neq \pm 1$, then $\dfrac{\dfrac{2x^2 - 2}{x - 1}}{2(x + 1)} =$

    (A) $x + 1$ (B) 1 (C) $x^2 - 1$ (D) $x - 1$ (E) 2

11. If $\left(x^2 - 4\right)\left(\dfrac{4}{x} - 5\right) = 0$, then $x =$

    (A) -4 (B) -1 (C) $-4/5$ (D) $4/5$ (E) 4

12. If $m = 3^{n-1} = 3^{3n+1}$, what is the value of $\dfrac{m}{n}$?

    (A) 0 (B) $-1/20$ (C) $-1/10$ (D) $-1/9$ (E) -2

13. For all $p \neq 1/4$ define $p*$ by the equation $p* = \dfrac{\dfrac{p}{2}}{4p - 1}$. If $q = 1*$, then $q* =$

    (A) $-5/7$ (B) $-1/3$ (C) $-1/4$ (D) $2/3$ (E) $3/4$

14. If $\dfrac{1}{x} + \dfrac{1}{y} \neq 0$, then which one of the following is equal to the negative reciprocal of $\dfrac{1}{x} + \dfrac{1}{y}$?

(A) $\dfrac{xy}{x + y}$ (B) $-\dfrac{x + y}{xy}$ (C) $-(x + y)$ (D) $\dfrac{x - y}{xy}$ (E) $\dfrac{-xy}{x + y}$

15. Let x and y be prime numbers such that $x > y$. If $q = x/y$, then q must be
    (A)   An integer greater than one.
    (B)   An integer less than one.
    (C)   A fraction less than one.
    (D)   A fraction greater than one.
    (E)   An even number.

Answers and Solutions to Problem Set K

1. $\dfrac{\frac{2}{4}}{\frac{3}{3}} = 2\cdot\dfrac{3}{4} = \dfrac{6}{4} = \dfrac{3}{2}$. The answer is (C).

2. Begin with $\dfrac{5}{6}$ and $\dfrac{4}{5}$. Cross-multiplying gives 25 versus 24. Hence, $\dfrac{5}{6} > \dfrac{4}{5}$. Continuing in this manner will show that $\dfrac{5}{6}$ is the greatest fraction listed. The answer is (A).

3. First, factor the expression $\dfrac{x^2+6x+9}{x+3}\cdot\dfrac{x^2-9}{x-3}$:

$$\frac{(x+3)(x+3)}{x+3}\cdot\frac{(x+3)(x-3)}{x-3}$$

Next, cancel the $x+3$ and the $x-3$:

$$(x+3)\cdot(x+3)$$

or

$$(x+3)^2$$

The answer is (C).

4. $\dfrac{\frac{1}{4}}{\frac{4}{3}-1} = \dfrac{\frac{1}{4}}{\frac{4}{3}-\frac{3}{3}} = \dfrac{\frac{1}{4}}{\frac{1}{3}} = 3$. The answer is (D).

5. Since squaring a fraction between 0 and 1 makes it smaller, we know Statement I is true. This eliminates both (B) and (C). Also, since taking the square root of a fraction between 0 and 1 makes it larger, we know Statement III is false. This eliminates (E). To analyze Statement II, we'll use substitution. Since $0 < x < 1$, we need only check one fraction, say, $x = \dfrac{1}{2}$. Then $\dfrac{1}{x^2} = \dfrac{1}{\left(\frac{1}{2}\right)^2} = \dfrac{1}{\left(\frac{1}{4}\right)} = 1\cdot\dfrac{4}{1} = 4$. Now,

$\dfrac{1}{2} < 4$. Hence, Statement II is true, and the answer is (D).

6. Let's take the first number in each pair, form its reciprocal, and then try to reduce it to the second number. Now, $1 \Rightarrow \dfrac{1}{1} = 1$. Hence, the pair 1 and 1 are reciprocals of each other. Next,

$\dfrac{1}{11} \Rightarrow \dfrac{1}{\frac{1}{11}} = 1\cdot\dfrac{11}{1} = 11 \neq -11$. Hence, the pair $\dfrac{1}{11}$ and -11 are not reciprocals of each other. Finally,

$\sqrt{5} \Rightarrow \dfrac{1}{\sqrt{5}} = \dfrac{1}{\sqrt{5}}\cdot\dfrac{\sqrt{5}}{\sqrt{5}} = \dfrac{\sqrt{5}}{5}$. Hence, the pair $\sqrt{5}$ and $\dfrac{\sqrt{5}}{5}$ are reciprocals of each other. The answer is (D).

7. $\dfrac{6^4-6^3}{5} = \dfrac{6^3(6-1)}{5} = \dfrac{6^3\cdot5}{5} = 6^3$. The answer is (B).

8. $\dfrac{1}{1-\dfrac{1}{1-\dfrac{1}{2}}} = \dfrac{1}{1-\dfrac{1}{\dfrac{2}{2}-\dfrac{1}{2}}} = \dfrac{1}{1-\dfrac{1}{\dfrac{1}{2}}} = \dfrac{1}{1-2} = \dfrac{1}{-1} = -1$. The answer is (B).

9. $\dfrac{1}{10^9} - \dfrac{1}{10^{10}} = \dfrac{1}{10^9} - \dfrac{1}{10^9} \cdot \dfrac{1}{10} = \dfrac{1}{10^9}\left(1-\dfrac{1}{10}\right) = \dfrac{1}{10^9}\left(\dfrac{9}{10}\right) = \dfrac{9}{10^{10}}$. The answer is (D).

10. $\dfrac{\dfrac{2x^2-2}{x-1}}{2(x+1)} = \dfrac{2x^2-2}{x-1} \cdot \dfrac{1}{2(x+1)} = \dfrac{2(x^2-1)}{x-1} \cdot \dfrac{1}{2(x+1)} = \dfrac{2(x+1)(x-1)}{x-1} \cdot \dfrac{1}{2(x+1)} = \dfrac{2}{2} \cdot \dfrac{x+1}{x+1} \cdot \dfrac{x-1}{x-1} = 1$.

The answer is (B).

11. From the equation $\left(x^2-4\right)\left(\dfrac{4}{x}-5\right) = 0$, we get $x^2-4 = 0$ or $\dfrac{4}{x}-5 = 0$. Consider the equation $x^2-4 = 0$ first. Factoring gives

$$(x+2)(x-2) = 0$$

Setting each factor to zero gives

$$x+2 = 0 \quad \text{or} \quad x-2 = 0$$

Hence, $x = 2$ or $x = -2$. But neither number is offered as an answer-choice. So we turn to the equation $\dfrac{4}{x}-5 = 0$. Adding 5 to both sides yields

$$\dfrac{4}{x} = 5$$

Multiplying both sides by x gives $\qquad 4 = 5x$

Dividing both sides by 5 gives $\qquad \dfrac{4}{5} = x$

The answer is (D).

12. $$3^{n-1} = 3^{3n+1}$$
$$n-1 = 3n+1$$
$$-2n = 2$$
$$n = -1$$

Since $n = -1$, $m = 3^{n-1} = 3^{-1-1} = 3^{-2} = \dfrac{1}{3^2} = \dfrac{1}{9}$. Hence, $\dfrac{m}{n} = \dfrac{\dfrac{1}{9}}{-1} = -\dfrac{1}{9}$, and the answer is (D).

13. $q = 1* = \dfrac{\dfrac{1}{2}}{4 \cdot 1 - 1} = \dfrac{\dfrac{1}{2}}{3} = \dfrac{1}{2} \cdot \dfrac{1}{3} = \dfrac{1}{6}$. Hence, $\qquad q* = \dfrac{\dfrac{1}{6}}{4 \cdot \dfrac{1}{6} - 1} = \dfrac{\dfrac{1}{6} \cdot \dfrac{1}{2}}{\dfrac{2}{3} - 1} = \dfrac{\dfrac{1}{12}}{-\dfrac{1}{3}} = \dfrac{1}{12}\left(-\dfrac{3}{1}\right) = -\dfrac{3}{12} = -\dfrac{1}{4}$

The answer is (C).

14. Forming the negative reciprocal of $\dfrac{1}{x} + \dfrac{1}{y}$ yields

$$\dfrac{-1}{\dfrac{1}{x} + \dfrac{1}{y}}$$

Adding the fractions in the denominator yields

$$\dfrac{-1}{\dfrac{y + x}{xy}}$$

Reciprocating the denominator yields

$$-1 \cdot \dfrac{xy}{x + y}$$

Or

$$\dfrac{-xy}{x + y}$$

The answer is (E).

15. Since x and y are prime numbers and $x > y$, we know that $x > y > 0$. Dividing this inequality by y yields $x/y > y/y > 0/y$. Reducing yields $x/y > 1$. Since x and y are prime numbers, they will not have any common factors that could reduce x/y to an integer. Therefore, x/y is an irreducible fraction greater than one. The answer is (D).

Equations

When simplifying algebraic expressions, we perform operations within parentheses first and then exponents and then multiplication and then division and then addition and lastly subtraction. This can be remembered by the mnemonic:

PEMDAS
Please Excuse My Dear Aunt Sally

When solving equations, however, we apply the mnemonic in reverse order: **SADMEP**. This is often expressed as follows: inverse operations in inverse order. The goal in solving an equation is to isolate the variable on one side of the equal sign (usually the left side). This is done by identifying the main operation—addition, multiplication, etc.—and then performing the opposite operation.

Example: Solve the following equation for x: $2x + y = 5$

Solution: The main operation is addition (remember addition now comes before multiplication, SADMEP), so subtracting y from both sides yields

$$2x + y - y = 5 - y$$

Simplifying yields $$2x = 5 - y$$

The only operation remaining on the left side is multiplication. Undoing the multiplication by dividing both sides by 2 yields

$$\frac{2x}{2} = \frac{5-y}{2}$$

Canceling the 2 on the left side yields $$x = \frac{5-y}{2}$$

Example: Solve the following equation for x: $3x - 4 = 2(x - 5)$

Solution: Here x appears on both sides of the equal sign, so let's move the x on the right side to the left side. But the x is trapped inside the parentheses. To release it, distribute the 2:

$$3x - 4 = 2x - 10$$

Now, subtracting $2x$ from both sides yields[*]

$$x - 4 = -10$$

Finally, adding 4 to both sides yields

$$x = -6$$

We often manipulate equations without thinking about what the equations actually say. The ACT likes to test this oversight. Equations are packed with information. Take for example the simple equation $3x + 2 = 5$. Since 5 is positive, the expression $3x + 2$ must be positive as well. An equation means that the terms on either side of the equal sign are equal in every way. Hence, any property one side of an equation has the

---

[*] Note, students often mistakenly add $2x$ to both sides of this equation because of the minus symbol between $2x$ and 10. But $2x$ is positive, so we subtract it. This can be seen more clearly by rewriting the right side of the equation as $-10 + 2x$.

other side will have as well. Following are some immediate deductions that can be made from simple equations.

Equation	Deduction
$y - x = 1$	$y > x$
$y^2 = x^2$	$y = \pm x$, or $|y| = |x|$. That is, x and y can differ only in sign.
$y^3 = x^3$	$y = x$
$y = x^2$	$y \geq 0$
$\dfrac{y}{x^2} = 1$	$y > 0$
$\dfrac{y}{x^3} = 2$	Both x and y are positive or both x and y are negative.
$x^2 + y^2 = 0$	$y = x = 0$
$3y = 4x$ and $x > 0$	$y > x$ and y is positive.
$3y = 4x$ and $x < 0$	$y < x$ and y is negative.
$y = \sqrt{x+2}$	$y \geq 0$ and $x \geq -2$
$y = 2x$	y is even
$y = 2x + 1$	y is odd
$yx = 0$	$y = 0$ or $x = 0$, or both

 In Algebra, you solve an equation for, say, y by isolating y on one side of the equality symbol. On the ACT, however, you are often asked to solve for an entire term, say, $3 - y$ by isolating it on one side.

Example: If $a + 3a$ is 4 less than $b + 3b$, then $a - b =$

(A) -4 (B) -1 (C) $1/5$ (D) $1/3$ (E) 2

Translating the sentence into an equation gives $a + 3a = b + 3b - 4$

Combining like terms gives $4a = 4b - 4$

Subtracting $4b$ from both sides gives $4a - 4b = -4$

Finally, dividing by 4 gives $a - b = -1$

Hence, the answer is (B).

 Sometimes on the ACT, a system of 3 equations will be written as one long "triple" equation. For example, the three equations $x = y$, $y = z$, $x = z$, can be written more compactly as $x = y = z$.

Example: If $w \neq 0$ and $w = 2x = \sqrt{2}y$, what is the value of $w - x$ in terms of y ?

(A) $2y$ (B) $\dfrac{\sqrt{2}}{2}y$ (C) $\sqrt{2y}$ (D) $\dfrac{4}{\sqrt{2}}y$ (E) y

The equation $w = 2x = \sqrt{2}y$ stands for three equations: $w = 2x$, $2x = \sqrt{2}y$, and $w = \sqrt{2}y$. From the last equation, we get $w = \sqrt{2}y$; and from the second equation, we get $x = \dfrac{\sqrt{2}}{2}y$. Hence,

$w - x = \sqrt{2}y - \dfrac{\sqrt{2}}{2}y = \dfrac{2}{2}\sqrt{2}y - \dfrac{\sqrt{2}}{2}y = \dfrac{2\sqrt{2}y - \sqrt{2}y}{2} = \dfrac{\sqrt{2}y}{2}$. Hence, the answer is (B).

Often on the ACT, you can solve a system of two equations in two unknowns by merely adding or subtracting the equations—instead of solving for one of the variables and then substituting it into the other equation.

Example: If p and q are positive, $p^2 + q^2 = 16$, and $p^2 - q^2 = 8$, then $q =$

(A) 2   (B) 4   (C) 8   (D) $2\sqrt{2}$ (E) $2\sqrt{6}$

Subtract the second equation from the first:

$$p^2 + q^2 = 16$$
$$(-) \quad p^2 - q^2 = 8$$
$$2q^2 = 8$$

Dividing both sides of the equation by 2 gives $\qquad q^2 = 4$

Finally, taking the square root of both sides gives $\qquad q = \pm 2$

Hence, the answer is (A).

METHOD OF SUBSTITUTION (Four-Step Method)

Although on the ACT you can often solve a system of two equations in two unknowns by merely adding or subtracting the equations, you still need to know a standard method for solving these types of systems.

The four-step method will be illustrated with the following system:

$$2x + y = 10$$
$$5x - 2y = 7$$

1) *Solve one of the equations for one of the variables*:

   Solving the top equation for y yields $y = 10 - 2x$.

2) *Substitute the result from Step 1 into the other equation*:

   Substituting $y = 10 - 2x$ into the bottom equation yields $5x - 2(10 - 2x) = 7$.

3) *Solve the resulting equation*:

$$5x - 2(10 - 2x) = 7$$
$$5x - 20 + 4x = 7$$
$$9x - 20 = 7$$
$$9x = 27$$
$$x = 3$$

4) *Substitute the result from Step 3 into the equation derived in Step 1*:

   Substituting $x = 3$ into $y = 10 - 2x$ yields $y = 10 - 2(3) = 10 - 6 = 4$.

Hence, the solution of the system of equations is the ordered pair (3, 4).

Problem Set L:

1. If $a > 0$ and $6a = 5b$, which of the following must be true?

    (A) $a = \frac{6}{5}b$ (B) $ab < 0$ (C) $a > b$ (D) $b = \frac{5}{6}a$ (E) $b > a$

2. If $p - q + r = 4$ and $p + q + r = 8$, then $p + r =$

    (A) 2   (B) 4   (C) 6   (D) 8   (E) 10

3. Suppose $x = y - 2 = \frac{y+5}{2}$. Then x equals

    (A) 1/3   (B) 1   (C) 7/6   (D) 2   (E) 7

4. Let $p = 3^{q+1}$ and $q = 2r$. Then $\frac{p}{3^2} =$

    (A) 3^{2r-1} (B) 3^{2r} (C) 3   (D) r (E) 3^{2r+1}

5. k is a constant in the equation $\frac{u-v}{k} = 8$. If $u = 18$ when $v = 2$, then what is the value of u when $v = 4$?

    (A) –3   (B) 0   (C) 10   (D) 23/2   (E) 20

6. If $x = 3y = 4z$, which of the following must equal $6x$?

    I. $18y$ II. $3y + 20z$ III. $\frac{4y+10z}{3}$

    (A) I only   (B) II only   (C) III only   (D) I and II only   (E) I and III only

7. Let $P = (x + y)k$. If $P = 10$ and $k = 3$, what is the average of x and y?

    (A) 0   (B) 1/2   (C) 5/3   (D) 10/3   (E) 7/2

8. Let $\frac{x}{y} + \frac{w}{z} = 2$. Then the value of $\frac{y}{x} + \frac{z}{w}$ is

    (A)   1/2
    (B)   3/4
    (C)   1
    (D)   5
    (E)   It cannot be determined from the information given.

9. If 4 percent of $(p + q)$ is 8 and p is a positive integer, what is the greatest possible value of q?
    (A) 196   (B) 197   (C) 198   (D) 199   (E) 200

10. If $x^5 = 4$ and $x^4 = \frac{7}{y}$, then what is the value of x in terms of y?

    (A) $\frac{7}{4}y$ (B) $\frac{4}{7}y$ (C) $\frac{1}{7}y$ (D) $7y$ (E) $7 + \frac{5}{y}$

11.
$$2x + y = 3$$
$$3y = 9 - 6x$$

How many solutions does the above system of equations have?

(A)   None
(B)   One
(C)   Two
(D)   Four
(E)   An infinite number

12.   If $\dfrac{p}{19}$ is 1 less than 3 times $\dfrac{q}{19}$, then p equals which of the following expressions?

(A) $3q + 19$
(B) $3q + 38$
(C) $19/2$
(D) $3q - 38$
(E) $3q - 19$

13.   If n is a number such that $(-8)^{2n} = 2^{8+2n}$, then $n =$

(A) $1/2$
(B) 2
(C) $3/2$
(D) 4
(E) 5

14.   If $m = 3^{n-1}$ and $3^{4n-1} = 27$, what is the value of $\dfrac{m}{n}$?

(A) 0
(B) 1
(C) $7/3$
(D) $9/2$
(E) 6

15.   If $s + S \neq 0$ and $\dfrac{1}{3} = \dfrac{1}{4}\dfrac{s-S}{s+S}$, then what is s in terms of S?

(A) $s = S + 3$
(B) $s = 4S$
(C) $s = S/12$
(D) $s = -7S$
(E) $s = 4S - 6$

16.   If $3^x = 81$, then $\left(3^{x+3}\right)\left(4^{x+1}\right) =$

(A) $5(7)^5$
(B) $9(7)^5$
(C) $2(12)^4$
(D) $9(12)^5$
(E) $2(12)^7$

17.   If $x = y/2$ and $y = z/2$, then $\sqrt{x/z} =$

    (A)   4
    (B)   2
    (C)   1
    (D)   1/2
    (E)   1/4

18.   If $a = b/c$ and $b = a/c$, then $c =$

    (A) b/a
    (B) a/b
    (C) -1
    (D) a
    (E) $-b$

19.   If $x + 3y = 5$ and $3x + y = 7$, then $x + y =$

    (A)   1
    (B)   2
    (C)   3
    (D)   4
    (E)   5

20.   If $7x - y = 23$ and $7y - x = 31$, then $x + y =$

    (A)   4
    (B)   6
    (C)   7
    (D)   8
    (E)   9

21.   If $x + y = 4a/5$, $y + z = 7a/5$ and $z + x = 9a/5$, then $x + y + z =$

    (A) $7a/15$
    (B) a
    (C) $2a$
    (D) $3a$
    (E) $4a$

Answers and Solutions to Problem Set L

1. Dividing both sides of the equation $6a = 5b$ by 6 gives $a = \dfrac{5}{6}b$. Thus, a is a fraction of b. But b is greater than zero and therefore b is greater than a. (Note, had we been given that a was less than zero, then a would have been greater than b.) The answer is (E).

2. Adding the two equations $\begin{array}{l} p - q + r = 4 \\ p + q + r = 8 \end{array}$ gives $\qquad\qquad 2p + 2r = 12$

   Then dividing by 2 gives $\qquad\qquad\qquad\qquad\qquad\qquad p + r = 6$

   Hence, the answer is (C).

3. Clearing fractions in the equation $y - 2 = \dfrac{y+5}{2}$ gives $\qquad 2(y - 2) = y + 5$

   Distributing the 2 gives $\qquad\qquad\qquad\qquad\qquad\qquad 2y - 4 = y + 5$

   Subtracting y and adding 4 to both sides gives $\qquad\qquad y = 9$

   Now, replacing y with 9 in the equation $x = y - 2$ gives $\qquad x = y - 2 = 9 - 2 = 7$

   Hence, the answer is (E).

4. Replacing p with 3^{q+1} in the expression $\dfrac{p}{3^2}$ gives $\qquad \dfrac{p}{3^2} = \dfrac{3^{q+1}}{3^2} = 3^{q+1-2} = 3^{q-1}$

   Now, replacing q with $2r$ in the expression 3^{q-1} gives $\qquad 3^{q-1} = 3^{2r-1}$

   Hence, the answer is (A).

5. Substituting $u = 18$ and $v = 2$ into the equation $\dfrac{u - v}{k} = 8$ gives $\qquad \dfrac{18 - 2}{k} = 8$

   Subtracting gives $\qquad\qquad\qquad\qquad\qquad\qquad\qquad\qquad \dfrac{16}{k} = 8$

   Multiplying both sides of this equation by k gives $\qquad\qquad 16 = 8k$

   Dividing by 8 gives $\qquad\qquad\qquad\qquad\qquad\qquad\qquad\qquad 2 = k$

   With this value for k, the original equation becomes $\qquad \dfrac{u - v}{2} = 8$

   Now, we are asked to find u when $v = 4$.

   Replacing v with 4 in the equation $\dfrac{u - v}{2} = 8$ gives $\qquad \dfrac{u - 4}{2} = 8$

   Multiplying by 2 gives $\qquad\qquad\qquad\qquad\qquad\qquad\qquad u - 4 = 16$

   Adding 4 gives $\qquad\qquad\qquad\qquad\qquad\qquad\qquad\qquad u = 20$

   Hence, the answer is (E).

6. The equation $x = 3y = 4z$ contains three equations:

$$x = 3y$$
$$3y = 4z$$
$$x = 4z$$

   Multiplying both sides of the equation $x = 3y$ by 6 gives $6x = 18y$. Hence, Statement I is true. This eliminates (B) and (C). Next, $3y + 20z = 3y + 5(4z)$. Substituting x for $3y$ and for $4z$ in this equation gives $3y + 20z = 3y + 5(4z) = x + 5x = 6x$. Hence, Statement II is true. This eliminates (A) and (E). Hence, by process of elimination, the answer is (D).

7. Plugging $P = 10$ and $k = 3$ into the equation $P = (x + y)k$ gives $10 = (x + y)3$. Dividing by 3 gives $x + y = \dfrac{10}{3}$. Finally, to form the average, divide both sides of this equation by 2: $\dfrac{x + y}{2} = \dfrac{10}{6} = \dfrac{5}{3}$. Hence, the answer is (C).

8. There are many different values for w, x, y, and z such that $\dfrac{x}{y} + \dfrac{w}{z} = 2$. Two particular cases are listed below:

If $x = y = w = z = 1$, then $\dfrac{x}{y} + \dfrac{w}{z} = \dfrac{1}{1} + \dfrac{1}{1} = 1 + 1 = 2$ and $\dfrac{y}{x} + \dfrac{z}{w} = \dfrac{1}{1} + \dfrac{1}{1} = 1 + 1 = 2$.

If $x = 3$, $y = 2$, $w = 1$, and $z = 2$, then $\dfrac{x}{y} + \dfrac{w}{z} = \dfrac{3}{2} + \dfrac{1}{2} = \dfrac{3+1}{2} = \dfrac{4}{2} = 2$ and $\dfrac{y}{x} + \dfrac{z}{w} = \dfrac{2}{3} + \dfrac{2}{1} = \dfrac{2}{3} + \dfrac{2}{1} \cdot \dfrac{3}{3} = \dfrac{2}{3} + \dfrac{6}{3} = \dfrac{2+6}{3} = \dfrac{8}{3}$

This is a double case. Hence, the answer is (E).

9. Translating the clause "4 percent of $(p + q)$ is 8" into a mathematical expression yields
$$.04(p + q) = 8$$
Dividing both sides of this equation by .04 yields
$$p + q = \dfrac{8}{.04} = 200$$
Subtracting p from both sides yields
$$q = 200 - p$$
This expression will be greatest when p is as small as possible. This is when $p = 1$:
$$q = 200 - 1 = 199$$
The answer is (D).

10. The expression $x^5 = 4$ can be rewritten as
$$x \cdot x^4 = 4$$
Replacing x^4 in this expression with $\dfrac{7}{y}$ yields
$$x \cdot \dfrac{7}{y} = 4$$
Multiplying both sides of this equation by y gives
$$x \cdot 7 = 4 \cdot y$$
Dividing both sides of this equation by 7 yields
$$x = \dfrac{4}{7} \cdot y$$
Hence, the answer is (B).

11. Start with the bottom equation $3y = 9 - 6x$:

Dividing by 3 yields $\qquad\qquad$ $y = 3 - 2x$

Adding $2x$ yields $\qquad\qquad$ $2x + y = 3$

Notice that this is the top equation in the system. Hence, the system is only one equation in two different forms. Thus, there are an infinite number of solutions. For example, the pair $x = 2$, $y = -1$ is a solution as is the pair $x = 0$, $y = 3$. The answer is (E).

12. The clause " $\frac{p}{19}$ *is 1 less than 3 times* $\frac{q}{19}$ " translates into:

$$\frac{p}{19} = 3 \cdot \frac{q}{19} - 1$$

Multiplying both sides of this equation by 19 gives

$$p = 3 \cdot q - 19$$

The answer is (E).

13. Since the right side of the equation is positive, the left side must also be positive. Thus, $(-8)^{2n}$ is equal to

$$8^{2n}$$

This in turn can be written as

$$\left(2^3\right)^{2n}$$

Multiplying the exponents gives

$$2^{6n}$$

Plugging this into the original equation gives

$$2^{6n} = 2^{8+2n}$$

Now, since the bases are the same, the exponents must be equal:

$$6n = 8 + 2n$$

Solving this equation gives

$$n = 2$$

The answer is (B).

14.
$$3^{4n-1} = 27$$
$$3^{4n-1} = 3^3$$
$$4n - 1 = 3$$
$$4n = 4$$
$$n = 1$$

Since $n = 1$, $m = 3^{n-1} = 3^{1-1} = 3^0 = 1$. Hence, $\frac{m}{n} = \frac{1}{1} = 1$, and the answer is (B).

15. First, clear fractions by multiplying both sides by $12(s + S)$: $4(s + S) = 3(s - S)$

Next, distribute the 3 and 4: $4s + 4S = 3s - 3S$

Finally, subtract $3s$ and $4S$ from both sides: $s = -7S$

The answer is (D).

16. $3^x = 81 = 3^4$. Hence, $x = 4$. Replacing x with 4 in the expression $\left(3^{x+3}\right)\left(4^{x+1}\right)$ yields

$$\left(3^{4+3}\right)\left(4^{4+1}\right) =$$

$$3^7 \cdot 4^5 =$$

$$3^2 \cdot 3^5 \cdot 4^5 =$$

$$3^2 (3 \cdot 4)^5 =$$

$$9(12)^5$$

The answer is (D).

17. We are given the equations: $x = y/2$
$y = z/2$

Solving the bottom equation for z yields $z = 2y$. Replacing x and z in the expression $\sqrt{x/z}$ with $y/2$ and $2y$, respectively, yields

$$\sqrt{x/z} = \sqrt{\frac{y/2}{2y}} = \sqrt{\frac{y}{2} \cdot \frac{1}{2y}} = \sqrt{\frac{1}{4}} = \frac{1}{2}$$

The answer is (D).

18. We are given $a = b/c$
$b = a/c$

Replacing b in the top equation with a/c (since $b = a/c$ according to the bottom equation) yields

$$a = \frac{a/c}{c}$$

$$a = \frac{a}{c} \cdot \frac{1}{c}$$

$$a = \frac{a}{c^2}$$

$$1 = \frac{1}{c^2} \qquad \text{(by canceling } a \text{ from both sides)}$$

$$c^2 = 1$$

$$c = \pm\sqrt{1} = \pm 1$$

Since one of the two possible answers is -1, the answer is (C).

19. Forming a system from the two given equations yields

$$x + 3y = 5$$
$$3x + y = 7$$

Adding the two equations yields

$$4x + 4y = 12$$

$$4(x + y) = 12 \qquad\qquad \text{by factoring out 4}$$

$$x + y = 12/4 = 3 \qquad\qquad \text{by dividing by 4}$$

The answer is (C).

20. Aligning the system of equations vertically yields

$$7x - y = 23$$
$$7y - x = 31$$

Adding the system of equations yields

$(7x - y) + (7y - x) = 23 + 31$	
$(7x - x) + (7y - y) = 54$	by collecting like terms
$6x + 6y = 54$	by adding like terms
$6(x + y) = 54$	by factoring out 6
$x + y = 9$	by dividing both sides by 6

The answer is (E).

21. Writing the system of given equations vertically yields

$$x + y = 4a/5$$
$$y + z = 7a/5$$
$$z + x = 9a/5$$

Adding the three equations yields

$(x + y) + (y + z) + (z + x) = 4a/5 + 7a/5 + 9a/5$	
$2x + 2y + 2z = 20a/5$	by adding like terms
$2(x + y + z) = 4a$	
$x + y + z = 2a$	by dividing both sides by 2

The answer is (C).

Averages

Problems involving averages are very common on the ACT. They can be classified into four major categories as follows.

 The average of N numbers is their sum divided by N, that is, $average = \dfrac{sum}{N}$.

Example 1: What is the average of x, $2x$, and 6?
  (A) $x/2$
  (B) $2x$
  (C) $\dfrac{x+2}{6}$
  (D) $x + 2$
  (E) $\dfrac{x+2}{3}$

By the definition of an average, we get $\dfrac{x + 2x + 6}{3} = \dfrac{3x + 6}{3} = \dfrac{3(x+2)}{3} = x + 2$. Hence, the answer is (D).

 Weighted average: **The average between two sets of numbers is closer to the set with more numbers.**

Example 2: If on a test three people answered 90% of the questions correctly and two people answered 80% correctly, then the average for the group is not 85% but rather $\dfrac{3 \cdot 90 + 2 \cdot 80}{5} = \dfrac{430}{5} = 86$.
Here, 90 has a weight of 3—it occurs 3 times. Whereas 80 has a weight of 2—it occurs 2 times. So the average is closer to 90 than to 80 as we have just calculated.

 Using an average to find a number.

Sometimes you will be asked to find a number by using a given average. An example will illustrate.

Example 3: If the average of five numbers is -10, and the sum of three of the numbers is 16, then what is the average of the other two numbers?

  (A) –33   (B) –1   (C) 5   (D) 20   (E) 25

Let the five numbers be a, b, c, d, e. Then their average is $\dfrac{a+b+c+d+e}{5} = -10$. Now three of the numbers have a sum of 16, say, $a + b + c = 16$. So substitute 16 for $a + b + c$ in the average above: $\dfrac{16 + d + e}{5} = -10$. Solving this equation for $d + e$ gives $d + e = -66$. Finally, dividing by 2 (to form the average) gives $\dfrac{d+e}{2} = -33$. Hence, the answer is (A).

Note! $Average\ Speed = \dfrac{Total\ Distance}{Total\ Time}$

Although the formula for average speed is simple, few people solve these problems correctly because most fail to find both the <u>total distance</u> and the <u>total time</u>.

Example 4:   In traveling from city A to city B, John drove for 1 hour at 50 mph and for 3 hours at 60 mph. What was his average speed for the whole trip?

    (A)   50
    (B) $53\frac{1}{2}$
    (C)   55
    (D)   56
    (E) $57\frac{1}{2}$

The total distance is $1 \cdot 50 + 3 \cdot 60 = 230$. And the total time is 4 hours. Hence,

$$Average\ Speed = \frac{Total\ Distance}{Total\ Time} = \frac{230}{4} = 57\frac{1}{2}$$

The answer is (E). Note, the answer is not the mere average of 50 and 60. Rather the average is closer to 60 because he traveled longer at 60 mph (3 hrs) than at 50 mph (1 hr).

Problem Set M:

1.   If the average of p and $4p$ is 10, then $p =$
    (A) 1   (B) 3   (C) 4   (D) 10   (E) 18

2.   The average of six consecutive integers in increasing order of size is $9\frac{1}{2}$. What is the average of the last three integers?
    (A) 8   (B) $9\frac{1}{2}$ (C) 10   (D) 11   (E) 19

3.   If S denotes the sum and A the average of the consecutive positive integers 1 through n, then which of the following must be true?
    I. $A = S/n$
    II. $S = A/n$
    III. $A - S = n$
    (A)   I only
    (B)   II only
    (C)   III only
    (D)   I and II only
    (E)   I, II, and III

4.   Cars X and Y leave City A at the same time and travel the same route to City B. Car X takes 30 minutes to complete the trip and car Y takes 20 minutes. Which of the following must be true?
    I.   The average miles per hour at which car X traveled was greater than the average miles per hour at which car Y traveled.
    II. The distance between the cities is 30 miles.
    III. The average miles per hour at which car Y traveled was greater than the average miles per hour at which car X traveled.
    (A)   I only
    (B)   II only
    (C)   III only
    (D)   I and II only
    (E)   I and III only

5. If $p + q = r$, what is the average of p, q, and r ?

    (A) $\dfrac{r}{3}$

    (B) $\dfrac{p+q}{3}$

    (C) $\dfrac{2r}{3}$

    (D) $\dfrac{r}{2}$

    (E) $\dfrac{p+q}{2}$

6. Suppose a train travels x miles in y hours and 15 minutes. Its average speed in miles per hour is

    (A) $\dfrac{y+15}{x}$

    (B) $x\left(y-\dfrac{1}{4}\right)$

    (C) $\dfrac{x}{y+\dfrac{1}{4}}$

    (D) $\dfrac{x}{y+15}$

    (E) $\dfrac{y+\dfrac{1}{4}}{x}$

7. The average of five numbers is 6.9. If one of the numbers is deleted, the average of the remaining numbers is 4.4. What is the value of the number deleted?

    (A) 6.8   (B) 7.4   (C) 12.5   (D) 16.9   (E) 17.2

8. The average of four numbers is 20. If one of the numbers is removed, the average of the remaining numbers is 15. What number was removed?

    (A) 10   (B) 15   (C) 30   (D) 35   (E) 45

9. The average of two numbers is $\pi/2$, and one of the numbers is x. What is the other number in terms of x ?

    (A) $\dfrac{\pi}{2} - x$ (B) $\dfrac{\pi}{2} + x$ (C) $\pi - x$ (D) $\pi + x$ (E) $2\pi + x$

10. A shopper spends \$25 to purchase floppy disks at 50¢ each. The next day, the disks go on sale for 30¢ each and the shopper spends \$45 to purchase more disks. What was the average price per disk purchased?

    (A) 25¢   (B) 30¢   (C) 35¢   (D) 40¢   (E) 45¢

11. The average of 8 numbers is A, and one of the numbers is 14. If 14 is replaced with 28, then what is the new average in terms of A ?

    (A) $A + \dfrac{7}{4}$ (B) $A + \dfrac{1}{2}$ (C) $A + 2$ (D) $2A + 1$ (E) $A + 4$

Answers and Solutions to Problem Set M

1. Since the average of p and $4p$ is 10, we get

$$\frac{p + 4p}{2} = 10$$

Combining the p's gives

$$\frac{5p}{2} = 10$$

Multiplying by 2 yields

$$5p = 20$$

Finally, dividing by 5 gives

$$p = 4$$

The answer is (C).

2. We have six consecutive integers whose average is $9\frac{1}{2}$, so we have the first three integers less than $9\frac{1}{2}$ and the first three integers greater than $9\frac{1}{2}$. That is, we are dealing with the numbers 7, 8, 9, 10, 11, 12. Clearly, the average of the last three numbers in this list is 11. Hence, the answer is (D).

3. The average of the consecutive positive integers 1 through n is $A = \dfrac{1 + 2 + \ldots + n}{n}$. Now, we are given that S denotes the sum of the consecutive positive integers 1 through n, that is, $S = 1 + 2 + \cdots + n$. Plugging this into the formula for the average gives $A = \dfrac{S}{n}$. Hence, Statement I is true, which eliminates (B) and (C). Next, solving the equation $A = \dfrac{S}{n}$ for S yields $S = A \cdot n$. Thus, Statement II is false, which eliminates (D) and (E). Therefore, the answer is (A).

4. The average speed at which car X traveled is $\dfrac{\text{Total Distance}}{30}$.

The average speed at which car Y traveled is $\dfrac{\text{Total Distance}}{20}$.

The two fractions have the same numerators, and the denominator for car Y is smaller. Hence, the average miles per hour at which car Y traveled is greater than the average miles per hour at which car X traveled. Thus, Statement I is false and Statement III is true. As to Statement II, we do not have enough information to calculate the distance between the cities. Hence, Statement II need not be true. The answer is (C).

5. The average of p, q, and r is $\dfrac{p + q + r}{3}$. Replacing $p + q$ with r gives $\dfrac{r + r}{3} = \dfrac{2r}{3}$. The answer is (C).

6. Often on the ACT you will be given numbers in different units. When this occurs, you must convert the numbers into the same units. (This is obnoxious but it does occur on the ACT, so be alert to it.) In this problem, we must convert 15 minutes into hours: $15 \cdot \dfrac{1}{60} = \dfrac{1}{4} \, hr$. Hence, the average speed is

$\dfrac{\text{Total Distance}}{\text{Total Time}} = \dfrac{x}{y + \dfrac{1}{4}}$. The answer is (C).

7. Forming the average of the five numbers gives

$$\frac{v + w + x + y + z}{5} = 6.9$$

Let the deleted number be z. Then forming the average of the remaining four numbers gives

$$\frac{v + w + x + y}{4} = 4.4$$

Multiplying both sides of this equation by 4 gives

$$v + w + x + y = 17.6$$

Plugging this value into the original average gives

$$\frac{17.6 + z}{5} = 6.9$$

Solving this equation for z gives

$$z = 16.9$$

The answer is (D).

8.   Let the four numbers be a, b, c, and d. Since their average is 20, we get

$$\frac{a + b + c + d}{4} = 20$$

Let d be the number that is removed. Since the average of the remaining numbers is 15, we get

$$\frac{a + b + c}{3} = 15$$

Solving for $a + b + c$ yields

$$a + b + c = 45$$

Substituting this into the first equation yields

$$\frac{45 + d}{4} = 20$$

Multiplying both sides of this equation by 4 yields

$$45 + d = 80$$

Subtracting 45 from both sides of this equation yields

$$d = 35$$

The answer is (D).

9.   Let the other number be y. Since the average of the two numbers is $\dfrac{\pi}{2}$, we get

$$\frac{x + y}{2} = \frac{\pi}{2}$$

Multiplying both sides of this equation by 2 yields

$$x + y = \pi$$

Subtracting x from both sides of this equation yields

$$y = \pi - x$$

The answer is (C).

10. This is a weighted-average problem because more disks were purchased on the second day. Let x be the number of disks purchased on the first day. Then $.50x = 25$. Solving for x yields $x = 50$. Let y be the number of disks purchased on the second day. Then $.30y = 45$. Solving for y yields $y = 150$. Forming the weighted average, we get

$$Average\ Cost = \frac{Total\ Cost}{Total\ Number} = \frac{25 + 45}{50 + 150} = \frac{70}{200} = .35$$

The answer is (C).

11. Let the seven unknown numbers be represented by $x_1, x_2, \cdots, x_7$. Forming the average of the eight numbers yields

$$\frac{x_1 + x_2 + \cdots + x_7 + 14}{8} = A$$

Replacing 14 with 28 (= 14 + 14), and forming the average yields

$$\frac{x_1 + x_2 + \cdots + x_7 + (14 + 14)}{8}$$

Breaking up the fraction into the sum of two fractions yields

$$\frac{x_1 + x_2 + \cdots + x_7 + 14}{8} + \frac{14}{8}$$

Since $\dfrac{x_1 + x_2 + \cdots + x_7 + 14}{8} = A$, this becomes

$$A + \frac{14}{8}$$

Reducing the fraction yields

$$A + \frac{7}{4}$$

The answer is (A).

Ratio & Proportion

RATIO

A ratio is simply a fraction. The following notations all express the ratio of x to y: $x:y$, $x \div y$, or $\frac{x}{y}$.

Writing two numbers as a ratio provides a convenient way to compare their sizes. For example, since $\frac{3}{\pi} < 1$, we know that 3 is less than π. A ratio compares two numbers. Just as you cannot compare apples and oranges, so to must the numbers you are comparing have the same units. For example, you cannot form the ratio of 2 feet to 4 yards because the two numbers are expressed in different units—feet vs. yards. It is quite common for the ACT to ask for the ratio of two numbers that are expressed in different units. Before you form any ratio, make sure the two numbers are expressed in the same units.

Example 1: What is the ratio of 2 feet to 4 yards?

        (A) 1:9   (B) 1:8   (C) 1:7   (D) 1:6   (E) 1:5

The ratio cannot be formed until the numbers are expressed in the same units. Let's turn the yards into feet. Since there are 3 feet in a yard, 4 yards = 4×3 feet = 12 feet. Forming the ratio yields

$$\frac{2 \; feet}{12 \; feet} = \frac{1}{6} \; or \; 1:6$$

The answer is (D).

Note, taking the reciprocal of a fraction usually changes its size. For example, $\frac{3}{4} \neq \frac{4}{3}$. So order is important in a ratio: $3:4 \neq 4:3$.

PROPORTION

A proportion is simply an equality between two ratios (fractions). For example, the ratio of x to y is equal to the ratio of 3 to 2 is translated as

$$\frac{x}{y} = \frac{3}{2}$$

or in ratio notation,

$$x:y::3:2$$

Two variables are *directly proportional* if one is a constant multiple of the other:

$$y = kx$$

where k is a constant.

The above equation shows that as x increases (or decreases) so does y. This simple concept has numerous applications in mathematics. For example, in constant velocity problems, distance is directly proportional to time: $d = vt$, where v is a constant. Note, sometimes the word *directly* is suppressed.

Example 2: If the ratio of *y* to *x* is equal to 3 and the sum of *y* and *x* is 80, what is the value of *y*?

(A) −10 (B) −2 (C) 5 (D) 20 (E) 60

Translating *"the ratio of y to x is equal to 3"* into an equation yields

$$\frac{y}{x} = 3$$

Translating *"the sum of y and x is 80"* into an equation yields

$$y + x = 80$$

Solving the first equation for *y* gives *y* = 3*x*. Substituting this into the second equation yields

$$3x + x = 80$$
$$4x = 80$$
$$x = 20$$

Hence, $y = 3x = 3 \cdot 20 = 60$. The answer is (E).

In many word problems, as one quantity increases (decreases), another quantity also increases (decreases). This type of problem can be solved by setting up a *direct* proportion.

Example 3: If Biff can shape 3 surfboards in 50 minutes, how many surfboards can he shape in 5 hours?

(A) 16 (B) 17 (C) 18 (D) 19 (E) 20

As time increases so does the number of shaped surfboards. Hence, we set up a direct proportion. First, convert 5 hours into minutes: *5 hours = 5 × 60 minutes = 300 minutes*. Next, let *x* be the number of surfboards shaped in 5 hours. Finally, forming the proportion yields

$$\frac{3}{50} = \frac{x}{300}$$

$$\frac{3 \cdot 300}{50} = x$$

$$18 = x$$

The answer is (C).

Example 4: On a map, 1 inch represents 150 miles. What is the actual distance between two cities if they are $3\frac{1}{2}$ inches apart on the map?

(A) 225 (B) 300 (C) 450 (D) 525 (E) 600

As the distance on the map increases so does the actual distance. Hence, we set up a direct proportion. Let *x* be the actual distance between the cities. Forming the proportion yields

$$\frac{1\,in}{150\,mi} = \frac{3\frac{1}{2}\,in}{x\,mi}$$

$$x = 3\frac{1}{2} \times 150$$

$$x = 525$$

The answer is (D).

Note, you need not worry about how you form the direct proportion so long as the order is the same on both sides of the equal sign. The proportion in Example 4 could have been written as $\frac{1\,in}{3\frac{1}{2}\,in} = \frac{150\,mi}{x\,mi}$. In this case, the order is inches to inches and miles to miles. However, the following is not a direct proportion because the order is not the same on both sides of the equal sign: $\frac{1\,in}{150\,mi} = \frac{x\,mi}{3\frac{1}{2}\,in}$. In this case, the order is inches to miles on the left side of the equal sign but miles to inches on the right side.

If one quantity increases (or decreases) while another quantity decreases (or increases), the quantities are said to be *inversely* proportional. The statement "*y* is inversely proportional to *x*" is written as

$$y = \frac{k}{x}$$

where *k* is a constant.

Multiplying both sides of $y = \frac{k}{x}$ by *x* yields

$$yx = k$$

Hence, in an inverse proportion, the product of the two quantities is constant. Therefore, instead of setting ratios equal, we set products equal.

In many word problems, as one quantity increases (decreases), another quantity decreases (increases). This type of problem can be solved by setting up a product of terms.

Example 5:   If 7 workers can assemble a car in 8 hours, how long would it take 12 workers to assemble the same car?

(A) 3hrs   (B) $3\frac{1}{2}$ hrs   (C) $4\frac{2}{3}$ hrs   (D) 5hrs   (E) $6\frac{1}{3}$ hrs

As the number of workers increases, the amount time required to assemble the car decreases. Hence, we set the products of the terms equal. Let *x* be the time it takes the 12 workers to assemble the car. Forming the equation yields

$$7 \cdot 8 = 12 \cdot x$$
$$\frac{56}{12} = x$$
$$4\frac{2}{3} = x$$

The answer is (C).

To summarize: if one quantity increases (decreases) as another quantity also increases (decreases), set ratios equal. If one quantity increases (decreases) as another quantity decreases (increases), set products equal.

The concept of proportion can be generalized to three or more ratios. *A*, *B*, and *C* are in the ratio 3:4:5 means $\frac{A}{B} = \frac{3}{4}$, $\frac{A}{C} = \frac{3}{5}$, and $\frac{B}{C} = \frac{4}{5}$.

Example 6:   In the figure to the right, the angles *A*, *B*, *C* of the triangle are in the ratio 5:12:13. What is the measure of angle A?

(A)   15
(B)   27
(C)   30
(D)   34
(E)   40

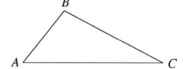

Since the angle sum of a triangle is 180°, *A* + *B* + *C* = 180. Forming two of the ratios yields

$$\frac{A}{B} = \frac{5}{12} \qquad \frac{A}{C} = \frac{5}{13}$$

Solving the first equation for *B* yields $B = \frac{12}{5}A$

Solving the second equation for *C* yields $C = \frac{13}{5}A$

Hence, $180 = A + B + C = A + \frac{12}{5}A + \frac{13}{5}A = 6A$. Therefore, $180 = 6A$, or $A = 30$. The answer is choice (C).

Problem Set N:

1. What is the ratio of 2 ft. 3 in. to 2 yds?

    (A) 1/4   (B) 1/3   (C) 3/8   (D) 1/2   (E) 3/4

2. The ratio of two numbers is 10 and their difference is 18. What is the value of the smaller number?

    (A) 2   (B) 5   (C) 10   (D) 21   (E) 27

3. If the degree measures of two angles of an isosceles triangle are in the ratio 1:3, what is the degree measure of the largest angle if it is not a base angle?

    (A) 26°   (B) 36°   (C) 51°   (D) 92°   (E) 108°

4. A jet uses 80 gallons of fuel to fly 320 miles. At this rate, how many gallons of fuel are needed for a 700 mile flight?

    (A) 150   (B) 155   (C) 160   (D) 170   (E) 175

5. Two boys can mow a lawn in 2 hours and 30 minutes If they are joined by three other boys, how many hours will it take to mow the lawn?

    (A) 1 hr.   (B) $1\frac{1}{4}$ hrs.   (C) $1\frac{1}{2}$ hrs.   (D) $1\frac{3}{4}$ hrs.   (E) 2 hrs.

6. A recipe requires $\frac{1}{2}$ lb. of shortening and 14 oz. of flour. If the chef accidentally pours in 21 oz. of flour, how many ounces of shortening should be added?

    (A) 9   (B) 10   (C) 11   (D) 12   (E) 13

7. If w widgets cost d dollars, then at this rate how many dollars will 2000 widgets cost?

    (A) $\dfrac{wd}{2000}$ (B) $\dfrac{2000w}{d}$ (C) $\dfrac{2000d}{w}$ (D) $\dfrac{d}{2000w}$ (E) $\dfrac{2000}{wd}$

8. In the system of equations to the right, $z \neq 0$. What is ratio of x to z?

    $$x + 2y - z = 1$$
    $$3x - 2y - 8z = -1$$

    (A) −9/4   (B) −1/3   (C) 1/3   (D) 4/9   (E) 9/4

9. If a sprinter takes 30 steps in 9 seconds, how many steps does he take in 54 seconds?

    (A) 130   (B) 170   (C) 173   (D) 180   (E) 200

10. If $5x = 6y$, then the ratio of x to y is

    (A) 5:11   (B) 5:6   (C) 1:1   (D) 6:5   (E) 11:6

Answers and Solutions to Problem Set N

1. First change all the units to inches: 2 ft. 3 in. = 27 in., and 2 yds. = 72 in. Forming the ratio yields

$$\frac{2\,ft.\ 3\,in.}{2\,yds.} = \frac{27\,in.}{72\,in.} = \frac{3}{8}$$

The answer is (C).

2. Let x and y denote the numbers. Then $\frac{x}{y} = 10$ and $x - y = 18$. Solving the first equation for x and plugging it into the second equation yields

$$10y - y = 18$$

$$9y = 18$$

$$y = 2$$

Plugging this into the equation $x - y = 18$ yields $x = 20$. Hence, y is the smaller number. The answer is (A).

3. Let x and y denote the angles:

Then $\frac{x}{y} = \frac{1}{3}$ and since the angle sum of a triangle is 180°, $x + x + y = 180$. Solving the first equation for y and plugging it into the second equation yields

$$2x + 3x = 180$$

$$5x = 180$$

$$x = 36$$

Plugging this into the equation $\frac{x}{y} = \frac{1}{3}$ yields $y = 108$. The answer is (E).

4. This is a direct proportion: as the distance increases, the gallons of fuel consumed also increases. Setting ratios equal yields

$$\frac{80\,gal.}{320\,mi.} = \frac{x\,gal.}{700\,mi.}$$

$$\frac{700 \cdot 80}{320} = x$$

$$175 = x$$

The answer is (E).

5. This is an inverse proportion: as the number of boys increases the time required to complete the job decreases. Setting products equal yields

$$2 \times 2.5 = 5 \times t$$

$$1 = t$$

The answer is (A).

6. This is a direct proportion: as the amount of flour increases so must the amount of shortening. First change $\frac{1}{2}$ lb. into 8 oz., Setting ratios equal yields

$$\frac{8}{14} = \frac{x}{21}$$

$$\frac{21 \cdot 8}{14} = x$$

$$12 = x$$

The answer is (D).

7. Most students struggle with this type of problem, and the ACT considers them to be difficult. However, if you can identify whether a problem is a direct proportion or an inverse proportion, then it is not so challenging. In this problem, as the number of widgets increases so does the absolute cost. This is a direct proportion, and therefore we set ratios equal:

$$\frac{w}{d} = \frac{2000}{x}$$

Cross multiplying yields

$$w \cdot x = 2000 \cdot d$$

Dividing by w yields

$$x = \frac{2000d}{w}$$

The answer is (C).

8. This is considered to be a hard problem. Begin by adding the two equations:

$$x + 2y - z = 1$$
$$\underline{3x - 2y - 8z = -1}$$
$$4x - 9z = 0$$
$$4x = 9z$$
$$\frac{x}{z} = \frac{9}{4}$$

The answer is (E).

9. This is a direct proportion: as the time increases so does the number of steps that the sprinter takes. Setting ratios equal yields

$$\frac{30}{9} = \frac{x}{54}$$

$$\frac{30 \cdot 54}{9} = x$$

$$180 = x$$

The answer is (D).

10. Dividing the equation $5x = 6y$ by $5y$ yields

$$\frac{x}{y} = \frac{6}{5} \qquad \text{ratio of } x \text{ to } y$$

or in ratio notation

$$x : y = 6 : 5$$

The answer is (D).

Exponents & Roots

EXPONENTS

Exponents afford a convenient way of expressing long products of the same number. The expression b^n is called a power and it stands for $b \times b \times b \times \cdots \times b$, where there are n factors of b. b is called the base, and n is called the exponent. By definition, $b^0 = 1$.

There are six rules that govern the behavior of exponents:

Rule 1: $x^a \cdot x^b = x^{a+b}$ Example, $2^3 \cdot 2^2 = 2^{3+2} = 2^5 = 32$. Caution, $x^a + x^b \neq x^{a+b}$

Rule 2: $\left(x^a\right)^b = x^{ab}$ Example, $\left(2^3\right)^2 = 2^{3 \cdot 2} = 2^6 = 64$

Rule 3: $(xy)^a = x^a \cdot y^a$ Example, $(2y)^3 = 2^3 \cdot y^3 = 8y^3$

Rule 4: $\left(\dfrac{x}{y}\right)^a = \dfrac{x^a}{y^a}$ Example, $\left(\dfrac{x}{3}\right)^2 = \dfrac{x^2}{3^2} = \dfrac{x^2}{9}$

Rule 5: $\dfrac{x^a}{x^b} = x^{a-b}$, if $a > b$.   Example, $\dfrac{2^6}{2^3} = 2^{6-3} = 2^3 = 8$

            $\dfrac{x^a}{x^b} = \dfrac{1}{x^{b-a}}$, if $b > a$.   Example, $\dfrac{2^3}{2^6} = \dfrac{1}{2^{6-3}} = \dfrac{1}{2^3} = \dfrac{1}{8}$

Rule 6: $x^{-a} = \dfrac{1}{x^a}$ Example, $z^{-3} = \dfrac{1}{z^3}$ Caution, a negative exponent does not make the number negative; it merely indicates that the base should be reciprocated. For example, $3^{-2} \neq -\dfrac{1}{3^2} \ or - \dfrac{1}{9}$.

Problems involving these six rules are common on the ACT, and they are often listed as hard problems. However, the process of solving these problems is quite mechanical: simply apply the six rules until they can no longer be applied.

Example 1:   If $x \neq 0$, $\dfrac{x\left(x^5\right)^2}{x^4} =$

         (A) x^5 (B) x^6 (C) x^7 (D) x^8 (E) x^9

First, apply the rule $\left(x^a\right)^b = x^{ab}$ to the expression $\dfrac{x\left(x^5\right)^2}{x^4}$:

$$\dfrac{x \cdot x^{5 \cdot 2}}{x^4} = \dfrac{x \cdot x^{10}}{x^4}$$

Next, apply the rule $x^a \cdot x^b = x^{a+b}$:

$$\dfrac{x \cdot x^{10}}{x^4} = \dfrac{x^{11}}{x^4}$$

Finally, apply the rule $\dfrac{x^a}{x^b} = x^{a-b}$:

$$\frac{x^{11}}{x^4} = x^{11-4} = x^7$$

The answer is (C).

Note: Typically, there are many ways of solving these types of problems. For this example, we could have begun with Rule 5, $\dfrac{x^a}{x^b} = \dfrac{1}{x^{b-a}}$:

$$\frac{x\left(x^5\right)^2}{x^4} = \frac{\left(x^5\right)^2}{x^{4-1}} = \frac{\left(x^5\right)^2}{x^3}$$

Then apply Rule 2, $\left(x^a\right)^b = x^{ab}$:

$$\frac{\left(x^5\right)^2}{x^3} = \frac{x^{10}}{x^3}$$

Finally, apply the other version of Rule 5, $\dfrac{x^a}{x^b} = x^{a-b}$:

$$\frac{x^{10}}{x^3} = x^7$$

Example 2: $\dfrac{3 \cdot 3 \cdot 3 \cdot 3}{9 \cdot 9 \cdot 9 \cdot 9} =$

(A) $\left(\dfrac{1}{3}\right)^4$ (B) $\left(\dfrac{1}{3}\right)^3$ (C) $\dfrac{1}{3}$ (D) $\dfrac{4}{9}$ (E) $\dfrac{4}{3}$

Canceling the common factor 3 yields $\dfrac{1 \cdot 1 \cdot 1 \cdot 1}{3 \cdot 3 \cdot 3 \cdot 3}$, or $\dfrac{1}{3} \cdot \dfrac{1}{3} \cdot \dfrac{1}{3} \cdot \dfrac{1}{3}$. Now, by the definition of a power, $\dfrac{1}{3} \cdot \dfrac{1}{3} \cdot \dfrac{1}{3} \cdot \dfrac{1}{3} = \left(\dfrac{1}{3}\right)^4$ Hence, the answer is (A).

Example 3: $\dfrac{6^4}{3^2} =$

(A) 2^4 (B) $2^3 \cdot 3$ (C) 6^2 (D) $2^4 \cdot 3^2$ (E) $2^2 \cdot 3^4$

First, factor the top of the fraction:

$$\frac{(2 \cdot 3)^4}{3^2}$$

Next, apply the rule $(xy)^a = x^a \cdot y^a$:

$$\frac{2^4 \cdot 3^4}{3^2}$$

Finally, apply the rule $\dfrac{x^a}{x^b} = x^{a-b}$:

$$2^4 \cdot 3^2$$

Hence, the answer is (D).

ROOTS

The symbol $\sqrt[n]{b}$ is read the *n*th root of *b*, where *n* is called the index, *b* is called the base, and $\sqrt{}$ is called the radical. $\sqrt[n]{b}$ denotes that number which raised to the *n*th power yields *b*. In other words, *a* is the *n*th root of *b* if $a^n = b$. For example, $\sqrt{9} = 3$* because $3^2 = 9$, and $\sqrt[3]{-8} = -2$ because $(-2)^3 = -8$. Even roots occur in pairs: both a positive root and a negative root. For example, $\sqrt[4]{16} = 2$ since $2^4 = 16$, and $\sqrt[4]{16} = -2$ since $(-2)^4 = 16$. Odd roots occur alone and have the same sign as the base: $\sqrt[3]{-27} = -3$ since $(-3)^3 = -27$. If given an even root, you are to assume it is the positive root. However, if you introduce even roots by solving an equation, then you <u>must</u> consider both the positive and negative roots:

$$x^2 = 9$$
$$\sqrt{x^2} = \pm\sqrt{9}$$
$$x = \pm 3$$

Square roots and cube roots can be simplified by removing perfect squares and perfect cubes, respectively. For example,

$$\sqrt{8} = \sqrt{4 \cdot 2} = \sqrt{4}\sqrt{2} = 2\sqrt{2}$$
$$\sqrt[3]{54} = \sqrt[3]{27 \cdot 2} = \sqrt[3]{27}\sqrt[3]{2} = 3\sqrt[3]{2}$$

Radicals are often written with fractional exponents. The expression $\sqrt[n]{b}$ can be written as $b^{1/n}$. This can be generalized as follows:

$$b^{m/n} = \left(\sqrt[n]{b}\right)^m = \sqrt[n]{b^m}$$

Usually, the form $\left(\sqrt[n]{b}\right)^m$ is better when calculating because the part under the radical is smaller in this case. For example, $27^{2/3} = \left(\sqrt[3]{27}\right)^2 = 3^2 = 9$. Using the form $\sqrt[n]{b^m}$ would be much harder in this case: $27^{2/3} = \sqrt[3]{27^2} = \sqrt[3]{729} = 9$. Most students know the value of $\sqrt[3]{27}$, but few know the value of $\sqrt[3]{729}$.

If *n* is even, then

$$\sqrt[n]{x^n} = |x|$$

For example, $\sqrt[4]{(-2)^4} = |-2| = 2$. With odd roots, the absolute value symbol is not needed. For example, $\sqrt[3]{(-2)^3} = \sqrt[3]{-8} = -2$.

To solve radical equations, just apply the rules of exponents to undo the radicals. For example, to solve the radical equation $x^{2/3} = 4$, we cube both sides to eliminate the cube root:

$$\left(x^{2/3}\right)^3 = 4^3$$
$$x^2 = 64$$
$$\sqrt{x^2} = \sqrt{64}$$
$$|x| = 8$$
$$x = \pm 8$$

---

* With square roots, the index is not written, $\sqrt[2]{9} = \sqrt{9}$.

The following rules are useful for manipulating roots:

$$\sqrt[n]{xy} = \sqrt[n]{x}\,\sqrt[n]{y} \qquad\qquad \text{For example, } \sqrt{3x} = \sqrt{3}\,\sqrt{x}\,.$$

$$\sqrt[n]{\frac{x}{y}} = \frac{\sqrt[n]{x}}{\sqrt[n]{y}} \qquad\qquad \text{For example, } \sqrt[3]{\frac{x}{8}} = \frac{\sqrt[3]{x}}{\sqrt[3]{8}} = \frac{\sqrt[3]{x}}{2}\,.$$

Caution: $\sqrt[n]{x+y} \ne \sqrt[n]{x} + \sqrt[n]{y}$. For example, $\sqrt{x+5} \ne \sqrt{x} + \sqrt{5}$. Also, $\sqrt{x^2 + y^2} \ne x + y$. This common mistake occurs because it is similar to the following valid property: $\sqrt{(x+y)^2} = x + y$ (If $x + y$ can be negative, then it must be written with the absolute value symbol: $|x + y|$). Note, in the valid formula, it's the whole term, $x + y$, that is squared, not the individual x and y.

To add two roots, both the index and the base must be the same. For example, $\sqrt[3]{2} + \sqrt[4]{2}$ cannot be added because the indices are different, nor can $\sqrt{2} + \sqrt{3}$ be added because the bases are different. However, $\sqrt[3]{2} + \sqrt[3]{2} = 2\sqrt[3]{2}$. In this case, the roots can be added because both the indices and bases are the same. Sometimes radicals with different bases can actually be added once they have been simplified to look alike. For example, $\sqrt{28} + \sqrt{7} = \sqrt{4 \cdot 7} + \sqrt{7} = \sqrt{4}\,\sqrt{7} + \sqrt{7} = 2\sqrt{7} + \sqrt{7} = 3\sqrt{7}\,.$

You need to know the approximations of the following roots: $\sqrt{2} \approx 1.4 \qquad \sqrt{3} \approx 1.7 \qquad \sqrt{5} \approx 2.2$

Example 4: Given the system $\begin{array}{c} x^2 = 4 \\ y^3 = -8 \end{array}$, which of the following is NOT necessarily true?

(A) $y < 0$ (B) $x < 5$ (C) y is an integer (D) $x > y$ (E) $\dfrac{x}{y}$ is an integer

$y^3 = -8$ yields one cube root, $y = -2$. However, $x^2 = 4$ yields two square roots, $x = \pm 2$. Now, if $x = 2$, then $x > y$; but if $x = -2$, then $x = y$. Hence, choice (D) is not necessarily true. The answer is (D).

Example 5: If $x < 0$ and y is 5 more than the square of x, which one of the following expresses x in terms of y?

(A) $x = \sqrt{y - 5}$ (B) $x = -\sqrt{y - 5}$ (C) $x = \sqrt{y + 5}$ (D) $x = \sqrt{y^2 - 5}$ (E) $x = -\sqrt{y^2 - 5}$

Translating the expression *"y is 5 more than the square of x"* into an equation yields:

$$y = x^2 + 5$$

$$y - 5 = x^2$$

$$\pm\sqrt{y - 5} = x$$

Since we are given that $x < 0$, we take the negative root, $-\sqrt{y - 5} = x$. The answer is (B).

RATIONALIZING

A fraction is not considered simplified until all the radicals have been removed from the denominator. If a denominator contains a single term with a square root, it can be rationalized by multiplying both the numerator and denominator by that square root. If the denominator contains square roots separated by a plus or minus sign, then multiply both the numerator and denominator by the conjugate, which is formed by merely changing the sign between the roots.

Example: Rationalize the fraction $\dfrac{2}{3\sqrt{5}}$.

Multiply top and bottom of the fraction by $\sqrt{5}$:
$$\frac{2}{3\sqrt{5}} \cdot \frac{\sqrt{5}}{\sqrt{5}} = \frac{2\sqrt{5}}{3 \cdot \sqrt{25}} = \frac{2\sqrt{5}}{3 \cdot 5} = \frac{2\sqrt{5}}{15}$$

Example: Rationalize the fraction $\dfrac{2}{3-\sqrt{5}}$.

Multiply top and bottom of the fraction by the conjugate $3+\sqrt{5}$:
$$\frac{2}{3-\sqrt{5}} \cdot \frac{3+\sqrt{5}}{3+\sqrt{5}} = \frac{2(3+\sqrt{5})}{3^2 + 3\sqrt{5} - 3\sqrt{5} - (\sqrt{5})^2} = \frac{2(3+\sqrt{5})}{9-5} = \frac{2(3+\sqrt{5})}{4} = \frac{3+\sqrt{5}}{2}$$

Problem Set O:

1.   If $x \neq 0$, $\left(\dfrac{2y^3}{x^2}\right)^4 \cdot x^{10} =$

   (A) $16y^{12}x^2$ (B) $8y^7x^2$ (C) $16\dfrac{y^{12}}{x^8}$ (D) $8\dfrac{y^{12}}{x^8}$ (E) $\dfrac{y^{12}}{16x^8}$

2. $\sqrt{(31-6)(16+9)} =$

   (A) 5   (B) 10   (C) 25   (D) 50   (E) 625

3.   What is the largest integer n such that 2^n is a factor of 20^8?

   (A) 1   (B) 2   (C) 4   (D) 8   (E) 16

4. $\dfrac{55^5}{5^{55}} =$

   (A) $\dfrac{11}{5^{50}}$ (B) $\dfrac{11}{5^{55}}$ (C) $\dfrac{11^5}{5^{50}}$ (D) $\dfrac{11^5}{5^5}$ (E) $\dfrac{11^5}{5}$

5.   If $x = 1/9$, then $\sqrt{x} - x^2 =$

   (A) 0   (B) 1/9   (C) 26/81   (D) 1/3   (E) 1

6. $\left(9^x\right)^3 =$

    (A) 3^{3x} (B) 3^{2+3x} (C) 3^{6x} (D) $729x^3$ (E) 9^{x^3}

7. If $x = 4$, then $-2^{2\sqrt{x}} + 2 =$

    (A) -14 (B) -8 (C) -2 (D) 0 (E) 18

8. $\sqrt{\dfrac{25 + 10x + x^2}{2}} =$

    (A) $\dfrac{\sqrt{2}(5-x)}{2}$ (B) $\dfrac{\sqrt{5+x}}{\sqrt{2}}$ (C) $\dfrac{\sqrt{2}(5+x)}{2}$ (D) $\dfrac{5+x}{2}$ (E) $\dfrac{5-x}{2}$

9. $\dfrac{2+\sqrt{5}}{2-\sqrt{5}} =$

    (A) $-9 - 4\sqrt{5}$ (B) $-1 - \dfrac{4}{9}\sqrt{5}$ (C) $1 + \dfrac{4}{9}\sqrt{5}$ (D) $9 + 4\sqrt{5}$ (E) 20

10. $2^{12} + 2^{12} + 2^{12} + 2^{12} =$

    (A) 4^{12} (B) 2^{14} (C) 2^{16} (D) 4^{16} (E) 2^{48}

11. $\left(\dfrac{\left(x^2 y\right)^3 z}{xyz}\right)^3 =$

    (A) $x^8 y^5$ (B) xy^6 (C) $x^{15} y^6 z$ (D) $x^3 y^6$ (E) $x^{15} y^6$

12. If $2^{2x} = 16^{x+2}$, what is the value of x ?

    (A) -4 (B) -2 (C) 0 (D) 2 (E) 4

13. If $(x-y)^{\frac{1}{3}} = (x+y)^{-\frac{1}{3}}$, then which one of the following must be true?

    (A) $x = 1$ (B) $y = 1$ (C) $x^2 - y^2 = 1$ (D) $x + y^2 = 1$ (E) $x^2 - 2xy + y^2 = 1$

Answers and Solutions to Problem Set O

1. $$\left(\frac{2y^3}{x^2}\right)^4 \cdot x^{10} = \frac{\left(2y^3\right)^4}{\left(x^2\right)^4} \cdot x^{10} = \qquad \text{by the rule } \left(\frac{x}{y}\right)^a = \frac{x^a}{y^a}$$

    $$\frac{2^4 \cdot \left(y^3\right)^4}{\left(x^2\right)^4} \cdot x^{10} = \qquad \text{by the rule } (xy)^a = x^a \cdot y^a$$

    $$\frac{2^4 \cdot y^{12}}{x^8} \cdot x^{10} = \qquad \text{by the rule } \left(x^a\right)^b = x^{ab}$$

    $$2^4 \cdot y^{12} \cdot x^2 = \qquad \text{by the rule } \frac{x^a}{x^b} = x^{a-b}$$

    $$16 \cdot y^{12} \cdot x^2$$

The answer is (A).

2. $$\sqrt{(31-6)(16+9)} =$$
    $$\sqrt{25 \cdot 25} =$$
    $$\sqrt{25}\sqrt{25} =$$
    $$5 \cdot 5 =$$
    $$25$$

The answer is (C).

3. Begin by completely factoring 20:

    $$20^8 = (2 \cdot 2 \cdot 5)^8 =$$
    $$2^8 \cdot 2^8 \cdot 5^8 = \qquad \text{by Rule 3, } (xy)^a = x^a \cdot y^a *$$
    $$2^{16} \cdot 5^8 \qquad \text{by Rule 1, } x^a \cdot x^b = x^{a+b}$$

The expression 2^{16} represents all the factors of 20^8 of the form 2^n. Hence, 16 is the largest such number, and the answer is (E).

4. Begin by factoring 55 in the top of the fraction:

    $$\frac{55^5}{5^{55}} = \frac{(5 \cdot 11)^5}{5^{55}} =$$
    $$\frac{5^5 \cdot 11^5}{5^{55}} = \qquad \text{by Rule 3, } (xy)^a = x^a \cdot y^a$$
    $$\frac{11^5}{5^{50}} \qquad \text{by Rule 5, } \frac{x^a}{x^b} = \frac{1}{x^{b-a}}$$

The answer is (C).

5. $\sqrt{x} - x^2 = \sqrt{\frac{1}{9}} - \left(\frac{1}{9}\right)^2 = \frac{1}{3} - \frac{1}{81} = \frac{27}{27} \cdot \frac{1}{3} - \frac{1}{81} = \frac{27-1}{81} = \frac{26}{81}$ The answer is (C).

---

*   Note, Rule 3 can be extended to any number of terms by repeatedly applying the rule. For example, $(xyz)^a = \left(\left[xy\right]z\right)^a = \left[xy\right]^a \cdot z^a = x^a y^a z^a$.

6.

$$\left(9^x\right)^3 = 9^{3x} = \qquad \text{by the rule } \left(x^a\right)^b = x^{ab}$$

$$\left(3^2\right)^{3x} = \qquad \text{since } 9 = 3^2$$

$$3^{6x} \qquad \text{again by the rule } \left(x^a\right)^b = x^{ab}$$

The answer is (C). Note, this is considered to be a hard problem.

7. Plugging $x = 4$ into the expression $-2^{2\sqrt{x}} + 2$ yields

$$-2^{2\sqrt{4}} + 2 = -2^{2 \cdot 2} + 2 = -2^4 + 2 = -16 + 2 = -14$$

The answer is (A).

8.

$$\sqrt{\frac{25 + 10x + x^2}{2}} = \sqrt{\frac{(5+x)^2}{2}} = \qquad \text{since } 25 + 10x + x^2 \text{ factors into } (5+x)^2$$

$$\frac{\sqrt{(5+x)^2}}{\sqrt{2}} = \qquad \text{by the rule } \sqrt[n]{\frac{x}{y}} = \frac{\sqrt[n]{x}}{\sqrt[n]{y}}$$

$$\frac{5+x}{\sqrt{2}} = \qquad \text{since } \sqrt{x^2} = x$$

$$\frac{5+x}{\sqrt{2}} \cdot \frac{\sqrt{2}}{\sqrt{2}} = \qquad \text{rationalizing the denominator}$$

$$\frac{\sqrt{2}(5+x)}{2}$$

Hence, the answer is (C).

9. $\dfrac{2+\sqrt{5}}{2-\sqrt{5}} = \dfrac{2+\sqrt{5}}{2-\sqrt{5}} \cdot \dfrac{2+\sqrt{5}}{2+\sqrt{5}} = \dfrac{4 + 4\sqrt{5} + 5}{4 - 5} = \dfrac{9 + 4\sqrt{5}}{-1} = -9 - 4\sqrt{5}$. Hence, the answer is (A).

10. $2^{12} + 2^{12} + 2^{12} + 2^{12} = 4 \cdot 2^{12} = 2^2 \cdot 2^{12} = 2^{2+12} = 2^{14}$. The answer is (B).

11. $\left(\dfrac{\left(x^2 y\right)^3 z}{xyz}\right)^3 = \left(\dfrac{\left(x^2 y\right)^3}{xy}\right)^3 = \left(\dfrac{\left(x^2\right)^3 y^3}{xy}\right)^3 = \left(\dfrac{x^6 y^3}{xy}\right)^3 = \left(x^5 y^2\right)^3 = \left(x^5\right)^3 \left(y^2\right)^3 = x^{15} y^6$

Hence, the answer is (E).

12. Our goal here is to write both sides of the equation in terms of the base 2 and then equate the exponents. To that end, write 16 as 2^4:

$$2^{2x} = \left(2^4\right)^{x+2}$$
$$2^{2x} = 2^{4(x+2)}$$

Since we have written both sides of the equation in terms of the base 2, we now equate the exponents:

$$2x = 4(x+2)$$
$$2x = 4x + 8$$
$$-2x = 8$$
$$x = -4$$

The answer is (A).

13. First, let's reciprocate the expression $(x+y)^{-\frac{1}{3}}$ to eliminate the negative exponent:

$$(x-y)^{\frac{1}{3}} = \frac{1}{(x+y)^{\frac{1}{3}}}$$

Cubing both sides of this equation to eliminate the cube roots yields

$$x - y = \frac{1}{x+y}$$

Multiplying both sides of this equation by $x + y$ yields

$$(x-y)(x+y) = 1$$

Multiplying out the left side of this equation yields

$$x^2 - xy + xy + y^2 = 1$$

Reducing yields

$$x^2 + y^2 = 1$$

The answer is (C).

Factoring

To factor an algebraic expression is to rewrite it as a product of two or more expressions, called factors. In general, any expression on the ACT that can be factored should be factored, and any expression that can be unfactored (multiplied out) should be unfactored.

DISTRIBUTIVE RULE

The most basic type of factoring involves the distributive rule:

$$ax + ay = a(x + y)$$

When this rule is applied from left to right, it is called factoring. When the rule is applied from right to left, it is called distributing.

For example, $3h + 3k = 3(h + k)$, and $5xy + 45x = 5xy + 9 \cdot 5x = 5x(y + 9)$. The distributive rule can be generalized to any number of terms. For three terms, it looks like $ax + ay + az = a(x + y + z)$. For example, $2x + 4y + 8 = 2x + 2 \cdot 2y + 2 \cdot 4 = 2(x + 2y + 4)$. For another example, $x^2 y^2 + xy^3 + y^5 = y^2(x^2 + xy + y^3)$.

Example 1: If $x - y = 9$, then $\left(x - \dfrac{y}{3} \right) - \left(y - \dfrac{x}{3} \right) =$

(A) -4 (B) -3 (C) 0 (D) 12 (E) 27

$$\left(x - \frac{y}{3} \right) - \left(y - \frac{x}{3} \right) =$$

$$x - \frac{y}{3} - y + \frac{x}{3} = \qquad \text{by distributing the negative sign}$$

$$\frac{4}{3}x - \frac{4}{3}y = \qquad \text{by combining the fractions}$$

$$\frac{4}{3}(x - y) = \qquad \text{by factoring out the common factor } \frac{4}{3}$$

$$\frac{4}{3}(9) = \qquad \text{since } x - y = 9$$

$$12$$

The answer is (D).

Example 2: $\dfrac{2^{20} - 2^{19}}{2^{11}} =$

(A) $2^9 - 2^{19}$ (B) $\dfrac{1}{2^{11}}$ (C) 2^8 (D) 2^{10} (E) 2^{28}

$$\frac{2^{20} - 2^{19}}{2^{11}} = \frac{2^{19+1} - 2^{19}}{2^{11}} =$$

$$\frac{2^{19} \cdot 2^1 - 2^{19}}{2^{11}} = \qquad \text{by the rule } x^a \cdot x^b = x^{a+b}$$

$$\frac{2^{19}(2 - 1)}{2^{11}} = \qquad \text{by the distributive property } ax + ay = a(x + y)$$

$$\frac{2^{19}}{2^{11}} =$$

$$2^8 \qquad \text{by the rule } \frac{x^a}{x^b} = x^{a-b}$$

The answer is (C).

DIFFERENCE OF SQUARES

One of the most important formulas on the ACT is the difference of squares:

$$\boxed{x^2 - y^2 = (x + y)(x - y)}$$

Caution: a sum of squares, $x^2 + y^2$, does not factor.

Example 3:   If $x \neq -2$, then $\dfrac{8x^2 - 32}{4x + 8} =$

(A) $2(x - 2)$ (B) $2(x - 4)$ (C) $8(x + 2)$ (D) $x - 2$ (E) $x + 4$

In most algebraic expressions involving multiplication or division, you won't actually multiply or divide, rather you will factor and cancel, as in this problem.

$$\frac{8x^2 - 32}{4x + 8} =$$

$$\frac{8(x^2 - 4)}{4(x + 2)} = \qquad \text{by the distributive property } ax + ay = a(x + y)$$

$$\frac{8(x + 2)(x - 2)}{4(x + 2)} = \qquad \text{by the difference of squares } x^2 - y^2 = (x + y)(x - y)$$

$$2(x - 2) \qquad \text{by canceling common factors}$$

The answer is (A).

PERFECT SQUARE TRINOMIALS

Like the difference of squares formula, perfect square trinomial formulas are very common on the ACT.

$$x^2 + 2xy + y^2 = (x + y)^2$$
$$x^2 - 2xy + y^2 = (x - y)^2$$

For example, $x^2 + 6x + 9 = x^2 + 2(3x) + 3^2 = (x + 3)^2$. Note, in a perfect square trinomial, the middle term is twice the product of the square roots of the outer terms.

Example 4:   If $r^2 - 2rs + s^2 = 4$, then $(r - s)^6 =$

(A) −4   (B) 4   (C) 8   (D) 16   (E) 64

$$r^2 - 2rs + s^2 = 4$$

$$(r - s)^2 = 4 \qquad \text{by the formula } x^2 - 2xy + y^2 = (x - y)^2$$

$$\left[(r - s)^2 \right]^3 = 4^3 \qquad \text{by cubing both sides of the equation}$$

$$(r - s)^6 = 64 \qquad \text{by the rule } \left(x^a \right)^b = x^{ab}$$

The answer is (E).

GENERAL TRINOMIALS

$$x^2 + (a + b)x + ab = (x + a)(x + b)$$

The expression $x^2 + (a + b)x + ab$ tells us that we need two numbers whose product is the last term and whose sum is the coefficient of the middle term. Consider the trinomial $x^2 + 5x + 6$. Now, two factors of 6 are 1 and 6, but $1 + 6 \neq 5$. However, 2 and 3 are also factors of 6, and $2 + 3 = 5$. Hence, $x^2 + 5x + 6 = (x + 2)(x + 3)$.

Example 5:   Which of the following could be a solution of the equation $x^2 - 7x - 18 = 0$?

(A) −1   (B) 0   (C) 2   (D) 7   (E) 9

Now, both 2 and −9 are factors of 18, and $2 + (-9) = -7$. Hence, $x^2 - 7x - 18 = (x + 2)(x - 9) = 0$. Setting each factor equal to zero yields $x + 2 = 0$ and $x - 9 = 0$. Solving these equations yields $x = -2$ and 9. The answer is (E).

COMPLETE FACTORING

When factoring an expression, first check for a common factor, then check for a difference of squares, then for a perfect square trinomial, and then for a general trinomial.

Example 6:   Factor the expression $2x^3 - 2x^2 - 12x$ completely.

Solution: First check for a common factor: $2x$ is common to each term. Factoring $2x$ out of each term yields $2x(x^2 - x - 6)$. Next, there is no difference of squares, and $x^2 - x - 6$ is not a perfect square trinomial since x does not equal twice the product of the square roots of x^2 and 6. Now, −3 and 2 are factors of −6 whose sum is −1. Hence, $2x(x^2 - x - 6)$ factors into $2x(x - 3)(x + 2)$.

Problem Set P:

1.   If $3y + 5 = 7x$, then $21y - 49x =$

(A) -40 (B) -35 (C) -10 (D) 0 (E) 15

2.   If $x - y = p$, then $2x^2 - 4xy + 2y^2 =$

(A) p (B) $2p$ (C) $4p$ (D) p^2 (E) $2p^2$

3.   If $p \neq 0$ and $p = \sqrt{2pq - q^2}$, then in terms of q, $p =$

(A) q (B) q^2 (C) $2q$ (D) $-2q$ (E) $q/4$

4.   If $\dfrac{x^2 + 2x - 10}{5} = 1$, then x could equal

(A) -5 (B) -3 (C) 0 (D) 10 (E) 15

5.   What is the absolute value of twice the difference of the roots of the equation $5y^2 - 20y + 15 = 0$?

(A) 0 (B) 1 (C) 2 (D) 3 (E) 4

6.   If $x \neq -2$, then $\dfrac{7x^2 + 28x + 28}{(x + 2)^2} =$

(A) 7 (B) 8 (C) 9 (D) 10 (E) 11

7. $\dfrac{7^9 + 7^8}{8} =$

(A) $1/8$ (B) $7/8$ (C) $\dfrac{7^7}{8}$ (D) 7^8 (E) 7^9

8.   If $x + y = 10$ and $x - y = 5$, then $x^2 - y^2 =$

(A) 50 (B) 60 (C) 75 (D) 80 (E) 100

9. $x(x - y) - z(x - y) =$

(A) $x - y$ (B) $x - z$ (C) $(x - y)(x - z)$ (D) $(x - y)(x + z)$ (E) $(x - y)(z - x)$

10.   If $(x - y)^2 = x^2 + y^2$, then which one of the following statements must also be true?

I. $x = 0$
II. $y = 0$
III. $xy = 0$

(A) None   (B) I only   (C) II only   (D) III only   (E) II and III only

11. If x and y are prime numbers such that $x > y > 2$, then $x^2 - y^2$ must be divisible by which one of the following numbers?

   (A)   3
   (B)   4
   (C)   5
   (D)   9
   (E)   12

12. If $\dfrac{x+y}{x-y} = \dfrac{1}{2}$, then $\dfrac{xy + x^2}{xy - x^2} =$

   (A)   −4.2
   (B)   −1/2
   (C)   1.1
   (D)   3
   (E)   5.3

13. If $x + y = 2\sqrt{xy}$, then which one of the following must be true?

   (A) $x < y$
   (B) $x = 2$
   (C) $x = y$
   (D) $x > y$
   (E) $x = 4$

Answers and Solutions to Problem Set P

1. First, interchanging 5 and $7x$ in the expression $3y + 5 = 7x$ yields $3y - 7x = -5$. Next, factoring $21y - 49x$ yields

$$21y - 49x =$$
$$7 \cdot 3y - 7 \cdot 7x =$$
$$7(3y - 7x) =$$
$$7(-5) = \qquad \text{since } 3y - 7x = -5$$
$$-35$$

The answer is (B).

2.
$$2x^2 - 4xy + 2y^2 =$$
$$2\left(x^2 - 2xy + y^2\right) = \qquad \text{by factoring out the common factor 2}$$
$$2(x - y)^2 = \qquad \text{by the formula } x^2 - 2xy + y^2 = (x - y)^2$$
$$2p^2 \qquad \text{since } x - y = p$$

The answer is (E).

3.
$$p = \sqrt{2pq - q^2}$$
$$p^2 = 2pq - q^2 \qquad \text{by squaring both sides}$$
$$p^2 - 2pq + q^2 = 0 \qquad \text{by subtracting } 2pq \text{ and adding } q^2 \text{ to both sides}$$
$$(p - q)^2 = 0 \qquad \text{by the formula } x^2 - 2xy + y^2 = (x - y)^2$$
$$p - q = 0 \qquad \text{by taking the square root of both sides}$$
$$p = q \qquad \text{by adding } q \text{ to both sides}$$

The answer is (A).

4.
$$\frac{x^2 + 2x - 10}{5} = 1$$
$$x^2 + 2x - 10 = 5 \qquad \text{by multiplying both sides by 5}$$
$$x^2 + 2x - 15 = 0 \qquad \text{by subtracting 5 from both sides}$$
$$(x + 5)(x - 3) = 0 \qquad \text{since } 5 \cdot 3 = 15 \text{ and } 5 - 3 = 2$$
$$x + 5 = 0 \text{ and } x - 3 = 0 \qquad \text{by setting each factor equal to zero}$$
$$x = -5 \text{ and } x = 3$$

The answer is (A).

5. Begin by factoring out the common factor in the equation $5y^2 - 20y + 15 = 0$:

$$5\left(y^2 - 4y + 3\right) = 0$$

Dividing both sides of this equation by 5 yields $y^2 - 4y + 3 = 0$
Since $3 + 1 = 4$, the trinomial factors into $(y - 3)(y - 1) = 0$
Setting each factor equal to zero yields $y - 3 = 0$ and $y - 1 = 0$

Solving these equations yields $y = 3$ and $y = 1$. Now, the difference of 3 and 1 is 2 and twice 2 is 4. Further, the difference of 1 and 3 is -2 and twice -2 is -4. Now, the absolute value of both 4 and -4 is 4. The answer is (E).

6.
$$\frac{7x^2 + 28x + 28}{(x+2)^2} =$$

$$\frac{7\left(x^2 + 4x + 4\right)}{(x+2)^2} = \qquad \text{by factoring out 7}$$

$$\frac{7(x+2)^2}{(x+2)^2} = \qquad \text{by the formula } x^2 + 2xy + y^2 = (x+y)^2$$

$$7 \qquad \text{by canceling the common factor } (x+2)^2$$

The answer is (A).

7.
$$\frac{7^9 + 7^8}{8} =$$

$$\frac{7^8 \cdot 7 + 7^8}{8} = \qquad \text{since } 7^9 = 7^8 \cdot 7$$

$$\frac{7^8(7+1)}{8} = \qquad \text{by factoring out the common factor } 7^8$$

$$\frac{7^8(8)}{8} =$$

$$7^8$$

Hence, the answer is (D). Note, this is considered to be a very hard problem.

8.
$$x^2 - y^2 =$$

$$(x+y)(x-y) = \qquad \text{since } x^2 - y^2 \text{ is a difference of squares}$$

$$(10)(5) = \qquad \text{since } x + y = 10 \text{ and } x - y = 5$$

$$50$$

The answer is (A). This problem can also be solved by adding the two equations. However, that approach will lead to long, messy fractions. Writers of the ACT put questions like this one on the ACT to see whether you will discover the short cut. The premise being that those students who do not see the short cut will take longer to solve the problem and therefore will have less time to finish the test.

9. Noticing that $x - y$ is a common factor, we factor it out:
$$x(x - y) - z(x - y) = (x - y)(x - z)$$

The answer is (C).

Method II
Sometimes a complicated expression can be simplified by making a substitution. In the expression $x(x - y) - z(x - y)$ replace $x - y$ with w:
$$xw - zw$$

Now, the structure appears much simpler. Factoring out the common factor w yields
$$w(x - z)$$

Finally, re-substitute $x - y$ for w:
$$(x - y)(x - z)$$

10. $(x - y)^2 = x^2 + y^2$

   $x^2 - 2xy + y^2 = x^2 + y^2$ by the formula $x^2 - 2xy + y^2 = (x - y)^2$

   $-2xy = 0$ by subtracting x^2 and y^2 from both sides of the equation

   $xy = 0$ by dividing both sides of the equation by -2

Hence, Statement III is true, which eliminates choices (A), (B), and (C). However, Statement II is false. For example, if $y = 5$ and $x = 0$, then $xy = 0 \cdot 5 = 0$. A similar analysis shows that Statement I is false. The answer is (D).

11. The Difference of Squares formula yields $x^2 - y^2 = (x + y)(x - y)$. Now, both x and y must be odd because 2 is the only even prime and $x > y > 2$. Remember that the sum (or difference) of two odd numbers is even. Hence, $(x + y)(x - y)$ is the product of two even numbers and therefore is divisible by 4. To show this explicitly, let $x + y = 2p$ and let $x - y = 2q$. Then $(x + y)(x - y) = 2p \cdot 2q = 4pq$. Since we have written $(x + y)(x - y)$ as a multiple of 4, it is divisible by 4. The answer is (B).

Method II (substitution):
Let $x = 5$ and $y = 3$, then $x > y > 2$ and $x^2 - y^2 = 5^2 - 3^2 = 25 - 9 = 16$. Since 4 is the only number listed that divides evenly into 16, the answer is (B).

12. Solution:

   $\dfrac{xy + x^2}{xy - x^2} =$

   $\dfrac{x(y + x)}{x(y - x)} =$ by factoring out x from both the top and bottom expressions

   $\dfrac{y + x}{y - x} =$ by canceling the common factor x

   $\dfrac{x + y}{-(x - y)} =$ by factoring out the negative sign in the bottom and then rearranging

   $-\dfrac{x + y}{x - y} =$ by recalling that a negative fraction can be written three ways: $\dfrac{a}{-b} = -\dfrac{a}{b} = \dfrac{-a}{b}$

   $-\dfrac{1}{2}$ by replacing $\dfrac{x + y}{x - y}$ with $\dfrac{1}{2}$

The answer is (B).

13. The only information we have to work with is the equation $x + y = 2\sqrt{xy}$. Since radicals are awkward to work with, let's square both sides of this equation to eliminate the radical:

$$\left(x+y\right)^2 = \left(2\sqrt{xy}\right)^2$$

Applying the Perfect Square Trinomial Formula to the left side and simplifying the right side yields

$$x^2 + 2xy + y^2 = 4xy$$

Subtracting $4xy$ from both sides yields

$$x^2 - 2xy + y^2 = 0$$

Using the Perfect Square Trinomial Formula again yields

$$\left(x - y\right)^2 = 0$$

Taking the square root of both sides yields

$$\sqrt{\left(x-y\right)^2} = \pm\sqrt{0}$$

Simplifying yields

$$x - y = 0$$

Finally, adding y to both sides yields

$$x = y$$

The answer is (C).

Algebraic Expressions

A mathematical expression that contains a variable is called an algebraic expression. Some examples of algebraic expressions are x^2, $3x - 2y$, $2z(y^3 - \frac{1}{z^2})$. Two algebraic expressions are called like terms if both the variable parts and the exponents are identical. That is, the only parts of the expressions that can differ are the coefficients. For example, $5y^3$ and $\frac{3}{2}y^3$ are like terms, as are $x + y^2$ and $-7(x + y^2)$. However, x^3 and y^3 are not like terms, nor are $x - y$ and $2 - y$.

ADDING & SUBTRACTING ALGEBRAIC EXPRESSIONS

Only like terms may be added or subtracted. To add or subtract like terms, merely add or subtract their coefficients:

$$x^2 + 3x^2 = (1 + 3)x^2 = 4x^2$$

$$2\sqrt{x} - 5\sqrt{x} = (2 - 5)\sqrt{x} = -3\sqrt{x}$$

$$.5\left(x + \frac{1}{y}\right)^2 + .2\left(x + \frac{1}{y}\right)^2 = (.5 + .2)\left(x + \frac{1}{y}\right)^2 = .7\left(x + \frac{1}{y}\right)^2$$

$$\left(3x^3 + 7x^2 + 2x + 4\right) + \left(2x^2 - 2x - 6\right) = 3x^3 + (7 + 2)x^2 + (2 - 2)x + (4 - 6) = 3x^3 + 9x^2 - 2$$

You may add or multiply algebraic expressions in any order. This is called the commutative property:

$$\boxed{x + y = y + x}$$

$$\boxed{xy = yx}$$

For example, $-2x + 5x = 5x + (-2x) = (5 - 2)x = 3x$ and $(x - y)(-3) = (-3)(x - y) = (-3)x - (-3)y = -3x + 3y$.

Caution: the commutative property does not apply to division or subtraction: $2 = 6 \div 3 \neq 3 \div 6 = \frac{1}{2}$ and $-1 = 2 - 3 \neq 3 - 2 = 1$.

When adding or multiplying algebraic expressions, you may regroup the terms. This is called the associative property:

$$\boxed{x + (y + z) = (x + y) + z}$$

$$\boxed{x(yz) = (xy)z}$$

Notice in these formulas that the variables have not been moved, only the way they are grouped has changed: on the left side of the formulas the last two variables are grouped together, and on the right side of the formulas the first two variables are grouped together.

For example, $(x - 2x) + 5x = (x + [-2x]) + 5x = x + (-2x + 5x) = x + 3x = 4x$

and

$2(12x) = (2 \cdot 12)x = 24x$

The associative property doesn't apply to division or subtraction: $4 = 8 \div 2 = 8 \div (4 \div 2) \neq (8 \div 4) \div 2 = 2 \div 2 = 1$

and

$-6 = -3 - 3 = (-1 - 2) - 3 \neq -1 - (2 - 3) = -1 - (-1) = -1 + 1 = 0.$

Notice in the first example that we changed the subtraction into negative addition: $(x - 2x) = (x + [- 2x])$. This allowed us to apply the associative property over addition.

PARENTHESES

When simplifying expressions with nested parentheses, work from the inner most parentheses out:

$$5x + (y - (2x - 3x)) = 5x + (y - (-x)) = 5x + (y + x) = 6x + y$$

Sometimes when an expression involves several pairs of parentheses, one or more pairs are written as brackets. This makes the expression easier to read:

$$2x(x - [y + 2(x - y)]) =$$
$$2x(x - [y + 2x - 2y]) =$$
$$2x(x - [2x - y]) =$$
$$2x(x - 2x + y) =$$
$$2x(-x + y) =$$
$$-2x^2 + 2xy$$

ORDER OF OPERATIONS: (PEMDAS)

When simplifying algebraic expressions, perform operations within parentheses first and then exponents and then multiplication and then division and then addition and lastly subtraction. This can be remembered by the mnemonic:

PEMDAS
Please **E**xcuse **M**y **D**ear **A**unt **S**ally

This mnemonic isn't quite precise enough. Multiplication and division are actually tied in order of operation, as is the pair addition and subtraction. When multiplication and division, or addition and subtraction, appear at the same level in an expression, perform the operations from left to right. For example, $6 \div 2 \times 4 = (6 \div 2) \times 4 = 3 \times 4 = 12$. To emphasize this left-to-right order, we can use parentheses in the mnemonic: **PE(MD)(AS)**.

Example 1: $2 - \left(5 - 3^3[4 \div 2 + 1]\right) =$

(A) -21 (B) 32 (C) 45 (D) 60 (E) 78

$2 - \left(5 - 3^3[4 \div 2 + 1]\right) =$

$\quad 2 - \left(5 - 3^3[2 + 1]\right) =$ By performing the division within the innermost parentheses

$\quad\quad 2 - \left(5 - 3^3[3]\right) =$ By performing the addition within the innermost parentheses

$\quad\quad\quad 2 - (5 - 27[3]) =$ By performing the exponentiation

$\quad\quad\quad\quad 2 - (5 - 81) =$ By performing the multiplication within the parentheses

$\quad\quad\quad\quad\quad 2 - (-76) =$ By performing the subtraction within the parentheses

$\quad\quad\quad\quad\quad\quad 2 + 76 =$ By multiplying the two negatives

$\quad\quad\quad\quad\quad\quad\quad 78$

The answer is (E).

FOIL MULTIPLICATION

You may recall from algebra that when multiplying two expressions you use the FOIL method: **First, Outer, Inner, Last:**

$$(x + y)(x + y) = xx + xy + xy + yy$$

Simplifying the right side yields $(x + y)(x + y) = x^2 + 2xy + y^2$. For the product $(x - y)(x - y)$ we get $(x - y)(x - y) = x^2 - 2xy + y^2$. These types of products occur often, so it is worthwhile to memorize the formulas. Nevertheless, you should still learn the FOIL method of multiplying because the formulas do not apply in all cases.

Examples (FOIL):

$$(2 - y)(x - y^2) = 2x - 2y^2 - xy + yy^2 = 2x - 2y^2 - xy + y^3$$

$$\left(\frac{1}{x} - y\right)\left(x - \frac{1}{y}\right) = \frac{1}{x}x - \frac{1}{x}\frac{1}{y} - xy + y\frac{1}{y} = 1 - \frac{1}{xy} - xy + 1 = 2 - \frac{1}{xy} - xy$$

$$\left(\frac{1}{2} - y\right)^2 = \left(\frac{1}{2} - y\right)\left(\frac{1}{2} - y\right) = \left(\frac{1}{2}\right)^2 - 2\left(\frac{1}{2}\right)y + y^2 = \frac{1}{4} - y + y^2$$

DIVISION OF ALGEBRAIC EXPRESSIONS

When dividing algebraic expressions, the following formula is useful:

$$\frac{x + y}{z} = \frac{x}{z} + \frac{y}{z}$$

This formula generalizes to any number of terms.

Examples:

$$\frac{x^2 + y}{x} = \frac{x^2}{x} + \frac{y}{x} = x^{2-1} + \frac{y}{x} = x + \frac{y}{x}$$

$$\frac{x^2 + 2y - x^3}{x^2} = \frac{x^2}{x^2} + \frac{2y}{x^2} - \frac{x^3}{x^2} = x^{2-2} + \frac{2y}{x^2} - x^{3-2} = x^0 + \frac{2y}{x^2} - x = 1 + \frac{2y}{x^2} - x$$

When there is more than a single variable in the denomination, we usually factor the expression and then cancel, instead of using the above formula.

Example 2: $\dfrac{x^2 - 2x + 1}{x - 1} =$

    (A) $x + 1$ (B) $-x - 1$ (C) $-x + 1$ (D) $x - 1$ (E) $x - 2$

$\dfrac{x^2 - 2x + 1}{x - 1} = \dfrac{(x - 1)(x - 1)}{x - 1} = x - 1$. The answer is (D).

Problem Set Q:

1. $\left(x^2 + 2\right)\left(x - x^3\right) =$

    (A) $x^4 - x^2 + 2$ (B) $-x^5 - x^3 + 2x$ (C) $x^5 - 2x$ (D) $3x^3 + 2x$ (E) $x^5 + x^3 + 2x$

2. $-2\left(3 - x\left[\dfrac{5 + y - 2}{x}\right] - 7 + 2 \cdot 3^2\right) =$

    (A) $2y - 11$ (B) $2y + 1$ (C) $x - 2$ (D) $x + 22$ (E) $2y - 22$

3. For all real numbers a and b, where $a \cdot b \neq 0$, let $a \lozenge b = ab - 1$, which of the following must be true?

    I. $a \lozenge b = b \lozenge a$

    II. $\dfrac{a \lozenge a}{a} = 1 \lozenge 1$

    III. $(a \lozenge b) \lozenge c = a \lozenge (b \lozenge c)$

    (A) I only   (B) II only   (C) III only   (D) I and II only   (E) I and III only

4. $\left(x + \dfrac{1}{2}\right)^2 - (2x - 4)^2 =$

    (A) $-3x^2 - 15x + \dfrac{65}{4}$ (B) $3x^2 + 16x$ (C) $-3x^2 + 17x - \dfrac{63}{4}$ (D) $5x^2 + \dfrac{65}{4}$ (E) $3x^2$

5. If $x = 2$ and $y = -3$, then $y^2 - \left(x - \left[y + \dfrac{1}{2}\right]\right) - 2 \cdot 3 =$

    (A) $-39/2$ (B) $-3/2$ (C) 0   (D) 31   (E) 43

6. $4(xy)^3 + \left(x^3 - y^3\right)^2 =$

    (A) $x^3 - y^3$ (B) $\left(x^2 + y^2\right)^3$ (C) $\left(x^3 + y^3\right)^3$ (D) $\left(x^3 - y^3\right)^2$ (E) $\left(x^3 + y^3\right)^2$

7. If $\dfrac{a}{b} = -\dfrac{2}{3}$, then $\dfrac{b - a}{a} =$

    (A) $-5/2$ (B) $-5/3$ (C) $-1/3$ (D) 0   (E) 7

8. The operation $*$ is defined for all non-zero x and y by the equation $x * y = \dfrac{x}{y}$. Then the expression $(x - 2)^2 * x$ is equal to

    (A) $x - 4 + \dfrac{4}{x}$ (B) $4 + \dfrac{4}{x}$ (C) $\dfrac{4}{x}$ (D) $1 + \dfrac{4}{x}$ (E) $1 - 4x + \dfrac{4}{x}$

9. $\left(2 + \sqrt{7}\right)\left(4 - \sqrt{7}\right)(-2x) =$

    (A) $78x - 4x\sqrt{7}$ (B) $\sqrt{7}x$ (C) $-2x - 4x\sqrt{7}$ (D) $-2x$ (E) $4x\sqrt{7}$

10. If the operation $*$ is defined for all non-zero x and y by the equation $x * y = (xy)^2$, then $(x * y) * z =$

    (A) $x^2 y^2 z^2$ (B) $x^4 y^4 z^2$ (C) $x^2 y^4 z^2$ (D) $x^4 y^2 z^2$ (E) $x^4 y^4 z^4$

11.   If $p = z + 1/z$ and $q = z - 1/z$, where z is a real number not equal to zero, then $(p + q)(p - q) =$

    (A)   2
    (B)   4
    (C) z^2
    (D) $\dfrac{1}{z^2}$
    (E) $z^2 - \dfrac{1}{z^2}$

12.   If $x^2 + y^2 = xy$, then $(x + y)^4 =$

    (A) xy
    (B) $x^2 y^2$
    (C) $9x^2 y^2$
    (D) $\left(x^2 + y^2\right)^2$
    (E) $x^4 + y^4$

13. $(2 + x)(2 + y) - (2 + x) - (2 + y) =$

    (A) $2y$
    (B) xy
    (C) $x + y$
    (D) $x - y$
    (E) $x + y + xy$

14.   If $x^2 + y^2 = 2ab$ and $2xy = a^2 + b^2$, with $a, b, x, y > 0$, then $x + y =$

    (A) ab
    (B) $a - b$
    (C) $a + b$
    (D) $\sqrt{a^2 + b^2}$
    (E) $\sqrt{a^2 - b^2}$

Answers and Solutions to Problem Set Q

1. $\left(x^2+2\right)\left(x-x^3\right)=x^2x-x^2x^3+2x-2x^3=x^3-x^5+2x-2x^3=-x^5-x^3+2x$. Thus, the answer is (B).

2.
$$-2\left(3-x\left[\frac{5+y-2}{x}\right]-7+2\cdot3^2\right)=$$
$$-2\left(3-x\left[\frac{3+y}{x}\right]-7+2\cdot3^2\right)=$$
$$-2\left(3-[3+y]-7+2\cdot3^2\right)=$$
$$-2\left(3-3-y-7+2\cdot3^2\right)=$$
$$-2(3-3-y-7+2\cdot9)=$$
$$-2(3-3-y-7+18)=$$
$$-2(-y+11)=$$
$$2y-22$$

The answer is (E).

3. $a\Diamond b=ab-1=ba-1=b\Diamond a$. Thus, I is true, which eliminates (B) and (C).

$\dfrac{a\Diamond a}{a}=\dfrac{aa-1}{a}\ne1\cdot1-1=1-1=0=1\Diamond1$. Thus, II is false, which eliminates (D).

$(a\Diamond b)\Diamond c=(ab-1)\Diamond c=(ab-1)c-1=abc-c-1\ne a\Diamond(bc-1)=a(bc-1)-1=abc-a-1=a\Diamond(b\Diamond c)$. Thus, III is false, which eliminates (E). Hence, the answer is (A).

4.
$$\left(x+\frac{1}{2}\right)^2-(2x-4)^2=$$
$$x^2+2x\frac{1}{2}+\left(\frac{1}{2}\right)^2-\left[(2x)^2-2(2x)4+4^2\right]=$$
$$x^2+x+\frac{1}{4}-4x^2+16x-16=$$
$$-3x^2+17x-\frac{63}{4}$$

Hence, the answer is (C).

5.
$$y^2-\left(x-\left[y+\frac{1}{2}\right]\right)-2\cdot3=$$
$$(-3)^2-\left(2-\left[-3+\frac{1}{2}\right]\right)-2\cdot3=$$
$$(-3)^2-\left(2-\left[-\frac{5}{2}\right]\right)-2\cdot3=$$
$$(-3)^2-\left(2+\frac{5}{2}\right)-2\cdot3=$$
$$(-3)^2-\frac{9}{2}-2\cdot3=$$
$$9-\frac{9}{2}-2\cdot3=$$

$$9 - \frac{9}{2} - 6 =$$

$$3 - \frac{9}{2} =$$

$$-\frac{3}{2}$$

The answer is (B).

6.

$$4(xy)^3 + \left(x^3 - y^3\right)^2 =$$

$$4x^3 y^3 + \left(x^3\right)^2 - 2x^3 y^3 + \left(y^3\right)^2 =$$

$$\left(x^3\right)^2 + 2x^3 y^3 + \left(y^3\right)^2 =$$

$$\left(x^3 + y^3\right)^2$$

The answer is (E).

7.
$$\frac{b-a}{a} = \frac{b}{a} - \frac{a}{a} = \frac{b}{a} - 1 = \frac{-3}{2} - 1 = \frac{-3}{2} - \frac{2}{2} = \frac{-3-2}{2} = \frac{-5}{2}.$$ The answer is (A).

8. $(x-2)^2 * x = \dfrac{(x-2)^2}{x} = \dfrac{x^2 - 4x + 4}{x} = \dfrac{x^2}{x} - \dfrac{4x}{x} + \dfrac{4}{x} = x - 4 + \dfrac{4}{x}.$ The answer is (A).

9.

$$\left(2 + \sqrt{7}\right)\left(4 - \sqrt{7}\right)(-2x) =$$

$$\left(2 \cdot 4 - 2\sqrt{7} + 4\sqrt{7} - \sqrt{7}\sqrt{7}\right)(-2x) =$$

$$\left(8 + 2\sqrt{7} - 7\right)(-2x) =$$

$$\left(1 + 2\sqrt{7}\right)(-2x) =$$

$$1(-2x) + 2\sqrt{7}(-2x) =$$

$$-2x - 4x\sqrt{7}$$

The answer is (C).

10. $(x * y) * z = (xy)^2 * z = \left((xy)^2 z\right)^2 = \left((xy)^2\right)^2 z^2 = (xy)^4 z^2 = x^4 y^4 z^2.$ The answer is (B).

11. Since we are given that $p = z + 1/z$ and $q = z - 1/z$,

$$p + q = (z + 1/z) + (z - 1/z) = z + 1/z + z - 1/z = 2z.$$
$$p - q = (z + 1/z) - (z - 1/z) = z + 1/z - z + 1/z = 2/z.$$

Therefore, $(p + q)(p - q) = (2z)(2/z) = 4.$ The answer is (B).

12. Adding $2xy$ to both sides of the equation $x^2 + y^2 = xy$ yields

$$x^2 + y^2 + 2xy = 3xy$$
$$(x + y)^2 = 3xy \qquad \text{from the formula } (x + y)^2 = x^2 + 2xy + y^2$$

Squaring both sides of this equation yields

$$(x + y)^4 = (3xy)^2 = 9x^2y^2$$

The answer is (C).

13. Solution:

$$(2 + x)(2 + y) - (2 + x) - (2 + y) =$$
$$4 + 2y + 2x + xy - 2 - x - 2 - y =$$
$$x + y + xy$$

The answer is (E).

14. Writing the system of equations vertically yields

$$x^2 + y^2 = 2ab$$
$$2xy = a^2 + b^2$$

Adding the equations yields

$$x^2 + 2xy + y^2 = a^2 + 2ab + b^2$$

Applying the Perfect Square Trinomial formula to both the sides of the equation yields

$$(x + y)^2 = (a + b)^2$$
$$x + y = a + b \qquad \text{by taking the square root of both sides and noting all numbers are positive}$$

The answer is (C).

Percents

Problems involving percent are common on the ACT. The word *percent* means "divided by one hundred."
When you see the word "percent," or the symbol %, remember it means $\frac{1}{100}$. For example,

$$25 \text{ percent}$$
$$\downarrow \quad \downarrow$$
$$25 \times \frac{1}{100} = \frac{1}{4}$$

To convert a decimal into a percent, move the decimal point two places to the right. For example,

$$0.25 = 25\%$$
$$0.023 = 2.3\%$$
$$1.3 = 130\%$$

Conversely, to convert a percent into a decimal, move the decimal point two places to the left. For example,

$$47\% = .47$$
$$3.4\% = .034$$
$$175\% = 1.75$$

To convert a fraction into a percent, first change it into a decimal (by dividing the denominator [bottom] into the numerator [top]) and then move the decimal point two places to the right. For example,

$$\frac{7}{8} = 0.875 = 87.5\%$$

Conversely, to convert a percent into a fraction, first change it into a decimal and then change the decimal into a fraction. For example,

$$80\% = .80 = \frac{80}{100} = \frac{4}{5}$$

Following are the most common fractional equivalents of percents:

$$33\frac{1}{3}\% = \frac{1}{3} \qquad\qquad 20\% = \frac{1}{5}$$

$$66\frac{1}{3}\% = \frac{2}{3} \qquad\qquad 40\% = \frac{2}{5}$$

$$25\% = \frac{1}{4} \qquad\qquad 60\% = \frac{3}{5}$$

$$50\% = \frac{1}{2} \qquad\qquad 80\% = \frac{4}{5}$$

Note!   **Percent problems often require you to translate a sentence into a mathematical equation.**

Example 1:   What percent of 25 is 5?
        (A) 10%   (B) 20%   (C) 30%   (D) 35%   (E) 40%

Translate the sentence into a mathematical equation as follows:

$$\begin{array}{cccccc} \text{What} & \text{percent} & \text{of} & 25 & \text{is} & 5 \\ \downarrow & \downarrow & \downarrow & \downarrow & \downarrow & \downarrow \\ x & \dfrac{1}{100} & \cdot & 25 & = & 5 \end{array}$$

$$\frac{25}{100}x = 5$$

$$\frac{1}{4}x = 5$$

$$x = 20$$

The answer is (B).

Example 2:   2 is 10% of what number
        (A) 10   (B) 12   (C) 20   (D) 24   (E) 32

Translate the sentence into a mathematical equation as follows:

$$\begin{array}{cccccc} 2 & \text{is} & 10 & \% & \text{of} & \underline{\text{what number}} \\ \downarrow & \downarrow & \downarrow & \downarrow & \downarrow & \downarrow \\ 2 & = & 10 & \dfrac{1}{100} & \cdot & x \end{array}$$

$$2 = \frac{10}{100}x$$

$$2 = \frac{1}{10}x$$

$$20 = x$$

The answer is (C).

Example 3:   What percent of *a* is 3*a* ?
        (A) 100%   (B) 150%   (C) 200%   (D) 300%   (E) 350%

Translate the sentence into a mathematical equation as follows:

$$\begin{array}{cccccc} \text{What} & \text{percent} & \text{of} & a & \text{is} & 3a \\ \downarrow & \downarrow & \downarrow & \downarrow & \downarrow & \downarrow \\ x & \dfrac{1}{100} & \cdot & a & = & 3a \end{array}$$

$$\frac{x}{100} \cdot a = 3a$$

$$\frac{x}{100} = 3 \quad \text{(by canceling the } a\text{'s)}$$

$$x = 300$$

The answer is (D).

Example 4:   If there are 15 boys and 25 girls in a class, what percent of the class is boys?

    (A)   10%
    (B)   15%
    (C)   18%
    (D)   25%
    (E)   37.5%

The total number of students in the class is $15 + 25 = 40$. Now, translate the main part of the sentence into a mathematical equation:

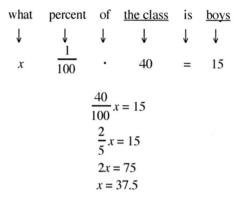

what	percent	of	the class	is	boys
↓	↓	↓	↓	↓	↓
x	$\dfrac{1}{100}$	$\cdot$	40	$=$	15

$$\frac{40}{100}x = 15$$
$$\frac{2}{5}x = 15$$
$$2x = 75$$
$$x = 37.5$$

The answer is (E).

Note!   **Often you will need to find the percent of increase (or decrease). To find it, calculate the increase (or decrease) and divide it by the original amount:**

$$\textbf{Percent of change: } \frac{Amount\ of\ change}{Original\ amount} \times 100\%$$

Example 5:   The population of a town was 12,000 in 1980 and 16,000 in 1990. What was the percent increase in the population of the town during this period?

    (A) $33\dfrac{1}{3}\%$
    (B)   50%
    (C)   75%
    (D)   80%
    (E)   120%

The population increased from 12,000 to 16,000. Hence, the change in population was 4,000. Now, translate the main part of the sentence into a mathematical equation:

Percent of change:
$$\frac{Amount\ of\ change}{Original\ amount} \times 100\% =$$
$$\frac{4000}{12000} \times 100\% =$$
$$\frac{1}{3} \times 100\% = \quad \text{(by canceling 4000)}$$
$$33\frac{1}{3}\%$$

The answer is (A).

Problem Set R:

1.   John spent $25, which is 15 percent of his monthly wage. What is his monthly wage?

(A) $80   (B) 166\frac{2}{3}$ (C) $225   (D) $312.5   (E) $375

2.   If a = 4b, what percent of 2a is 2b?

(A) 10%   (B) 20%   (C) 25%   (D) 26%   (E) 40%

3.   If $p = 5q > 0$, then 40 percent of $3p$ equals

(A) 6q   (B) 5.52q   (C) 13.3q   (D) 9q   (E) 20.1q

4.   A jar contains 24 blue balls and 40 red balls. Which one of the following is 50% of the blue balls?

(A) 10   (B) 11   (C) 12   (D) 13   (E) 14

5.   In a company with 180 employees, 108 of the employees are female. What percent of the employees are male?

(A) 5%   (B) 25%   (C) 35%   (D) 40%   (E) 60%

6.   John bought a shirt, a pair of pants, and a pair of shoes, which cost $10, $20, and $30, respectively. What percent of the total expense was spent for the pants?

(A) $16\frac{2}{3}$%   (B) 20%   (C) 30%   (D) $33\frac{1}{3}$%   (E) 60%

7.   Last year Jenny was 5 feet tall, and this year she is 5 feet 6 inches. What is the percent increase of her height?

(A) 5%   (B) 10%   (C) 15%   (D) 20%   (E) 40%

8.   Last month the price of a particular pen was $1.20. This month the price of the same pen is $1.50. What is the percent increase in the price of the pen?

(A) 5%   (B) 10%   (C) 25%   (D) 30%   (E) $33\frac{1}{3}$%

9.   Stella paid $1,500 for a computer after receiving a 20 percent discount. What was the price of the computer before the discount?

(A) $300   (B) $1,500   (C) $1,875   (D) $2,000   (E) $3,000

10.   A town has a population growth rate of 10% per year. The population in 1990 was 2000. What was the population in 1992?

(A) 1600   (B) 2200   (C) 2400   (D) 2420   (E) 4000

11.   In a class of 200 students, forty percent are girls. Twenty-five percent of the boys and 10 percent of the girls signed up for a tour to Washington DC. What percent of the class signed up for the tour?

(A) 19%   (B) 23%   (C) 25%   (D) 27%   (E) 35%

12.   If 15% of a number is 4.5, then 45% of the same number is

(A) 1.5   (B) 3.5   (C) 13.5   (D) 15   (E) 45

Answers and Solutions to Problem Set R

1.   Consider the first sentence: John spent \$25, which is 15 percent of his monthly wage. Now, translate the main part of the sentence into a mathematical equation as follows:

25	is	15	%	of	his monthly wage
↓	↓	↓	↓	↓	↓
25	=	15	$\frac{1}{100}$	·	x

$$25 = \frac{15}{100}x$$

$$2500 = 15x$$

$$x = \frac{2500}{15} = \frac{500}{3} = 166\frac{2}{3}$$

The answer is (B).

2.   Translate the main part of the sentence into a mathematical equation as follows:

What	percent	of	2a	is	2b
↓	↓		↓	↓	↓
x	$\frac{1}{100}$	·	$2a$	=	$2b$

$$\frac{x}{100} \cdot 2a = 2b$$

$$\frac{x}{100} \cdot 2(4b) = 2b \qquad \text{(substituting } a = 4b)$$

$$\frac{x}{100} \cdot 8 = 2 \qquad \text{(canceling } b \text{ from both sides)}$$

$$\frac{8x}{100} = 2$$

$$8x = 200$$

$$x = 25$$

The answer is (C).

Remark: You can substitute $b = a/4$ instead of $a = 4b$. Whichever letter you substitute, you will get the same answer. However, depending on the question, one substitution may be easier than another.

3.   Since more than one letter is used in this question, we need to substitute one of the letters for the other to minimize the number of unknown quantities (letters).

40	percent	of	3p
↓	↓	↓	↓
40	$\frac{1}{100}$	×	$3p$

$$= \frac{40}{100} \times 3p$$

$$= \frac{40}{100} \times 3(5q) \qquad \text{(substituting } p = 5q)$$

$$= \frac{600q}{100}$$

$$= 6q$$

The answer is (A).

4.

50	%	of	the blue balls
↓	↓	↓	↓
50	$\dfrac{1}{100}$	×	24

$= \dfrac{50 \times 24}{100}$

$= \dfrac{1200}{100}$

$= 12$

The answer is (C).

5.   Since female employees are 108 out of 180, there are $180 - 108 = 72$ male employees. Now, translate the main part of the sentence into a mathematical equation as follows:

What	percent	of	the employees	are	male
↓	↓	↓	↓	↓	↓
x	$\dfrac{1}{100}$	·	180	=	72

$\dfrac{180}{100}x = 72$

$\dfrac{100}{180} \times \dfrac{180}{100}x = \dfrac{100}{180} \times 72$

$x = 40$

The answer is (D).

6.   The total expense is the sum of expenses for the shirt, pants, and shoes, which is $10 + $20 + $30 = $60. Now, translate the main part of the sentence into a mathematical equation:

What	percent	of	the total expense	was spent for	the pants
↓	↓	↓	↓	↓	↓
x	$\dfrac{1}{100}$	·	60	=	20

$\dfrac{60}{100}x = 20$

$60x = 2000$ (by multiplying both sides of the equation by 100)

$x = \dfrac{2000}{60}$ (by dividing both sides of the equation by 60)

$x = \dfrac{100}{3} = 33\dfrac{1}{3}$

The answer is (D).

7. First, express all the numbers in the same units (inches):

The original height is $5 \text{ feet} = 5 \text{ feet} \times \dfrac{12 \text{ inches}}{1 \text{ feet}} = 60 \text{ inches}$

The change in height is $(5 \text{ feet } 6 \text{ inches}) - (5 \text{ feet}) = 6 \text{ inches}$.
Now, use the formula for percent of change.

Percent of change: $\dfrac{\textit{Amount of change}}{\textit{Original amount}} \times 100\% =$

$\dfrac{6}{60} \times 100\% =$

$\dfrac{1}{10} \times 100\% =$ (by canceling 6)

10%

The answer is (B).

8. The change in price is $\$1.50 - \$1.20 = \$.30$. Now, use the formula for percent of change.

$\dfrac{\textit{Amount of change}}{\textit{Original amount}} \times 100\% =$

$\dfrac{.30}{1.20} \times 100\% =$

$\dfrac{1}{4} \times 100\% =$

25%

The answer is (C).

9. Let x be the price before the discount. Since Stella received a 20 percent discount, she paid 80 percent of the original price. Thus, 80 percent of the original price is $\$1,500$. Now, translate this sentence into a mathematical equation:

80	percent	of	the original price	is	$\$1,500$
↓	↓	↓	↓	↓	↓
80	$\dfrac{1}{100}$	·	x	=	1500

$\dfrac{80}{100} x = 1500$

$\dfrac{100}{80} \dfrac{80}{100} x = \dfrac{100}{80} 1500$ (by multiplying both sides by the reciprocal of $\dfrac{80}{100}$)

$x = 1875$

The answer is (C).

10. Since the population increased at a rate of 10% per year, the population of any year is the population of the previous year + 10% of that same year. Hence, the population in 1991 is the population of 1990 + 10% of the population of 1990:

$$2000 + 10\% \text{ of } 2000 =$$
$$2000 + 200 =$$
$$2200$$

Similarly, the population in 1992 is the population of 1991 + 10% of the population of 1991:

$$2200 + 10\% \text{ of } 2200 =$$
$$2200 + 220 =$$
$$2420$$

Hence, the answer is (D).

11. Let g be the number of girls, and b the number of boys. Calculate the number of girls in the class:

<u>Girls</u>	are	40	percent	of	<u>the class</u>
↓	↓	↓	↓	↓	↓
g	=	40	$\frac{1}{100}$	×	200

$$g = \frac{40}{100} \times 200 = 80$$

The number of boys equals the total number of students minus the number of girls:

$$b = 200 - 80 = 120$$

Next, calculate the number of boys and girls who signed up for the tour:

25 percent of boys ($\frac{25}{100} \times 120 = 30$) and 10 percent of girls ($\frac{10}{100} \times 80 = 8$) signed up for the tour. Thus, $30 + 8 = 38$ students signed up. Now, translate the main part of the question with a little modification into a mathematical equation:

What	percent	of	<u>the class</u>	is	<u>the students who signed up for the tour</u>
↓	↓	↓	↓	↓	↓
x	$\frac{1}{100}$	·	200	=	38

$$\frac{200}{100}x = 38$$

$$x = 19$$

The answer is (A).

12. Let x be the number of which the percentage is being calculated. Then 15% of the number x is $.15x$. We are told this is equal to 4.5. Hence,

$$.15x = 4.5$$

Solving this equation by dividing both sides by .15 yields

$$x = \frac{4.5}{.15} = 30$$

Now, 45% of 30 is

$$.45(30)$$

Multiplying out this expression gives 13.5. The answer is (C).

Graphs

Questions involving graphs are common on the ACT. Rarely do these questions involve any significant calculating. Usually, the solution is merely a matter of interpreting the graph.

Questions 1-4 refer to the following graphs.

SALES AND EARNINGS OF CONSOLIDATED CONGLOMERATE

Sales
(in millions of dollars)

Earnings
(in millions of dollars)

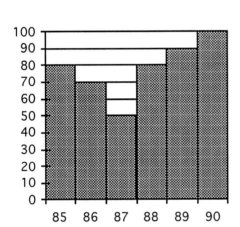
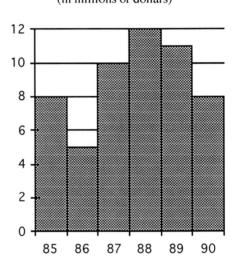

Note: Figure drawn to scale.

1. During which year was the company's earnings 10 percent of its sales?

    (A) 85   (B) 86   (C) 87   (D) 88   (E) 90

Reading from the graph, we see that in 1985 the company's earnings were $8 million and its sales were $80 million. This gives

$$\frac{8}{10} = \frac{1}{10} = \frac{10}{100} = 10\%$$

The answer is (A).

2. During the years 1986 through 1988, what were the average earnings per year?

    (A) 6 million   (B) 7.5 million   (C) 9 million   (D) 10 million   (E) 27 million

The graph yields the following information:

Year	Earnings
1986	$5 million
1987	$10 million
1988	$12 million

Forming the average yields $\dfrac{5+10+12}{3} = \dfrac{27}{3} = 9$. The answer is (C).

3.   In which year did sales increase by the greatest percentage over the previous year?

(A) 86   (B) 87   (C) 88   (D) 89   (E) 90

To find the percentage increase (or decrease), divide the numerical change by the original amount. This yields

Year	Percentage increase
86	$\dfrac{70-80}{80} = \dfrac{-10}{80} = \dfrac{-1}{8} = -12.5\%$
87	$\dfrac{50-70}{70} = \dfrac{-20}{70} = \dfrac{-2}{7} \approx -29\%$
88	$\dfrac{80-50}{50} = \dfrac{30}{50} = \dfrac{3}{5} = 60\%$
89	$\dfrac{90-80}{80} = \dfrac{10}{80} = \dfrac{1}{8} = 12.5\%$
90	$\dfrac{100-90}{90} = \dfrac{10}{90} = \dfrac{1}{9} \approx 11\%$

The largest number in the right-hand column, 60%, corresponds to the year 1988. The answer is (C).

4.   If Consolidated Conglomerate's earnings are less than or equal to 10 percent of sales during a year, then the stockholders must take a dividend cut at the end of the year. In how many years did the stockholders of Consolidated Conglomerate suffer a dividend cut?

(A) None   (B) One   (C) Two   (D) Three   (E) Four

Calculating 10 percent of the sales for each year yields

Year	10% of Sales (millions)	Earnings (millions)
85	$.10 \times 80 = 8$	8
86	$.10 \times 70 = 7$	5
87	$.10 \times 50 = 5$	10
88	$.10 \times 80 = 8$	12
89	$.10 \times 90 = 9$	11
90	$.10 \times 100 = 10$	8

Comparing the right columns shows that earnings were 10 percent or less of sales in 1985, 1986, and 1990. The answer is (D).

Problem Set S:

Questions 1–5 refer to the following graphs.

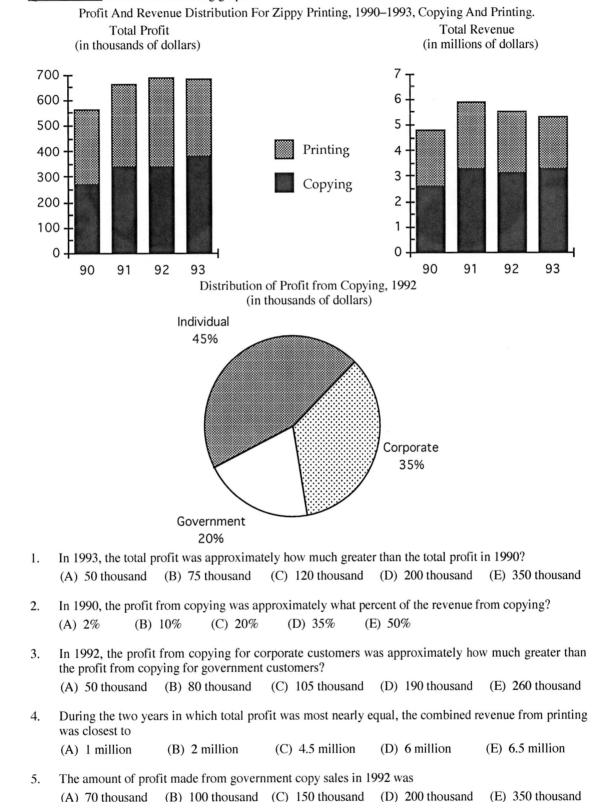

Profit And Revenue Distribution For Zippy Printing, 1990–1993, Copying And Printing.

Total Profit
(in thousands of dollars)

Total Revenue
(in millions of dollars)

Distribution of Profit from Copying, 1992
(in thousands of dollars)

1. In 1993, the total profit was approximately how much greater than the total profit in 1990?

    (A) 50 thousand   (B) 75 thousand   (C) 120 thousand   (D) 200 thousand   (E) 350 thousand

2. In 1990, the profit from copying was approximately what percent of the revenue from copying?

    (A) 2%   (B) 10%   (C) 20%   (D) 35%   (E) 50%

3. In 1992, the profit from copying for corporate customers was approximately how much greater than the profit from copying for government customers?

    (A) 50 thousand   (B) 80 thousand   (C) 105 thousand   (D) 190 thousand   (E) 260 thousand

4. During the two years in which total profit was most nearly equal, the combined revenue from printing was closest to

    (A) 1 million   (B) 2 million   (C) 4.5 million   (D) 6 million   (E) 6.5 million

5. The amount of profit made from government copy sales in 1992 was

    (A) 70 thousand   (B) 100 thousand   (C) 150 thousand   (D) 200 thousand   (E) 350 thousand

<u>Questions 6–10</u> refer to the following graphs.

DISTRIBUTION OF CRIMINAL ACTIVITY BY CATEGORY OF CRIME FOR COUNTRY X IN 1990
AND PROJECTED FOR 2000.

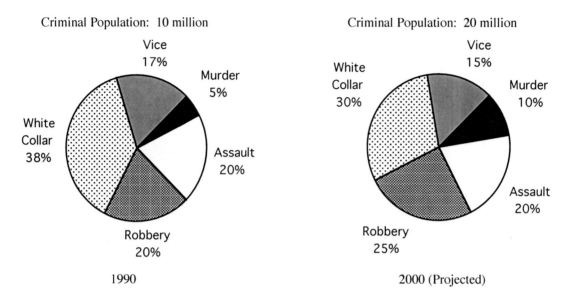

6.   What is the projected number of white-collar criminals in 2000?

    (A)   1 million
    (B)   3.8 million
    (C)   6 million
    (D)   8 million
    (E)   10 million

7.   The ratio of the number of robbers in 1990 to the number of projected robbers in 2000 is

    (A) 2/5   (B) 3/5   (C) 1   (D) 3/2   (E) 5/2

8.   From 1990 to 2000, there is a projected decrease in the number of criminals for which of the following categories?
    I. Vice
    II. Assault
    III. White Collar
    (A) None   (B) I only   (C) II only   (D) II and III only   (E) I, II, and III

9.   What is the approximate projected percent increase between 1990 and 2000 in the number of criminals involved in vice?

    (A) 25%   (B) 40%   (C) 60%   (D) 75%   (E) 85%

10.   The projected number of Robbers in 2000 will exceed the number of white-collar criminals in 1990 by

    (A) 1.2 million   (B) 2.3 million   (C) 3.4 million   (D) 5.8 million   (E) 7.2 million

Questions 11–15 refer to the following graph.

SALES BY CATEGORY FOR GRAMMERCY PRESS, 1980–1989
(in thousands of books)

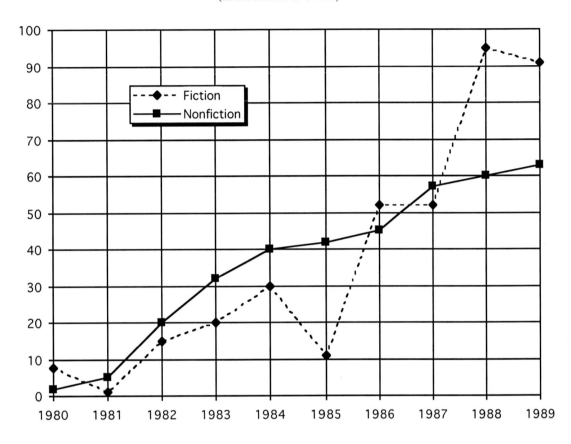

11. In how many years did the sales of nonfiction titles exceed the sales of fiction titles ?

     (A) 2   (B) 3   (C) 4   (D) 5   (E) 6

12. Which of the following best approximates the amount by which the increase in sales of fiction titles from 1985 to 1986 exceeded the increase in sales of fiction titles from 1983 to 1984?

     (A)   31.5   thousand
     (B)   40   thousand
     (C)   49.3   thousand
     (D)   50.9   thousand
     (E)   68   thousand

13. Which of the following periods showed a continual increase in the sales of fiction titles?

     (A) 1980–1982   (B) 1982–1984   (C) 1984–1986   (D) 1986–1988   (E) 1987–1989

14. What was the approximate average number of sales of fiction titles from 1984 to 1988?

     (A) 15 thousand   (B) 30 thousand   (C) 40 thousand   (D) 48 thousand   (E) 60 thousand

15. By approximately what percent did the sale of nonfiction titles increase from 1984 to 1987?

     (A) 42%   (B) 50%   (C) 70%   (D) 90%   (E) 110%

Questions 16–20 refer to the following graph.

AUTOMOBILE ACCIDENTS IN COUNTRY X: 1990 TO 1994
(in ten thousands)

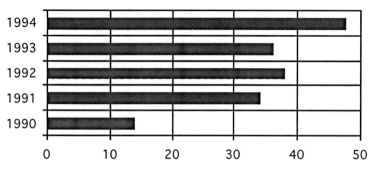

CARS IN COUNTRY X
(in millions)

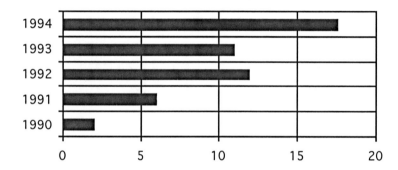

16. Approximately how many millions of cars were in Country X in 1994?

   (A) 1.0   (B) 4.7   (C) 9.0   (D) 15.5   (E) 17.5

17. The amount by which the number of cars in 1990 exceeded the number of accidents in 1991 was approximately

   (A) 0.3 million   (B) 0.7 million   (C) 1.0 million   (D) 1.7 million   (E) 2.5 million

18. The number of accidents in 1993 was approximately what percentage of the number of cars?

   (A) 1%   (B) 1.5%   (C) 3%   (D) 5%   (E) 10%

19. In which of the following years will the number of accidents exceed 500 thousand?

   (A)   1994
   (B)   1995
   (C)   1998
   (D)   2000
   (E)   It cannot be determined from the information given.

20. If no car in 1993 was involved in more than four accidents, what is the minimum number of cars that could have been in accidents in 1993?

   (A) 50 thousand   (B) 60 thousand   (C) 70 thousand   (D) 80 thousand   (E) 90 thousand

Questions 21–25 refer to the following graphs.

DISTRIBUTION OF IMPORTS AND EXPORTS FOR COUNTRY X IN 1994.

Imports
200 million items

Exports
100 million items

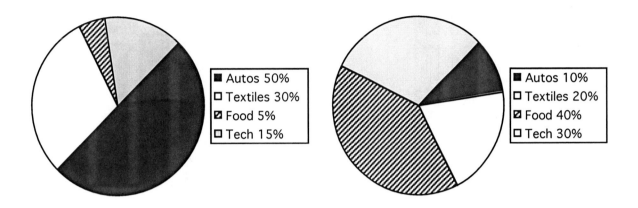

■ Autos 50%
□ Textiles 30%
▨ Food 5%
□ Tech 15%

■ Autos 10%
□ Textiles 20%
▨ Food 40%
□ Tech 30%

21. How many autos did Country X export in 1994?

   (A)   10 million
   (B)   15 million
   (C)   16 million
   (D)   20 million
   (E)   30 million

22. In how many categories did the total number of items (import and export) exceed 75 million?

   (A) 1   (B) 2   (C) 3   (D) 4   (E) none

23. The ratio of the number of technology items imported in 1994 to the number of textile items exported in 1994 is

   (A) 1/3   (B) 3/5   (C) 1   (D) 6/5   (E) 3/2

24. If in 1995 the number of autos exported was 16 million, then the percent increase from 1994 in the number of autos exported is

   (A) 40%   (B) 47%   (C) 50%   (D) 60%   (E) 65%

25. In 1994, if twice as many autos imported to Country X broke down as autos exported from Country X and 20 percent of the exported autos broke down, what percent of the imported autos broke down?

   (A) 1%   (B) 1.5%   (C) 2%   (D) 4%   (E) 5.5%

Answers and Solutions to Problem Set S

Questions 1–5 refer to the following graphs.

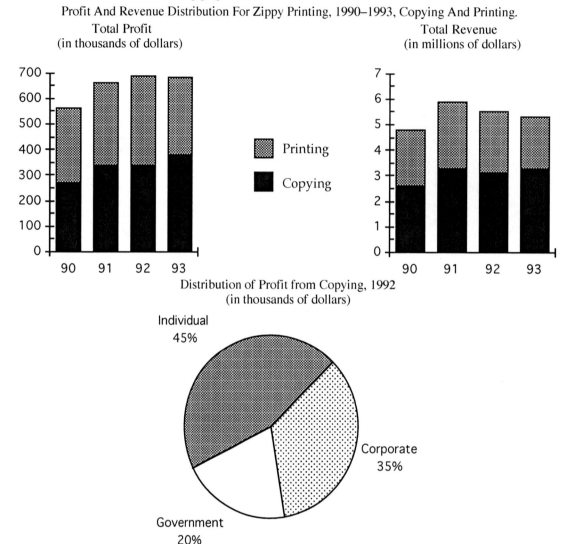

Profit And Revenue Distribution For Zippy Printing, 1990–1993, Copying And Printing.

1. In 1993, the total profit was approximately how much greater than the total profit in 1990?

    (A) 50 thousand   (B) 75 thousand   (C) 120 thousand   (D) 200 thousand   (E) 350 thousand

Remember, rarely does a graph question involve significant computation. For this question, we need merely to read the bar graph. The Total Profit graph shows that in 1993 approximately 680 thousand was earned, and in 1990 approximately 560 thousand was earned. Subtracting these numbers yields 680 – 560 = 120. The answer is (C).

2. In 1990, the profit from copying was approximately what percent of the revenue from copying?

    (A) 2%   (B) 10%   (C) 20%   (D) 35%   (E) 50%

The Total Revenue graph indicates that in 1990 the revenue from copying was about $2,600,000. The Total Profit graph shows the profit from copying in that same year was about $270,000. The profit margin is

$$\frac{\text{Profit}}{\text{Revenue}} = \frac{270,000}{2,600,000} \approx 10\%$$

The answer is (B).

3. In 1992, the profit from copying for corporate customers was approximately how much greater than the profit from copying for government customers?

    (A) 50 thousand (B) 80 thousand (C) 105 thousand (D) 190 thousand (E) 260 thousand

From the chart, the profit in 1992 was approximately $700,000 of which 35% x $700,000 = $245,000 was from corporate customers and 20% x $700,000 = $140,000 was from government customers. Subtracting these amounts yields $245,000 – $140,000 = $105,000. The answer is (C).

4. During the two years in which total profit was most nearly equal, the combined revenue from printing was closest to

    (A) 1 million (B) 2 million (C) 4.5 million (D) 6 million (E) 6.5 million

The Total Profit graph shows that 1992 and 1993 are clearly the two years in which total profit was most nearly equal. Turning to the Total Revenue graph, we see that in 1992 the revenue from printing sales was approximately 2.5 million, and that in 1993 the revenue from printing sales was approximately 2 million. This gives a total of 4.5 million in total printing sales revenue for the period. The answer is (C).

5. The amount of profit made from government copy sales in 1992 was

    (A) 70 thousand (B) 100 thousand (C) 150 thousand (D) 200 thousand (E) 350 thousand

The Total Profit graph shows that Zippy Printing earned about $340,000 from copying in 1992. The Pie Chart indicates that 20% of this was earned from government sales. Multiplying these numbers gives $340,000 \times 20\% \approx \$70,000$. The answer is (A).

Questions 6–10 refer to the following graphs.

DISTRIBUTION OF CRIMINAL ACTIVITY BY CATEGORY OF CRIME FOR COUNTRY X IN 1990 AND PROJECTED FOR 2000.

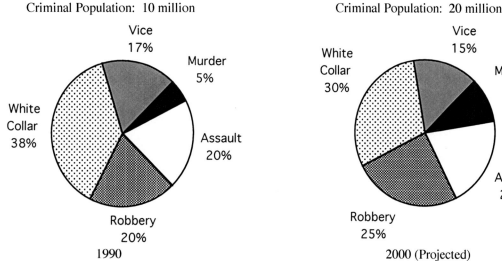

Criminal Population: 10 million

1990

Criminal Population: 20 million

2000 (Projected)

6. What is the projected number of white-collar criminals in 2000?

    (A) 1 million
    (B) 3.8 million
    (C) 6 million
    (D) 8 million
    (E) 10 million

From the projected-crime graph, we see that the criminal population will be 20 million and of these 30 percent are projected to be involved in white-collar crime. Hence, the number of white-collar criminals is $(30\%)(20 \; million) = (.30)(20 \; million) = 6 \; million$. The answer is (C).

7.   The ratio of the number of robbers in 1990 to the number of projected robbers in 2000 is

    (A) $\dfrac{2}{5}$ (B) $\dfrac{3}{5}$ (C) 1   (D) $\dfrac{3}{2}$ (E) $\dfrac{5}{2}$

In 1990, there were 10 million criminals and 20% were robbers. Thus, the number of robbers in 1990 was
$$(20\%)(10 \text{ million}) = (.20)(10 \text{ million}) = 2 \text{ million}$$
In 2000, there are projected to be 20 million criminals of which 25% are projected to be robbers. Thus, the number of robbers in 2000 is projected to be
$$(25\%)(20 \text{ million}) = (.25)(20 \text{ million}) = 5 \text{ million}$$
Forming the ratio of the above numbers yields
$$\frac{number\ of\ robbers\ in\ 1990}{number\ of\ robbers\ in\ 2000} = \frac{2}{5}$$

The answer is (A).

8.   From 1990 to 2000, there is a projected decrease in the number of criminals for which of the following categories?
    I.   Vice
    II. Assault
    III. White Collar

    (A) None   (B) I only   (C) II only   (D) II and III only   (E) I, II, and III

The following table lists the number of criminals by category for 1990 and 2000 and the projected increase or decrease:

Category	Number in 1990 (millions)	Number in 2000 (millions)	Projected increase (millions)	Projected decrease (millions)
Vice	1.7	3	1.3	None
Assault	2	4	2	None
White Collar	3.8	6	2.2	None

As the table displays, there is a projected increase (not decrease) in all three categories. Hence, the answer is (A).

9.   What is the approximate projected percent increase between 1990 and 2000 in the number of criminals involved in vice?

    (A) 25%   (B) 40%   (C) 60%   (D) 75%   (E) 85%

Remember, to calculate the percentage increase, find the absolute increase and divide it by the original number. Now, in 1990, the number of criminals in vice was 1.7 million, and in 2000 it is projected to be 3 million. The absolute increase is thus:
$$3 - 1.7 = 1.3$$
Hence the projected percent increase in the number of criminals in vice is
$$\frac{absolute\ increase}{original\ number} = \frac{1.3}{1.7} \approx 75\%.$$

The answer is (D).

10.   The projected number of Robbers in 2000 will exceed the number of white-collar criminals in 1990 by

    (A) 1.2 million   (B) 2.3 million   (C) 3.4 million   (D) 5.8 million   (E) 7.2 million

In 1990, the number of white-collar criminals was (38%)(10 million) = 3.8 million. From the projected-crime graph, we see that the criminal population in the year 2000 will be 20 million and of these (25%)(20 million) = 5 million will be robbers. Hence, the projected number of Robbers in 2000 will exceed the number of white-collar criminals in 1990 by 5 – 3.8 = 1.2 million. The answer is (A).

Questions 11–15 refer to the following graph.

SALES BY CATEGORY FOR GRAMMERCY PRESS, 1980–1989
(in thousands of books)

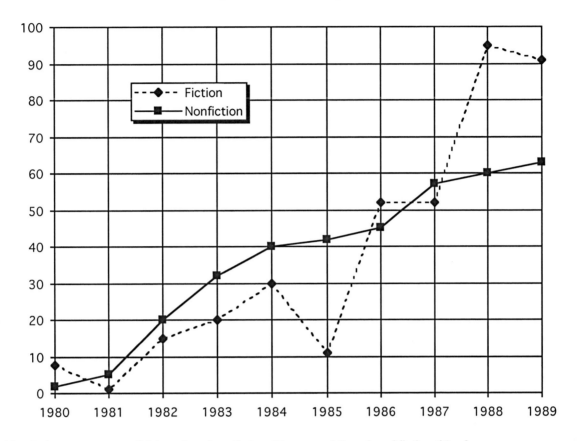

11. In how many years did the sales of nonfiction titles exceed the sales of fiction titles ?

   (A) 2   (B) 3   (C) 4   (D) 5   (E) 6

The graph shows that nonfiction sales exceeded fiction sales in '81, '82, '83, '84, '85, and '87. The answer is (E).

12. Which of the following best approximates the amount by which the increase in sales of fiction titles from 1985 to 1986 exceeded the increase in sales of fiction titles from 1983 to 1984?

   (A) 31.5   thousand
   (B)   40   thousand
   (C) 49.3   thousand
   (D) 50.9   thousand
   (E)   68   thousand

The graph shows that the increase in sales of fiction titles from 1985 to 1986 was approximately 40 thousand and the increase in sales of fiction titles from 1983 to 1984 was approximately 10 thousand. Hence, the difference is 40 – 10 = 30. Choice (A) is the only answer-choice close to 30 thousand.

13. Which of the following periods showed a continual increase in the sales of fiction titles?

   (A) 1980–1982   (B) 1982–1984   (C) 1984–1986   (D) 1986–1988   (E) 1987–1989

According to the chart, sales of fiction increased from 15,000 to 20,000 to 30,000 between 1982 and 1984. The answer is (B).

14.   What was the approximate average number of sales of fiction titles from 1984 to 1988?

   (A) 15 thousand   (B) 30 thousand   (C) 40 thousand   (D) 48 thousand   (E) 60 thousand

The following chart summarizes the sales for the years 1984 to 1988:

Year	Sales
1984	30 thousand
1985	11 thousand
1986	52 thousand
1987	52 thousand
1988	95 thousand

Forming the average yields:

$$\frac{30+11+52+52+95}{5}=48$$

The answer is (D).

   Note, it is important to develop a feel for how the writers of the ACT approximate when calculating. We used 52 thousand to calculate the sales of fiction in 1986, which is the actual number. But from the chart, it is difficult to tell whether the actual number is 51, 52, or 53 thousand. However, using any of the these numbers, the average would still be nearer to 40 than to any other answer-choice.

15.   By approximately what percent did the sale of nonfiction titles increase from 1984 to 1987?

   (A) 42%   (B) 50%   (C) 70%   (D) 90%   (E) 110%

Recall that the percentage increase (decrease) is formed by dividing the absolute increase (decrease) by the original amount:

$$\frac{57-40}{40}=.425$$

The answer is (A).

Questions 16–20 refer to the following graph.

AUTOMOBILE ACCIDENTS IN COUNTRY X: 1990 TO 1994
(in ten thousands)

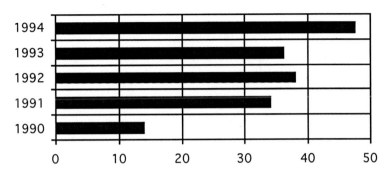

CARS IN COUNTRY X
(in millions)

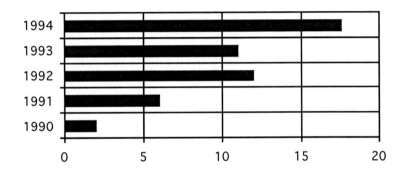

16. Approximately how many millions of cars were in Country X in 1994?

    (A) 1.0   (B) 4.7   (C) 9.0   (D) 15.5   (E) 17.5

In the bottom chart, the bar for 1994 ends half way between 15 and 20. Thus, there were about 17.5 million cars in 1994. The answer is (E).

17. The amount by which the number of cars in 1990 exceeded the number of accidents in 1991 was approximately

    (A) 0.3 million   (B) 0.7 million   (C) 1.0 million   (D) 1.7 million   (E) 2.5 million

From the bottom chart, there were 2 million cars in 1990; and from the top chart, there were 340 thousand accidents in 1991. Forming the difference yields

$$2,000,000 - 340,000 = 1,660,000$$

Rounding 1.66 million off yields 1.7 million. The answer is (D).

18. The number of accidents in 1993 was approximately what percentage of the number of cars?

    (A) 1%   (B) 1.5%   (C) 3%   (D) 5%   (E) 10%

From the charts, the number of accidents in 1993 was 360,000 and the number of cars was 11,000,000. Forming the percentage yields

$$\frac{360,000}{11,000,000} \approx 3\%$$

The answer is (C).

19. In which of the following years will the number of accidents exceed 500 thousand?

(A) 1994
(B) 1995
(C) 1998
(D) 2000
(E) It cannot be determined from the information given.

From the graphs, there is no way to predict what will happen in the future. The number of accidents could continually decrease after 1994. The answer is (E).

20. If no car in 1993 was involved in more than four accidents, what is the minimum number of cars that could have been in accidents in 1993?

(A) 50 thousand   (B) 60 thousand   (C) 70 thousand   (D) 80 thousand   (E) 90 thousand

The number of cars involved in accidents will be minimized when each car has exactly 4 accidents. Now, from the top chart, there were 360,000 accidents in 1993. Dividing 360,000 by 4 yields

$$\frac{360,000}{4} = 90,000$$

The answer is (E).

Questions 21–25 refer to the following graphs.

DISTRIBUTION OF IMPORTS AND EXPORTS FOR COUNTRY X IN 1994.

Imports
200 million items

Exports
100 million items

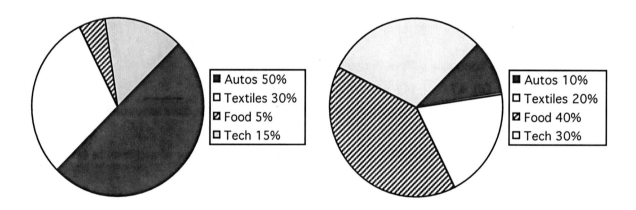

Autos 50%
Textiles 30%
Food 5%
Tech 15%

Autos 10%
Textiles 20%
Food 40%
Tech 30%

21. How many autos did Country X export in 1994?

(A) 10 million
(B) 15 million
(C) 16 million
(D) 20 million
(E) 30 million

The graph shows that 100 million items were exported in 1994 and 10% were autos. Hence, 10 million autos were exported. The answer is (A).

22. In how many categories did the total number of items (import and export) exceed 75 million?

(A) 1   (B) 2   (C) 3   (D) 4   (E) none

The chart shows that only autos and textiles exceeded 75 million total items. The answer is (B).

23. The ratio of the number of technology items imported in 1994 to the number of textile items exported in 1994 is

(A) $\dfrac{1}{3}$ (B) $\dfrac{3}{5}$ (C) 1   (D) $\dfrac{6}{5}$ (E) $\dfrac{3}{2}$

In 1994, there were 200 million items imported of which 15% were technology items. Thus, the number of technology items imported was

$$(15\%)(200 \text{ million}) = (.15)(200 \text{ million}) = 30 \text{ million}$$

In 1994, there were 100 million items exported of which 20% were textile items. Thus, the number of textile items exported was

$$(20\%)(100 \text{ million}) = (.20)(100 \text{ million}) = 20 \text{ million}$$

Forming the ratio of the above numbers yields

$$\frac{number\ of\ \text{technology}\ items\ imported}{number\ of\ textile\ items\ \exp orted} = \frac{30}{20} = \frac{3}{2}$$

The answer is (E).

24. If in 1995 the number of autos exported was 16 million, then the percent increase from 1994 in the number of autos exported is

(A) 40%   (B) 47%   (C) 50%   (D) 60%   (E) 65%

Remember, to calculate the percentage increase, find the absolute increase and divide it by the original number. Now, in 1994, the number of autos exported was 10 million (100x10%), and in 1995 it was 16 million. The absolute increase is thus:

$$16 - 10 = 6$$

Hence the percent increase in the number of autos exported is

$$\frac{absolute\ increase}{original\ number} = \frac{6}{10} = 60\%$$

The answer is (D).

25. In 1994, if twice as many autos imported to Country X broke down as autos exported from Country X and 20 percent of the exported autos broke down, what percent of the imported autos broke down?

(A) 1%   (B) 1.5%   (C) 2%   (D) 4%   (E) 5.5%

If 20% of the exports broke down, then 2 million autos broke down (20%x10). Since "twice as many autos imported to Country X broke down as autos exported from Country X," 4 million imported autos broke down. Further, Country X imported 100 million autos (50%x200). Forming the percentage yields $\dfrac{4}{100} = 0.04 = 4\%$. The answer is (D).

Word Problems

Before we begin solving word problems, we need to be very comfortable with translating words into mathematical symbols. Following is a partial list of words and their mathematical equivalents.

Concept	Symbol	Words	Example	Translation
equality	=	is	2 plus 2 is 4	$2 + 2 = 4$
		equals	x minus 5 equals 2	$x - 5 = 2$
		is the same as	multiplying x by 2 is the same as dividing x by 7	$2x = x/7$
addition	+	sum	the sum of y and π is 20	$y + \pi = 20$
		plus	x plus y equals 5	$x + y = 5$
		add	how many marbles must John add to collection F so that he has 13 marbles	$x + P = 13$
		increase	a number is increased by 10%	$x + 10\%x$
		more	the perimeter of the square is 3 more than the area	$P = 3 + A$
subtraction	−	minus	x minus y	$x - y$
		difference	the difference of x and y is 8	$\left|x - y\right| = 8$
		subtracted	x subtracted from y	$y - x$ *
		less than	the circumference is 5 less than the area	$C = A - 5$
multiplication	$\times$ or $\cdot$	times	the acceleration is 5 times the velocity	$a = 5v$
		product	the product of two consecutive integers	$x(x + 1)$
		of	x is 125% of y	$x = 125\%y$
division	÷	quotient	the quotient of x and y is 9	$x \div y = 9$
		divided	if x is divided by y, the result is 4	$x \div y = 4$

Although exact steps for solving word problems cannot be given, the following guidelines will help:

(1) First, choose a variable to stand for the least unknown quantity, and then try to write the other unknown quantities in terms of that variable.

For example, suppose we are given that Sue's age is 5 years less than twice Jane's and the sum of their ages is 16. Then Jane's age would be the least unknown, and we let $x = $ *Jane's age*. Expressing Sue's age in terms of x gives *Sue's age* $= 2x - 5$.

(2) Second, write an equation that involves the expressions in Step 1. Most (though not all) word problems pivot on the fact that two quantities in the problem are equal. Deciding which two quantities should be set equal is usually the hardest part in solving a word problem since it can require considerable ingenuity to discover which expressions are equal.

For the example above, we would get $(2x - 5) + x = 16$.

(3) Third, solve the equation in Step 2 and interpret the result.

For the example above, we would get by adding the x's: $3x - 5 = 16$

Then adding 5 to both sides gives $3x = 21$

Finally, dividing by 3 gives $x = 7$

Hence, Jane is 7 years old and Sue is $2x - 5 = 2 \cdot 7 - 5 = 9$ years old.

---

* Notice that with "minus" and "difference" the terms are subtracted in the same order as they are written, from left to right (x minus $y \longrightarrow x - y$). However, with "subtracted" and "less than," the order of subtraction is reversed (x subtracted from $y \longrightarrow y - x$). Many students translate "subtracted from" in the wrong order.

MOTION PROBLEMS

Virtually, all motion problems involve the formula *Distance* = *Rate* × *Time*, or

$$D = R \times T$$

Overtake: In this type of problem, one person catches up with or overtakes another person. The key to these problems is that at the moment one person overtakes the other they have traveled the same distance.

Example: Scott starts jogging from point X to point Y. A half-hour later his friend Garrett who jogs 1 mile per hour slower than twice Scott's rate starts from the same point and follows the same path. If Garrett overtakes Scott in 2 hours, how many miles will Garrett have covered?

(A) $2\frac{1}{5}$ (B) $3\frac{1}{3}$ (C) 4   (D) 6   (E) $6\frac{2}{3}$

Following Guideline 1, we let *r* = *Scott's rate*. Then 2*r* – 1 = *Garrett's rate*. Turning to Guideline 2, we look for two quantities that are equal to each other. When Garrett overtakes Scott, they will have traveled the same distance. Now, from the formula $D = R \times T$, Scott's distance is $D = r \times 2\frac{1}{2}$

and Garrett's distance is $D = (2r - 1)2 = 4r - 2$

Setting these expressions equal to each other gives $4r - 2 = r \times 2\frac{1}{2}$

Solving this equation for *r* gives $r = \frac{4}{3}$

Hence, Garrett will have traveled $D = 4r - 2 = 4\left(\frac{4}{3}\right) - 2 = 3\frac{1}{3}$ miles. The answer is (B).

Opposite Directions: In this type of problem, two people start at the same point and travel in opposite directions. The key to these problems is that the total distance traveled is the sum of the individual distances traveled.

Example: Two people start jogging at the same point and time but in opposite directions. If the rate of one jogger is 2 mph faster than the other and after 3 hours they are 30 miles apart, what is the rate of the faster jogger?

(A) 3   (B) 4   (C) 5   (D) 6   (E) 7

Let *r* be the rate of the slower jogger. Then the rate of the faster jogger is *r* + 2. Since they are jogging for 3 hours, the distance traveled by the slower jogger is $D = rt = 3r$, and the distance traveled by the faster jogger is 3(*r* + 2). Since they are 30 miles apart, adding the distances traveled gives

$$3r + 3(r + 2) = 30$$
$$3r + 3r + 6 = 30$$
$$6r + 6 = 30$$
$$6r = 24$$
$$r = 4$$

Hence, the rate of the faster jogger is *r* + 2 = 4 + 2 = 6. The answer is (D).

Round Trip: The key to these problems is that the distance going is the same as the distance returning.

Example: A cyclist travels 20 miles at a speed of 15 miles per hour. If he returns along the same path and the entire trip takes 2 hours, at what speed did he return?

(A) 15 mph   (B) 20 mph   (C) 22 mph   (D) 30 mph   (E) 34 mph

Solving the formula $D = R \times T$ for T yields $T = \dfrac{D}{R}$. For the first half of the trip, this yields $T = \dfrac{20}{15} = \dfrac{4}{3}$ hours. Since the entire trip takes 2 hours, the return trip takes $2 - \dfrac{4}{3}$ hours, or $\dfrac{2}{3}$ hours. Now, the return trip is also 20 miles, so solving the formula $D = R \times T$ for R yields $R = \dfrac{D}{T} = \dfrac{20}{\frac{2}{3}} = 20 \cdot \dfrac{3}{2} = 30$. The answer is (D).

Compass Headings: In this type of problem, typically two people are traveling in perpendicular directions. The key to these problems is often the Pythagorean Theorem.

Example: At 1 PM, Ship A leaves port heading due west at x miles per hour. Two hours later, Ship B is 100 miles due south of the same port and heading due north at y miles per hour. At 5 PM, how far apart are the ships?

(A) $\sqrt{(4x)^2 + (100 + 2y)^2}$

(B) $x + y$

(C) $\sqrt{x^2 + y^2}$

(D) $\sqrt{(4x)^2 + (2y)^2}$

(E) $\sqrt{(4x)^2 + (100 - 2y)^2}$

Since Ship A is traveling at x miles per hour, its distance traveled at 5 PM is $D = rt = 4x$. The distance traveled by Ship B is $D = rt = 2y$. This can be represented by the following diagram:

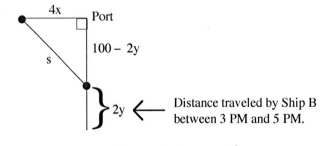

Applying the Pythagorean Theorem yields $s^2 = (4x)^2 + (100 - 2y)^2$. Taking the square root of this equation gives $s = \sqrt{(4x)^2 + (100 - 2y)^2}$. The answer is (E).

Circular Motion: In this type of problem, the key is often the arc length formula $S = R\theta$, where S is the arc length (or distance traveled), R is the radius of the circle, and θ is the angle.

Example: The figure to the right shows the path of a car moving around a circular racetrack. How many miles does the car travel in going from point A to point B ?

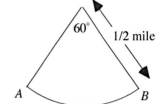

(A) $\pi/6$ (B) $\pi/3$ (C) π (D) 30   (E) 60

When calculating distance, degree measure must be converted to radian measure. To convert degree measure to radian measure, multiply by the conversion factor $\dfrac{\pi}{180}$. Multiplying $60°$ by $\dfrac{\pi}{180}$ yields $60 \cdot \dfrac{\pi}{180} = \dfrac{\pi}{3}$. Now, the length of arc traveled by the car in moving from point A to point B is S. Plugging this information into the formula $S = R\theta$ yields $S = \dfrac{1}{2} \cdot \dfrac{\pi}{3} = \dfrac{\pi}{6}$. The answer is (A).

Example: If a wheel is spinning at 1200 revolutions per minute, how many revolutions will it make in t seconds?

(A) $2t$ (B) $10t$ (C) $20t$ (D) $48t$ (E) $72t$

Since the question asks for the number of revolutions in t seconds, we need to find the number of revolutions per second and multiply that number by t. Since the wheel is spinning at 1200 revolutions per minute and there are 60 seconds in a minute, we get $\dfrac{1200 \text{ revolutions}}{60 \text{ seconds}} = 20 \text{ rev/sec}$. Hence, in t seconds, the wheel will make $20t$ revolutions. The answer is (C).

WORK PROBLEMS

The formula for work problems is *Work = Rate × Time*, or $W = R \times T$. The amount of work done is usually 1 unit. Hence, the formula becomes $1 = R \times T$. Solving this for R gives $R = \dfrac{1}{T}$.

Example: If Johnny can mow the lawn in 30 minutes and with the help of his brother, Bobby, they can mow the lawn 20 minutes, how long would it take Bobby working alone to mow the lawn?

(A) 1/2 hour   (B) 3/4 hour   (C) 1 hour   (D) 3/2 hours   (E) 2 hours

Let $r = 1/t$ be Bobby's rate. Now, the rate at which they work together is merely the sum of their rates:

$$\textit{Total Rate = Johnny's Rate + Bobby's Rate}$$

$$\frac{1}{20} = \frac{1}{30} + \frac{1}{t}$$

$$\frac{1}{20} - \frac{1}{30} = \frac{1}{t}$$

$$\frac{30 - 20}{30 \cdot 20} = \frac{1}{t}$$

$$\frac{1}{60} = \frac{1}{t}$$

$$t = 60$$

Hence, working alone, Bobby can do the job in 1 hour. The answer is (C).

Example: A tank is being drained at a constant rate. If it takes 3 hours to drain $\dfrac{6}{7}$ of its capacity, how much longer will it take to drain the tank completely?

(A) 1/2 hour   (B) 3/4 hour   (C) 1 hour   (D) 3/2 hours   (E) 2 hours

Since 6/7 of the tank's capacity was drained in 3 hours, the formula $W = R \times T$ becomes $\dfrac{6}{7} = R \times 3$.
Solving for R gives $R = 2/7$. Now, since 6/7 of the work has been completed, 1/7 of the work remains.
Plugging this information into the formula $W = R \times T$ gives $\dfrac{1}{7} = \dfrac{2}{7} \times T$. Solving for T gives $T = 1/2$. The answer is (A).

MIXTURE PROBLEMS

The key to these problems is that the combined total of the concentrations in the two parts must be the same as the whole mixture.

Example: How many ounces of a solution that is 30 percent salt must be added to a 50-ounce solution that is 10 percent salt so that the resulting solution is 20 percent salt?

(A) 20   (B) 30   (C) 40   (D) 50   (E) 60

Let x be the ounces of the 30 percent solution. Then $30\%x$ is the amount of salt in that solution. The final solution will be $50 + x$ ounces, and its concentration of salt will be $20\%(50 + x)$. The original amount of salt in the solution is $10\% \cdot 50$. Now, the concentration of salt in the original solution plus the concentration of salt in the added solution must equal the concentration of salt in the resulting solution:

$$10\% \cdot 50 + 30\%x = 20\%(50 + x)$$

Multiply this equation by 100 to clear the percent symbol and then solving for x yields $x = 50$. The answer is (D).

COIN PROBLEMS

The key to these problems is to keep the quantity of coins distinct from the value of the coins. An example will illustrate.

Example: Laura has 20 coins consisting of quarters and dimes. If she has a total of $3.05, how many dimes does she have?

(A) 3   (B) 7   (C) 10   (D) 13   (E) 16

Let D stand for the number of dimes, and let Q stand for the number of quarters. Since the total number of coins in 20, we get $D + Q = 20$, or $Q = 20 - D$. Now, each dime is worth 10¢, so the value of the dimes is $10D$. Similarly, the value of the quarters is $25Q = 25(20 - D)$. Summarizing this information in a table yields

	Dimes	Quarters	Total
Number	D	$20 - D$	20
Value	$10D$	$25(20 - D)$	305

Notice that the total value entry in the table was converted from $3.05 to 305¢. Adding up the value of the dimes and the quarters yields the following equation:

$$10D + 25(20 - D) = 305$$
$$10D + 500 - 25D = 305$$
$$-15D = -195$$
$$D = 13$$

Hence, there are 13 dimes, and the answer is (D).

AGE PROBLEMS

Typically, in these problems, we start by letting x be a person's current age and then the person's age a years ago will be $x - a$ and the person's age a years in future will be $x + a$. An example will illustrate.

Example: John is 20 years older than Steve. In 10 years, Steve's age will be half that of John's. What is Steve's age?

(A) 2   (B) 8   (C) 10   (D) 20   (E) 25

Steve's age is the most unknown quantity. So we let x = Steve's age and then $x + 20$ is John's age. Ten years from now, Steve and John's ages will be $x + 10$ and $x + 30$, respectively. Summarizing this information in a table yields

	Age now	**Age in 10 years**
Steve	x	$x + 10$
John	$x + 20$	$x + 30$

Since "in 10 years, Steve's age will be half that of John's," we get

$$\frac{1}{2}(x + 30) = x + 10$$
$$x + 30 = 2(x + 10)$$
$$x + 30 = 2x + 20$$
$$x = 10$$

Hence, Steve is 10 years old, and the answer is (C).

INTEREST PROBLEMS

These problems are based on the formula

$$\text{INTEREST} = \text{AMOUNT} \times \text{TIME} \times \text{RATE}$$

Often, the key to these problems is that the interest earned from one account plus the interest earned from another account equals the total interest earned:

Total Interest = (Interest from first account) + (Interest from second account)

An example will illustrate.

Example: A total of $1200 is deposited in two savings accounts for one year, part at 5% and the remainder at 7%. If $72 was earned in interest, how much was deposited at 5%?

(A) 410   (B) 520   (C) 600   (D) 650   (E) 760

Let x be the amount deposited at 5%. Then $1200 - x$ is the amount deposited at 7%. The interest on these investments is $.05x$ and $.07(1200 - x)$. Since the total interest is $72, we get

$$.05x + .07(1200 - x) = 72$$
$$.05x + 84 - .07x = 72$$
$$-.02x + 84 = 72$$
$$-.02x = -12$$
$$x = 600$$

The answer is (C).

Problem Set T:

1. Seven years ago, Scott was 3 times as old as Kathy was at that time. If Scott is now 5 years older than Kathy, how old is Scott?

    (A) 12 ½   (B) 13   (C) 13 ½   (D) 14   (E) 14 ½

Duals

2. A dress was initially listed at a price that would have given the store a profit of 20 percent of the wholesale cost. After reducing the asking price by 10 percent, the dress sold for a net profit of 10 dollars. What was the wholesale cost of the dress?

    (A) 200   (B) 125   (C) 100   (D) 20   (E) 10

3. A dress was initially listed at a price that would have given the store a profit of 20 percent of the wholesale cost. The dress sold for 50 dollars. What was the wholesale cost of the dress?

    (A) 100   (B) 90   (C) 75   (D) 60   (E) Not enough information to decide

Duals

4. The capacity of glass X is 80 percent of the capacity of glass Y. Further, glass X contains 6 ounces of punch and is half-full, while glass Y is full. Glass Y contains how many more ounces of punch than glass X?

    (A) 1   (B) 3   (C) 6   (D) 9   (E) Not enough information to decide

5. The capacity of glass X is 80 percent of the capacity of glass Y. Further, Glass X is 70 percent full, and glass Y is 30 percent full. Glass X contains how many more ounces of punch than glass Y?

    (A) 1   (B) 3   (C) 6   (D) 8   (E) Not enough information to decide

6. Car X traveled from city A to city B in 30 minutes. The first half of the distance was covered at 50 miles per hour, and the second half of the distance was covered at 60 miles per hour. What was the average speed of car X?

    (A) 200/11   (B) 400/11   (C) 500/11   (D) 600/11   (E) 700/11

7. Steve bought some apples at a cost of $.60 each and some oranges at a cost of $.50 each. If he paid a total of $4.10 for a total of 8 apples and oranges, how many apples did Steve buy?

    (A) 1   (B) 2   (C) 3   (D) 5   (E) 6

8. Cyclist M leaves point P at 12 noon and travels in a straight path at a constant velocity of 20 miles per hour. Cyclist N leaves point P at 2 PM, travels the same path at a constant velocity, and overtakes M at 4 PM. What was the average speed of N?

    (A) 15   (B) 24   (C) 30   (D) 35   (E) 40

9. A pair of pants and matching shirt cost $52.50. The pants cost two and a half times as much as the shirt. What is the cost of the shirt alone?

    (A) 10   (B) 15   (C) 20   (D) 27   (E) 30

10. Jennifer and Alice are 4 miles apart. If Jennifer starts walking toward Alice at 3 miles per hour and at the same time Alice starts walking toward Jennifer at 2 miles per hour, how much time will pass before they meet?

    (A) 20 minutes   (B) 28 minutes   (C) 43 minutes   (D) 48 minutes   (E) 60 minutes

11. If Robert can assemble a model car in 30 minutes and Craig can assemble the same model car in 20 minutes, how long would it take them, working together, to assemble the model car?

    (A) 12 minutes   (B) 13 minutes   (C) 14 minutes   (D) 15 minutes   (E) 16 minutes

12. How many ounces of nuts costing 80 cents a pound must be mixed with nuts costing 60 cents a pound to make a 10-ounce mixture costing 70 cents a pound?

    (A) 3   (B) 4   (C) 5   (D) 7   (E) 8

13. Tom is 10 years older than Carrie. However, 5 years ago Tom was twice as old as Carrie. How old is Carrie?

    (A) 5   (B) 10   (C) 12   (D) 15   (E) 25

14. Two cars start at the same point and travel in opposite directions. If one car travels at 45 miles per hour and the other at 60 miles per hour, how much time will pass before they are 210 miles apart?

    (A) .5 hours   (B) 1 hour   (C) 1.5 hours   (D) 2 hours   (E) 2.5 hours

15. If the value of x quarters is equal to the value of $x + 32$ nickels, $x =$

    (A) 8   (B) 11   (C) 14   (D) 17   (E) 20

16. Steve has $5.25 in nickels and dimes. If he has 15 more dimes than nickels, how many nickels does he have?

    (A) 20   (B) 25   (C) 27   (D) 30   (E) 33

17. Cathy has equal numbers of nickels and quarters worth a total of $7.50. How many coins does she have?

    (A) 20   (B) 25   (C) 50   (D) 62   (E) 70

18. Richard leaves to visit his friend who lives 200 miles down Interstate 10. One hour later his friend Steve leaves to visit Richard via Interstate 10. If Richard drives at 60 mph and Steve drives at 40 mph, how many miles will Steve have driven when they cross paths?

    (A) 56   (B) 58   (C) 60   (D) 65   (E) 80

19. At 1 PM, Ship A leaves port traveling 15 mph. Three hours later, Ship B leaves the same port in the same direction traveling 25 mph. At what time does Ship B pass Ship A?

    (A) 8:30 PM   (B) 8:35 PM   (C) 9 PM   (D) 9:15 PM   (E) 9:30 PM

20. In x hours and y minutes a car traveled z miles. What is the car's speed in miles per hour?

    (A) $\dfrac{z}{60 + y}$ (B) $\dfrac{60z}{60x + y}$ (C) $\dfrac{60}{60 + y}$ (D) $\dfrac{z}{x + y}$ (E) $\dfrac{60 + y}{60z}$

21. A 30% discount reduces the price of a commodity by $90. If the discount is reduced to 20%, then the price of the commodity will be

    (A) $180   (B) $210   (C) $240   (D) $270   (E) $300

22. In a class of 40 students, the number of students who passed the math exam is equal to half the number of students who passed the science exam. Each student in the class passed at least one of the two exams. If 5 students passed both exams, then the number of students who passed the math exam is

    (A) 5   (B) 10   (C) 15   (D) 20   (E) 25

23. A train of length l, traveling at a constant velocity, passes a pole in t seconds. If the same train traveling at the same velocity passes a platform in $3t$ seconds, then the length of the platform is

    (A) 0.5l (B) l (C) 1.5l (D) 2l (E) 3l

24. If two workers can assemble a car in 8 hours and a third worker can assemble the same car in 12 hours, then how long would it take the three workers together to assemble the car?

    (A) $\frac{5}{12}$ hrs

    (B) $2\frac{2}{5}$ hrs

    (C) $2\frac{4}{5}$ hrs

    (D) $3\frac{1}{2}$ hrs

    (E) $4\frac{4}{5}$ hrs

25. The age of B is half the sum of the ages of A and C. If B is 2 years younger than A and C is 32 years old, then the age of B must be

    (A) 28
    (B) 30
    (C) 32
    (D) 34
    (E) 36

26. The ages of three people are such that the age of one person is twice the age of the second person and three times the age of the third person. If the sum of the ages of the three people is 33, then the age of the youngest person is

    (A) 3
    (B) 6
    (C) 9
    (D) 11
    (E) 18

Answers and Solutions to Problem Set T

1.   Let S be Scott's age and K be Kathy's age. Then translating the sentence *"If Scott is now 5 years older than Kathy, how old is Scott"* into an equation yields

$$S = K + 5$$

Now, Scott's age 7 years ago can be represented as $S = -7$, and Kathy's age can be represented as $K = -7$. Then translating the sentence *"Seven years ago, Scott was 3 times as old as Kathy was at that time"* into an equation yields $S - 7 = 3(K - 7)$.

Combining this equation with $S = K + 5$ yields the system:

$$S - 7 = 3(K - 7)$$
$$S = K + 5$$

Solving this system gives $S = 14\frac{1}{2}$. The answer is (E).

2.   Since the store would have made a profit of 20 percent on the wholesale cost, the original price P of the dress was 120 percent of the cost: $P = 1.2C$. Now, translating *"After reducing the asking price by 10 percent, the dress sold for a net profit of 10 dollars"* into an equation yields:

$$P - .1P = C + 10$$

Simplifying gives $.9P = C + 10$

Solving for P yields $P = \dfrac{C + 10}{.9}$

Plugging this expression for P into $P = 1.2C$ gives

$$\frac{C + 10}{.9} = 1.2C$$

Solving this equation for C yields $C = 125$. The answer is (B).

3.   There is not sufficient information since the selling price is not related to any other information. Note, the phrase "initially listed" implies that there was more than one asking price. If it wasn't for that phrase, the information would be sufficient. The answer is (E).

4.   Since *"the capacity of glass X is 80 percent of the capacity of glass Y,"* we get

$$X = .8Y$$

Since *"glass X contains 6 ounces of punch and is half-full,"* the capacity of glass X is 12 ounces. Plugging this into the equation yields

$$12 = .8Y$$

$$\frac{12}{.8} = Y$$

$$15 = Y$$

Hence, glass Y contains $15 - 6 = 9$ more ounces of punch than glass X. The answer is (D).

5.   Now, there is not sufficient information to solve the problem since it does not provide any absolute numbers. The following diagram shows two situations: one in which Glass X contains 5.2 more ounces of punch than glass Y, and one in which Glass X contains 2.6 more ounces than glass Y.

Scenario I (Glass X contains 5.2 more ounces than glass Y.)

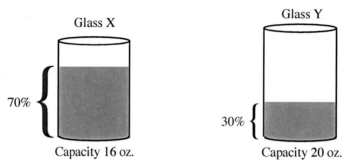

Scenario II (Glass X contains 2.6 more ounces than glass Y.)

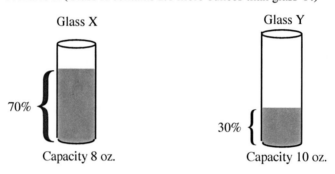

The answer is (E).

6.   Recall that *Average Speed* $= \dfrac{\text{Total Distance}}{\text{Total Time}}$. Now, the setup to the question gives the total time for the trip—30 minutes. Hence, to answer the question, we need to find the distance of the trip.

Let t equal the time for the first half of the trip. Then since the whole trip took 30 minutes (or $\dfrac{1}{2}$ hour), the second half of the trip took $\dfrac{1}{2} - t$ hours. Now, from the formula *Distance* $=$ *Rate* $\times$ *Time* , we get for the first half of the trip:

$$\frac{d}{2} = 50 \cdot t$$

And for the second half of the trip, we get

$$\frac{d}{2} = 60\left(\frac{1}{2} - t\right)$$

Solving this system yields

$$d = \frac{300}{11}$$

Hence, the *Average Speed* $= \dfrac{\text{Total Distance}}{\text{Total Time}} = \dfrac{300/11}{1/2} = \dfrac{600}{11}$. The answer is (D).

7.   Let x denote the number of apples bought, and let y denote the number of oranges bought. Then, translating the sentence *"Steve bought some apples at a cost of $.60 each and some oranges at a cost of $.50 each"* into an equation yields

$$.60x + .50y = 4.10$$

Since there are two variables and only one equation, the key to this problem is finding a second equation that relates x and y. Since he bought a total of 8 apples and oranges, we get

$$x + y = 8$$

Solving this system yields $x = 1$. Hence, he bought one apple, and the answer is (A).

8.   Recall the formula *Distance = Rate × Time* , or $D = R \cdot T$. From the second sentence, we get for Cyclist N:

$$D = R \cdot 2$$

Now, Cyclist M traveled at 20 miles per hour and took 4 hours. Hence, Cyclist M traveled a total distance of

$$D = R \cdot T = 20 \cdot 4 = 80 \text{ miles}$$

Since the cyclists covered the same distance at the moment they met, we can plug this value for D into the equation $D = R \cdot 2$:

$$80 = R \cdot 2$$
$$40 = R$$

The answer is (E).

9.   Let p denote the cost of the pants, and let s denote the cost of the shirt. Then from the question setup, $p + s = 52.50$.

Translating *"The pants cost two and a half times as much as the shirt"* into an equation gives $p = 2.5s$. Plugging this into the above equation gives

$$2.5s + s = 52.50$$

$$3.5s = 52.50$$

$$s = 15$$

The answer is (B).

10.   Let the distance Jennifer walks be x. Then since they are 4 miles apart, Alice will walk $4 - x$ miles. The key to this problem is that when they meet each person will have walked for an equal amount of time. Solving the equation $D = R \times T$ for T yields $T = \dfrac{D}{R}$. Hence,

$$\frac{x}{3} = \frac{4-x}{2}$$
$$2x = 3(4-x)$$
$$2x = 12 - 3x$$
$$5x = 12$$
$$x = \frac{12}{5}$$

Therefore, the time that Jennifer walks is $T = \dfrac{D}{R} = \dfrac{12/5}{3} = \dfrac{12}{5} \times \dfrac{1}{3} = \dfrac{4}{5}$ of an hour. Converting this into minutes gives $\dfrac{4}{5} \times 60 = 48$ minutes. The answer is (D).

11. ILet t be the time it takes the boys, working together, to assemble the model car. Then their combined rate is $\frac{1}{t}$, and their individual rates are $\frac{1}{30}$ and $\frac{1}{20}$. Now, their combined rate is merely the sum of their individual rates:

$$\frac{1}{t} = \frac{1}{30} + \frac{1}{20}$$

Solving this equation for t yields $t = 12$. The answer is (A).

12. Let x be the amount of nuts at 80 cents a pound. Then $10 - x$ is the amount of nuts at 60 cents a pound. The cost of the 80-cent nuts is $80x$, the cost of the 60-cent nuts is $60(10 - x)$, and the cost of the mixture is $70(10)$ cents. Since the cost of the mixture is the sum of the costs of the 70- and 80-cent nuts, we get

$$80x + 60(10 - x) = 70(10)$$

Solving this equation for x yields $x = 5$. The answer is (C).

13. Let C be Carrie's age. Then Tom's age is $C + 10$. Now, 5 years ago, Carrie's age was $C - 5$ and Tom's age was $(C + 10) - 5 = C + 5$. Since at that time, Tom was twice as old as Carrie, we get $5 + C = 2(C - 5)$. Solving this equation for C yields $C = 15$. The answer is (D).

14. Since the cars start at the same time, the time each has traveled is the same. Let t be the time when the cars are 210 miles apart. The equation $D = R \times T$, yields

$$210 = 45 \cdot t + 60 \cdot t$$
$$210 = 105 \cdot t$$
$$2 = t$$

The answer is (D).

15. The value of the x quarters is $25x$, and the value of the $x + 32$ nickels is $5(x + 32)$. Since these two quantities are equal, we get

$$25x = 5(x + 32)$$
$$25x = 5x + 160$$
$$20x = 160$$
$$x = 8$$

The answer is (A).

16. Let N stand for the number of nickels. Then the number of dimes is $N + 15$. The value of the nickels is $5N$, and the value of the dimes is $10(N + 15)$. Since the total value of the nickels and dimes is 525¢, we get

$$5N + 10(N + 15) = 525$$
$$15N + 150 = 525$$
$$15N = 375$$
$$N = 25$$

Hence, there are 25 nickels, and the answer is (B).

17. Let x stand for both the number of nickels and the number of quarters. Then the value of the nickels is $5x$ and the value of the quarters is $25x$. Since the total value of the coins is \$7.50, we get

$$5x + 25x = 750$$
$$30x = 750$$
$$x = 25$$

Hence, she has $x + x = 25 + 25 = 50$ coins. The answer is (C).

18. Let t be time that Steve has been driving. Then $t + 1$ is time that Richard has been driving. Now, the distance traveled by Steve is $D = rt = 40t$, and Richard's distance is $60(t + 1)$. At the moment they cross paths, they will have traveled a combined distance of 200 miles. Hence,

$$40t + 60(t + 1) = 200$$
$$40t + 60t + 60 = 200$$
$$100t + 60 = 200$$
$$100t = 140$$
$$t = 1.4$$

Therefore, Steve will have traveled $D = rt = 40(1.4) = 56$ miles. The answer is (A).

19. Let t be time that Ship B has been traveling. Then $t + 3$ is time that Ship A has been traveling. The distance traveled by Ship B is $D = rt = 25t$, and Ship A's distance is $15(t + 3)$. At the moment Ship B passes Ship A, they will have traveled the same distance. Hence,

$$25t = 15(t + 3)$$
$$25t = 15t + 45$$
$$10t = 45$$
$$t = 4.5$$

Since Ship B left port at 4 PM and overtook Ship A in 4.5 hours, it passed Ship A at 8:30 PM. The answer is (A).

20. Since the time is given in mixed units, we need to change the minutes into hours. Since there are 60 minutes in an hour, y minutes is equivalent to $\dfrac{y}{60}$ hours. Hence, the car's travel time, "x hours and y minutes," is $x + \dfrac{y}{60}$ hours. Plugging this along with the distance traveled, z, into the formula $d = rt$ yields

$$z = r\left(x + \frac{y}{60}\right)$$
$$z = r\left(\frac{60}{60}x + \frac{y}{60}\right)$$
$$z = r\left(\frac{60x + y}{60}\right)$$
$$\frac{60z}{60x + y} = r$$

The answer is (B).

21. Let the original price of the commodity be x. The reduction in price due to the 30% discount is $0.3x$. It is given that the 30% discount reduced the price of the commodity by $90. Expressing this as an equation yields

$$0.3x = 90$$

Solving for x yields

$$x = 300$$

Hence, the original price of the commodity was $300. The value of a 20% discount on $300 is

$$.20(300) = 60$$

Hence, the new selling price of the commodity is

$$\$300 - \$60 = \$240$$

The answer is (C).

22. Let x represent the number of students in the class who passed the math exam. Since it is given that the number of students who passed the math exam is half the number of students who passed the science exam, the number of students in the class who passed the science exam is $2x$. It is given that 5 students passed both exams. Hence, the number of students who passed only the math exam is $(x - 5)$, and the number of students who passed only the science exam is $(2x - 5)$. Since it is given that each student in the class passed at least one of the two exams, the number of students who failed both exams is 0.

We can divide the class into four groups:

    1) Group of students who passed only the math exam: $(x - 5)$
    2) Group of students who passed only the science exam: $(2x - 5)$
    3) Group of students who passed both exams: 5
    4) Group of students who failed both exams: 0

The sum of the number of students from each of these four categories is equal to the number of students in the class—40. Expressing this as an equation yields

$$(x - 5) + (2x - 5) + 5 + 0 = 40$$
$$3x - 5 = 40$$
$$3x = 45$$
$$x = 15$$

Thus, the number of students who passed the math exam is 15. The answer is (C).

23. The distance traveled by the train while passing the pole is l (which is the length of the train). The train takes t seconds to pass the pole. Recall the formula velocity = distance/time. Applying this formula, we get

$$\text{velocity} = \frac{l}{t}$$

While passing the platform, the train travels a distance of $l + x$, where x is the length of the platform. The train takes $3t$ seconds at the velocity of l/t to cross the platform. Recalling the formula distance = velocity × time and substituting the values for the respective variables, we get

$$l + x = \frac{l}{t} \times 3t \qquad \text{by substitution}$$
$$l + x = 3l \qquad \text{by canceling } t$$
$$x = 2l \qquad \text{by subtracting } l \text{ from both sides}$$

Hence, the length of the platform is $2l$. The answer is (D).

24. The fraction of work done in 1 hour by the first two people working together is 1/8. The fraction of work done in 1 hour by the third person is 1/12. When the three people work together, the total amount of work done in 1 hour is 1/8 + 1/12 = 5/24. The time taken by the people working together to complete the job is

$$\frac{1}{\text{fraction of work done per unit time}} =$$

$$\frac{1}{\frac{5}{24}} =$$

$$\frac{24}{5} =$$

$$4\frac{4}{5}$$

The answer is (E).

25. Let a represent the age of A and let c represent the age of C. If b represents the age of B, then according to the question $b = \dfrac{a+c}{2}$. We are told that B is 2 years younger than A. This generates the equation $a = b + 2$. We know that the age of C is 32. Substituting these values into the equation $b = \dfrac{a+c}{2}$ yields $b = \dfrac{(b+2)+32}{2}$. Solving this equation for b yields $b = 34$. The answer is (D).

26. Let a represent the age of the oldest person, b the age of the age of second person, and c the age of youngest person. The age of first person is twice the age of the second person and three times the age of the third person. This can be expressed as $a = 2b$ and $a = 3c$. Solving these equations for b and c yields $b = a/2$ and $c = a/3$. The sum of the ages of the three people is $a + b + c = 33$. Substituting for b and c in this equation, we get

$$a + a/2 + a/3 = 33$$
$$6a + 3a + 2a = 198 \qquad \text{by multiplying both sides by 6}$$
$$11a = 198$$
$$a = 198/11 = 18 \qquad \text{by dividing both sides by 11}$$

Since $c = a/3$, we get

$$c = a/3 = 18/3 = 6$$

The answer is (B).

Sequences & Series

A sequence is an ordered list of numbers. The following is a sequence of odd numbers:

$$1, 3, 5, 7, \ldots$$

A term of a sequence is identified by its position in the sequence. In the above sequence, 1 is the first term, 3 is the second term, etc. The ellipsis symbol (...) indicates that the sequence continues forever.

Example 1: In sequence S, the 3rd term is 4, the 2nd term is three times the 1st, and the 3rd term is four times the 2nd. What is the 1st term in sequence S?

   (A) 0   (B) 1/3   (C) 1   (D) 3/2   (E) 4

We know *"the 3rd term of S is 4,"* and that *"the 3rd term is four times the 2nd."* This is equivalent to saying the 2nd term is 1/4 the 3rd term: $\frac{1}{4} \cdot 4 = 1$. Further, we know *"the 2nd term is three times the 1st."* This is equivalent to saying the 1st term is $\frac{1}{3}$ the 2nd term: $\frac{1}{3} \cdot 1 = \frac{1}{3}$. Hence, the first term of the sequence is fully determined:

$$\frac{1}{3}, 1, 4$$

The answer is (B).

Example 2: Except for the first two numbers, every number in the sequence –1, 3, –3, ... is the product of the two immediately preceding numbers. How many numbers of this sequence are odd?

   (A) one   (B) two   (C) three   (D) four   (E) more than four

Since *"every number in the sequence –1, 3, –3, ... is the product of the two immediately preceding numbers,"* the forth term of the sequence is –9 = 3(–3). The first 6 terms of this sequence are

$$-1, 3, -3, -9, 27, -243, \ldots$$

At least six numbers in this sequence are odd: –1, 3, –3, –9, 27, –243. The answer is (E).

Arithmetic Progressions

An arithmetic progression is a sequence in which the difference between any two consecutive terms is the same. This is the same as saying: each term exceeds the previous term by a fixed amount. For example, 0, 6, 12, 18, ... is an arithmetic progression in which the common difference is 6. The sequence 8, 4, 0, –4, ... is arithmetic with a common difference of –4.

Example 3: The seventh number in a sequence of numbers is 31 and each number after the first number in the sequence is 4 less than the number immediately preceding it. What is the fourth number in the sequence?

(A) 15   (B) 19   (C) 35   (D) 43   (E) 51

Since each number *"in the sequence is 4 less than the number immediately preceding it,"* the sixth term is 31 + 4 = 35; the fifth number in the sequence is 35 + 4 = 39; and the fourth number in the sequence is 39 + 4 = 43. The answer is (D). Following is the sequence written out:

$$55, 51, 47, 43, 39, 35, 31, 27, 23, 19, 15, 11, \ldots$$

Sequence Formulas

Students with strong backgrounds in mathematics may prefer to solve sequence problems by using formulas.

Since each term of an arithmetic progression *"exceeds the previous term by a fixed amount,"* we get the following:

first term	$a + 0d$	where a is the first term and d is the common difference
second term	$a + 1d$	
third term	$a + 2d$	
fourth term	$a + 3d$	
	$\ldots$	
nth term	$a + (n - 1)d$	This formula generates the nth term

The sum of the first n terms of an arithmetic sequence is

$$\frac{n}{2}\left[2a + (n - 1)d\right]$$

Geometric Progressions

A geometric progression is a sequence in which the ratio of any two consecutive terms is the same. Thus, each term is generated by multiplying the preceding term by a fixed number. For example, $-3, 6, -12, 24, \ldots$ is a geometric progression in which the common ratio is -2. The sequence $32, 16, 8, 4, \ldots$ is geometric with common ratio $1/2$.

Example 4: What is the sixth term of the sequence $90, -30, 10, -10/3, \ldots$?

(A) 1/3
(B) 0
(C) −10/27
(D) −3
(E) −100/3

Since the common ratio between any two consecutive terms is $-\frac{1}{3}$, the fifth term is $\frac{10}{9} = \left(-\frac{1}{3}\right) \cdot \left(-\frac{10}{3}\right)$.

Hence, the sixth number in the sequence is $-\frac{10}{27} = \left(-\frac{1}{3}\right) \cdot \left(\frac{10}{9}\right)$. The answer is (C).

Sequence Formulas

Since each term of a geometric progression *"is generated by multiplying the preceding term by a fixed number,"* we get the following:

first term	a	
second term	ar^1	where r is the common ratio
third term	ar^2	
fourth term	ar^3	

. . .

nth term $a_n = ar^{n-1}$ This formula generates the nth term

The sum of the first n terms of an geometric sequence is

$$\frac{a\left(1-r^n\right)}{1-r}$$

SERIES

A series is simply the sum of the terms of a sequence. The following is a series of even numbers formed from the sequence 2, 4, 6, 8, . . . :

$$2 + 4 + 6 + 8 + \cdots$$

A term of a series is identified by its position in the series. In the above series, 2 is the first term, 4 is the second term, etc. The ellipsis symbol (. . .) indicates that the series continues forever.

Example 5: The sum of the squares of the first n positive integers $1^2 + 2^2 + 3^2 + \ldots + n^2$ is $\frac{n(n+1)(2n+1)}{6}$. What is the sum of the squares of the first 9 positive integers?

  (A) 90 (B) 125 (C) 200 (D) 285 (E) 682

We are given a formula for the sum of the squares of the first n positive integers. Plugging $n = 9$ into this formula yields

$$\frac{n(n+1)(2n+1)}{6} = \frac{9(9+1)(2\cdot9+1)}{6} = \frac{9(10)(19)}{6} = 285$$

The answer is (D).

Example 6: For all integers $x > 1$, $\langle x \rangle = 2x + (2x-1) + (2x-2) + \ldots + 2 + 1$. What is the value   of $\langle 3 \rangle \cdot \langle 2 \rangle$?

  (A) 60 (B) 116 (C) 210 (D) 263 (E) 478

$\langle 3 \rangle = 2(3) + (2\cdot3-1) + (2\cdot3-2) + (2\cdot3-3) + (2\cdot3-4) + (2\cdot3-5) = 6+5+4+3+2+1 = 21$

$\langle 2 \rangle = 2(2) + (2\cdot2-1) + (2\cdot2-2) + (2\cdot2-3) = 4+3+2+1 = 10$

Hence, $\langle 3 \rangle \cdot \langle 2 \rangle = 21 \cdot 10 = 210$, and the answer is (C).

Problem Set U:

1. By dividing 21 into 1, the fraction $\frac{1}{21}$ can be written as a repeating decimal: 0.476190476190 . . . where the block of digits 476190 repeats. What is the 54th digit following the decimal point?

    (A) 0   (B) 4   (C) 6   (D) 7   (E) 9

2. The positive integers P, Q, R, S, and T increase in order of size such that the value of each successive integer is one more than the preceding integer and the value of T is 6. What is the value of R?

    (A) 0   (B) 1   (C) 2   (D) 3   (E) 4

3. Let u represent the sum of the integers from 1 through 20, and let v represent the sum of the integers from 21 through 40. What is the value of $v - u$?

    (A) 21   (B) 39   (C) 200   (D) 320   (E) 400

4. In the pattern of dots to the right, each row after the first row has two more dots than the row immediately above it. Row 6 contains how many dots?

    (A) 6   (B) 8   (C) 10   (D) 11   (E) 12

5. In sequence S, all odd numbered terms are equal and all even numbered terms are equal. The first term in the sequence is $\sqrt{2}$ and the second term is –2. What is approximately the sum of two consecutive terms of the sequence?

    (A) –2   (B) –0.6   (C) 0   (D) 2   (E) 0.8

6. The sum of the first n even, positive integers is $2 + 4 + 6 + \cdots + 2n$ is $n(n + 1)$. What is the sum of the first 20 even, positive integers?

    (A) 120   (B) 188   (C) 362   (D) 406   (E) 420

7. In the array of numbers to the right, each number above the bottom row is equal to three times the number immediately below it. What is value of $x + y$?

27	x	81	–108
9	–18	27	–36
3	–6	y	–12
1	–2	3	–4

    (A) –45   (B) –15   (C) –2   (D) 20   (E) 77

8. The first term of a sequence is 2. All subsequent terms are found by adding 3 to the immediately preceding term and then multiplying the sum by 2. Which of the following describes the terms of the sequence?

    (A) Each term is odd   (B) Each term is even   (C) The terms are: even, odd, even, odd, etc.
    (D) The terms are: even, odd, odd, odd, etc.   (E) The terms are: even, odd, odd, even, odd, odd, etc.

9. Except for the first two numbers, every number in the sequence –1, 3, 2, . . . is the sum of the two immediately preceding numbers. How many numbers of this sequence are even?

    (A) none   (B) one   (C) two   (D) three   (E) more than three

10. In the sequence w, x, y, 30, adding any one of the first three terms to the term immediately following it yields $w/2$. What is the value of w ?

    (A) –60   (B) –30   (C) 0   (D) 5   (E) 25

Answers and Solutions to Problem Set U

1.   The sixth digit following the decimal point is the number zero: 0.476190476190 . . . Since the digits repeat in blocks of six numbers, 0 will appear in the space for all multiples of six. Since 54 is a multiple of six, the 54th digit following the decimal point is 0. The answer is (A).

2.   We know that T is 6; and therefore from the fact that *"each successive integer is one more than the preceding integer"* we see that S is 5. Continuing in this manner yields the following unique sequence:

$$
\begin{array}{ccccc}
P & Q & R & S & T \\
2 & 3 & 4 & 5 & 6
\end{array}
$$

Hence, the value of R is 4. The answer is (E).

3.   Forming the series for u and v yields

$$u = 1 + 2 + \cdots + 19 + 20$$
$$v = 21 + 22 + \cdots + 39 + 40$$

Subtracting the series for u from the series for v yields

$$v - u = \underbrace{20 + 20 + \cdots + 20 + 20}_{20 \text{ times}} = 20 \cdot 20 = 400$$

The answer is (E).

4.   Extending the dots to six rows yields

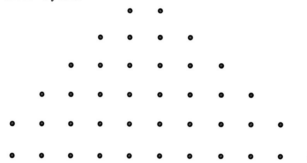

Row 6 has twelve dots. Hence, the answer is (E).

5.   Since the *"the first term in the sequence is $\sqrt{2}$"* and *"all odd numbered terms are equal,"* all odd numbered terms equal $\sqrt{2}$. Since the *"the second term is –2"* and *"all even numbered terms are equal,"* all even numbered terms equal –2. Hence, the sum of any two consecutive terms of the sequence is $\sqrt{2} + (-2) \approx -0.6$ (remember, $\sqrt{2} \approx 1.4$). The answer is (B).

6.   We are given a formula for the sum of the first n even, positive integers. Plugging $n = 20$ into this formula yields

$$n(n + 1) = 20(20 + 1) = 20(21) = 420$$

The answer is (E).

7.   Since *"each number above the bottom row is equal to three times the number immediately below it,"* $x = 3(-18) = -54$ and $y = 3(3) = 9$. Hence, $x + y = -54 + 9 = -45$. The answer is (A).

8.   The first term is even, and all subsequent terms are found by multiplying a number by 2. Hence, all terms of the sequence are even. The answer is (B). Following is the sequence:

$$2, 10, 26, 58, \ldots$$

9.   Since *"every number in the sequence* $-1, 3, 2, \ldots$ *is the sum of the two immediately preceding numbers,"* the forth term of the sequence is $5 = 3 + 2$. The first 12 terms of this sequence are

$$-1, 3, 2, 5, 7, 12, 19, 31, 50, 81, 131, 212, \ldots$$

At least four numbers in this sequence are even: 2, 12, 50, and 212. The answer is (E).

10.   Since *"adding any one of the first three terms to the term immediately following it yields* $\frac{w}{2}$*,"* we get

$$w + x = \frac{w}{2}$$

$$x + y = \frac{w}{2}$$

$$y + 30 = \frac{w}{2}$$

Subtracting the last equation from the second equation yields $x - 30 = 0$. That is $x = 30$. Plugging $x = 30$ into the first equation yields

$$w + 30 = \frac{w}{2}$$

Multiplying both sides by 2 yields $2w + 60 = w$

Subtracting w from both sides yields $w + 60 = 0$

Finally, subtracting 60 from both sides yields $w = -60$

The answer is (A).

Counting

Counting may have been one of humankind's first thought processes; nevertheless, counting can be deceptively hard. In part, because we often forget some of the principles of counting, but also because counting can be inherently difficult.

 When counting elements that are in overlapping sets, the total number will equal the number in one group plus the number in the other group minus the number common to both groups. Venn diagrams are very helpful with these problems.

Example 1: If in a certain school 20 students are taking math and 10 are taking history and 7 are taking both, how many students are taking either math or history?

(A) 20   (B) 22   (C) 23   (D) 25   (E) 29

Solution:

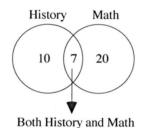

Both History and Math

By the principle stated above, we add 10 and 20 and then subtract 7 from the result. Thus, there are $(10 + 20) - 7 = 23$ students. The answer is (C).

 The number of integers between two integers <u>inclusive</u> is one more than their difference.

Example 2: How many integers are there between 49 and 101, inclusive?

(A) 50   (B) 51   (C) 52   (D) 53   (E) 54

By the principle stated above, the number of integers between 49 and 101 inclusive is $(101 - 49) + 1 = 53$. The answer is (D). To see this more clearly, choose smaller numbers, say, 9 and 11. The difference between 9 and 11 is 2. But there are three numbers between them inclusive—9, 10, and 11—one more than their difference.

 Fundamental Principle of Counting: **If an event occurs *m* times, and each of the *m* events is followed by a second event which occurs *k* times, then the first event follows the second event *m · k* times.**

The following diagram illustrates the fundamental principle of counting for an event that occurs 3 times with each occurrence being followed by a second event that occurs 2 times for a total of $3 \cdot 2 = 6$ events:

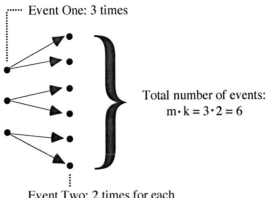

Event One: 3 times

Total number of events:
m·k = 3·2 = 6

Event Two: 2 times for each
occurrence of Event One

Example 3: A drum contains 3 to 5 jars each of which contains 30 to 40 marbles. If 10 percent of the marbles are flawed, what is the greatest possible number of flawed marbles in the drum?

(A) 51   (B) 40   (C) 30   (D) 20   (E) 12

There is at most 5 jars each of which contains at most 40 marbles; so by the fundamental counting principle, there is at most $5 \cdot 40 = 200$ marbles in the drum. Since 10 percent of the marbles are flawed, there is at most $20 = 10\% \cdot 200$ flawed marbles. The answer is (D).

MISCELLANEOUS COUNTING PROBLEMS

Example 4: In a legislative body of 200 people, the number of Democrats is 50 less than 4 times the number of Republicans. If one fifth of the legislators are neither Republican nor Democrat, how many of the legislators are Republicans?

(A) 42   (B) 50   (C) 71   (D) 95   (E) 124

Let D be the number of Democrats and let R be the number of Republicans. "One fifth of the legislators are neither Republican nor Democrat," so there are $\frac{1}{5} \cdot 200 = 40$ legislators who are neither Republican nor Democrat. Hence, there are $200 - 40 = 160$ Democrats and Republicans, or $D + R = 160$. Translating the clause "the number of Democrats is 50 less than 4 times the number of Republicans" into an equation yields $D = 4R - 50$. Plugging this into the equation $D + R = 160$ yields

$$4R - 50 + R = 160$$
$$5R - 50 = 160$$
$$5R = 210$$
$$R = 42$$

The answer is (A).

Example 5: Speed bumps are being placed at 20 foot intervals along a road 1015 feet long. If the first speed bump is placed at one end of the road, how many speed bumps are needed?

(A) 49   (B) 50   (C) 51   (D) 52   (E) 53

Since the road is 1015 feet long and the speed bumps are 20 feet apart, there are $\frac{1015}{20} = 50.75$, or 50 full sections in the road. If we ignore the first speed bump and associate the speed bump at the end of each section with that section, then there are 50 speed bumps (one for each of the fifty full sections). Counting the first speed bump gives a total of 51 speed bumps. The answer is (C).

SETS

A *set* is a collection of objects, and the objects are called *elements* of the set. You may be asked to form the *union* of two sets, which contains all the objects from either set. You may also be asked to form the *intersection* of two sets, which contains only the objects that are in both sets. For example, if
Set $A = \{1, 2, 5\}$ and Set $B = \{5, 10, 21\}$, then the union of sets A and B would be $\{1, 2, 5, 10, 21\}$ and the intersection would be $\{5\}$.

Problem Set V:

1. The number of integers between 29 and 69, inclusive is
    (A) 39   (B) 40   (C) 41   (D) 42   (E) 43

2. A school has a total enrollment of 150 students. There are 63 students taking French, 48 taking chemistry, and 21 taking both. How many students are taking <u>neither</u> French nor chemistry?
    (A) 60   (B) 65   (C) 71   (D) 75   (E) 97

3. The number of minutes in $1\frac{1}{3}$ hours is
    (A) 60   (B) 65   (C) 71   (D) 80   (E) 97

4. A web press prints 5 pages every 2 seconds. At this rate, how many pages will the press print in 7 minutes?
    (A) 350   (B) 540   (C) 700   (D) 950   (E) 1050

5. A school has a total enrollment of 90 students. There are 30 students taking physics, 25 taking English, and 13 taking both. What percentage of the students are taking either physics or English?
    (A) 30%   (B) 36%   (C) 47%   (D) 51%   (E) 58%

6. Callers 49 through 91 to a radio show won a prize. How many callers won a prize?
    (A) 42   (B) 43   (C) 44   (D) 45   (E) 46

7. A rancher is constructing a fence by stringing wire between posts 20 feet apart. If the fence is 400 feet long, how many posts must the rancher use?
    (A) 18   (B) 19   (C) 20   (D) 21   (E) 22

8. The number of marbles in x jars , each containing 15 marbles, plus the number of marbles in $3x$ jars , each containing 20 marbles is
    (A) $65x$ (B) $70x$ (C) $75x$ (D) $80x$ (E) $85x$

9. The number of integers from 2 to 10^3 , inclusive is
    (A) 997   (B) 998   (C) 999   (D) 1000   (E) 1001

10. In a small town, 16 people own Fords and 11 people own Toyotas. If exactly 15 people own only one of the two types of cars, how many people own both types of cars.
    (A) 2   (B) 6   (C) 7   (D) 12   (E) 14

Answers and Solutions to Problem Set V

1.   Since the number of integers between two integers inclusive is one more than their difference, we get $69 - 29 + 1 = 41$ integers. The answer is (C).

2.   First display the information in a Venn diagram:

French   Chemistry

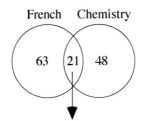

Both French and Chemistry

Adding the number of students taking French and the number of students taking chemistry and then subtracting the number of students taking both yields $(63 + 48) - 21 = 90$. This is the number of students enrolled in *either* French or chemistry or both. Since the total school enrollment is 150, there are $150 - 90 = 60$ students enrolled in *neither* French nor chemistry. The answer is (A).

3.   There are 60 minutes in an hour. Hence, there are $1\frac{1}{3} \cdot 60 = 80$ minutes in $1\frac{1}{3}$ hours. The answer is (D).

4.   Since there are 60 seconds in a minute and the press prints 5 pages every 2 seconds, the press prints $5 \cdot 30 = 150$ pages in one minute. Hence, in 7 minutes, the press will print $7 \cdot 150 = 1050$ pages. The answer is (E).

5.   First display the information in a Venn diagram:

Physics   English

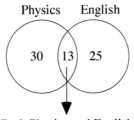

Both Physics and English

Adding the number of students taking physics and the number of students taking English and then subtracting the number of students taking both yields $(30 + 25) = -13 = 42$. This is the number of students enrolled in *either* physics or English or both. The total school enrollment is 90, so forming the ratio yields

$$\frac{physics \; or \; math \; enrollment}{total \; enrollment} = \frac{42}{90} \approx .47 = 47\%$$

The answer is (C).

6.   Since the number of integers between two integers inclusive is one more than their difference, $(91 - 49) + 1 = 43$ callers won a prize. The answer is (B).

7.   Since the fence is 400 feet long and the posts are 20 feet apart, there are $\dfrac{400}{20} = 20$ sections in the fence. Now, if we ignore the first post and associate the post at the end of each section with that section, then there are 20 posts (one for each of the twenty sections). Counting the first post gives a total of 21 posts. The answer is (D).

8.   The x jars have $15x$ marbles, and the $3x$ jars have $20 \cdot 3x = 60x$ marbles. Hence, there is a total of $15x + 60x = 75x$ marbles. The answer is (C).

9.   Since the number of integers between two integers inclusive is one more than their difference, we have $\left(10^3 - 2\right) + 1 = (1000 - 2) + 1 = 999$ integers. The answer is (C).

10.   This is a hard problem. Let x be the number of people who own both types of cars. Then the number of people who own only Fords is $16 - x$, and the number of people who own only Toyotas is $11 - x$. Adding these two expressions gives the number of people who own only one of the two types of cars, which we are are told is 15:

$$(16 - x) + (11 - x) = 15$$

Add like terms: $27 - 2x = 15$

Subtract 27 from both sides of the equation: $-2x = -12$

Finally, divide both sides of the equation by –2: $x = 6$

The answer is (B).

Probability & Statistics

PROBABILITY

We know what probability means, but what is its formal definition? Let's use our intuition to define it. If there is no chance that an event will occur, then its probability of occurring should be 0. On the other extreme, if an event is certain to occur, then its probability of occurring should be 100%, or 1. Hence, our *probability* should be a number between 0 and 1, inclusive. But what kind of number? Suppose your favorite actor has a 1 in 3 chance of winning the Oscar for best actor. This can be measured by forming the fraction 1/3. Hence, a *probability* is a fraction where the top is the number of ways an event can occur and the bottom is the total number of possible events:

$$P = \frac{Number\ of\ ways\ an\ event\ can\ occur}{Number\ of\ total\ possible\ events}$$

Example: *Flipping a coin*

What's the probability of getting heads when flipping a coin?

There is only one way to get heads in a coin toss. Hence, the top of the probability fraction is 1. There are two possible results: heads or tails. Forming the probability fraction gives 1/2.

Example: *Tossing a die*

What's the probability of getting a 3 when tossing a die?

A die (a cube) has six faces, numbered 1 through 6. There is only one way to get a 3. Hence, the top of the fraction is 1. There are 6 possible results: 1, 2, 3, 4, 5, and 6. Forming the probability fraction gives 1/6.

Example: *Drawing a card from a deck*

What's the probability of getting a king when drawing a card from a deck of cards?

A deck of cards has four kings, so there are 4 ways to get a king. Hence, the top of the fraction is 4. There are 52 total cards in a deck. Forming the probability fraction gives 4/52, which reduces to 1/13. Hence, there is 1 chance in 13 of getting a king.

Example: *Drawing marbles from a bowl*

What's the probability of drawing a blue marble from a bowl containing 4 red marbles, 5 blue marbles, and 5 green marbles?

There are five ways of drawing a blue marble. Hence, the top of the fraction is 5. There are 14 (= 4 + 5 + 5) possible results. Forming the probability fraction gives 5/14.

Example: *Drawing marbles from a bowl (second drawing)*

What's the probability of drawing a red marble from the same bowl, given that the first marble drawn was blue and was not placed back in the bowl?

There are four ways of drawing a red marble. Hence, the top of the fraction is 4. Since the blue marble from the first drawing was not replaced, there are only 4 blue marbles remaining. Hence, there are 13 (= 4 + 4 + 5) possible results. Forming the probability fraction gives 4/13.

Consecutive Probabilities

What's the probability of getting heads twice in a row when flipping a coin twice? Previously we calculated the probability for the first flip to be 1/2. Since the second flip is not affected by the first (these are called *mutually exclusive* events), its probability is also 1/2. Forming the product yields the probability of two heads in a row: $\frac{1}{2} \times \frac{1}{2} = \frac{1}{4}$.

What's the probability of drawing a blue marble and then a red marble from a bowl containing 4 red marbles, 5 blue marbles, and 5 green marbles? (Assume that the marbles are not replaced after being selected.) As calculated before, there is a 5/14 likelihood of selecting a blue marble first and a 4/13 likelihood of selecting a red marble second. Forming the product yields the probability of a red marble immediately followed by a blue marble: $\frac{5}{14} \times \frac{4}{13} = \frac{20}{182} = \frac{10}{91}$.

These two examples can be generalized into the following rule for calculating consecutive probabilities:

To calculate consecutive probabilities, multiply the individual probabilities.

This rule applies to two, three, or any number of consecutive probabilities.

Either-Or Probabilities

What's the probability of getting either heads or tails when flipping a coin once? Since the only possible outcomes are heads or tails, we expect the probability to be 100%, or 1: $\frac{1}{2} + \frac{1}{2} = 1$. Note that the events heads and tails are mutually exclusive. That is, if heads occurs, then tails cannot (and vice versa).

What's the probability of drawing a red marble or a green marble from a bowl containing 4 red marbles, 5 blue marbles, and 5 green marbles? There are 4 red marbles out of 14 total marbles. So the probability of selecting a red marble is 4/14 = 2/7. Similarly, the probability of selecting a green marble is 5/14. So the probability of selecting a red or green marble is $\frac{2}{7} + \frac{5}{14} = \frac{9}{14}$. Note again that the events are mutually exclusive. For instance, if a red marble is selected, then neither a blue marble nor a green marble is selected.

These two examples can be generalized into the following rule for calculating *either-or* probabilities:

To calculate *either-or* probabilities, add the individual probabilities (only if the events are mutually exclusive).

The probabilities in the two immediately preceding examples can be calculated more naturally by adding up the events that occur and then dividing by the total number of possible events. For the coin example, we get 2 events (heads or tails) divided by the total number of possible events, 2 (heads and tails): 2/2 = 1. For the marble example, we get 9 (= 4 + 5) ways the event can occur divided by 14 (= 4 + 5 + 5) possible events: 9/14.

If it's more natural to calculate the *either-or* probabilities above by adding up the events that occur and then dividing by the total number of possible events, why did we introduce a second way of calculating the probabilities? Because in some cases, you may have to add the individual probabilities. For example, you may be given the individual probabilities of two mutually exclusive events and be asked for the probability that either could occur. You now know to merely add their individual probabilities.

Geometric Probability

In this type of problem, you will be given two figures, with one inside the other. You'll then be asked what is the probability that a randomly selected point will be in the smaller figure. These problems are solved with the same principle we have been using: $Probability = \dfrac{desired\ outcome}{possible\ outcomes}$.

Example: In the figure to the right, the smaller square has sides of length 2 and the larger square has sides of length 4. If a point is chosen at random from the large square, what is the probability that it will be from the small square?

Applying the probability principle, we get $Probability = \dfrac{\text{area of the small square}}{\text{area of the large square}} = \dfrac{2^2}{4^2} = \dfrac{4}{16} = \dfrac{1}{4}$.

STATISTICS

Statistics is the study of the patterns and relationships of numbers and data. There are four main concepts that may appear on the test:

Median

When a set of numbers is arranged in order of size, the *median* is the middle number. For example, the median of the set {8, 9, 10, 11, 12} is 10 because it is the middle number. In this case, the median is also the mean (average). But this is usually not the case. For example, the median of the set {8, 9, 10, 11, 17} is 10 because it is the middle number, but the mean is $11 = \dfrac{8 + 9 + 10 + 11 + 17}{5}$. If a set contains an even number of elements, then the median is the average of the two middle elements. For example, the median of the set {1, 5, 8, 20} is $6.5 \left(= \dfrac{5 + 8}{2} \right)$.

Example: What is the median of 0, –2, 256 , 18, $\sqrt{2}$?

Arranging the numbers from smallest to largest (we could also arrange the numbers from the largest to smallest; the answer would be the same), we get –2, 0, $\sqrt{2}$, 18, 256. The median is the middle number, $\sqrt{2}$.

Mode

The *mode* is the number or numbers that appear most frequently in a set. Note that this definition allows a set of numbers to have more than one mode.

Example: What is the mode of 3, –4, 3 , 7, 9, 7.5 ?

The number 3 is the mode because it is the only number that is listed more than once.

Example: What is the mode of 2, π, 2 , –9, π, 5 ?

Both 2 and π are modes because each occurs twice, which is the greatest number of occurrences for any number in the list.

Range

The *range* is the distance between the smallest and largest numbers in a set. To calculate the range, merely subtract the smallest number from the largest number.

Example: What is the range of 2, 8, 1 , –6, π, 1/2 ?

The largest number in this set is 8, and the smallest number is –6. Hence, the range is 8 – (–6) = 8 + 6 = 14.

Standard Deviation

On the test, you are not expected to know the definition of standard deviation. However, you may be presented with the definition of standard deviation and then be asked a question based on the definition. To make sure we cover all possible bases, we'll briefly discuss this concept.

Standard deviation measures how far the numbers in a set vary from the set's mean. If the numbers are scattered far from the set's mean, then the standard deviation is large. If the numbers are bunched up near the set's mean, then the standard deviation is small.

Example: Which of the following sets has the larger standard deviation?

$$A = \{1, 2, 3, 4, 5\}$$
$$B = \{1, 4, 15, 21, 34\}$$

All the numbers in Set A are within 2 units of the mean, 3. All the numbers in Set B are greater than 5 units from the mean, 15 (except, or course, the mean itself). Hence, the standard deviation of Set B is greater.

Problem Set W:

1. The median is larger than the average for which one of the following sets of integers?

    (A) {8, 9, 10, 11, 12}
    (B) {8, 9, 10, 11, 13}
    (C) {8, 10, 10, 10, 12}
    (D) {10, 10, 10, 10, 10}
    (E) {7, 9, 10, 11, 12}

2. A hat contains 15 marbles, and each marble is numbered with one and only one of the numbers 1, 2, 3. From a group of 15 people, each person selects exactly 1 marble from the hat.

Numbered Marble	Number of People Who Selected The Marble
1	4
2	5
3	6

    What is the probability that a person selected at random picked a marble numbered 2 or greater?

    (A) 5/15　　(B) 9/15　　(C) 10/15　　(D) 11/15　　(E) 1

3. Sarah cannot completely remember her four-digit ATM pin number. She does remember the first two digits, and she knows that each of the last two digits is greater than 5. The ATM will allow her three tries before it blocks further access. If she randomly guesses the last two digits, what is the probability that she will get access to her account?

    (A) 1/2　　(B) 1/4　　(C) 3/16　　(D) 3/18　　(E) 1/32

4. If $x < y < z$, $z = ky$, $x = 0$, and the average of the numbers x, y, and z is 3 times the median, what is the value of k?

    (A) –2　　(B) 3　　(C) 5.5　　(D) 6　　(E) 8

5. Three positive numbers x, y, and z have the following relationships $y = x + 2$ and $z = y + 2$. When the median of x, y, and z is subtracted from the product of the smallest number and the median, the result is 0. What is the value of the largest number?

    (A) –2　　(B) π　　(C) 5　　(D) 8　　(E) 21/2

6. A jar contains only three types of objects: red, blue, and silver paper clips. The probability of selecting a red paper clip is 1/4, and the probability of selecting a blue paper clip is 1/6. What is the probability of selecting a silver paper clip?

    (A) 5/12　　(B) 1/2　　(C) 7/12　　(D) 3/4　　(E) 11/12

7. A bowl contains one marble labeled 0, one marble labeled 1, one marble labeled 2, and one marble labeled 3. The bowl contains no other objects. If two marbles are drawn randomly without replacement, what is the probability that they will add up to 3?

    (A) 1/12　　(B) 1/8　　(C) 1/6　　(D) 1/4　　(E) 1/3

8. A housing subdivision contains only two types of homes: ranch-style homes and townhomes. There are twice as many townhomes as ranch-style homes. There are 3 times as many townhomes with pools than without pools. What is the probability that a home selected at random from the subdivision will be a townhome with a pool?

    (A) 1/6　　(B) 1/5　　(C) 1/4　　(D) 1/3　　(E) 1/2

9. The figure to the right shows a small equilateral triangle inscribed in the large equilateral triangle. If a point is chosen at random from the large triangle, what is the probability that it will be from the small triangle?

    (A) 1/8　　(B) 1/5　　(C) 1/4　　(D) 1/3　　(E) 1/2

Answers and Solutions to Problem Set W

1. The median in all five answer-choices is 10. By symmetry, the average in answer-choices (A), (C), and (D) is 10 as well. The average in choice (B) is larger than 10 because 13 is further away from 10 than 8 is. Similarly, the average in choice (E) is smaller than 10 because 7 is further away from 10 than 12 is. The exact average is $\dfrac{7+9+10+11+12}{5} = \dfrac{49}{5} < 10$. The answer is (E).

2. There are 11 (= 5 + 6) people who selected a number 2 or number 3 marble, and there are 15 total people. Hence, the probability of selecting a number 2 or number 3 marble is 11/15, and the answer is (D).

3. Randomly guessing either of the last two digits does not affect the choice of the other, which means that these events are mutually exclusive and we are dealing with consecutive probabilities. Since each of the last two digits is greater than 5, Sarah has four digits to choose from: 6, 7, 8, 9. Her chance of guessing correctly on the first choice is 1/4, and on the second choice also 1/4. Her chance of guessing correctly on both choices is

$$\frac{1}{4} \cdot \frac{1}{4} = \frac{1}{16}$$

Since she gets three tries, the total probability is $\dfrac{1}{16} + \dfrac{1}{16} + \dfrac{1}{16} = \dfrac{3}{16}$. The answer is (C).

4. Since y is the middle number, it is the median. Forming the average of x, y, and z and setting it equal to 3 times the median yields

$$\frac{x+y+z}{3} = 3y$$

Replacing x with 0 and z with ky yields

$$\frac{0+y+ky}{3} = 3y$$

Multiplying both sides of this equation by 3 yields $\quad y + ky = 9y$

Subtracting $9y$ from both sides yields $\quad -8y + ky = 0$

Factoring out y yields $\quad y(-8 + k) = 0$

Since $y \neq 0$ (why?), $-8 + k = 0$. Hence, $k = 8$ and the answer is (E).

5. Plugging $y = x + 2$ into the equation $z = y + 2$ gives $z = (x + 2) + 2 = x + 4$. Hence, in terms of x, the three numbers x, y, and z are

$$x, x+2, x+4$$

Clearly, x is the smallest number. Further, since $x + 2$ is smaller than $x + 4$, $x + 2$ is the median. Subtracting the median from the product of the smallest number and the median and setting the result equal to 0 yields

$$x(x+2) - (x+2) = 0$$

Factoring out the common factor $x + 2$ yields

$$(x+2)(x-1) = 0$$

Setting each factor equal to 0 yields

$$x + 2 = 0 \ \text{ or } \ x - 1 = 0$$

Hence, $x = -2$ or $x = 1$. Since the three numbers are positive, x must be 1. Hence, the largest number is $x + 4 = 1 + 4 = 5$. The answer is (C).

6. First, let's calculate the probability of selecting a red or a blue paper clip. This is an either-or probability and is therefore the sum of the individual probabilities:

$$1/4 + 1/6 = 5/12$$

Now, since there are only three types of objects, the sum of their probabilities must be 1 (Remember that the sum of the probabilities of all possible outcomes is always 1):

$$P(r) + P(b) + P(s) = 1,$$

where r stands for red, b stands for blue, and s stands for silver.

Replacing $P(r) + P(b)$ with 5/12 yields $5/12 + P(s) = 1$

Subtracting 5/12 from both sides of this equation yields $P(s) = 1 - 5/12$

Performing the subtraction yields $P(s) = 7/12$

The answer is (C).

7.   The following list shows all 12 ways of selecting the two marbles:

(0, 1)	(1, 0)	(2, 0)	**(3, 0)**
(0, 2)	**(1, 2)**	**(2, 1)**	(3, 1)
(0, 3)	(1, 3)	(2, 3)	(3, 2)

The four pairs in bold are the only ones whose sum is 3. Hence, the probability that two randomly drawn marbles will have a sum of 3 is

$$4/12 = 1/3$$

The answer is (E).

8.   Since there are twice as many townhomes as ranch-style homes, the probability of selecting a townhome is 2/3.[*] Now, "there are 3 times as many townhomes with pools than without pools." So the probability that a townhome will have a pool is 3/4. Hence, the probability of selecting a townhome with a pool is

$$\frac{2}{3} \cdot \frac{3}{4} = \frac{1}{2}$$

The answer is (E).

9.   In the figure, it appears that the small inscribed triangle divides the large triangle into four congruent triangles. Hence, the probability that a point chosen at random from the large triangle will also be from the small triangle is 1/4. (As an exercise, prove that small inscribed triangle divides the large triangle into four congruent triangles.) The answer is (C).

---

[*] Caution: Were you tempted to choose 1/2 for the probability because there are "twice" as many townhomes? One-half (= 50%) would be the probability if there were an equal number of townhomes and ranch-style homes. Remember the probability of selecting a townhome is not the ratio of townhomes to ranch-style homes, but the ratio of townhomes to the total number of homes. To see this more clearly, suppose there are 3 homes in the subdivision. Then 2 would be townhomes and 1 would be a ranch-style home. So the ratio of townhomes to total homes would be 2/3.

Functions

DEFINITION

A function is a special relationship (correspondence) between two sets such that for each element x in its domain there is assigned one and <u>only one</u> element y in its range.

Notice that the correspondence has two parts:

1) For each x there is assigned *one* y. (This is the ordinary part of the definition.)

2) For each x there is assigned *only one* y. (This is the special part of the definition.)

The second part of the definition of a function creates the uniqueness of the assignment: There cannot be assigned two values of y to one x. In mathematics, uniqueness is very important. We know that $2 + 2 = 4$, but it would be confusing if $2 + 2$ could also equal something else, say 5. In this case, we could never be sure that the answer to a question was the *right* answer.

The correspondence between x and y is usually expressed with the function notation: $y = f(x)$, where y is called the *dependent variable* and x is called the *independent variable*. In other words, the value of y depends on the value of x plugged into the function. For example, the square root function can be written as $y = f(x) = \sqrt{x}$. To calculate the correspondence for $x = 4$, we get $y = f(4) = \sqrt{4} = 2$. That is, the square root function assigns the unique y value of 2 to the x value of 4. Most expressions can be turned into functions. For example, the expression $2^x - \dfrac{1}{x}$ becomes the function

$$f(x) = 2^x - \frac{1}{x}$$

DOMAIN AND RANGE

We usually identify a function with its correspondence, as in the example above. However, a function consists of three parts: a domain, a range, and correspondence between them.

➢ **The *domain* of a function is the set of x values for which the function is defined.**

For example, the function $f(x) = \dfrac{1}{x-1}$ is defined for all values of $x \neq 1$, which causes division by zero.

There is an infinite variety of functions with restricted domains, but only two types of restricted domains appear on the ACT: division by zero and even roots of negative numbers. For example, the function $f(x) = \sqrt{x-2}$ is defined only if $x - 2 \geq 0$, or $x \geq 2$. The two types of restrictions can be combined. For example, $f(x) = \dfrac{1}{\sqrt{x-2}}$. Here, $x - 2 \geq 0$ since it's under the square root symbol. Further $x - 2 \neq 0$, or $x \neq 2$, because that would cause division by zero. Hence, the domain is all $x > 2$.

*e **range** of a function is the set of y values that are assigned to the x values in the domain.*

ample, the range of the function $y = f(x) = x^2$ is $y \geq 0$ since a square is never negative. The range of the function $y = f(x) = x^2 + 1$ is $y \geq 1$ since $x^2 + 1 \geq 1$. You can always calculate the range of a function algebraically, but is usually better to graph the function and read off its range from the y values of the graph.

GRAPHS

The graph of a function is the set of ordered pairs $(x, f(x))$, where x is in the domain of f and $y = f(x)$.

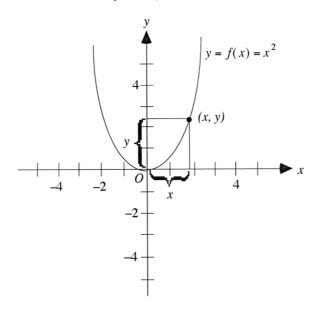

For this function, the domain is all x and the range is all $y \geq 0$ (since the graph touches the x-axis at the origin and is above the x-axis elsewhere).

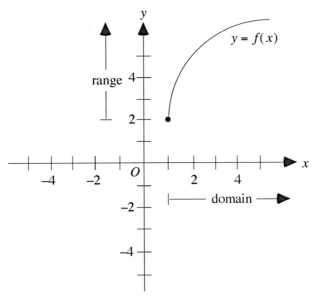

For this function, the domain is all $x \geq 1$ and the range is all $y \geq 2$.

TRANSLATIONS OF GRAPHS

Many graphs can be obtained by shifting a base graph around by adding positive or negative numbers to various places in the function. Take for example, the absolute value function $y = |x|$. Its graph is

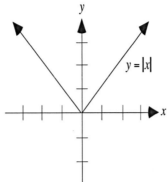

(Notice that sometimes an arrow is added to a graph to indicate the graph continues indefinitely and sometimes nothing is used. To indicate that a graph stops, a dot is added to the terminal point of the graph. Also, notice that the domain of the absolute value function is all x because you can take the absolute value of any number. The range is $y \geq 0$ because the graph touches the x-axis at the origin, is above the x-axis elsewhere, and increases indefinitely.)

To shift this base graph up one unit, we add 1 outside the absolute value symbol, $y = |x| + 1$:

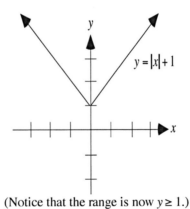

(Notice that the range is now $y \geq 1$.)

To shift the base graph down one unit, we subtract 1 outside the absolute value symbol, $y = |x| - 1$:

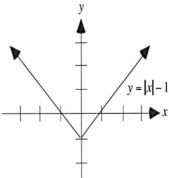

(Notice that the range is now $y \geq -1$.)

To shift the base graph to the right one unit, we subtract 1 inside the absolute value symbol, $y = |x - 1|$:

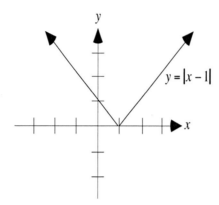

(Notice that the range did not change; it's still $y \geq 0$. Notice also that subtracting 1 moved the graph to right. Many students will mistakenly move the graph to the left because that's where the negative numbers are.)

To shift the base graph to the left one unit, we add 1 inside the absolute value symbol, $y = |x + 1|$:

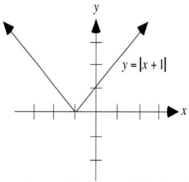

(Notice that the range did not change; it's still $y \geq 0$. Notice also that adding 1 moved the graph to left. Many students will mistakenly move the graph to the right because that's where the positive numbers are.)

The pattern of the translations above holds for all functions. So to move a function $y = f(x)$ up c units, add the positive constant c to the exterior of the function: $y = f(x) + c$. To move a function $y = f(x)$ to the right c units, subtract the constant c in interior of the function: $y = f(x - c)$. To summarize, we have

To shift up c units:	$y = f(x) + c$
To shift down c units:	$y = f(x) - c$
To shift to the right c units:	$y = f(x - c)$
To shift to the left c units:	$y = f(x + c)$

REFLECTIONS OF GRAPHS

Many graphs can be obtained by reflecting a base graph by multiplying various places in the function by negative numbers. Take for example, the square root function $y = \sqrt{x}$. Its graph is

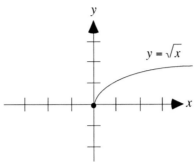

(Notice that the domain of the square root function is all $x \geq 0$ because you cannot take the square root of a negative number. The range is $y \geq 0$ because the graph touches the x-axis at the origin, is above the x-axis elsewhere, and increases indefinitely.)

To reflect this base graph about the x-axis, multiply the exterior of the square root symbol by negative one, $y = -\sqrt{x}$:

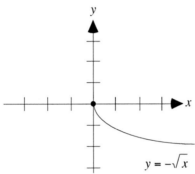

(Notice that the range is now $y \leq 0$ and the domain has not changed.)

To reflect the base graph about the y-axis, multiply the interior of the square root symbol by negative one, $y = \sqrt{-x}$:

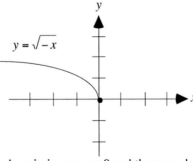

(Notice that the domain is now $x \leq 0$ and the range has not changed.)

The pattern of the reflections above holds for all functions. So to reflect a function $y = f(x)$ about the x-axis, multiply the exterior of the function by negative one: $y = -f(x)$. To reflect a function $y = f(x)$ about the y-axis, multiply the exterior of the function by negative one: $y = f(-x)$. To summarize, we have

To reflect about the x-axis: $\qquad y = -f(x)$

To reflect about the y-axis: $\qquad y = f(-x)$

Reflections and translations can be combined. Let's reflect the base graph of the square root function $y = \sqrt{x}$ about the *x*-axis, the *y*-axis and then shift it to the right 2 units and finally up 1 unit:

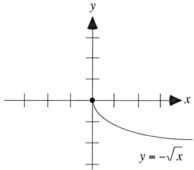

(Notice that the domain is still $x \geq 0$ and the range is now $y \leq 0$.)

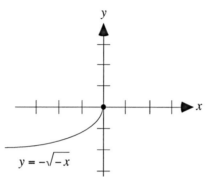

(Notice that the domain is now $x \leq 0$ and the range is still $y \leq 0$.)

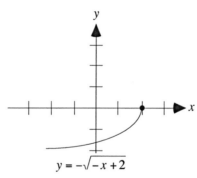

(Notice that the domain is now $x \leq 2$ and the range is still $y \leq 0$.)

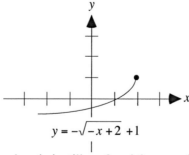

(Notice that the domain is still $x \leq 2$ and the range is now $y \leq 1$.)

EVALUATION AND COMPOSITION OF FUNCTIONS

EVALUATION

We have been using the function notation $f(x)$ intuitively; we also need to study what it actually means. You can think of the letter f in the function notation $f(x)$ as the name of the function. Instead of using the equation $y = x^3 - 1$ to describe the function, we can write $f(x) = x^3 - 1$. Here, f is the name of the function and $f(x)$ is the value of the function at x. So $f(2) = 2^3 - 1 = 8 - 1 = 7$ is the value of the function at 2. As you can see, this notation affords a convenient way of prompting the evaluation of a function for a particular value of x.

Any letter can be used as the independent variable in a function. So the above function could be written $f(p) = p^3 - 1$. This indicates that the independent variable in a function is just a "placeholder." The function could be written without a variable as follows:

$$f(\ ) = (\ )^3 - 1$$

In this form, the function can be viewed as an input/output operation. If 2 is put into the function $f(2)$, then $2^3 - 1$ is returned.

In addition to plugging numbers into functions, we can plug expressions into functions. Plugging $y + 1$ into the function $f(x) = x^2 - x$ yields

$$f(y + 1) = (y + 1)^2 - (y + 1)$$

You can also plug other expressions in terms of x into a function. Plugging $2x$ into the function $f(x) = x^2 - x$ yields

$$f(2x) = (2x)^2 - 2x$$

This evaluation can be troubling to students because the variable x in the function is being replaced by the same variable. But the x in function is just a placeholder. If the placeholder were removed from the function, the substitution would appear more natural. In $f(\ ) = (\ )^2 - (\ )$, we plug $2x$ into the left side $f(2x)$ and it returns the right side $(2x)^2 - 2x$.

COMPOSITION

We have plugged numbers into functions and expressions into functions; now let's plug in other functions. Since a function is identified with its expression, we have actually already done this. In the example above with $f(x) = x^2 - x$ and $2x$, let's call $2x$ by the name $g(x)$. In other words, $g(x) = 2x$. Then the composition of f with g (that is plugging g into f) is

$$f(g(x)) = f(2x) = (2x)^2 - 2x$$

For another example, let $f(x) = \dfrac{1}{x+1}$ and let $g(x) = x^2$. Then $f(g(x)) = \dfrac{1}{x^2+1}$ and $g(f(x)) = \left(\dfrac{1}{x+1}\right)^2$.

Once you see that the composition of functions merely substitutes one function into another, these problems can become routine. Notice that the composition operation $f(g(x))$ is performed from the inner parentheses out, not from left to right. In the operation $f(g(2))$, the number 2 is first plugged into the function g and then that result is plugged in the function f.

A function can also be composed with itself. That is, substituted into itself. Let $f(x) = \sqrt{x} - 2$. Then $f(f(x)) = \sqrt{\sqrt{x} - 2} - 2$.

Example: The graph of $y = f(x)$ is shown to the right. If $f(-1) = v$, then which one of the following could be the value of $f(v)$?

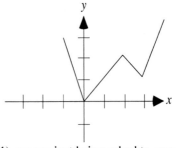

(A)   0
(B)   1
(C)   2
(D)   2.5
(E)   3

Since we are being asked to evaluate $f(v)$ and we are told that $v = f(-1)$, we are just being asked to compose f(x) with itself. That is, we need to calculate $f(f(-1))$. From the graph, $f(-1) = 3$. So $f(f(-1)) = f(3)$. Again, from the graph, $f(3) = 1$. So $f(f(-1)) = f(3) = 1$. The answer is (B).

QUADRATIC FUNCTIONS

Quadratic functions (parabolas) have the following form:

$$y = f(x) = ax^2 + bx + c$$

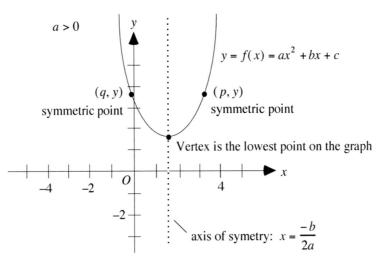

The lowest or highest point on a quadratic graph is called the vertex. The *x*–coordinate of the vertex occurs at $x = \dfrac{-b}{2a}$. This vertical line also forms the axis of symmetry of the graph, which means that if the graph were folded along its axis, the left and right sides of the graph would coincide.

In graphs of the form $y = f(x) = ax^2 + bx + c$ if $a > 0$, then the graph opens up.

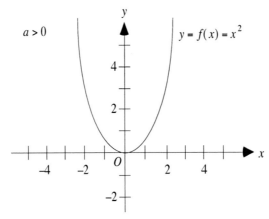

If $a < 0$, then the graph opens down.

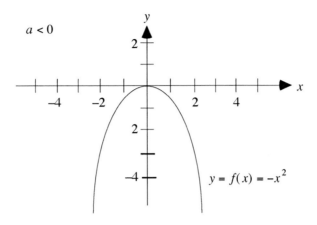

By completing the square, the form $y = ax^2 + bx + c$ can be written as $y = a(x - h)^2 + k$. You are not expected to know this form on the test. But it is a convenient form since the vertex occurs at the point (h, k) and the axis of symmetry is the line $x = h$.

We have been analyzing quadratic functions that are vertically symmetric. Though not as common, quadratic functions can also be horizontally symmetric. They have the following form:

$$x = g(y) = ay^2 + by + c$$

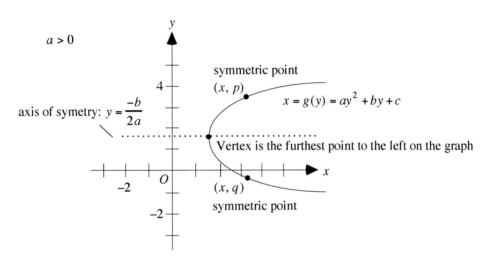

The furthest point to the left on this graph is called the vertex. The y-coordinate of the vertex occurs at $y = \dfrac{-b}{2a}$. This horizontal line also forms the axis of symmetry of the graph, which means that if the graph were folded along its axis, the top and bottom parts of the graph would coincide.

In graphs of the form $x = ay^2 + by + c$ if $a > 0$, then the graph opens to the right and if $a < 0$ then the graph opens to the left.

Example: The graph of $x = -y^2 + 2$ and the graph of the line k intersect at $(0, p)$ and $(1, q)$. Which one of the following is the smallest possible slope of line k?

(A) $-\sqrt{2} - 1$
(B) $-\sqrt{2} + 1$
(C) $\sqrt{2} - 1$
(D) $\sqrt{2} + 1$
(E) $\sqrt{2} + 2$

Let's make a rough sketch of the graphs. Expressing $x = -y^2 + 2$ in standard form yields $x = -1y^2 + 0 \cdot y + 2$. Since $a = -1$, $b = 0$, and $c = 2$, the graph opens to the left and its vertex is at $(2, 0)$.

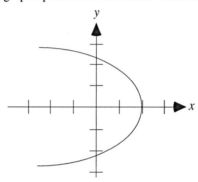

Since p and q can be positive or negative, there are four possible positions for line k (the y-coordinates in the graphs below can be calculated by plugging $x = 0$ and $x = 1$ into the function $x = -y^2 + 2$):

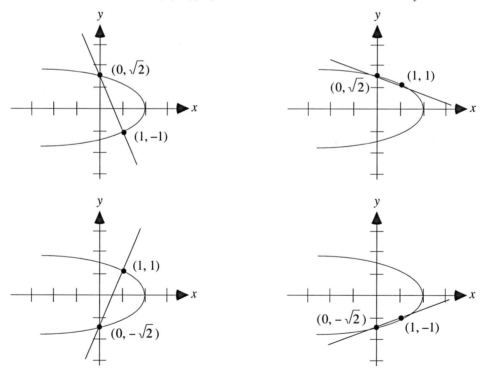

Since the line in the first graph has the steepest negative slope, it is the smallest possible slope. Calculating the slope yields

$$m = \frac{\sqrt{2} - (-1)}{0 - 1} = \frac{\sqrt{2} + 1}{-1} = -\left(\sqrt{2} + 1\right) = -\sqrt{2} - 1$$

The answer is (A).

CIRCLES

The standard form for a circle of radius r centered at (h, k) is

$$(x-h)^2 + (y-k)^2 = r^2$$

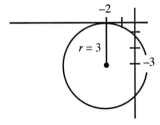

For instance, the equation of a circle of radius 4 centered at $(-1, 3)$ is

$$(x-(-1))^2 + (y-3)^2 = 2^2$$
$$(x+1)^2 + (y-3)^2 = 2^2$$

Note that a circle is not function because for some values of x, there is more than one value of y. For example, with the unit circle, $x^2 + y^2 = 1$, if $x = 0$, then $0^2 + y^2 = 1$, or $y^2 = 1$, or $y = \pm 1$. Since there are two values for y (-1 and $+1$), this is not a function.

Example: A circle of radius 3 in the (x, y) coordinate plane is tangent to x-axis at -2. If the y-coordinate of the center of the circle is negative, which one of the following is an equation of the circle?

(A) $x^2 + y^2 = 9$

(B) $x^2 + y^2 = 3$

(C) $(x-2)^2 + (y-3)^2 = 9$

(D) $(x-2)^2 + (y+3)^2 = 3$

(E) $(x+2)^2 + (y+3)^2 = 9$

Since the circle is tangent to x-axis at -2 and the y-coordinate of the center is negative, the center of the circle is in Quadrant III:

From the figure, it is clear that the center of the circle (h, k) is $(-2, -3)$. Plugging this information along with $r = 3$ into the formula for a circle yields

$$(x-(-2))^2 + (y-(-3))^2 = 3^2$$
$$(x+2)^2 + (y+3)^2 = 9$$

The answer is (E).

QUALITATIVE BEHAVIOR OF GRAPHS AND FUNCTIONS

In this rather vague category, you will be asked how a function and its graph are related. You may be asked to identify the zeros of a function based on its graph. The zeros, or roots, of a function are the *x*-coordinates of where it crosses the *x*-axis. Or you may be given two graphs and asked for what *x* values are their functions equal. The functions will be equal where they intersect.

Example: The graphs of $y = f(x)$ and $y = 1$ are shown to the right. For how many *x* values does $f(x)$ equal 1?

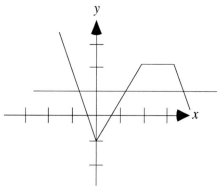

    (A)   0
    (B)   1
    (C)   2
    (D)   3
    (E)   4

The figure shows that the graphs intersect at three points. At each of these points, both graphs have a height, or *y*-coordinate, of 1. The points are approximately (–.8, 1), (1.2, 1), and (4, 1). Hence, $f(x) = 1$ for three *x* values. The answer is (D).

FUNCTIONS AS MODELS OF REAL-LIFE SITUATIONS

Functions can be used to predict the outcomes of certain physical events or real-life situations. For example, a function can predict the maximum height a projectile will reach when fired with an initial velocity, or the number of movie tickets that will be sold at a given price.

Example: The graph to the right shows the number of music CDs sold at various prices. At what price should the CDs be marked to sell the maximum number of CDs?

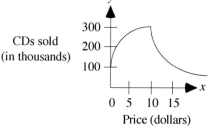

    (A)   0
    (B)   5
    (C)   10
    (D)   15
    (E)   20

As you read the graph from left to right, it shows that sales initially increase rapidly and then slow to a maximum of about 300,000. From there, sales drop precipitously and then slowly approach zero as the price continues to increase. From the graph, sales of 300,000 units on the *y*-axis correspond to a price of about $10 on the *x*-axis. The answer is (C).

Problem Set X:

$$g(x) = (2x - 3)^{1/4} + 1$$

1. In the function above, for what values of x is $g(x)$ a real number?
    (A) $x \geq 0$
    (B) $x \geq 1/2$
    (C) $x \geq 3/2$
    (D) $x \geq 2$
    (E) $x \geq 3$

x	-1	0	1	2
$f(x)$	1	3	1	-5

2. The table above shows the values of the quadratic function f for several values of x. Which one of the following best represents f?
    (A) $f(x) = -2x^2$
    (B) $f(x) = x^2 + 3$
    (C) $f(x) = -x^2 + 3$
    (D) $f(x) = -2x^2 - 3$
    (E) $f(x) = -2x^2 + 3$

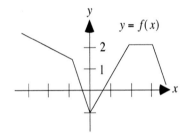

3. In the function above, if $f(k) = 2$, then which one of the following could be a value of k?
    (A) -1
    (B) 0
    (C) 0.5
    (D) 2.5
    (E) 4

4. Let the function h be defined by $h(x) = \sqrt{x} + 2$. If $3h(v) = 18$, then which one of the following is the value of $h\left(\dfrac{v}{4}\right)$?
    (A) -4
    (B) -1
    (C) 0
    (D) 2
    (E) 4

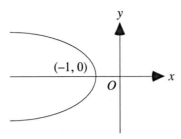

5.   The graph above shows a parabola that is symmetric about the *x*-axis. Which one of the following could be the equation of the graph?

   (A) $x = -y^2 - 1$
   (B) $x = -y^2$
   (C) $x = -y^2 + 1$
   (D) $x = y^2 - 1$
   (E) $x = (y + 1)^2$

6.   A pottery store owner determines that the revenue for sales of a particular item can be modeled by the function $r(x) = 50\sqrt{x} - 40$, where *x* is the number of the items sold. How many of the items must be sold to generate $110 in revenue?

   (A)   5
   (B)   6
   (C)   7
   (D)   8
   (E)   9

7.   At time $t = 0$, a projectile was fired upward from an initial height of 10 feet. Its height after *t* seconds is given by the function $h(t) = p - 10(q - t)^2$, where *p* and *q* are positive constants. If the projectile reached a maximum height of 100 feet when $t = 3$, then what was the height, in feet, of the projectile when $t = 4$?

   (A) 62   (B) 70   (C) 85   (D) 89   (E) 90

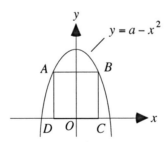

8.   The figure above shows the graph of $y = a - x^2$ for some constant *a*. If the square *ABCD* intersects the graph at points *A* and *B* and the area of the square is 16, what is the value of *a*?

   (A) 2   (B) 4   (C) 6   (D) 8   (E) 10

9.   If $f(x) = x^2 + x$, then $f(x - a) =$

   (A) $x^2 - (2a - 1)x + a^2 - a$
   (B) $x^2 - (2a + 1)x + a^2$
   (C) $x^2 + x - a^2 - a$
   (D) $x^2 + a^2$
   (E) $x^2 a^2$

Answers and Solutions to Problem Set X

$$g(x) = (2x - 3)^{1/4} + 1$$

1. In the function above, for what values of x is $g(x)$ a real number?
    (A) $x \geq 0$
    (B) $x \geq 1/2$
    (C) $x \geq 3/2$
    (D) $x \geq 2$
    (E) $x \geq 3$

Let's change the fractional notation to radical notation: $g(x) = \sqrt[4]{2x - 3} + 1$. Since we have an even root, the expression under the radical must be greater than or equal to zero. Hence, $2x - 3 \geq 0$. Adding 3 to both sides of this inequality yields $2x \geq 3$. Dividing both sides by 2 yields $x \geq 3/2$. The answer is (C).

x	−1	0	1	2
$f(x)$	1	3	1	−5

2. The table above shows the values of the quadratic function f for several values of x. Which one of the following best represents f?
    (A) $f(x) = -2x^2$
    (B) $f(x) = x^2 + 3$
    (C) $f(x) = -x^2 + 3$
    (D) $f(x) = -2x^2 - 3$
    (E) $f(x) = -2x^2 + 3$

We need to plug the x table values into each given function to find the one that returns the function values in the bottom row of the table. Let's start with $x = 0$ since zero is the easiest number to calculate with. According to the table $f(0) = 3$. This eliminates Choice (A) since $f(0) = -2(0)^2 = -2(0) = 0$; and it eliminates Choice (D) since $f(0) = -2(0)^2 - 3 = -2 \cdot 0 - 3 = 0 - 3 = -3$. Now, choose $x = 1$. The next easiest number to calculate with. According to the table $f(1) = 1$. This eliminates Choice (B) since $f(1) = 1^2 + 3 = 1 + 3 = 4$; and it eliminates Choice (C) since $f(1) = -(1)^2 + 3 = -1 + 3 = 2$. Hence, by process of elimination, the answer is (E).

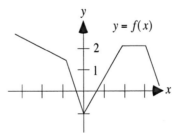

3. In the function above, if $f(k) = 2$, then which one of the following could be a value of k?
    (A) −1
    (B) 0
    (C) 0.5
    (D) 2.5
    (E) 4

The graph has a height of 2 for every value of x between 2 and 3; it also has a height of 2 at about $x = -2$. The only number offered in this interval is 2.5. This is illustrated by the dot and the thick line in the following graph:

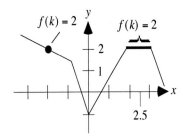

The answer is (D).

4. Let the function h be defined by $h(x) = \sqrt{x} + 2$. If $3h(v) = 18$, then which one of the following is the value of $h\left(\dfrac{v}{4}\right)$?

   (A) −4
   (B) −1
   (C) 0
   (D) 2
   (E) 4

Evaluating the function $h(x) = \sqrt{x} + 2$ at v yields $h(v) = \sqrt{v} + 2$. Plugging this into the equation $3h(v) = 18$ yields

$$3\left(\sqrt{v} + 2\right) = 18$$
$$\sqrt{v} + 2 = 6 \qquad \text{by dividing both sides by 3}$$
$$\sqrt{v} = 4 \qquad \text{by subtracting 2 from both sides}$$
$$\left(\sqrt{v}\right)^2 = 4^2 \qquad \text{by squaring both sides}$$
$$v = 16 \qquad \text{since } \left(\sqrt{v}\right)^2 = v$$

Plugging $v = 16$ into $h\left(\dfrac{v}{4}\right)$ yields

$$h\left(\frac{v}{4}\right) = h\left(\frac{16}{4}\right) = h(4) = \sqrt{4} + 2 = 2 + 2 = 4$$

The answer is (E).

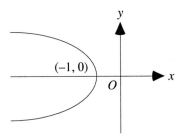

5. The graph above shows a parabola that is symmetric about the x-axis. Which one of the following could be the equation of the graph?

   (A) $x = -y^2 - 1$
   (B) $x = -y^2$
   (C) $x = -y^2 + 1$
   (D) $x = y^2 - 1$
   (E) $x = (y + 1)^2$

Since the graph is symmetric about the x-axis, its base graph is $x = y^2$. Since the graph opens to the left, we know that the exterior of the base function is multiplied by negative one: $-y^2$. Since the graph is shifted one unit to the left, we know that one is subtracted from the exterior of the function: $x = -y^2 - 1$. The answer is (A).

6.   A pottery store owner determines that the revenue for sales of a particular item can be modeled by the function $r(x) = 50\sqrt{x} - 40$, where x is the number of the items sold. How many of the items must be sold to generate \$110 in revenue?

(A)   5
(B)   6
(C)   7
(D)   8
(E)   9

We are asked to find the value of x for which revenue is \$110. In mathematical terms, we need to solve the equation $r(x) = 110$. Since $r(x) = 50\sqrt{x} - 40$, we get

$$50\sqrt{x} - 40 = 110$$
$$50\sqrt{x} = 150$$
$$\sqrt{x} = 3$$
$$\left(\sqrt{x}\right)^2 = 3^2$$
$$|x| = 9$$
$$x = 9 \quad \text{or} \quad x = -9$$

Since $x = -9$ has no physical interpretation for this problem, we know that $x = 9$. The answer is (E).

7.   At time $t = 0$, a projectile was fired upward from an initial height of 10 feet. Its height after t seconds is given by the function $h(t) = p - 10(q - t)^2$, where p and q are positive constants. If the projectile reached a maximum height of 100 feet when $t = 3$, then what was the height, in feet, of the projectile when $t = 4$?

(A) 62   (B) 70   (C) 85   (D) 89   (E) 90

Method I:
Recall that when a quadratic function is written in the form $y = a(x - h)^2 + k$, its vertex (in this case, the maximum height of the projectile) occurs at the point (h, k). So let's rewrite the function $h(t) = p - 10(q - t)^2$ in the form $h(t) = a(t - h)^2 + k$. Notice that we changed y to $h(t)$ and x to t.

$$h(t) = p - 10(q - t)^2$$
$$= -10(q - t)^2 + p$$
$$= -10(-[-q + t])^2 + p$$
$$= -10(-[t - q])^2 + p$$
$$= -10([-1]^2[t - q])^2 + p$$
$$= -10([+1][t - q])^2 + p$$
$$= -10(t - q)^2 + p$$

In this form, we can see that the vertex (maximum) occurs at the point (q, p). We are given that the maximum height of 100 occurs when t is 3. Hence, $q = 3$ and $p = 100$. Plugging this into our function yields

$$h(t) = -10(t - q)^2 + p = -10(t - 3)^2 + 100$$

We are asked to find the height of the projectile when $t = 4$. Evaluating our function at 4 yields

$$h(4) = -10(4-3)^2 + 100$$
$$= -10(1)^2 + 100$$
$$= -10 \cdot 1 + 100$$
$$= -10 + 100$$
$$= 90$$

The answer is (E).

Method II:
In this method, we are going to solve a system of two equations in two unknowns in order to determine the values of p and q in the function $h(t) = p - 10(q - t)^2$. At time $t = 0$, the projectile had a height of 10 feet. In other words, $h(0) = 10$. At time $t = 3$, the projectile had a height of 100 feet. In other words, $h(3) = 100$. Plugging this information into the function $h(t) = p - 10(q - t)^2$ yields

$$h(0) = 10 \quad \Rightarrow \quad 10 = p - 10(q - 0)^2$$
$$h(3) = 100 \quad \Rightarrow \quad 100 = p - 10(q - 3)^2$$

Now, we solve this system of equations by subtracting the bottom equation from the top equation:

$$10 = p - 10q^2$$
$$\underline{(-) \quad 100 = p - 10(q - 3)^2}$$
$$-90 = -10q^2 + 10(q - 3)^2$$

Solving this equation for q yields

$$-90 = -10q^2 + 10(q - 3)^2$$
$$-90 = -10q^2 + 10(q^2 - 6q + 9)$$
$$-90 = -10q^2 + 10q^2 - 60q + 90$$
$$-90 = -60q + 90$$
$$-180 = -60q$$
$$3 = q$$

Plugging $q = 3$ into the equation $10 = p - 10q^2$ yields

$$10 = p - 10 \cdot 3^2$$
$$10 = p - 10 \cdot 9$$
$$10 = p - 90$$
$$100 = p$$

Hence, the function $h(t) = p - 10(q - t)^2$ becomes $h(t) = 100 - 10(3 - t)^2$. We are asked to find the height of the projectile when $t = 4$. Evaluating this function at 4 yields

$$h(4) = 100 - 10(3 - 4)^2$$
$$= 100 - 10(-1)^2$$
$$= 100 - 10 \cdot 1$$
$$= 100 - 10$$
$$= 90$$

The answer is (E).

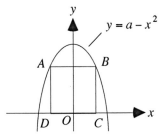

8.   The figure above shows the graph of $y = a - x^2$ for some constant a. If the square $ABCD$ intersects the graph at points A and B and the area of the square is 16, what is the value of a ?

(A) 2   (B) 4   (C) 6   (D) 8   (E) 10

Let s denote the length of a side of square $ABCD$. Since the area of the square is 16, we get $s^2 = 16$. Taking the square root of both sides of this equation yields $s = 4$. Hence, line segment AB has length 4. Since the parabola is symmetric about the y-axis, Point B is 2 units from the y-axis (as is Point A). That is, the x-coordinate of Point B is 2. Since line segment BC has length 4, the coordinates of Point B are (2, 4). Since the square and the parabola intersect at Point B, the point (2, 4) must satisfy the equation $y = a - x^2$:

$$4 = a - 2^2$$
$$4 = a - 4$$
$$8 = a$$

The answer is (D).

9.   If $f(x) = x^2 + x$, then $f(x - a) =$

(A) $x^2 - (2a - 1)x + a^2 - a$
(B) $x^2 - (2a + 1)x + a^2$
(C) $x^2 + x - a^2 - a$
(D) $x^2 + a^2$
(E) $x^2 a^2$

$$f(x - a) = (x - a)^2 + (x - a)$$
$$= x^2 - 2ax + a^2 + x - a$$
$$= x^2 - 2ax + x + a^2 - a$$
$$= x^2 - (2a - 1)x + a^2 - a$$

The answer is (A).

Logarithms

$$\log_b x = y \quad \text{if and only if} \quad b^y = x$$

Note that b is called the base, x is the number whose log is being calculated, and the result y is the log. Both x and b must be positive.

Students often find logs mysterious. Even after studying logs for a while, students may still ask, "what is a log?" It is nothing more than the definition above! Notice that on the right side of the definition that y (the log) is an exponent: it is the power to which you raise the base to get the number you are taking the log of. If this seems contrived, you're right. A log is a pure contrivance. Many subjects in mathematics are created this way. For instance, Trigonometry, which is just the naming of various ratios of the sides of a triangle with respect to an angle of the triangle.

Let's use this definition (rule) to calculate some logs:

1) $\log_2 8 = y$

    Here, the base b is 2, x is 8, and y is itself. Plugging this information into the right side of the definition yields

    $$2^y = 8$$

    Clearly, the solution to this equation is 3: $2^3 = 2 \cdot 2 \cdot 2 = 8$.

2) $\log_3 27$

    Here, we are being asked to find to what power do you raise 3 to get 27. Though y was not written in the problem, we will use it in the solution. Here, the base b is 3, and x is 27. Plugging this information into the right side of the definition yields

    $$3^y = 27$$

    Clearly, the solution to this equation is 3: $3^3 = 3 \cdot 3 \cdot 3 = 27$.

3) $\log_b 4 = 2$

    Here, we are not asked to calculate the log, which is 2. Instead, by the right-hand side of the definition, we are asked what number squared is 4 ($b^2 = 4$). Of course, the answer is 2, so $b = 2$. Note: the base is always positive, so –2 is not a possible answer.

Since logs are exponents, they should share the properties of exponents. When multiply two exponential expressions, you add their exponents: $x^m \cdot x^n = x^{m+n}$. The analogous rule for logs is

$$\log_b mn = \log_b m + \log_b n$$

Logs have many exotic properties, which is why students often find logs mysterious. However, these properties are easy to manipulate, which makes logs fundamentally easy—as long as you are not intimidated by the strange properties.

One of the more unusual properties is the "leap frog" rule (with this silly name, you are unlikely to forget the rule):

$$\log_b x^a = a \log_b x$$

Here, the exponent "leaps" in front of the log. For example, $\log_2 (x+1)^5 = 5\log_2 (x+1)$. Caution: to apply the "leap frog" rule, the exponent must be on just the argument, not the entire log: $(\log_3 x)^5 \neq 5\log_3 x$.

We have seen logs of base 2 and base 3; the most common base is base 10: $\log_{10} x$. It is called the *common log*, and often the base is not written:

$$\log_{10} x = \log x$$

Pop Quiz: $\log_b b^a =$

If you are struggling to solve this problem (and most students do the first time they see it), don't overlook the obvious. Go back to the definition of a log: the question is asking us to what power do we raise b to get b^a. Of course, the answer is a—it's staring us in the face. Or using the formal definition $b^y = b^a$, so equating exponents yields $y = a$. Whenever you are struggling with a logarithmic problem, stop and look for the simple concept or property that you are probably overlooking—again, logs are fundamentally easy.

Let's summarize the properties we have derived and add a few more.

Properties of Logs:

1) $\log_b xy = \log_b x + \log_b y$ Caution: $\log_b (x + y) \neq \log_b x + \log_b y$

2) $\log_b \dfrac{x}{y} = \log_b x - \log_b y$ Caution: $\log_b (x - y) \neq \log_b x - \log_b y$

3) $\log_b x^a = a \log_b x$ The "leap frog" rule

4) $\log_b b^a = a$

5) $\log_b 1 = 0$ This follows from the fact that $b^0 = 1$.

6) $\log_b b = 1$ This follows from the fact that $b^1 = b$.

Before doing any of the exercises at the end of this chapter, know these log properties cold.

Examples:

1) $\log_4(z+2) - \log_4 3 = 1$

   $\log_4 \dfrac{z+2}{3} = 1$ by Rule 2

   $4^1 = \dfrac{z+2}{3}$ by the definition of a log: $\log_b x = y$ if and only if $b^y = x$

   $12 = z + 2$

   $z = 10$

2) $\log x + \log(x-6) = \log 9$

   $\log x(x-6) = \log 9$ by Rule 1

   $x(x-6) = 9$ If two logs are equal, then their arguments are equal:
                     If $\log_b x = \log_b y$, then $x = y$. This fact is used often with logs.

   $x^2 - 6x = 9$

   $x^2 - 6x - 9 = 0$

   $(x-3)^2 = 0$

   $x - 3 = 0$ by taking the square root of both sides

   $x = 3$ Note: We have not yet determined that 3 is the solution. We have merely narrowed the infinite number of possible solutions to just one, 3. With simple equations, the potential solution is usually the solution. But, with more complex equations, such as logarithmic equations, the potential solution often is not a solution. We must plug potential solutions into the original equation to see whether they make the two sides of the equation equal. This is not a check; it is the final step in finding the solution. Plugging 3 into the original equation yields:

   $\log 6 + \log(3-6) = \log 6 + \log(-3)$ However, the log of a negative number does not exit, so the equation has no solutions.

3)   Write $\log x + \dfrac{1}{3}\log(z+4) - 3\log_b y^2$ as a single logarithm.

   First, apply the "leap frog" rule ($\log_b x^a = a\log_b x$):

$$\log x + \log(z+4)^{1/3} - \log_b\left(y^2\right)^3$$

   Next, apply Rule 1 ($\log_b xy = \log_b x + \log_b y$):

$$\log x(z+4)^{1/3} - \log_b y^6$$

   Finally, apply Rule 2 ($\log_b \dfrac{x}{y} = \log_b x - \log_b y$):

$$\log \dfrac{x(z+4)^{1/3}}{y^6}$$

4) Write $\log \sqrt[4]{x^2 - 1}$ as a sum of two logs.

First, change to fractional exponents:

$$\log\left(x^2 - 1\right)^{1/4}$$

Next, apply the "leap frog" rule ($\log_b x^a = a \log_b x$):

$$\frac{1}{4}\log\left(x^2 - 1\right)$$

Factoring the difference of squares $x^2 - 1$ yields

$$\frac{1}{4}\log(x + 1)(x - 1)$$

Applying Rule 1 ($\log_b xy = \log_b x + \log_b y$) yields

$$\frac{1}{4}\left[\log(x + 1) + \log(x - 1)\right]$$

Finally, distribute the 1/4:

$$\frac{1}{4}\log(x + 1) + \frac{1}{4}\log(x - 1)$$

Though the manipulations in this problem are a little odd, aren't they actually easy? This would be considered a hard problem on the ACT, not because it is inherently hard, but because most students would get it wrong.

SOLVING EXPONENTIAL EQUATIONS BY USING LOGS

Often, we solve exponential equations by equating exponents:

$2^{-1/x} = 8$

$2^{-1/x} = 2^3$

$-1/x = 3$ if the bases are equal (2), the exponents must be equal

$-1/3 = x$

But, what if the bases are not equal? In this case, we can use logs to solve the equation.

Example: Solve the equation $3^y = 5$.

In the previous example, we were able to write 8 in terms of the 2: $8 = 2^3$. However, we cannot write 5 in terms of 3, or vice versa. Taking the log of both sides of the equation[*] yields

$$\log 3^y = \log 5$$

Applying the "leap frog" rule yields

$$y \log 3 = \log 5$$

Finally, dividing both sides by $\log 3$ (which is just a number) yields

$$y = \frac{\log 5}{\log 3}$$

---

[*] Just as you can square both sides of an equation or multiply both sides of an equation, you can log both sides of an equation.

We used the common log (base 10) to solve this problem, but we can use any base for the log. Using $\log_3$ would be a more efficient way to solve the equation:

$$\log_3 3^y = \log_3 5$$
$$y = \log_3 5$$

Instead of solving this equation by taking the log of both sides, we can just use the definition of a log: $\log_b x = y$ if and only if $b^y = x$. Note that all definitions read both from left to right and from right to left. That's what the "if and only if" part of a definition means. Reading the definition from right to left, $3^y = 5$ indicates that the base is 3, the exponent is y, and 5 is the number that we are taking the log of. This yields

$$\log_3 5 = y$$

GRAPHS OF LOGARITHMIC FUNCTIONS

We will graph a typical logarithmic function by plotting points, but the ACT does not expect you to graph functions this way: they assume that you are familiar with the shapes of graphs of common functions, such as the log.

Graph of $y = \log_2 x$

x	1/8	1/4	1/2	1	2	4	8
$f(x) = \log_2 x$	−3	−2	−1	0	1	2	3

Plotting these points in the coordinate system and connecting them with a smooth curve yields the following graph:

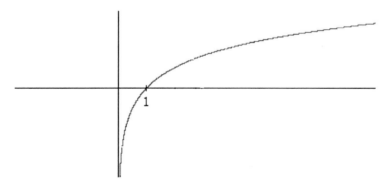

From the graph, notice that the domain (x values) consists of positive numbers only, and the range (y values) is all real numbers (negative, zero, and positive). This is the basic shape of all logarithmic functions with a base greater than 1. They all intersect the x-axis at (1, 0). Notice that the y-values of the graph (the range) increase[*] slowly when x is greater than 1. In fact, they increase extremely slowly. To get the y-value of the graph of the common log ($y = \log_{10} x$) to 10, you have to go out to 10 billion on the x-axis:

$\log_{10} x = 10 \implies x = 10^{10}$, which is 10 billion. On the other hand, the y-values increase rapidly for values of x smaller than 1 (notice that the y-axis is a vertical asymptote). Understanding of these types of graph properties is what the ACT tests.

---

[*] Note that we "read" graphs just as we read English—from left to right. So, as you view the graph from left to right, it is increasing (going up hill): at first rapidly and then very slowly.

Example: Sketch the graph of $y = 1 + 2\log(x - 3)$.

The number 1 shifts the graph of the common log ($\log_{10} x$) up 1 unit, the number 2 increases the height of the graph by a factor of 2, and the number 3 shifts the graph to the right 3 units:

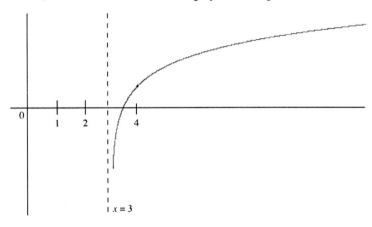

Example: Sketch the graph of $y = \log|x|$.

Usually, we cannot plug negative numbers into a log function. But here, the absolute value turns all negative numbers into positive numbers. So, for negative values of x, the graph looks the same as for positive values of x. This has the affect of reflecting the graph about the y-axis (Note: the y-axis is still the vertical asymptote since $|0| = 0$):

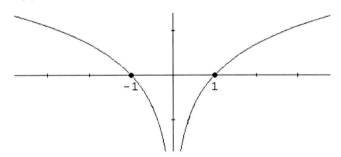

Example: The graphs of the functions $y = \log_3 x$ and $y = \dfrac{1}{2}(x - 1)$ are shown in the standard coordinate system below. For what real values of x is $\log_3 x > \dfrac{1}{2}(x - 1)$?

(A) $x < 1$ and $x > 3$ (B) $x < 0$ and $x > 3$ (C) $1 < x < 3$ (D) $1 < x < 2$ (E) $x < 3$

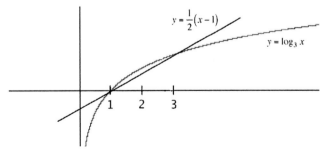

From the graph, we see that the graph of $y = \log_3 x$ is above the graph of $y = \dfrac{1}{2}(x - 1)$ for all values of x between 1 and 3. Hence, the answer is (C).

GRAPHS OF EXPONENTIAL FUNCTIONS

The exponential function can be viewed as the inverse of the logarithm function.

Interchanging x and y (which creates the inverse) in the left-hand side of the definition of the common log ($\log_{10} x = y$) yields

$$\log_{10} y = x$$

Now, use the definition of the logarithm ($\log_b x = y$ if and only if $b^y = x$) to convert this form to the exponential form:

$$y = 10^x$$

As with all inverse functions, we can obtain the graph of $y = 10^x$ by reflecting the graph of $y = \log_{10} x$ about the line $y = x$:

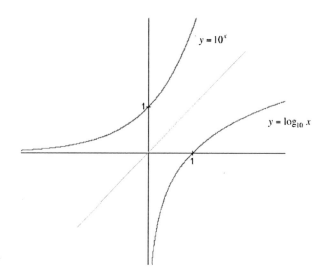

From the graph, notice that the domain (x values) includes all real numbers (negative, zero, and positive), and the range (y values) is only positive numbers. This is the basic shape of all exponential functions with a base greater than 1. They all intersect the y-axis at $(0, 1)$. Notice that the y-values of the graph (the range) increase[*] slowly when x is less than 0 (notice that the x-axis is a horizontal asymptote), and the y-values increase rapidly for values of x greater than 1. In fact, they increase extremely fast. To get the y-value of the graph of the exponential function ($y = 10^x$) to 10 billion, you have to go out to only 10 on the x-axis: $y = 10^{10}$, which is 10 billion. Notice that our analysis of the exponential function is the same as the logarithm function, just the roles of x and y have been interchanged. This is to be expected since they are inverses of each other.

---

[*] Note that we "read" graphs just as we read English—from left to right. So, as you view the graph from left to right, it is increasing (going up hill): at first rapidly and then very slowly.

Problem Set Y:

1. $\log_{10} \dfrac{1}{100} =$

    (A)   −2
    (B)   −1
    (C)   0
    (D)   1
    (E)   2

2.   Which one of the following values of x satisfies the equation $\log_x 16 = 2$?

    (A)   2
    (B)   4
    (C)   8
    (D)   10
    (E)   16

3.   Which one of the following real numbers satisfies the equation $(3^x)(9) = 27^2$?

    (A)   1
    (B)   2
    (C)   3
    (D)   4
    (E)   5

4.   If $\log_b x = u$ and $\log_b y = v$, then $\log_b \left(\dfrac{x}{y}\right)^3 =$

    (A) $uv/3$
    (B) $3uv$
    (C) $u - v$
    (D) $(u - v)/3$
    (E) $3(u - v)$

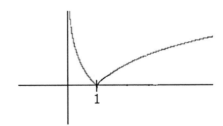

5.   Which one of the following functions could represent the graph?

    (A) $y = \dfrac{1}{2}\log(x - 1)$
    (B) $y = \log(x - 1)$
    (C) $y = \log x^2$
    (D) $y = (\log x)^4 + 2$
    (E) $y = (\log x)^2$

6.   Which one of the following sets of real numbers represents all the solutions of the equation
     $\log \sqrt{x} = \sqrt{\log x}$?

     (A)   {0, 10}
     (B)   {1, 100}
     (C)   {1, 10,000}
     (D)   {1, 2}
     (E)   {0, 4}

7.   Which one of the following expressions is equivalent to $\log \dfrac{x^2}{y^2} - 2\log y + \log \sqrt{xy}$?

     (A) $\dfrac{1}{2}\log \dfrac{x^5}{y^7}$

     (B) $\log \dfrac{x^{5/2}}{y^7}$

     (C) $\log \dfrac{x^5}{y^{7/2}}$

     (D) $\dfrac{5}{2}\log \dfrac{x}{y}$

     (E) $\log \dfrac{x}{y}$

8.   The base of a logarithm can be changed by using the following Change of Base Formula:
     $\log_b x = \dfrac{\log_a x}{\log_a b}$. With the aid of this formula what is the real number solution of the
     equation $\log_2 x + \log_4 x = 3$?

     (A)   1
     (B)   2
     (C)   3
     (D)   4
     (E)   5

9.   Which one of the following real numbers is a solution of the equation $x \log 3 + \log 4^x = 1$?

     (A) $\log 3$
     (B) $\dfrac{1}{\log 12}$
     (C) $\log 12$
     (D)   3
     (E)   4

10. The loudness of sound can be measured by the formula $\alpha = 10 \log\left(\dfrac{I}{I_0}\right)$, where I is the intensity level
     of the sound and I_o is a constant. What is the loudness of a sound with an intensity level 100 times
     greater than I_o ?

     (A)   1
     (B)   20
     (C)   100
     (D)   2,000
     (E)   10,000

Answers and Solutions to Problem Set Y

1. $\log_{10} \dfrac{1}{100} =$

   (A) -2
   (B) -1
   (C) 0
   (D) 1
   (E) 2

By the definition of a logarithm, $\log_{10} \dfrac{1}{100} = y$ if and only if

$$10^y = \frac{1}{100}$$
$$10^y = 100^{-1}$$
$$10^y = \left(10^2\right)^{-1}$$
$$10^y = 10^{2(-1)}$$
$$10^y = 10^{-2}$$
$$y = -2 \qquad \text{by equating exponents}$$

Hence, the answer is (A).

2.   Which one of the following values of x satisfies the equation $\log_x 16 = 2$?

   (A)   2
   (B)   4
   (C)   8
   (D)   10
   (E)   16

By the definition of a logarithm, $\log_x 16 = 2$ if and only if

$$x^2 = 16$$
$$x = \pm 4 \qquad \text{by taking the square root of both sides}$$

Since the base of a log must be positive, $x = 4$ and the answer is (B).

3.   Which one of the following real numbers satisfies the equation $\left(3^x\right)(9) = 27^2$?

   (A)   1
   (B)   2
   (C)   3
   (D)   4
   (E)   5

We don't need to use a log to solve this problem because all the numbers are powers of 3, so we will work to equate exponents:

$$\left(3^x\right)(9) = 27^2$$

$$\left(3^x\right)\left(3^2\right) = \left(3^3\right)^2$$

$$\left(3^x\right)\left(3^2\right) = 3^{3 \cdot 2} \qquad \text{by the rule } \left(x^a\right)^b = x^{ab}$$

$$3^{x+2} = 3^6 \qquad \text{by the rule } x^a x^b = x^{a+b}$$

$$x + 2 = 6 \qquad \text{by equating exponents}$$

$$x = 4$$

The answer is (D).

If you chose answer (B), you may have made the mistake of writing $\left(3^x\right)(9) = 27^x$.

If you chose answer (C), you may have made the mistake of writing $\left(3^3\right)^2 = 3^5$.

4.   If $\log_b x = u$ and $\log_b y = v$, then $\log_b\left(\dfrac{x}{y}\right)^3 =$

(A) $uv/3$
(B) $3uv$
(C) $u - v$
(D) $(u - v)/3$
(E) $3(u - v)$

$$\log_b\left(\dfrac{x}{y}\right)^3 =$$

$$3\log_b\left(\dfrac{x}{y}\right) = \qquad \text{by the rule } \log_b x^a = a \log_b x$$

$$3\left(\log_b x - \log_b y\right) = \qquad \text{by the rule } \log_b \dfrac{x}{y} = \log_b x - \log_b y$$

$$3(u - v) \qquad \text{by substituting } u \text{ for } \log_b x \text{ and } v \text{ for } \log_b y$$

Hence, the answer is (E).

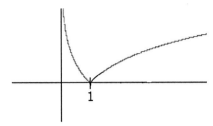

5.   Which one of the following functions could represent the graph?

(A) $y = \dfrac{1}{2}\log(x-1)$

(B) $y = \log(x-1)$

(C) $y = \log x^2$

(D) $y = (\log x)^4 + 2$

(E) $y = (\log x)^2$

The standard log ($y = \log x$) is negative between 0 and 1 (it is below the *x*-axis). But our graph is positive there (it is above the *x*-axis). One way to make it positive is to raise the standard function to an even exponent (even exponents turn negative expressions into positive ones). So, the answer is either (D) or (E). The expression in Choice (D), however, is always greater than or equal to 2 (why?), and, from the graph, the function is 0 when *x* is 1. Hence, by process of elimination, the answer is (E).

Don't make the mistake of choosing (C). $\log x^2$ is still negative between 0 and 1. The even exponent here is affecting just the *x*, not the entire function. For example,

$$\log\left(\frac{1}{10}\right)^2 = \log\left(10^{-1}\right)^2 = \log 10^{-2} = -2$$

6.   Which one of the following sets of real numbers represents all the solutions of the equation $\log\sqrt{x} = \sqrt{\log x}$?

(A)   {0, 10}

(B)   {1, 100}

(C)   {1, 10,000}

(D)   {1, 2}

(E)   {0, 4}

First, change to fractional exponents:

$$\log x^{1/2} = (\log x)^{1/2}$$

Using the "leap frog" rule ($\log_b x^a = a\log_b x$) on the left side of the equation yields

$$\frac{1}{2}\log x = (\log x)^{1/2}$$

Squaring both sides to eliminate the remaining exponent yields

$$\frac{1}{4}(\log x)^2 = \log x$$

Subtracting $\log x$ from both sides yields

$$\frac{1}{4}\left(\log x\right)^2 - \log x = 0$$

Factoring out $\log x$ yields

$$\log x\left(\frac{1}{4}\log x - 1\right) = 0$$

Setting each factor to zero yields

$$\log x = 0 \quad \text{or} \quad \frac{1}{4}\log x - 1 = 0$$

Or

$$\log x = 0 \quad \text{or} \quad \log x = 4$$

From the first equation, we get $x = 10^0 = 1$; and from the second equation, we get $x = 10^4 = 10,000$. Hence, the answer is (C).

7. Which one of the following expressions is equivalent to $\log \dfrac{x^2}{y^2} - 2\log y + \log\sqrt{xy}$?

(A) $\dfrac{1}{2}\log\dfrac{x^5}{y^7}$

(B) $\log\dfrac{x^{5/2}}{y^7}$

(C) $\log\dfrac{x^5}{y^{7/2}}$

(D) $\dfrac{5}{2}\log\dfrac{x}{y}$

(E) $\log\dfrac{x}{y}$

$$\log\frac{x^2}{y^2} - 2\log y + \log\sqrt{xy} =$$

$$\log\frac{x^2}{y^2} - 2\log y + \log(xy)^{1/2} =$$

$$\log\frac{x^2}{y^2} - \log y^2 + \log(xy)^{1/2} =$$

$$\log\frac{x^2/y^2}{y^2} + \log(xy)^{1/2} =$$

$$\log\frac{x^2/y^2}{y^2/1} + \log(xy)^{1/2} =$$

$$\log\left(\frac{x^2}{y^2}\cdot\frac{1}{y^2}\right) + \log(xy)^{1/2} =$$

$$\log\frac{x^2}{y^4} + \log(xy)^{1/2} =$$

$$\log\left(\frac{x^2}{y^4}\cdot(xy)^{1/2}\right) =$$

$$\log\left(\frac{x^2}{y^4}\cdot x^{1/2}\cdot y^{1/2}\right) =$$

$$\log\frac{x^{2+1/2}}{y^{4-1/2}} =$$

$$\log\frac{x^{5/2}}{y^{7/2}} =$$

$$\log\left(\frac{x^5}{y^7}\right)^{1/2} =$$

$$\frac{1}{2}\log\frac{x^5}{y^7}$$

The answer is (A).

8.   The base of a logarithm can be changed by using the following Change of Base Formula:
$\log_b x = \dfrac{\log_a x}{\log_a b}$. With the aid of this formula what is the real number solution of the
equation $\log_2 x + \log_4 x = 3$?

(A)   1
(B)   2
(C)   3
(D)   4
(E)   5

We cannot apply the rule $\log_b xy = \log_b x + \log_b y$ to the equation $\log_2 x + \log_4 x = 3$ because the bases are different, $2 \neq 4$. Let's use the change of base formula to write the base 4 log in terms of the base 2 log:

$$\log_4 x = \frac{\log_2 x}{\log_2 4} = \frac{\log_2 x}{2}$$

Plugging this result into the equation yields

$$\log_2 x + \frac{\log_2 x}{2} = 3$$

Multiplying the equation by 2 yields

$$2 \log_2 x + \log_2 x = 6$$

Adding like terms yields

$$3 \log_2 x = 6$$

Dividing by 3 yields

$$\log_2 x = 2$$

Applying the definition of a log yields

$$x = 2^2 = 4$$

The answer is (D). Note: This problem can also be solved efficiently by plugging the answer-choices into the equation.

9.   Which one of the following real numbers is a solution of the equation $x \log 3 + \log 4^x = 1$?

(A) $\log 3$

(B) $\dfrac{1}{\log 12}$

(C) $\log 12$

(D)   3

(E)   4

First, apply the "leap frog" rule ($\log_b x^a = a \log_b x$):

$$x \log 3 + x \log 4 = 1$$

Many students are intimated by equations like this one because of the odd looking logs in it. But the logs here are just numbers. If you were to replace the logs with the numbers 3 and 4, you would get the following simple linear equation:

$$x \cdot 3 + x \cdot 4 = 1$$

Since $\log 3$ and $\log 4$ are just numbers, our equation is also linear. Factoring out the common factor x yields

$$x(\log 3 + \log 4) = 1$$

Dividing both sides of this equation by $\log 3 + \log 4$ yields

$$x = \frac{1}{\log 3 + \log 4}$$

Finally, using the rule $\log_b xy = \log_b x + \log_b y$ to simplify the expression yields

$$x = \frac{1}{\log 3 \cdot 4} = \frac{1}{\log 12}$$

The answer is (B).

10. The loudness of sound can be measured by the formula $\alpha = 10\log\left(\dfrac{I}{I_0}\right)$, where I is the intensity level of the sound and I_o is a constant. What is the loudness of a sound with an intensity level 100 times greater than I_o ?

   (A)   1
   (B)   20
   (C)   100
   (D)   2,000
   (E)   10,000

Since the intensity is 100 times greater than I_o, $I = 100I_o$. Substituting this into the formula for loudness yields

$$\alpha = 10\log\left(\frac{I}{I_0}\right)$$
$$= 10\log\left(\frac{100I_0}{I_0}\right)$$
$$= 10\log 100$$
$$= 10(2)$$
$$= 20$$

The answer is (B).

Complex Numbers

In the previous chapter, we said that logs are fundamentally easy. Well, complex numbers are even easier, mainly, because they do not have the exotic properties of logs, and because, with a few exceptions, the rules for manipulating real numbers apply to complex numbers.

Complex number evolved from the need to solve equations like $x^2 + 1 = 0$, or $x^2 = -1$. Equations like this one occur frequently in Algebra, and they have no real number solutions. The only possible candidates for solutions of the equation $x^2 = -1$ are 1 and -1, but both equal $+1$ when squared. This prompts the following definition of a new number, *i*, called an *imaginary number*.

DEFINITION

$$i^2 = -1 \quad \text{or} \quad i = \sqrt{-1}$$

A number written in the form *a + bi* is called a *complex number*. In this complex number, *a* is called the real part, and *b* is called the imaginary part, but both *a* and *b* are always real numbers.

Example: Solve the equation $x^2 - 4x + 4 = -1$.

$$x^2 - 4x + 4 = -1$$
$$(x - 2)(x - 2) = -1$$
$$(x - 2)^2 = -1$$
$$\sqrt{(x - 2)^2} = \pm\sqrt{-1}$$
$$x - 2 = \pm i$$
$$x = 2 \pm i$$

There are formulas for adding, multiplying, etc. complex numbers, but they are unnecessary—just use the rules for real numbers, and each time $\sqrt{-1}$ appears, replace it with *i* and replace i^2 with -1.

Examples:

$$(3 - i) + (-4 + 5i) = (3 - 4) + (-1i + 5i) = (3 - 4) + (-1 + 5)i = -1 + 4i$$

$$\begin{aligned}
(1+i)\sqrt{-4} &= (1+i)\sqrt{4}i \\
&= (1+i)2i \\
&= 1(2i) + i(2i) \\
&= 2i + 2i^2 \\
&= 2i + 2(-1) \\
&= -2 + 2i
\end{aligned}$$

Probably the only algebraic formula for real numbers that you will see that is false for complex number is $\sqrt{x}\sqrt{y} = \sqrt{xy}$.

$$\boxed{\text{For complex numbers, } \sqrt{x}\sqrt{y} \neq \sqrt{xy}}$$

For example,

$$\sqrt{-2}\sqrt{-2} = \sqrt{2}i \cdot \sqrt{2}i = \left(\sqrt{2} \cdot \sqrt{2}\right)i^2 = 2(-1) = -2$$

$$\sqrt{(-2)(-2)} = \sqrt{4} = 2$$

To avoid this error, and others like it, always replace $\sqrt{-1}$ with i before performing any algebraic operations. For example,

$$\sqrt{-x}\sqrt{-y} = \sqrt{x}i \cdot \sqrt{y}i = \sqrt{x}\sqrt{y}\left(i^2\right) = \sqrt{xy}(-1) = -\sqrt{xy}$$

CONJUGATE

Because complex numbers are based on a radical, we often rationalize fractions involving complex numbers. This makes the conjugate important for complex numbers.

$$\boxed{\text{The conjugate of the complex number } a + bi \text{ is } a - bi.}$$

Example: $\dfrac{1}{1-i} = \dfrac{1}{1-i} \cdot \dfrac{1+i}{1+i} = \dfrac{1(1+i)}{(1-i)(1+i)} = \dfrac{1+i}{1+i-i-i^2} = \dfrac{1+i}{1+i-i-(-1)} = \dfrac{1+i}{1+i-i+1} = \dfrac{1+i}{2} = \dfrac{1}{2} + \dfrac{1}{2}i$

Because complex numbers have two parts (real and imaginary), they can be represented in the coordinate plane:

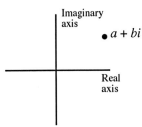

Example: $-1 - 4i$

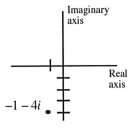

ABSOLUTE VALUE

With real numbers, the absolute value is the distance a number is from the origin. Likewise for complex numbers:

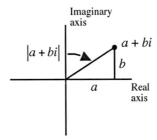

Applying The Pythagorean Theorem to the triangle in the figure gives

> **The absolute value of the complex number $a + bi$ is**
> $$|a + bi| = \sqrt{a^2 + b^2}$$

Notice that the absolute value of a complex number is a real number (the i does not appear in $\sqrt{a^2 + b^2}$).

Examples:

$$|-2 + 3i| = \sqrt{(-2)^2 + (3)^2} = \sqrt{4 + 9} = \sqrt{13}$$

$$|-5i| = |0 + (-5)i| = \sqrt{0^2 + (-5)^2} = \sqrt{0 + 25} = \sqrt{25} = 5$$

$$|0| = |0 + (0)i| = \sqrt{0^2 + 0^2} = \sqrt{0 + 0} = \sqrt{0} = 0$$

Problem Set Z:

1. $\dfrac{-1-2i}{3+2i} \cdot \dfrac{3-2i}{3-2i} =$

    (A) $-\dfrac{7}{10} - \dfrac{4}{10}i$

    (B) $\dfrac{7}{13} + \dfrac{4}{13}i$

    (C) $-\dfrac{7}{13} - \dfrac{4}{13}i$

    (D) $-\dfrac{7}{10} - \dfrac{4}{13}i$

    (E) $\dfrac{7}{13} - \dfrac{6}{13}i$

2. $\left(3 - \sqrt{-9}\right)\left(4 - \sqrt{-4}\right) =$

    (A) $6 - 18i$
    (B) $6 + 18i$
    (C) $-6 - 18i$
    (D) $6 - 6i$
    (E) $18 - 18i$

3. What are the complex solutions of the equation $x^2 - 6x + 9 = -4$?

    (A) $3 + 2i$ and $3 - 2i$
    (B) $-3 + 2i$ and $3 + 2i$
    (C) $-3 + 2i$ and $-3 + 2i$
    (D) $2 + 2i$ and $2 + 2i$
    (E) $3 + 2i$ and $3 + 2i$

4. $-\sqrt{-\dfrac{16}{49}} =$

    (A) $\dfrac{4}{7}i$

    (B) $-\dfrac{4}{7}i$

    (C) $\dfrac{4}{7}$

    (D) $\dfrac{4}{7}i^2$

    (E) $4i$

5. If $p = 1 + i$ and $q = 0.5 + 1.5i$, then which one of the following must be true?

    (A) $|p| = |q|$
    (B) $|p| > |q|$
    (C) $|p| \ge |q|$
    (D) $|p| < |q|$
    (E) $|p| \le |q|$

6. $\dfrac{1-i}{i} - \dfrac{2}{2+i} =$

    (A) $-\dfrac{3}{5}i$

    (B) $\dfrac{9}{2} + \dfrac{3}{2}i$

    (C) $\dfrac{9}{5} - \dfrac{3}{5}i$

    (D) $-\dfrac{9}{2} - \dfrac{3}{2}i$

    (E) $-\dfrac{9}{5} - \dfrac{3}{5}i$

7. The conjugate of a complex number $z = a + bi$ is often denoted by $\bar{z}$. That is, $\bar{z} = a - bi$. With this notation $\bar{z} = z$ if and only if

    (A) a is zero
    (B) z is a real number
    (C) $b = 1$
    (D) z is an irrational number
    (E) $a = b = 0$

8. If $z = a + bi$, then $\overline{z^2} =$

    (A) z
    (B) $\bar{z}$
    (C) z^2
    (D) $\left(\bar{z}\right)^2$
    (E) $z/2$

9. Which one of the complex numbers in the figure has the greatest absolute value?

    (A) z_1
    (B) z_2
    (C) z_3
    (D) z_4
    (E) z_5

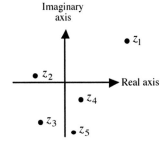

10. Two complex numbers are equal if and only if their real parts are equal and their imaginary parts are equal. That is, if $a + bi = c + di$, then $a = c$ and $b = d$. From this definition, what are the values of x and y in the equation $x^3 - (x - y)i = 8 - 2i$?

    (A) $x = -8, y = 1$
    (B) $x = 8, y = 2$
    (C) $x = -2, y = 2$
    (D) $x = 2, y = 3$
    (E) $x = 2, y = 0$

Answers and Solutions to Problem Set Z

1. $\dfrac{-1-2i}{3+2i} \cdot \dfrac{3-2i}{3-2i} =$

   (A) $-\dfrac{7}{10}-\dfrac{4}{10}i$

   (B) $\dfrac{7}{13}+\dfrac{4}{13}i$

   (C) $-\dfrac{7}{13}-\dfrac{4}{13}i$

   (D) $-\dfrac{7}{10}-\dfrac{4}{13}i$

   (E) $\dfrac{7}{13}-\dfrac{6}{13}i$

$$\dfrac{-1-2i}{3+2i} \cdot \dfrac{3-2i}{3-2i} = \dfrac{-3+2i-6i+4i^2}{9-6i+6i-4i^2}$$
$$= \dfrac{-3-4i+4(-1)}{9-4(-1)}$$
$$= \dfrac{-7-4i}{13}$$
$$-\dfrac{7}{13}-\dfrac{4}{13}i$$

The answer is (C).

2. $\left(3-\sqrt{-9}\right)\left(4-\sqrt{-4}\right) =$

   (A) $6-18i$
   (B) $6+18i$
   (C) $-6-18i$
   (D) $6-6i$
   (E) $18-18i$

$$\left(3-\sqrt{-9}\right)\left(4-\sqrt{-4}\right) = \left(3-\sqrt{9}i\right)\left(4-\sqrt{4}i\right)$$
$$= \left(3-3i\right)\left(4-2i\right)$$
$$= 12-6i-12i+6i^2$$
$$= 12-18i+6(-1)$$
$$= 6-18i$$

The answer is (A).

3. What are the complex solutions of the equation $x^2 - 6x + 9 = -4$?

   (A) $3 + 2i$ and $3 - i$
   (B) $-3 + 2i$ and $3 + 2i$
   (C) $-3 + 2i$ and $-3 + 2i$
   (D) $2 + 2i$ and $2 + 2i$
   (E) $3 + 2i$ and $3 - 2i$

$$x^2 - 6x + 9 = -4$$
$$(x - 3)(x - 3) = -4$$
$$(x - 3)^2 = -4$$
$$\sqrt{(x - 3)^2} = \pm\sqrt{-4}$$
$$x - 3 = \pm 2i$$
$$x = 3 \pm 2i$$

The answer is (E).

4. $-\sqrt{-\dfrac{16}{49}} =$

   (A) $\dfrac{4}{7}i$

   (B) $-\dfrac{4}{7}i$

   (C) $\dfrac{4}{7}$

   (D) $\dfrac{4}{7}i^2$

   (E) $4i$

$$-\sqrt{-\frac{16}{49}} = -\sqrt{\frac{16}{49}}i$$
$$= -\frac{\sqrt{16}}{\sqrt{49}}i$$
$$= -\frac{4}{7}i$$

The answer is (B).

5. If $p = 1 + i$ and $q = 0.5 + 1.5i$, then which one of the following must be true?

   (A) $|p| = |q|$
   (B) $|p| > |q|$
   (C) $|p| \geq |q|$
   (D) $|p| < |q|$
   (E) $|p| \leq |q|$

$$|p| = |1 + i| = |1 + 1i| = \sqrt{1^2 + 1^2} = \sqrt{1 + 1} = \sqrt{2}$$

$$|q| = |0.5 + 1.5i| = \sqrt{(0.5)^2 + (1.5)^2} = \sqrt{0.25 + 2.25} = \sqrt{2.5}$$

Since $\sqrt{2.5} > \sqrt{2}$, $|q| > |p|$ and the answer is (D).

6. $\dfrac{1-i}{i} - \dfrac{2}{2+i} =$

 (A) $-\dfrac{3}{5}i$

 (B) $\dfrac{9}{2} + \dfrac{3}{2}i$

 (C) $\dfrac{9}{5} - \dfrac{3}{5}i$

 (D) $-\dfrac{9}{2} - \dfrac{3}{2}i$

 (E) $-\dfrac{9}{5} - \dfrac{3}{5}i$

$$\frac{1-i}{i} - \frac{2}{2+i} = \frac{1-i}{i} \cdot \frac{i}{i} - \frac{2}{2+i} \cdot \frac{2-i}{2-i}$$

$$= \frac{(1-i)i}{i \cdot i} - \frac{2(2-i)}{(2+i)(2-i)}$$

$$= \frac{1i - i \cdot i}{i \cdot i} - \frac{2 \cdot 2 - 2i}{2 \cdot 2 - 2i + 2i - i \cdot i}$$

$$= \frac{i - i^2}{i^2} - \frac{4 - 2i}{4 - i^2}$$

$$= \frac{i - (-1)}{-1} - \frac{4 - 2i}{4 - (-1)}$$

$$= \frac{i + 1}{-1} - \frac{4 - 2i}{4 + 1}$$

$$= -\frac{i + 1}{1} - \frac{4 - 2i}{5}$$

$$= -\frac{i + 1}{1} \cdot \frac{5}{5} - \frac{4 - 2i}{5}$$

$$= -\frac{5i + 5}{5} - \frac{4 - 2i}{5}$$

$$= \frac{-5i - 5}{5} + \frac{-4 + 2i}{5}$$

$$= \frac{-5i - 5 - 4 + 2i}{5}$$

$$= \frac{-9 - 3i}{5}$$

$$= -\frac{9}{5} - \frac{3}{5}i$$

The answer is (E).

7. The conjugate of a complex number $z = a + bi$ is often denoted by $\bar{z}$. That is, $\bar{z} = a - bi$. With this notation $\bar{z} = z$ if and only if

   (A) a is zero
   (B) z is a real number
   (C) $b = 1$
   (D) z is an irrational number
   (E) $a = b = 0$

The equation $\bar{z} = z$ yields

$$\overline{a + bi} = a + bi$$

Applying the conjugate yields

$$a - bi = a + bi$$

Subtracting a from both sides of the equation yields

$$-bi = bi$$

Since a has been removed from the equation, its value is not constrained by the equation. Hence, a can have any value, which eliminates choices (A) and (E). Now, subtracting bi from both sides of the equation yields

$$-2bi = 0$$

Finally, dividing both sides of the equation by $-2i$ yields

$$b = 0$$

Hence, $z = a + bi = a + 0i = a + 0 = a$. Since a is always a real number, z is a real number. The answer is (B).

8. If $z = a + bi$, then $\overline{z^2} =$

   (A) z
   (B) $\bar{z}$
   (C) z^2
   (D) $(\bar{z})^2$
   (E) $z/2$

$$\overline{z^2} = \overline{(a + bi)^2}$$
$$= \overline{(a + bi)(a + bi)}$$
$$= \overline{a^2 + abi + abi + b^2i^2}$$
$$= \overline{a^2 + 2abi + b^2(-1)}$$
$$= \overline{a^2 - b^2 + 2abi}$$
$$= a^2 - b^2 - 2abi$$
$$= a^2 - 2abi - b^2$$
$$= (a - bi)(a - bi)$$
$$= (a - bi)^2$$
$$= \left(\overline{a + bi}\right)^2$$
$$= \left(\bar{z}\right)^2$$

The answer is (D).

9. Which one of the complex numbers in the figure has the greatest absolute value?

(A) z_1
(B) z_2
(C) z_3
(D) z_4
(E) z_5

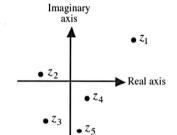

Remember: The absolute value of a complex number is its distance from the origin. Clearly, from the figure, point z_1 is the farthest from the origin. The answer is (A).

10. Two complex numbers are equal if and only if their real parts are equal and their imaginary parts are equal. That is, if $a + bi = c + di$, then $a = c$ and $b = d$. From this definition, what are the values of x and y in the equation $x^3 - (x - y)i = 8 - 2i$?

(A) $x = -8, y = 1$
(B) $x = 8, y = 2$
(C) $x = -2, y = 2$
(D) $x = 2, y = 3$
(E) $x = 2, y = 0$

Since the real parts must be equal and the imaginary parts must be equal, we get the following system of two equations:

$$x^3 = 8$$
$$-(x - y) = -2$$

Taking the cube root of both sides of the equation $x^3 = 8$ yields $x = 2$. Plugging this result into the equation $-(x - y) = -2$ yields

$$-(2 - y) = -2$$
$$2 - y = 2$$
$$-y = 0$$
$$y = 0$$

Hence, $x = 2$ and $y = 0$. The answer is (E).

Matrices

Matrices afford an efficient way of solving systems of equations. We won't study this method, however, because it is very unlikely on the test that you will be asked to solve a system of equations by using matrices. Instead, you will be given problems that require an understanding of the properties of matrices.

A *matrix* is just an array of numbers. Some examples are

$$\begin{bmatrix} 1 & 2 & 3 \end{bmatrix} \qquad \begin{bmatrix} 1 & 2 \\ 3 & 4 \end{bmatrix} \qquad \begin{bmatrix} a & b & c \\ d & e & f \\ g & h & i \end{bmatrix}$$

In general, an $m \times n$ matrix (m rows and n columns) is

$$\begin{bmatrix} a_{11} & a_{12} & a_{13} & \cdots & a_{1n} \\ a_{21} & a_{22} & a_{23} & \cdots & a_{2n} \\ a_{31} & a_{32} & a_{33} & \cdots & a_{3n} \\ \vdots & \vdots & \vdots & \ddots & \vdots \\ a_{m1} & a_{m2} & a_{m3} & \cdots & a_{mn} \end{bmatrix}$$

ADDING MATRICES

To add two matrices, just add their corresponding elements:

$$\begin{bmatrix} a & b \\ c & d \end{bmatrix} + \begin{bmatrix} e & f \\ g & h \end{bmatrix} = \begin{bmatrix} a+e & b+f \\ c+g & d+h \end{bmatrix}$$

Examples:

$$\begin{bmatrix} 1 & 2 \\ 3 & 4 \end{bmatrix} + \begin{bmatrix} 5 & 6 \\ 7 & 8 \end{bmatrix} = \begin{bmatrix} 1+5 & 2+6 \\ 3+7 & 4+8 \end{bmatrix} = \begin{bmatrix} 6 & 8 \\ 10 & 12 \end{bmatrix}$$

$$\begin{bmatrix} a & 0 & 2a \\ 0 & 0 & a \\ 1 & 3a & 0 \end{bmatrix} + \begin{bmatrix} a & 0 & 0 \\ 1 & 0 & 1 \\ 1 & 2a & 0 \end{bmatrix} = \begin{bmatrix} 2a & 0 & 2a \\ 1 & 0 & a+1 \\ 2 & 5a & 0 \end{bmatrix}$$

Note: To add matrices, they must be the same size—same number of rows and columns. You cannot add a 2×2 matrix and a 3×2 matrix.

SUBTRACTING MATRICES

To subtract two matrices, just subtract their corresponding elements:

$$\begin{bmatrix} a & b \\ c & d \end{bmatrix} - \begin{bmatrix} e & f \\ g & h \end{bmatrix} = \begin{bmatrix} a-e & b-f \\ c-g & d-h \end{bmatrix}$$

Examples:

$$\begin{bmatrix} 1 & 2 \\ 3 & 4 \end{bmatrix} - \begin{bmatrix} 5 & 6 \\ 7 & 8 \end{bmatrix} = \begin{bmatrix} 1-5 & 2-6 \\ 3-7 & 4-8 \end{bmatrix} = \begin{bmatrix} -4 & -4 \\ -4 & -4 \end{bmatrix}$$

$$\begin{bmatrix} a & 0 & 2a \\ 0 & 0 & a \\ 1 & 3a & 0 \end{bmatrix} - \begin{bmatrix} a & 0 & 0 \\ 1 & 0 & 1 \\ 1 & 2a & 0 \end{bmatrix} = \begin{bmatrix} 0 & 0 & 2a \\ -1 & 0 & a-1 \\ 0 & a & 0 \end{bmatrix}$$

Note: To subtract matrices, they must be the same size—same number of rows and columns. You cannot subtract a 2×2 matrix and a 3×2 matrix.

THE ZERO MATRIX

The *zero matrix*, appropriately enough, has zeros for all its entries:

$$\begin{bmatrix} 0 & 0 & 0 \end{bmatrix} \qquad \begin{bmatrix} 0 & 0 \\ 0 & 0 \end{bmatrix} \qquad \begin{bmatrix} 0 & 0 & 0 \\ 0 & 0 & 0 \\ 0 & 0 & 0 \end{bmatrix}$$

The zero matrix is the additive identity. That is, adding the zero matrix to any matrix leaves the matrix unchanged:

$$\begin{bmatrix} a & b \\ c & d \end{bmatrix} + \begin{bmatrix} 0 & 0 \\ 0 & 0 \end{bmatrix} = \begin{bmatrix} a+0 & b+0 \\ c+0 & d+0 \end{bmatrix} = \begin{bmatrix} a & b \\ c & d \end{bmatrix}$$

SCALAR MULTIPLICATION

To multiply a matrix by a number, just multiply each element of the matrix by the number:

$$2\begin{bmatrix} 1 & 0 \\ 3 & \pi \end{bmatrix} = \begin{bmatrix} 2\cdot1 & 2\cdot0 \\ 2\cdot3 & 2\cdot\pi \end{bmatrix} = \begin{bmatrix} 2 & 0 \\ 6 & 2\pi \end{bmatrix}$$

MULTIPLYING MATRICES

To multiply two matrices, multiply the elements in each row of the first matrix by the corresponding elements in each column of the second matrix.

$$\begin{bmatrix} a & b \\ c & d \end{bmatrix}\begin{bmatrix} e & f \\ g & h \end{bmatrix} = \begin{bmatrix} ae+bg & af+bh \\ ce+dg & cf+dh \end{bmatrix}$$

Examples:

$$[1 \quad 2]\begin{bmatrix} 3 \\ 4 \end{bmatrix} = [1 \cdot 3 + 2 \cdot 4] = [11]$$

$$\begin{bmatrix} 1 & 0 \\ 0 & 3 \end{bmatrix}\begin{bmatrix} 2 & 4 \\ 4 & 5 \end{bmatrix} = \begin{bmatrix} 1 \cdot 2 + 0 \cdot 4 & 1 \cdot 4 + 0 \cdot 5 \\ 0 \cdot 2 + 3 \cdot 4 & 0 \cdot 4 + 3 \cdot 5 \end{bmatrix} = \begin{bmatrix} 2 & 4 \\ 12 & 15 \end{bmatrix}$$

$$\begin{bmatrix} a & 0 & 2a \\ 0 & 0 & a \\ 1 & 3a & 0 \end{bmatrix}\begin{bmatrix} a & 0 & 0 \\ 1 & 0 & 1 \\ 1 & 2a & 0 \end{bmatrix} = \begin{bmatrix} a \cdot a + 0 \cdot 1 + 2a \cdot 1 & a \cdot 0 + 0 \cdot 0 + 2a \cdot 2a & a \cdot 0 + 0 \cdot 1 + 2a \cdot 0 \\ 0 \cdot a + 0 \cdot 1 + a \cdot 1 & 0 \cdot 0 + 0 \cdot 0 + a \cdot 2a & 0 \cdot 0 + 0 \cdot 1 + a \cdot 0 \\ 1 \cdot a + 3a \cdot 1 + 0 \cdot 1 & 1 \cdot 0 + 3a \cdot 0 + 0 \cdot 2a & 1 \cdot 0 + 3a \cdot 0 + 0 \cdot 0 \end{bmatrix} = \begin{bmatrix} a^2 + 2a & 4a^2 & 0 \\ a & 2a^2 & 0 \\ 4a & 0 & 0 \end{bmatrix}$$

Note: To multiply two matrices, the first matrix must have the same number of columns as the rows in the second matrix: $m \times n$ and $n \times p$. The result of the product will be a matrix of size $m \times p$. Also, matrix multiplication is not commutative. If A and B are matrices, then, in general, $AB \neq BA$.

APPLICATIONS OF MATRICES

Example: The number of people running for political office in a particular state is given by the following matrix:

$$\begin{array}{ccc} \text{Governor} & \text{Legislator} & \text{Controller} \\ [\ 10 & 90 & 6\ ] \end{array}$$

The percentage of candidates who will qualify to be on the ballot is given by the following matrix:

$$\begin{array}{c} \text{Governor} \\ \text{Legislator} \\ \text{Controller} \end{array}\begin{bmatrix} 40\% \\ 30\% \\ 50\% \end{bmatrix}$$

From these matrices, how many total candidates will qualify to be on the ballot?

(A) 34
(B) 35
(C) 37
(D) 40
(E) 52

This is a fairly complex and abstract problem. Yet, the ACT would not consider it hard, probably because there is only one natural way to solve it—multiply the matrices:

$$[10 \quad 90 \quad 6]\begin{bmatrix} 40\% \\ 30\% \\ 50\% \end{bmatrix} = [10 \cdot 40\% + 90 \cdot 30\% + 6 \cdot 50\%] = [4 + 27 + 3] = 34$$

The answer is (A).

Problem Set AA:

1. $\begin{bmatrix} 1 & 0 \\ 2 & 3 \end{bmatrix} + \begin{bmatrix} 5 & \sqrt{2} \\ -2 & 0 \end{bmatrix} =$

    (A) $\begin{bmatrix} 6 & \sqrt{2} \\ 0 & 0 \end{bmatrix}$

    (B) $\begin{bmatrix} 6 & \sqrt{2} \\ 0 & 3 \end{bmatrix}$

    (C) $\begin{bmatrix} -4 & -\sqrt{2} \\ 4 & 3 \end{bmatrix}$

    (D) $\begin{bmatrix} 6 & 2 \\ 0 & 3 \end{bmatrix}$

    (E) $\begin{bmatrix} 6 & \sqrt{2} \\ 0 & 0 \end{bmatrix}$

2. If $A = \begin{bmatrix} 1 & 2 \\ 2 & 0 \end{bmatrix}$ and $B = \begin{bmatrix} 0 & 3 \\ 1 & -1 \end{bmatrix}$ then $3A - B =$

    (A) $\begin{bmatrix} 3 & 3 \\ 5 & -1 \end{bmatrix}$

    (B) $\begin{bmatrix} 1 & 3 \\ 5 & 1 \end{bmatrix}$

    (C) $\begin{bmatrix} 3 & 3 \\ 5 & 1 \end{bmatrix}$

    (D) $\begin{bmatrix} 3 & 3 \\ -5 & 1 \end{bmatrix}$

    (E) $\begin{bmatrix} 3 & 3 \\ 5 & 0 \end{bmatrix}$

3. $\begin{bmatrix} 2 & 1 \\ 0 & -2 \end{bmatrix} \begin{bmatrix} 0 & 4 \\ -2 & 3 \end{bmatrix} =$

    (A) $\begin{bmatrix} -2 & 1 \\ 4 & -6 \end{bmatrix}$

    (B) $\begin{bmatrix} -2 & 0 \\ 0 & -6 \end{bmatrix}$

    (C) $\begin{bmatrix} -2 & 11 \\ 4 & 6 \end{bmatrix}$

    (D) $\begin{bmatrix} -2 & 11 \\ 4 & -6 \end{bmatrix}$

    (E) $\begin{bmatrix} 2 & 11 \\ 4 & 6 \end{bmatrix}$

4. What is the product of the matrices $\begin{bmatrix} x \\ 2x \\ 0 \end{bmatrix} \begin{bmatrix} 1 & 0 & 2 \end{bmatrix}$?

   (A) $\begin{bmatrix} x & 0 & 0 \end{bmatrix}$

   (B) $\begin{bmatrix} x \\ 0 \\ 0 \end{bmatrix}$

   (C) $\begin{bmatrix} x \end{bmatrix}$

   (D) $\begin{bmatrix} x & 0 & 0 \\ 2 & x & 0 \\ 0 & 4x & x \end{bmatrix}$

   (E) $\begin{bmatrix} x & 0 & 2x \\ 2x & 0 & 4x \\ 0 & 0 & 0 \end{bmatrix}$

5. What is the product of the matrices $\begin{bmatrix} x & 1 & 3x \end{bmatrix} \begin{bmatrix} x \\ 0 \\ 4 \end{bmatrix}$?

   (A) $\begin{bmatrix} x^2 \\ 1 \\ 12x \end{bmatrix}$

   (B) $\begin{bmatrix} x^2 \\ 0 \\ 12x \end{bmatrix}$

   (C) $\begin{bmatrix} x^2 + 12 \end{bmatrix}$

   (D) $\begin{bmatrix} x^2 + 12x \end{bmatrix}$

   (E) Does not exist

6. The number of each type of sandwich on the menu at the Mom & Pop Sandwich shop is given by the following matrix:

$$\begin{array}{ccc} \text{Tuna} & \text{Pastrami} & \text{Chicken} \\ \begin{bmatrix} 5 & 2 & 4 \end{bmatrix} \end{array}$$

The number of sides available for each sandwich is given by the following matrix:

$$\begin{array}{c} \text{Tuna} \\ \text{Pastrami} \\ \text{Chicken} \end{array} \begin{bmatrix} 5 \\ 3 \\ 2 \end{bmatrix}$$

From these matrices, how many total combinations of orders of one sandwich with one side are possible?

   (A) 30
   (B) 36
   (C) 39
   (D) 43
   (E) 59

Answers and Solutions to Problem Set AA

1. $\begin{bmatrix} 1 & 0 \\ 2 & 3 \end{bmatrix} + \begin{bmatrix} 5 & \sqrt{2} \\ -2 & 0 \end{bmatrix} =$

    (A) $\begin{bmatrix} 6 & \sqrt{2} \\ 0 & 0 \end{bmatrix}$

    (B) $\begin{bmatrix} 6 & \sqrt{2} \\ 0 & 3 \end{bmatrix}$

    (C) $\begin{bmatrix} -4 & -\sqrt{2} \\ 4 & 3 \end{bmatrix}$

    (D) $\begin{bmatrix} 6 & 2 \\ 0 & 3 \end{bmatrix}$

    (E) $\begin{bmatrix} 6 & \sqrt{2} \\ 0 & 0 \end{bmatrix}$

$$\begin{bmatrix} 1 & 0 \\ 2 & 3 \end{bmatrix} + \begin{bmatrix} 5 & \sqrt{2} \\ -2 & 0 \end{bmatrix} = \begin{bmatrix} 1+5 & 0+\sqrt{2} \\ 2+(-2) & 3+0 \end{bmatrix} = \begin{bmatrix} 6 & \sqrt{2} \\ 0 & 3 \end{bmatrix}$$

The answer is (B).

2. If $A = \begin{bmatrix} 1 & 2 \\ 2 & 0 \end{bmatrix}$ and $B = \begin{bmatrix} 0 & 3 \\ 1 & -1 \end{bmatrix}$ then $3A - B =$

    (A) $\begin{bmatrix} 3 & 3 \\ 5 & -1 \end{bmatrix}$

    (B) $\begin{bmatrix} 1 & 3 \\ 5 & 1 \end{bmatrix}$

    (C) $\begin{bmatrix} 3 & 3 \\ 5 & 1 \end{bmatrix}$

    (D) $\begin{bmatrix} 3 & 3 \\ -5 & 1 \end{bmatrix}$

    (E) $\begin{bmatrix} 3 & 3 \\ 5 & 0 \end{bmatrix}$

$$3A - B = 3\begin{bmatrix} 1 & 2 \\ 2 & 0 \end{bmatrix} - \begin{bmatrix} 0 & 3 \\ 1 & -1 \end{bmatrix}$$

$$= \begin{bmatrix} 3\cdot 1 & 3\cdot 2 \\ 3\cdot 2 & 3\cdot 0 \end{bmatrix} - \begin{bmatrix} 0 & 3 \\ 1 & -1 \end{bmatrix}$$

$$= \begin{bmatrix} 3 & 6 \\ 6 & 0 \end{bmatrix} - \begin{bmatrix} 0 & 3 \\ 1 & -1 \end{bmatrix}$$

$$= \begin{bmatrix} 3-0 & 6-3 \\ 6-1 & 0-(-1) \end{bmatrix}$$

$$= \begin{bmatrix} 3 & 3 \\ 5 & 1 \end{bmatrix}$$

The answer is (C).

3. $\begin{bmatrix} 2 & 1 \\ 0 & -2 \end{bmatrix}\begin{bmatrix} 0 & 4 \\ -2 & 3 \end{bmatrix} =$

   (A) $\begin{bmatrix} -2 & 1 \\ 4 & -6 \end{bmatrix}$

   (B) $\begin{bmatrix} -2 & 0 \\ 0 & -6 \end{bmatrix}$

   (C) $\begin{bmatrix} -2 & 11 \\ 4 & 6 \end{bmatrix}$

   (D) $\begin{bmatrix} -2 & 11 \\ 4 & -6 \end{bmatrix}$

   (E) $\begin{bmatrix} 2 & 11 \\ 4 & 6 \end{bmatrix}$

$$\begin{bmatrix} 2 & 1 \\ 0 & -2 \end{bmatrix}\begin{bmatrix} 0 & 4 \\ -2 & 3 \end{bmatrix} = \begin{bmatrix} 2 \cdot 0 + 1(-2) & 2 \cdot 4 + 1 \cdot 3 \\ 0 \cdot 0 + (-2)(-2) & 0 \cdot 4 + (-2) \cdot 3 \end{bmatrix}$$

$$= \begin{bmatrix} -2 & 11 \\ 4 & -6 \end{bmatrix}$$

The answer is (D).

4.   What is the product of the matrices $\begin{bmatrix} x \\ 2x \\ 0 \end{bmatrix}\begin{bmatrix} 1 & 0 & 2 \end{bmatrix}$?

   (A) $\begin{bmatrix} x & 0 & 0 \end{bmatrix}$

   (B) $\begin{bmatrix} x \\ 0 \\ 0 \end{bmatrix}$

   (C) $\begin{bmatrix} x \end{bmatrix}$

   (D) $\begin{bmatrix} x & 0 & 0 \\ 2 & x & 0 \\ 0 & 4x & x \end{bmatrix}$

   (E) $\begin{bmatrix} x & 0 & 2x \\ 2x & 0 & 4x \\ 0 & 0 & 0 \end{bmatrix}$

This problem is harder than it may appear at first glance. Many students mistakenly chose the answer to be (C). For the product to be defined, the number of columns of the first matrix must equal the number of rows of the second matrix. The first matrix in the problem has 1 column, and the second matrix has 1 row. So, the product is defined, and the result is a 3×3 matrix.

To form the product, we multiply the first row of $\begin{bmatrix} x \\ 2x \\ 0 \end{bmatrix}$ by the *first* column of $\begin{bmatrix} 1 & 0 & 2 \end{bmatrix}$. This yields

$x \cdot 1 = x$. Adding this calculation to our 3×3 matrix yields

$$\begin{bmatrix} x & - & - \\ - & - & - \\ - & - & - \end{bmatrix}$$

Now, multiply the first row of $\begin{bmatrix} x \\ 2x \\ 0 \end{bmatrix}$ by the *second* column of $\begin{bmatrix} 1 & 0 & 2 \end{bmatrix}$. This yields $x \cdot 0 = 0$. Adding this

calculation to our matrix yields

$$\begin{bmatrix} x & 0 & - \\ - & - & - \\ - & - & - \end{bmatrix}$$

Now, multiply the first row of $\begin{bmatrix} x \\ 2x \\ 0 \end{bmatrix}$ by the *third* column of $\begin{bmatrix} 1 & 0 & 2 \end{bmatrix}$. This yields $x \cdot 2 = 2x$. Adding this

calculation to our matrix yields

$$\begin{bmatrix} x & 0 & 2x \\ - & - & - \\ - & - & - \end{bmatrix}$$

Performing the same series of calculations for the second and third rows yields

$$\begin{bmatrix} x & 0 & 2x \\ 2x & 0 & 4x \\ 0 & 0 & 0 \end{bmatrix}$$

The answer is (E).

5. What is the product of the matrices $\begin{bmatrix} x & 1 & 3x \end{bmatrix}\begin{bmatrix} x \\ 0 \\ 4 \end{bmatrix}$?

(A) $\begin{bmatrix} x^2 \\ 1 \\ 12x \end{bmatrix}$

(B) $\begin{bmatrix} x^2 \\ 0 \\ 12x \end{bmatrix}$

(C) $\begin{bmatrix} x^2 + 12 \end{bmatrix}$

(D) $\begin{bmatrix} x^2 + 12x \end{bmatrix}$

(E) Does not exist

For the product to be defined, the number of columns of the first matrix must equal the number of rows of the second matrix. The first matrix in the problem has 3 columns, and the second matrix has 3 rows. So, the product is defined, and the result is a 1×1 matrix.

To form the product, we multiply the first and only row of $\begin{bmatrix} x & 1 & 3x \end{bmatrix}$ by the first and only column of $\begin{bmatrix} x \\ 0 \\ 4 \end{bmatrix}$. This yields

$$\begin{bmatrix} x & 1 & 3x \end{bmatrix} \begin{bmatrix} x \\ 0 \\ 4 \end{bmatrix} = \begin{bmatrix} x \cdot x + 1 \cdot 0 + 3x \cdot 4 \end{bmatrix}$$
$$= \begin{bmatrix} x^2 + 0 + 12x \end{bmatrix}$$
$$= \begin{bmatrix} x^2 + 12x \end{bmatrix}$$

The answer is (D).

6.   The number of each type of sandwich on the menu at the Mom & Pop Sandwich shop is given by the following matrix:

$$\begin{array}{ccc} \text{Tuna} & \text{Pastrami} & \text{Chicken} \\ \begin{bmatrix} 5 & 2 & 4 \end{bmatrix} \end{array}$$

The number of sides available for each sandwich is given by the following matrix:

$$\begin{array}{c} \text{Tuna} \\ \text{Pastrami} \\ \text{Chicken} \end{array} \begin{bmatrix} 5 \\ 3 \\ 2 \end{bmatrix}$$

From these matrices, how many total combinations of orders of one sandwich with one side are possible?

(A)   30
(B)   36
(C)   39
(D)   43
(E)   59

The only option we have in this problem is to multiply the matrices:

$$\begin{bmatrix} 5 & 2 & 4 \end{bmatrix} \begin{bmatrix} 5 \\ 3 \\ 2 \end{bmatrix} = \begin{bmatrix} 5 \cdot 5 + 2 \cdot 3 + 4 \cdot 2 \end{bmatrix} = \begin{bmatrix} 25 + 6 + 8 \end{bmatrix} = 39$$

Hence, there are 39 combinations of one sandwich with one side. The answer is (C).

Trigonometry

Trigonometry is one of the least elegant math topics. It is just the naming of various ratios of the sides of a triangle with respect to an angle of the triangle. These simple ratios lead to an enormous number properties, formulas, and applications, most of which you do not need to know for the ACT. Though the basic definitions, you must know cold.

The ACT pretty consistently asks only three or four trig questions. Two of which are just straightforward applications of the basic definitions of sin, cos, etc. This is probably because many students take the test at the end of their junior year or at the beginning of their senior year, so many are just starting their studies of trig.

TRIGONOMETRIC FUNCTIONS AND FORMULAS YOU MUST KNOW

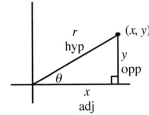

$$\sin\theta = \frac{opp}{hyp} = \frac{y}{r} \qquad \csc\theta = \frac{hyp}{opp} = \frac{r}{y} = \frac{1}{\sin\theta}$$

$$\cos\theta = \frac{adj}{hyp} = \frac{x}{r} \qquad \sec\theta = \frac{hyp}{adj} = \frac{r}{x} = \frac{1}{\cos\theta}$$

$$\tan\theta = \frac{opp}{adj} = \frac{y}{x} = \frac{\sin\theta}{\cos\theta} \qquad \cot\theta = \frac{adj}{hyp} = \frac{x}{y} = \frac{1}{\tan\theta}$$

Example: Given right triangle $\triangle ABC$, what is the value of $\cos B$?

(A) c/a
(B) a/c
(C) b/c
(D) b/a
(E) c/b

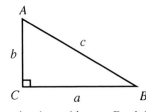

On the test, you will probably get a trig problem as simple as this one. By definition,

$$\cos B = \frac{adj}{hyp} = \frac{a}{c}$$

The answer is (B).

Example: Given right triangle $\triangle ABC$, what is the value of $\tan A$?

(A) $\dfrac{\sqrt{1-x^2}}{x}$

(B) $\sqrt{1-x^2}$

(C) $\dfrac{1}{x}$

(D) $\dfrac{1}{\sqrt{1-x^2}}$

(E) $\dfrac{x}{\sqrt{1-x^2}}$

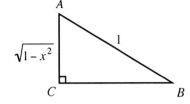

In order to calculate $\tan A$, we need the length of segment CB. Applying The Pythagorean Theorem to $\triangle ABC$ yields

$$1^2 = \left(\sqrt{1-x^2}\right)^2 + \left(\overline{CB}\right)^2$$

$$1 = 1 - x^2 + \left(\overline{CB}\right)^2$$

$$x^2 = \left(\overline{CB}\right)^2$$

$$x = \overline{CB}$$

Now, applying the definition of the tangent yields

$$\tan A = \frac{opp}{adj} = \frac{CB}{AC} = \frac{x}{\sqrt{1-x^2}}$$

The answer is (E).

TRIGONOMETRIC IDENTITIES YOU SHOULD BE FAMILIAR WITH, BUT PROBABLY DO NOT NEED TO MEMORIZE

Sum or Difference formulas:

$$\sin(x \pm y) = \sin x \cos y \pm \cos x \sin y$$

$$\cos(x \pm y) = \cos x \cos y \mp \sin x \sin y$$

$$\tan(x \pm y) = \frac{\tan x \pm \tan y}{1 \mp \tan x \tan y}$$

Double Angle formulas:

$$\sin 2\theta = 2 \sin \theta \cos \theta$$

$$\cos 2\theta = 1 - 2\sin^2 \theta$$

$$= 2\cos^2 \theta - 1$$

$$= \cos^2 \theta - \sin^2 \theta$$

$$\tan 2\theta = \frac{2\tan\theta}{1 - \tan^2 \theta}$$

Pythagorean formulas:

$$\sin^2\theta + \cos^2\theta = 1$$

$$\tan^2\theta + 1 = \sec^2\theta$$

$$\cot^2\theta + 1 = \csc^2\theta$$

Example: If $x = a\sin\theta$ for $-\pi/2 < \theta < \pi/2$ and $a > 0$, then $\dfrac{\sqrt{a^2 - x^2}}{x} =$

(A) $\tan\theta$

(B) $\cot\theta$

(C) $a\tan\theta$

(D) $a\cot\theta$

(E) $\dfrac{\tan\theta}{a}$

Replacing x with $a\sin\theta$ in the expression $\dfrac{\sqrt{a^2 - x^2}}{x}$ yields

$$\frac{\sqrt{a^2 - x^2}}{x} = \frac{\sqrt{a^2 - (a\sin\theta)^2}}{a\sin\theta}$$

$$= \frac{\sqrt{a^2 - a^2\sin^2\theta}}{a\sin\theta}$$

$$= \frac{\sqrt{a^2(1 - \sin^2\theta)}}{a\sin\theta}$$

$$= \frac{\sqrt{a^2\cos^2\theta}}{a\sin\theta}$$

$$= \frac{a\cos\theta}{a\sin\theta}$$

$$= \frac{\cos\theta}{\sin\theta}$$

$$= \cot\theta$$

The answer is (B).

Half Angle formulas:

$$\sin^2\theta = \frac{1}{2}(1 - \cos 2\theta)$$

$$\cos^2\theta = \frac{1}{2}(1 + \cos 2\theta)$$

$$\sin\frac{\theta}{2} = \pm\sqrt{\frac{1 - \cos\theta}{2}}$$

$$\cos\frac{\theta}{2} = \pm\sqrt{\frac{1 + \cos\theta}{2}}$$

$$\tan\frac{\theta}{2} = \frac{\sin\theta}{1 + \cos\theta} = \frac{1 - \cos\theta}{\sin\theta}$$

Sum and Product formulas:

$$\sin x \cos y = \frac{1}{2}[\sin(x+y) + \sin(x-y)]$$

$$\cos x \sin y = \frac{1}{2}[\sin(x+y) - \sin(x-y)]$$

$$\cos x \cos y = \frac{1}{2}[\cos(x+y) + \cos(x-y)]$$

$$\sin x \sin y = \frac{1}{2}[\cos(x-y) - \cos(x+y)]$$

$$\sin x + \sin y = 2\sin\left(\frac{x+y}{2}\right)\cos\left(\frac{x-y}{2}\right)$$

$$\sin x - \sin y = 2\cos\left(\frac{x+y}{2}\right)\sin\left(\frac{x-y}{2}\right)$$

$$\cos x + \cos y = 2\cos\left(\frac{x+y}{2}\right)\cos\left(\frac{x-y}{2}\right)$$

$$\cos x - \cos y = -2\sin\left(\frac{x+y}{2}\right)\sin\left(\frac{x-y}{2}\right)$$

Reduction formulas:

$$\sin(-\theta) = -\sin\theta$$
$$\cos(-\theta) = \cos\theta$$
$$\sin\theta = -\sin(\theta - \pi)$$
$$\cos\theta = -\cos(\theta - \pi)$$

Conversion factors:

$$1° = \frac{\pi}{180} \text{ radians}$$

$$1 \text{ radian} = \frac{180°}{\pi}$$

FORMULAS FOR SOLVING NONRIGHT TRIANGLES

Law of Cosines:

$$c^2 = a^2 + b^2 - 2ab\cos C$$
where a, b, and c are the sides of the triangle and C is the angle opposite side c

The Law of Cosines is one of the favorite formulas of the ACT writers. There is a good chance you will see it on your test. You don't need to memorize the formula. If you do get a problem that requires the Law of Cosines, the formula will be given to you. The ACT is more concerned about measuring the mathematical skills you have developed than how many formulas you have memorized. So, you need to understand how the formula can be used.

Example: Given right triangle $\triangle ABC$, what is the length of side AB ?

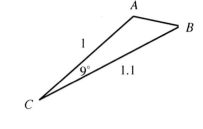

(A) $\sqrt{1^2 + (1.1)^2}$

(B) $\sqrt{1^2 - (1.1)^2}$

(C) $\sqrt{1^2 + (1.1)^2 - 2(1)(1.1)\cos 9°}$

(D) $\sqrt{1^2 + (1.1)^2 + 2(1)(1.1)\cos 9°}$

(E) $\sqrt{1^2 + (1.1)^2 - 2(1)(1.1)\cos(90 - 9)°}$

Since side AB is opposite angle C, the Law of Cosines yields

$$AB^2 = a^2 + b^2 - 2ab\cos C$$

Letting $a = 1$, $b = 1.1$ (or you can let $a = 1.1$ and $b = 1$), and $C = 9°$ yields

$$AB^2 = 1^2 + (1.1)^2 - 2(1)(1.1)\cos 9°$$

Finally, taking the square root of both sides of this equation yields

$$AB = \sqrt{1^2 + (1.1)^2 - 2(1)(1.1)\cos 9°}$$

The answer is (C).

Law of Sines:

$$\frac{\sin A}{a} = \frac{\sin B}{b} = \frac{\sin C}{c}$$ where angle A is oppsite side a, etc.

TRIGONOMETRIC VALUES FOR SPECIAL ANGLES

Angle	$\sin\theta$	$\cos\theta$	$\tan\theta$	$\cot\theta$	$\sec\theta$	$\csc\theta$
0 or 0°	0	1	0	Undefined	1	Undefined
$\pi/6$ or 30°	1/2	$\sqrt{3}/2$	$\sqrt{3}/3$	$\sqrt{3}$	$2\sqrt{3}/3$	2
$\pi/4$ or 45°	$\sqrt{2}/2$	$\sqrt{2}/2$	1	1	$\sqrt{2}$	$\sqrt{2}$
$\pi/3$ or 60°	$\sqrt{3}/2$	1/2	$\sqrt{3}$	$\sqrt{3}/3$	2	$2\sqrt{3}/3$

Example: What is $\sin\dfrac{\pi}{8}$ given that $\sin\dfrac{\theta}{2}=\sqrt{\dfrac{1-\cos\theta}{2}}$?

(Note: You can use any of the values in the above table.)

(A) $2-\sqrt{2}$

(B) $\sqrt{2}$

(C) $\dfrac{\sqrt{2-\sqrt{2}}}{4}$

(D) $\sqrt{2-\sqrt{2}}$

(E) $\dfrac{\sqrt{2-\sqrt{2}}}{2}$

Our goal here is to write $\dfrac{\pi}{8}$ as half of one of the special angles in the table so that we can use the given

Half Angle Formula: $\sin\dfrac{\theta}{2}=\sqrt{\dfrac{1-\cos\theta}{2}}$. Now, $\dfrac{\pi}{8}=\dfrac{\pi}{2\cdot4}=\dfrac{1}{2}\left(\dfrac{\pi}{4}\right)=\dfrac{\pi/4}{2}$, so replacing θ in the formula

with $\dfrac{\pi}{4}$ yields

$$\sin\frac{\pi}{8}=\sin\frac{\pi/4}{2}$$

$$=\sqrt{\frac{1-\cos\pi/4}{2}}$$

$$=\sqrt{\frac{1-\dfrac{\sqrt{2}}{2}}{2}}\qquad\text{from the table } \cos\pi/4=\frac{\sqrt{2}}{2}$$

$$=\sqrt{\frac{\dfrac{2}{2}-\dfrac{\sqrt{2}}{2}}{2}}$$

$$=\sqrt{\frac{\dfrac{2-\sqrt{2}}{2}}{2}}$$

$$=\sqrt{\frac{2-\sqrt{2}}{4}}$$

$$=\frac{\sqrt{2-\sqrt{2}}}{2}$$

The answer is (E).

Problem Set BB:

1. In the right triangle $\triangle ABC$, the length of side AC is 2. If the cosine of angle A is 1/2, then what is the length of the hypotenuse AB ?

    (A) 4
    (B) $\dfrac{4}{\sqrt{3}}$
    (C) $\sqrt{3}$
    (D) 2
    (E) 1

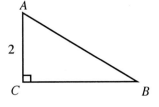

2. In the right triangle $\triangle ABC$ shown, $\dfrac{\sec B}{\sin a}$ =

    (A) 1
    (B) a/c
    (C) $\left(\dfrac{c}{a}\right)^2$
    (D) c^2
    (E) a^2

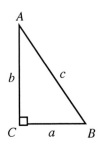

3. If $\cos A = \dfrac{b}{c}$, $b > 0$, and $0 < A < \pi/2$, then $\sin A$ =

    (A) $\dfrac{c}{\sqrt{c^2 - b^2}}$
    (B) c/b
    (C) $\dfrac{\sqrt{c^2 + b^2}}{c}$
    (D) $\dfrac{\sqrt{c^2 - b^2}}{c}$
    (E) $\sqrt{c^2 - b^2}$

4. In the right triangle shown, the secant of one of the angles is c/a. What is the tangent of this angle?

    (A) $\dfrac{a}{\sqrt{c^2 - a^2}}$
    (B) $\dfrac{\sqrt{c^2 - a^2}}{a}$
    (C) $\dfrac{\sqrt{c^2 - a^2}}{c}$
    (D) $\sqrt{c^2 - a^2}$
    (E) c/a

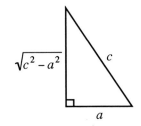

5. Given right triangle $\triangle ABC$, what is the value
    of csc A ?

    (A) $\dfrac{2}{\sqrt{5}}$

    (B) $\dfrac{\sqrt{5}}{2}$

    (C) $\dfrac{3}{2}$

    (D) $\sqrt{5}$

    (E) $\dfrac{1}{2}$

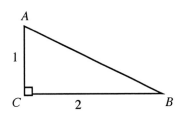

6. What is $\tan\dfrac{\pi}{12}$ given that $\tan(x-y) = \dfrac{\tan x - \tan y}{1 + \tan x \tan y}$ and $\dfrac{\pi}{12} = \dfrac{\pi}{3} - \dfrac{\pi}{4}$?

    (Note: You can use the values in the table below.)

θ	$\tan \theta$
$\pi/4$	1
$\pi/3$	$\sqrt{3}$

    (A) $\dfrac{\sqrt{3}-1}{1+\sqrt{3}}$

    (B) $\dfrac{\sqrt{3}+1}{1+\sqrt{3}}$

    (C) $\dfrac{\sqrt{3}+1}{1-\sqrt{3}}$

    (D) $\dfrac{\sqrt{3}-1}{\sqrt{3}}$

    (E) $\dfrac{\sqrt{3}}{1+\sqrt{3}}$

Answers and Solutions to Problem Set BB

1. In the right triangle $\triangle ABC$, the length of side AC is 2. If the cosine of angle A is 1/2, then what is the length of the hypotenuse AB ?

    (A)   4
    (B) $\dfrac{4}{\sqrt{3}}$
    (C) $\sqrt{3}$
    (D)   2
    (E)   1

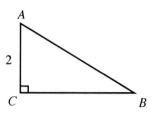

From the definition of cosine, we get

$$\cos A = \frac{adj}{hyp} = \frac{2}{AB}$$

Since we are given that $\cos A = \dfrac{1}{2}$, this becomes

$$\frac{2}{AB} = \frac{1}{2}$$

Solving this equation yields $AB = 4$, and the answer is (A).

2. In the right triangle $\triangle ABC$ shown, $\dfrac{\sec B}{\sin a} =$

    (A)   1
    (B) a/c
    (C) $\left(\dfrac{c}{a}\right)^2$
    (D) c^2
    (E) a^2

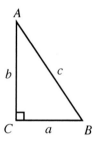

From the definitions of secant and sine, we get

$$\frac{\sec B}{\sin A} = \frac{{}^{hyp}\!/_{adj}}{{}^{opp}\!/_{hyp}} = \frac{{}^{c}\!/_{a}}{{}^{a}\!/_{c}} = \frac{c}{a} \cdot \frac{c}{a} = \left(\frac{c}{a}\right)^2$$

The answer is (C).

3. If $\cos A = \dfrac{b}{c}$, $b > 0$, and $0 < A < \pi/2$, then $\sin A =$

(A) $\dfrac{c}{\sqrt{c^2 - b^2}}$

(B) c/b

(C) $\dfrac{\sqrt{c^2 + b^2}}{c}$

(D) $\dfrac{\sqrt{c^2 - b^2}}{c}$

(E) $\sqrt{c^2 - b^2}$

In a triangle, the cosine is the ratio of the adjacent side to the hypotenuse, so we get

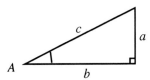

In order to determine $\sin A$, we must find the length of side a. Applying The Pythagorean Theorem to the triangle yields $c^2 = a^2 + b^2$. Solving this equation for a yields $a = \sqrt{c^2 - b^2}$, so the figure becomes

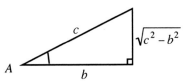

Hence, $\sin A = \dfrac{opp}{hyp} = \dfrac{\sqrt{c^2 - b^2}}{c}$. The answer is (D).

4. In the right triangle shown, the secant of one of the angles is c/a. What is the tangent of this angle?

(A) $\dfrac{a}{\sqrt{c^2 - a^2}}$

(B) $\dfrac{\sqrt{c^2 - a^2}}{a}$

(C) $\dfrac{\sqrt{c^2 - a^2}}{c}$

(D) $\sqrt{c^2 - a^2}$

(E) c/a

Since the secant is the hypotenuse divided by the adjacent side, we are dealing with the angle at the lower right-hand corner of the triangle. Let's label it B:

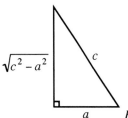

From the definition of tangent, we get

$$\tan B = \frac{opp}{adj} = \frac{\sqrt{c^2 - a^2}}{a}$$

The answer is (B).

5. Given right triangle $\triangle ABC$, what is the value of csc A ?

(A) $\dfrac{2}{\sqrt{5}}$

(B) $\dfrac{\sqrt{5}}{2}$

(C) $\dfrac{3}{2}$

(D) $\sqrt{5}$

(E) $\dfrac{1}{2}$

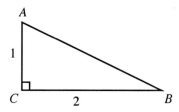

In order to calculate csc A, we need the length of the hypotenuse AB. Applying The Pythagorean Theorem to $\triangle ABC$ yields

$$AB^2 = 1^2 + 2^2$$
$$AB^2 = 5$$
$$AB = \sqrt{5}$$

Now, applying the definition of the cosecant to angle A yields

$$\csc A = \frac{hyp}{opp} = \frac{AB}{CB} = \frac{\sqrt{5}}{2}$$

The answer is (B).

6. What is $\tan\dfrac{\pi}{12}$ given that $\tan(x-y) = \dfrac{\tan x - \tan y}{1 + \tan x \tan y}$ and $\dfrac{\pi}{12} = \dfrac{\pi}{3} - \dfrac{\pi}{4}$?

(Note: You can use the values in the table below.)

θ	$\tan\theta$
$\pi/4$	1
$\pi/3$	$\sqrt{3}$

(A) $\dfrac{\sqrt{3}-1}{1+\sqrt{3}}$

(B) $\dfrac{\sqrt{3}+1}{1+\sqrt{3}}$

(C) $\dfrac{\sqrt{3}+1}{1-\sqrt{3}}$

(D) $\dfrac{\sqrt{3}-1}{\sqrt{3}}$

(E) $\dfrac{\sqrt{3}}{1+\sqrt{3}}$

Replacing $\dfrac{\pi}{12}$ with $\dfrac{\pi}{3} - \dfrac{\pi}{4}$ in the expression $\tan\dfrac{\pi}{12}$ yields

$$\tan\frac{\pi}{12} = \tan\left(\frac{\pi}{3} - \frac{\pi}{4}\right)$$

$$= \frac{\tan\dfrac{\pi}{3} - \tan\dfrac{\pi}{4}}{1 + \tan\dfrac{\pi}{3}\tan\dfrac{\pi}{4}} \qquad \text{since } \tan(x-y) = \frac{\tan x - \tan y}{1 + \tan x \tan y}$$

$$= \frac{\sqrt{3}-1}{1+\sqrt{3}\cdot 1} \qquad \text{from the table}$$

$$= \frac{\sqrt{3}-1}{1+\sqrt{3}}$$

The answer is (A).

Permutations & Combinations

Suppose you must seat 3 of 5 delegates in 3 chairs. And suppose you are interested in the order in which they sit. You will first select 3 of the 5 delegates, and then choose the order in which they sit. The first act is a combination, the second is a permutation. Effectively, the permutation comes after the combination. The delegates in each combination can be ordered in different ways, which can be called permutations of the combination.

Now, if you can select 3 of the 5 delegates in m ways and each selection can be ordered in n ways, then the total number of possible arrangements (permutations) is $m \cdot n$.

Now, let's count the number of permutations of 3 objects taken from a set of 4 objects {A, B, C, D}. Let's call the set {A, B, C, D} a base set.

We must first choose 3 objects from the base set, which yields the following selections:

$$\{A, B, C\}, \{B, C, D\}, \{A, C, D\}, \{A, B, D\}$$

These are combinations. We have 4 selections (combinations) here.

If {E1, E2, E3} represents one of the four combinations above, then the following are its possible permutations:

E1	E2	E3
E1	E3	E2
E2	E1	E3
E2	E3	E1
E3	E1	E2
E3	E2	E1

You can use this scheme to find the permutations of each of the 4 selections (combinations) we formed above. For example, for the selection {A, B, C}, the following are the six permutations:

$$A - B - C$$
$$A - C - B$$
$$B - A - C$$
$$B - C - A$$
$$C - A - B$$
$$C - B - A$$

Thus, we have 6 permutations for each selection. For practice, you may wish to list the permutations for the remaining 3 selections: {B, C, D}, {A, C, D}, and {A, B, D}.

Summary:
Here, {A, B, C, D} is the base set. We formed 4 combinations that use 3 elements each. Then we formed 6 permutations for each of the 4 combinations. Hence, the problem has in total $6 + 6 + 6 + 6 = 4 \times 6 = 24$ permutations.

Note 1: A combination might have multiple permutations. The reverse is never true.

Note 2: A permutation is an ordered combination.

Note 3: With combinations, AB = BA. With permutations, AB ≠ BA.

Combinations and their Permutations

Here is another discussion of the distinction between permutations and combinations. The concept is repeated here because it forms the basis for the rest of the chapter.

Combinations are the selections (subsets) of a base set.

For example, the possible combinations of two elements each of the set {A, B} are

A, B or B, A
(Both are the same combination)

The permutations (the combination ordered in different ways) of the combination are

A – B and B – A
(The permutations are different)

How to distinguish between a Combination and a Permutation

At the risk of redundancy, here is yet another discussion of the distinction between permutations and combinations.

As combinations, {A, B, C} and {B, A, C} are the same because each has the same number of each type of object: A, B, and C as in the base set.

But, as permutations, A – B – C and B – A – C are not the same because the ordering is different, though each has the same number of each type of object: A, B, and C as in the base set In fact, no two arrangements that are not identical are ever the same permutation.

Hence, with combinations, look for selections, while with permutations, look for arrangements.

The following definitions will help you distinguish between Combinations and Permutations

Permutations are *arrangements* (order is important) of objects formed from an original set (base set) such that each new arrangement has an order different from the original set. So, the positions of objects is important.

Combinations are sets of objects formed by *selecting* (order not important) objects from an original set (base set).

To help you remember, think "Permutation … Position."

Combinations with Repetitions: Permutations with Repetitions

Here, repetition of objects is allowed in selections or the arrangements.

Suppose you have the base set {A, B, C}. Allowing repetitions, the objects can repeat in the combinations (selections).

Hence, the allowed *selections* of 2 elements are {A, A}, {A, B} or {B, A}, {B, B}, {B, C} or {C, B}, {C, C}, {C, A} or {A, C} in total 6.

The corresponding *permutations* are

A – A for {A, A}
A – B and B – A for {A, B}
B – B for {B, B}
B – C and C – B for {B, C}
C – C for {C, C}
C – A and A – C for {C, A}

The total number of combinations is 6, and the total number of permutations is 9. We have 3 objects to choose for 2 positions; allowing repetitions, the calculation is $3^2 = 9$.

Note that {A, B} and {B, A} are the same combination because each has an equal number of A's and B's.

By allowing repetitions, you can chose the same object more than once and therefore can have the same object occupying different positions.

In general, *permutation* means "permutation without repetition," unless stated otherwise.

Indistinguishable Objects

Suppose we replace C in the base set {A, B, C} with A. Then, we have {A, B, A}. Now the A's in the first and third positions of the set are indistinguishable and make some of the combinations and permutations formed earlier involving C redundant (because some identical combinations and permutations will be formed). Hence, replacing distinguishable objects with indistinguishable ones reduces the number of combinations and permutations.

Combinations (repetition not allowed) with Indistinguishable Objects

Consider the set {A, B, A}. Here, for example, ABA (2 A's and 1 B as in the base set) is an allowed combination but ABB (containing 2 B's not as in base set) is not because B occurs only once in the base set.

All the allowed permutations are listed in Table IV.

Permutations (repetition not allowed) with Indistinguishable Objects

The corresponding permutations are listed in Table IV.

Observe that {A, B, C} has permutations ABC, ACB, BAC, BCA, CAB, and CBA (6 permutations); and {A, B, A} has permutations ABA, AAB, BAA, ~~BAA~~, ~~AAB~~, and ~~ABA~~ (we crossed out the last three permutations because they are identical to the first three). So, there are 3 permutations.

Combinations (repetition allowed) with Indistinguishable Objects

Again, consider the set {A, B, A}. Here, for example, ABA is an allowed combination and ABB is an allowed combination.

All the allowed permutations are listed in Table III.

Permutations (repetition allowed) with Indistinguishable Objects

The corresponding permutations are listed in Table III.

Summary:

➤ Repetition problems have the objects repeating in the combinations or permutations that are formed from a base set.

➤ Problems with indistinguishable objects, instead, have the objects repeating in the base set itself.

➤ Allowing repetition increases the number of selections (combinations) and therefore the number of permutations.

➤ Using indistinguishable objects in the base set reduces the number of selections (combinations) and the number of permutations.

Table I
The base set is {A, B, C}
Permutations with Repetitions allowed. [n = 3, r = 3]

First Position (3 ways allowed: A, B, C)	Second Position (3 ways allowed: A, B, C)	Third Position (3 ways allowed: A, B, C)	Word Formed	Count
A	A	A	AAA	1
		B	AAB	2
		C	AAC	3
	B	A	ABA	4
		B	ABB	5
		C	ABC	6
	C	A	ACA	7
		B	ACB	8
		C	ACC	9
B	A	A	BAA	10
		B	BAB	11
		C	BAC	12
	B	A	BBA	13
		B	BBB	14
		C	BBC	15
	C	A	BCA	16
		B	BCB	17
		C	BCC	18
C	A	A	CAA	19
		B	CAB	20
		C	CAC	21
	B	A	CBA	22
		B	CBB	23
		C	CBC	24
	C	A	CCA	25
		B	CCB	26
		C	CCC	27

Total number of ways: 27

Table II
The base set is {A, B, C}
The Permutations (not allowing Repetitions) are as follows [n = 3, r = 3].
Shaded entries are redundant and therefore not counted. (That is, we pick
only the entries in which no object is repeated.) Shaded entries the ones
having the same object repeating and therefore not counted.

First Position (3 ways allowed: A, B, C)	Second Position (3 ways allowed: A, B, C)	Third Position (3 ways allowed: A, B, C)	Word Formed	Count
A	A	A	AAA	A repeat
		B	AAB	A repeat
		C	AAC	A repeat
	B	A	ABA	A repeat
		B	ABB	B repeat
		C	ABC	1
	C	A	ACA	A repeat
		B	ACB	2
		C	ACC	C repeat
B	A	A	BAA	A repeat
		B	BAB	B repeat
		C	BAC	3
	B	A	BBA	B repeat
		B	BBB	B repeat
		C	BBC	B repeat
	C	A	BCA	4
		B	BCB	B repeat
		C	BCC	C repeat
C	A	A	CAA	A repeat
		B	CAB	5
		C	CAC	C repeat
	B	A	CBA	6
		B	CBB	B repeat
		C	CBC	C repeat
	C	A	CCA	C repeat
		B	CCB	C repeat
		C	CCC	C repeat

Total number of ways: 6

There is only 1 combination (without repetition), because any of the 6 words (ABC or ACB or BAC or BCA or CAB or CBA) formed in the above table is the same combination (is a single combination).

Permutations (repetition allowed) using Indistinguishable Objects

By replacing C with A in the base set {A, B, C}, we get {A, B, A}. Reducing the repetitive permutations yields

Table III
The Permutations (allowing Repetitions) are as follows [$n = 3$, $r = 3$],
and two of the three objects are indistinguishable. The table is derived
by replacing C with A in Table I and eliminating the repeating entries.
Shaded entries are redundant and therefore not counted. (That is, we
pick only one of the indistinguishable permutations.)

First Position (3 ways allowed: A, B, C)	Second Position (3 ways allowed: A, B, C)	Third Position (3 ways allowed: A, B, C)	Word Formed	Count
A	A	A	AAA	1
		B	AAB	2
		A	AAA	already counted
	B	A	ABA	3
		B	ABB	4
		A	ABA	already counted
	A	A	AAA	already counted
		B	AAB	already counted
		A	AAA	already counted
B	A	A	BAA	5
		B	BAB	6
		A	BAA	already counted
	B	A	BBA	7
		B	BBB	8
		A	BBA	already counted
	A	A	BAA	already counted
		B	BAB	already counted
		A	BAA	already counted
A	A	A	AAA	already counted
		B	AAB	already counted
		A	AAA	already counted
	B	A	ABA	already counted
		B	ABB	already counted
		A	ABA	already counted
	A	A	AAA	already counted
		B	AAB	already counted
		A	AAA	already counted

Total number of ways: 8

Permutations (repetition not allowed) with Indistinguishable Objects

Indistinguishable objects are items that repeat in the original set. For example, replace C in the above set with A. Then the new base set would be {A, B, A}. Hence, if we replace C with A in the Table II, we get the repetitions in the permutations. Reducing the repetitive permutations yields

Table IV
The Permutations (not allowing Repetitions) with Indistinguishable objects are as follows [$n = 3$, $r = 3$]. The table is derived by replacing C with A in Table II and eliminating the repeating entries. Shaded entries are redundant and therefore not counted. (That is, we pick only one of the indistinguishable permutations)

First Position (3 ways allowed: A, B, C)	Second Position (3 ways allowed: A, B, C)	Third Position (3 ways allowed: A, B, C)	Word Formed	Count
A	B	A	ABA	1
	A	B	AAB	2
B	A	A	BAA	3
	A	A	BAA	already counted
A	A	B	AAB	already counted
	A	A	ABA	already counted

Total number of ways: 3

So far, we have discussed the types of the problems. When trying to solve a problem, it is very helpful to identify its type. Once this is done, we need to count the number of possibilities.

Distinction between Indistinguishable Objects Problems and Repetition Problems

Suppose you are to arrange the letters of the word SUCCESS.

The base set is {S, U, C, C, E, S, S}. There are 3 S's, which are indistinguishable objects. Hence, the letter S, can be used a maximum of 3 times in forming a new word if repetition is not allowed. So, SSSSUCE is not a possible arrangement.

If repetition is allowed, you can use S as many times as you wish, regardless of the number of S's in the base word (for example, even if there is only 1 S, you can use it up to maximum allowed times). Hence, SSSSSSS is a possible arrangement.

Counting

There are three models of counting we can use.

We already discussed that if there are m combinations possible from a base set and if there are n permutations possible for each combination, then the total number of permutations possible is $m \cdot n$.

This is also clear from the *Fundamental Principle of Counting*.

Model 1:
The Fundamental Principle of Counting:

Construct a tree diagram (we used tables above) to keep track of all possibilities. Each decision made produces a new branch. Finally, count all the allowed possibilities.

The previous tables are examples of tree diagrams. They can represent possibilities as trees. The possibilities are also counted in the tables.

Model 2:

Divide a work into mutually independent jobs and multiply the number of ways of doing each job to find the total number of ways the work can be done. For example, if you are to position three letters in 3 slots, you can divide the work into the jobs as

1) Choose one of three letters A, B, and C for the first position
2) Choose one of the remaining 2 letters for the second position
3) Choose the only remaining letter for the third position

This can be done in $3 \times 2 \times 1 = 6$ ways. The model is a result of the Fundamental Principle of Counting.

Model 3:

Models 1 and 2 are fundamental. Model 3 uses at least one of the first two models. Here, we use the following formula:

Total Number of Permutations = Number of Combinations × Number of Permutations of Each Combination

Predominantly, we use the model for calculating combinations. The total number of permutations and the number of permutations for each combination can be calculated using either or both models 1 and 2 in many cases.

Cyclic Permutations

A *cyclic permutation* is a permutation that shifts all elements of a given ordered set by a certain amount, with the elements that are shifted off the end inserted back at the beginning in the same order, i.e., cyclically. In other words, a rotation.

For example, {A, B, C, D}, {B, C, D, A}, {C, D, A, B}, and {D, A, B, C} are different linear permutations but the same cyclic permutation. The permutations when arranged in cyclic order, starting from, say, A and moving clockwise, yield the same arrangement {A, B, C, D}. The following figure helps visualize this.

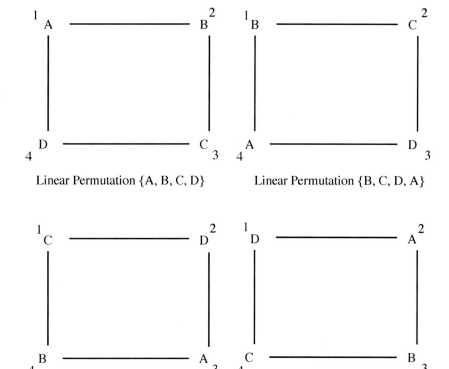

Cyclic arrangements of the cyclic permutations.

For the r placement positions (for the example in the figure, r equals 4), we get r permutations, each is an equivalent cyclic permutation. Hence, the number of cyclic permutations equals

(The number of ordinary permutations) $\div r$

Hence, for $_nP_r$ permutations, $_nP_r \div r$ cyclic permutations exist. Simply said, r linear permutations would be same cyclic permutation.

Also, {A, B, C, D} and {A, C, B, D} are different linear permutations and different cyclic permutations, because arranging them in cyclic order yields different sequences.

Factorial

The **factorial** of a non-negative integer n, denoted by n!, is the product of all positive integers less than or equal to n. That is, $n! = n(n-1)(n-2)\cdots 3 \cdot 2 \cdot 1$. For example, $4! = 4 \cdot 3 \cdot 2 \cdot 1 = 24$. Note: 0! is defined to be 1.

Formulas

Verify that the following formulas apply to the scenarios mentioned above. These formulas should be memorized.

Formula 1: If you have n items to choose from and you choose r of them, then the number of permutations *with repetitions allowed* is

$$n \cdot n \cdot \ldots n = n^r$$
$$(r \text{ times})$$

Formula 2: The formula for permutations *with repetitions not allowed* is

$$_nP_r = \frac{n!}{(n-r)!}$$

Formula 3: The formula for combinations *with repetitions not allowed* is

$$_nC_r = \frac{n!}{r!(n-r)!}$$

Formula 4: We know that k *distinguishable* objects have $k!$ *different* arrangements (permutations). But a set of k *indistinguishable* objects, will have only 1 *indistinguishable* permutation. Hence, if we have P permutations for k *distinguishable* objects, we will have $\frac{P}{k!}$ permutations for k *indistinguishable* objects because we now treat the earlier $k!$ arrangements as one.

The case is similar when we have more than one set of indistinguishable objects. Suppose the word ABCDEF has $_nP_r$ permutations (not allowing repetitions); then the word AAABBC will have $\frac{_nP_r}{3! \cdot 2!}$ permutations because here we have a set of 3 indistinguishable objects A and a set of 2 indistinguishable objects B.

There are formulas for the other problem models, but they are not needed for the test. We can always use the Fundamental Principal of Counting for them.

Formula 5: For r linear positions (for the example in the figure, r equals 4), we get r permutations, each of which is an equivalent cyclic permutation. Hence, the number of cyclic permutations is

(The number of ordinary permutations) $\div r$

The formulas in this section will be referenced while we solve the problems.

Problem Solving Strategy

In permutation and combination problems, it is very important to recognize the type of problem. Many students mistakenly approach a combination problem as a permutation, and vice versa. The steps below will help you determine the problem type.

Solving a permutation or combination problem involves two steps:

1) Recognizing the problem type: permutation vs. combination.
2) Using formulas or models to count the possibilities.

We have three questions to ask ourselves in order to identify the problem type:

1) **Is it a permutation or combination?**
   Check any two typical arrangements with the same combination. If the two arrangements are counted only once, it is a combination problem. Otherwise, it is a permutation.

   For example, if you are asked for a lock code, then 321 and 123 could be two possibilities, and the two numbers are formed from the same combination (Same number of 1's, 2's, and 3's). So, lock codes must be permutations.

   For another example, suppose you have 5 balls numbering 1 through 5. If you are asked to select 3 out of the 5 balls and you are only interested in the numbers on the balls, not the order in which they are taken, then you have a combination problem.

   Problems that by definition connote ordering (though not directly stated) are permutations. For example, 3 digits form a 3-digit number. Here, the 3-digit number connotes ordering. For another example, if you are to answer 3 questions, you probably would not be asked to answer a particular question more than once. So, you would not allow repetition in the calculations. Though not often needed, such logical assumptions are allowed and sometimes expected.

   If the problem itself defines slots for the arrangements, it is a permutation problem. Words like "arrange" define slots for the arrangements. We will explain this in more detail later in the problems.

   Generally, "arrangements" refer to permutations, and "selections" refer to combinations. These words often flag the problem type.

   Other words indicating permutations are "alteration," "shift," "transformation," and "transmutation," all of which connote ordering.

   For example:
   In how many ways can the letters of the word XYZ be *transformed* to form new words?
   In how many ways can the letters of the word XYZ be *altered* to form new words?

   Some words indicating combinations are "aggregation," "alliance," "association," "coalition," "composition," "confederation," "gang," "league," and "union," (all of which have nothing to do with arrangements but instead connote selections.)

   For example:
   In how many ways can a coalition of 2 countries be formed from 4 countries?
   (Here, a coalition is the same whether you say country A and B are a coalition or country B and country A are a coalition.)

2)   **Are repetitions allowed?**
Check whether, based on the problem description, the results of a permutation/combination can have repetitions.

For example:
If you are to list countries in a coalition, you can hardly list a country twice.
(Here, repetition automatically is not allowed unless specified otherwise.)

If you have 3 doors to a room, you could use the same door for both entering and exiting.
(Here, repetition is automatically allowed.)

3)   **Are there any indistinguishable objects in the base set?**
Check the base set: the objects from which a permutation or a combination are drawn. If any indistinguishable objects (repetitions at base set level) are available, collect them. This is easy since it only requires finding identical objects in a base set, which is usually given.

For example, if the original question is to find the words formed from the word GARGUNTUNG, then, in this step, you collect the information: G exists thrice, U exists twice, and so on.

Once the problem type is recognized, use the corresponding formula or model to solve it.

Problem Set CC:

1.   There are 3 doors to a lecture room. In how many ways can a lecturer enter and leave the room?

    (A)   1
    (B)   3
    (C)   6
    (D)   9
    (E)   12

2.   There are 3 doors to a lecture room. In how many ways can a lecturer enter the room from one door and leave from another door?

    (A)   1
    (B)   3
    (C)   6
    (D)   9
    (E)   12

3.   How many possible combinations can a 3-digit safe code have?

    (A) $_9C_3$
    (B) $_9P_3$
    (C) 3^9
    (D) 9^3
    (E) 10^3

4.   Goodwin has 3 different colored pants and 2 different colored shirts. In how many ways can he choose a pair of pants and a shirt?

    (A)   2
    (B)   3
    (C)   5
    (D)   6
    (E)   12

5.   In how many ways can 2 doors be selected from 3 doors?

    (A)   1
    (B)   3
    (C)   6
    (D)   9
    (E)   12

6.   In how many ways can 2 doors be selected from 3 doors for entering and leaving a room?

    (A)   1
    (B)   3
    (C)   6
    (D)   9
    (E)   12

7.   In how many ways can a room be entered and exited from the 3 doors to the room?

    (A)   1
    (B)   3
    (C)   6
    (D)   9
    (E)   12

8. There are 5 doors to a lecture room. Two are red and the others are green. In how many ways can a lecturer enter the room and leave the room from different colored doors?

   (A) 1
   (B) 3
   (C) 6
   (D) 9
   (E) 12

9. Four pool balls—A, B, C, D—are randomly arranged in a straight line. What is the probability that the order will actually be A, B, C, D ?

   (A) 1/4
   (B) $\dfrac{1}{_4C_4}$
   (C) $\dfrac{1}{_4P_4}$
   (D) 1/2!
   (E) 1/3!

10. A basketball team has 11 players on its roster. Only 5 players can be on the court at one time. How many different groups of 5 players can the team put on the floor?

    (A) 5^{11}
    (B) $_{11}C_5$
    (C) $_{11}P_5$
    (D) 11^5
    (E) $11! \cdot 5!$

11. How many different 5-letter words can be formed from the word ORANGE using each letter only once?

    (A) $_6P_6$
    (B) 36
    (C) $_6C_6$
    (D) 6^6
    (E) $_6P_5$

12. How many unequal 5-digit numbers can be formed using each digit of the number 11235 only once?

    (A) 5!
    (B) $_5P_3$
    (C) $\dfrac{_5C_5}{2!}$
    (D) $\dfrac{_5P_5}{2! \cdot 3!}$
    (E) $\dfrac{_5C_5}{2! \cdot 3!}$

13. How many different six-digit numbers can be formed using all of the following digits:

    3, 3, 4, 4, 4, 5

    (A) 10
    (B) 20
    (C) 30
    (D) 36
    (E) 60

14. This is how Edward's Lotteries work. First, 9 different numbers are selected. Tickets with exactly 6 of the 9 numbers randomly selected are printed such that no two tickets have the same set of numbers. Finally, the winning ticket is the one containing the 6 numbers drawn from the 9 randomly. There is exactly one winning ticket in the lottery system. How many tickets can the lottery system print?

(A) $_9P_6$
(B) $_9P_3$
(C) $_9C_9$
(D) $_9C_6$
(E) 6^9

15. How many different strings of letters can be made by reordering the letters of the word SUCCESS?

(A) 20
(B) 30
(C) 40
(D) 60
(E) 420

16. A company produces 8 different types of candies, and sells the candies in gift packs. How many different gift packs containing exactly 3 different candy types can the company put on the market?

(A) $_8C_2$
(B) $_8C_3$
(C) $_8P_2$
(D) $_8P_3$
(E) $\dfrac{_8P_3}{2!}$

17. Fritz is taking an examination that consists of two parts, A and B, with the following instructions:

Part A contains three questions, and a student must answer two.
Part B contains four questions, and a student must answer two.
Part A must be completed before starting Part B.

In how many ways can the test be completed?

(A) 12
(B) 15
(C) 36
(D) 72
(E) 90

18. A menu offers 2 entrees, 3 main courses, and 3 desserts. How many different combinations of dinner can be made? (A dinner must contain an entrée, a main course, and a dessert.)

(A) 12
(B) 15
(C) 18
(D) 21
(E) 24

19. In how many ways can 3 red marbles, 2 blue marbles, and 5 yellow marbles be placed in a row?

(A) $3! \cdot 2! \cdot 5!$

(B) $\dfrac{12!}{10!}$

(C) $\dfrac{10!}{3!} \cdot \dfrac{10!}{2!} \cdot \dfrac{10!}{5!}$

(D) $\dfrac{10!}{3! \cdot 2! \cdot 5!}$

(E) $\dfrac{10!}{\left(3! \cdot 2! \cdot 5!\right)^2}$

20. The retirement plan for a company allows employees to invest in 10 different mutual funds. Six of the 10 funds grew by at least 10% over the last year. If Sam randomly selected 4 of the 10 funds, what is the probability that 3 of Sam's 4 funds grew by at least 10% over last year?

(A) $\dfrac{_6C_3}{_{10}C_4}$

(B) $\dfrac{_6C_3 \cdot _4C_1}{_{10}C_4}$

(C) $\dfrac{_6C_3 \cdot _4C_1}{_{10}P_4}$

(D) $\dfrac{_6P_3 \cdot _4P_1}{_{10}C_4}$

(E) $\dfrac{_6P_3 \cdot _4P_1}{_{10}P_4}$

21. The retirement plan for a company allows employees to invest in 10 different mutual funds. Six of the 10 funds grew by at least 10% over the last year. If Sam randomly selected 4 of the 10 funds, what is the probability that *at least* 3 of Sam's 4 funds grew by at least 10% over the last year?

(A) $\dfrac{_6C_3}{_{10}C_4}$

(B) $\dfrac{_6C_3 \cdot _4C_1}{_{10}C_4}$

(C) $\dfrac{_6C_3 \cdot _4C_1 + _6C_4}{_{10}P_4}$

(D) $\dfrac{_6P_3 \cdot _4P_1}{_{10}C_4}$

(E) $\dfrac{_6C_3 \cdot _4C_1 + _6C_4}{_{10}C_4}$

22. In how many ways can the letters of the word ACUMEN be rearranged such that the vowels always appear together?

(A) $3! \cdot 3!$

(B) $\dfrac{6!}{2!}$

(C) $\dfrac{4! \cdot 3!}{2!}$

(D) $4! \cdot 3!$

(E) $\dfrac{3! \cdot 3!}{2!}$

23. In how many ways can the letters of the word ACCLAIM be rearranged such that the vowels always appear together?

    (A) $\dfrac{7!}{2!\cdot 2!}$

    (B) $\dfrac{4!\cdot 3!}{2!\cdot 2!}$

    (C) $\dfrac{4!\cdot 3!}{2!}$

    (D) $\dfrac{5!}{2!\cdot 2!}$

    (E) $\dfrac{5!}{2!}\cdot\dfrac{3!}{2!}$

24. In how many ways can the letters of the word GARGANTUNG be rearranged such that all the G's appear together?

    (A) $\dfrac{8!}{3!\cdot 2!\cdot 2!}$

    (B) $\dfrac{8!}{2!\cdot 2!}$

    (C) $\dfrac{8!\cdot 3!}{2!\cdot 2!}$

    (D) $\dfrac{8!}{2!\cdot 3!}$

    (E) $\dfrac{10!}{3!\cdot 2!\cdot 2!}$

25. In how many ways can the letters of the word GOSSAMERE be rearranged such that all S's and M's appear in the middle?

    (A) $\dfrac{9!}{2!\cdot 2!}$

    (B) $\dfrac{{}_7P_6}{2!\cdot 2!}$

    (C) $\dfrac{{}_7P_6}{2!}\cdot\dfrac{{}_3P_3}{2!}$

    (D) $\dfrac{{}_6P_6}{2!}\cdot\dfrac{{}_3P_3}{2!}$

    (E) $\dfrac{{}_{10}P_6}{2!}\cdot\dfrac{{}_3P_3}{2!}$

26. How many different four-letter words can be formed (the words need not be meaningful) using the letters of the word GREGARIOUS such that each word starts with G and ends with R?

    (A) ${}_8P_2$

    (B) $\dfrac{{}_8P_2}{2!\cdot 2!}$

    (C) ${}_8P_4$

    (D) $\dfrac{{}_8P_4}{2!\cdot 2!}$

    (E) $\dfrac{{}_{10}P_2}{2!\cdot 2!}$

27. A coin is tossed five times. What is the probability that the fourth toss would turn a head?

    (A) $\dfrac{1}{_5P_3}$

    (B) $\dfrac{1}{_5P_9}$

    (C) $\dfrac{1}{2}$

    (D) $\dfrac{1}{2!}$

    (E) $\dfrac{1}{2^3}$

28. In how many of ways can 5 balls be placed in 4 tins if any number of balls can be placed in any tin?

    (A) $_5C_4$
    (B) $_5P_4$
    (C) 5^4
    (D) 4^5
    (E) 5^5

29. On average, a sharpshooter hits the target once every 3 shots. What is the probability that he will hit the target in 4 shots?

    (A)   1
    (B)   1/81
    (C)   1/3
    (D)   65/81
    (E)   71/81

30. On average, a sharpshooter hits the target once every 3 shots. What is the probability that he will not hit the target until 4th shot?

    (A)   1
    (B)   8/81
    (C)   16/81
    (D)   65/81
    (E)   71/81

31. A new word is to be formed by randomly rearranging the letters of the word ALGEBRA. What is the probability that the new word has consonants occupying only the positions currently occupied by consonants in the word ALGEBRA?

    (A)   2/120
    (B)   1/24
    (C)   1/6
    (D)   2/105
    (E)   1/35

32. Chelsea has 5 roses and 2 jasmines. A bouquet of 3 flowers is to be formed. In how many ways can it be formed if at least one jasmine must be in the bouquet?

    (A)   5
    (B)   20
    (C)   25
    (D)   35
    (E)   40

33.   In how many ways can 3 boys and 2 girls be selected from a group of 6 boys and 5 girls?

(A)   10
(B)   20
(C)   50
(D)   100
(E)   200

34.   In how many ways can a committee of 5 members be formed from 4 women and 6 men such that at least 1 woman is a member of the committee?

(A)   112
(B)   156
(C)   208
(D)   246
(E)   252

35.   In how many ways can 5 boys and 4 girls be arranged in a line so that there will be a boy at the beginning and at the end?

(A) $\dfrac{3!}{5!} \cdot 7!$

(B) $\dfrac{5!}{6!} \cdot 7!$

(C) $\dfrac{5!}{3!} \cdot 7!$

(D) $\dfrac{3!}{5!} \cdot 7!$

(E) $\dfrac{5!}{7!} \cdot 7!$

36.   In how many ways can the letters of the word MAXIMA be arranged such that all vowels are together?

(A)   12
(B)   18
(C)   30
(D)   36
(E)   72

37.   In how many ways can the letters of the word MAXIMA be arranged such that all vowels are together and all consonants are together?

(A)   12
(B)   18
(C)   30
(D)   36
(E)   42

38.   In how many ways can 4 boys and 4 girls be arranged in a row such that no two boys and no two girls are next to each other?

(A)   1032
(B)   1152
(C)   1254
(D)   1432
(E)   1564

39. In how many ways can 4 boys and 4 girls be arranged in a row such that boys and girls alternate their positions (that is, boy girl)?

    (A)   1032
    (B)   1152
    (C)   1254
    (D)   1432
    (E)   1564

40. The University of Maryland, University of Vermont, and Emory University have each 4 soccer players. If a team of 9 is to be formed with an equal number of players from each university, how many number of ways can the selections be done?

    (A)   3
    (B)   4
    (C)   12
    (D)   16
    (E)   25

41. In how many ways can 5 persons be seated around a circular table?

    (A)   5
    (B)   24
    (C)   25
    (D)   30
    (E)   120

42. In how many ways can 5 people from a group of 6 people be seated around a circular table?

    (A)   56
    (B)   80
    (C)   100
    (D)   120
    (E)   144

43. What is the probability that a word formed by randomly rearranging the letters of the word ALGAE is the word ALGAE itself?

    (A)   1/120
    (B)   1/60
    (C)   2/7
    (D)   2/5
    (E)   1/30

Answers and Solutions to Problem Set CC

1.   There are 3 doors to a lecture room. In how many ways can a lecturer enter and leave the room?

   (A)   1
   (B)   3
   (C)   6
   (D)   9
   (E)   12

Recognizing the Problem:

1) Is it a permutation or a combination problem?
Here, order is important. Suppose A, B, and C are the three doors. Entering by door A and leaving by door B is not the same way as entering by door B and leaving by door A. Hence, AB ≠ BA implies the problem is a *permutation* (order is important).

2) Are repetitions allowed?
Since the lecturer can enter and exit through the same door, *repetition* is allowed.

3) Are there any indistinguishable objects in the base set?
Doors are different. They are not indistinguishable, so *no indistinguishable objects*.

Hence, we have a permutation problem, with repetition allowed and no indistinguishable objects.

Method I (Using known formula for the scenario):
Apply Formula 1, n^r, from the Formula section. Here, $n = 3$, (three doors to choose from), $r = 2$, 2 slots (one for entry door, one for exit door).

Hence, $n^r = 3^2 = 9$, and the answer is (D).

Method II (Model 2):
The lecturer can enter the room in 3 ways and exit in 3 ways. So, in total, the lecturer can enter and leave the room in 9 (= 3 · 3) ways. The answer is (D). This problem allows repetition: the lecturer can enter by a door and exit by the same door.

Method III (Model 3):
Let the 3 doors be A, B, and C. We must choose 2 doors: one to enter and one to exit. This can be done in 6 ways: {A, A}, {A, B}, {B, B}, {B, C}, {C, C}, and {C, A}. Now, the order of the elements is important because entering by A and leaving by B is not same as entering by B and leaving by A. Let's permute the combinations, which yields

$$A - A$$
$$A - B \text{ and } B - A$$
$$\{B, B\}$$
$$B - C \text{ and } C - B$$
$$C - C$$
$$C - A \text{ and } A - C$$

The total is 9, and the answer is (D).

2.   There are 3 doors to a lecture room. In how many ways can a lecturer enter the room from one door and leave from another door?

   (A)   1
   (B)   3
   (C)   6
   (D)   9
   (E)   12

This problem is the same as the previous one, except entering and leaving must be done by different doors (since the doors are different, repetition is not allowed).

Hence, we have a permutation (there are two slots individually defined: one naming the entering door and one naming the leaving door), without repetition, and no indistinguishable objects (doors are different).

Recognizing the Problem:

1) Is it a permutation or a combination problem?
Here, order is important. Suppose A, B, and C are the three doors. Entering by door B and leaving by door C is not same as entering by door C and leaving by door B. Hence, BC ≠ CB implies the problem is a *permutation* (order is important).

2) Are repetitions allowed?
We must count the number of possibilities in which the lecturer enters and exits by different doors, so *repetition is not allowed*.

3) Are there any indistinguishable objects in the base set?
Doors are different. They are not indistinguishable, so *no indistinguishable objects*.

Hence, we have a permutation problem, with repetition not allowed and no indistinguishable objects.

Method I (Using known formula for the scenario):
Apply Formula 2, $_nP_r$, from the Formula section. Here, $n = 3$ (three doors to choose), $r = 2$ slots (one for entry door, one for exit door) to place them in.

The calculation is

$$_nP_r = {_3P_2} =$$
$$\frac{3!}{(3-2)!} =$$
$$\frac{3!}{1!} =$$
$$\frac{3 \cdot 2 \cdot 1}{1} =$$
$$6$$

The answer is (C).

Method II (Model 2):
The lecturer can enter the room in 3 ways and exit in 2 ways (not counting the door entered). Hence, in total, the number of ways is $3 \cdot 2 = 6$ (by Model 2) or by the Fundamental Principle of Counting $2 + 2 + 2 = 6$. The answer is (C). This is a problem with repetition not allowed.

Method III (Model 3):
Let the 3 doors be A, B, and C. Hence, the base set is {A, B, C}. We have to choose 2 doors—one to enter and one to exit. This can be done in 3 ways: {A, B}, {B, C}, {C, A} [The combinations {A, A}, {B, B}, and {C, C} were eliminated because repetition is not allowed]. Now, the order of the permutation is

important because entering by A and leaving by B is not considered same as entering by B and leaving by A. Let's permute the combinations:

$$\{A, B\}$$
$$\{A, C\}$$
$$\{B, A\}$$
$$\{B, C\}$$
$$\{C, A\}$$
$$\{C, B\}$$

The total is 6, and the answer is (C).

3.   How many possible combinations can a 3-digit safe code have?

   (A) $_9C_3$
   (B) $_9P_3$
   (C) 3^9
   (D) 9^3
   (E) 10^3

The safe combination could be 433 or 334; the combinations are the same, but their ordering is different. Since order is important for the safe combinations, this is a permutation problem.

A safe code can be made of any of the numbers $\{0, 1, 2, 3, 4, 5, 6, 7, 8, 9\}$. No two objects in the set are indistinguishable. Hence, the base set does not have any indistinguishable objects.

Repetitions of numbers in the safe code are possible. For example, 334 is a possible safe code.

Hence, the problem is a permutation, with repetition and no indistinguishable objects. Hence, use Formula 1, n^r [here, $n = 10$, $r = 3$]. The number of codes is $10^3 = 1000$. The answer is (E).

Safe codes allow 0 to be first digit. Here, the same arrangement rules apply to each of the 3 digits. So, this is a uniform arrangement problem. We can use any formula or model here. But there are non-uniform arrangement problems. For example, if you are to form a 3-digit number, the first digit has an additional rule: it cannot be 0 (because in this case the number would actually be 2-digit number). In such scenarios, we need to use model I or II. The number of ways the digits can be formed by model II is

$$9 \cdot 10 \cdot 10 = 900$$

4.   Goodwin has 3 different colored pants and 2 different colored shirts. In how many ways can he choose a pair of pants and a shirt?

   (A)   2
   (B)   3
   (C)   5
   (D)   6
   (E)   12

Model 2:
The pants can be selected in 3 ways and the shirt in 2 ways. Hence, the pair can be selected in $3 \cdot 2 = 6$ ways. The answer is (D).

5.   In how many ways can 2 doors be selected from 3 doors?

   (A)   1
   (B)   3
   (C)   6
   (D)   9
   (E)   12

It appears that order is not important in this problem: the doors are mentioned but not defined. Also, since we are *selecting* doors, it is a combination problem.

The base set is the 3 doors [$n = 3$]. The doors are different, so there are no indistinguishable objects in the base set.

The arranged sets are the 2 doors [$r = 2$] we select. A door cannot be selected twice because "we select 2 doors" clearly means 2 different doors.

Hence, the problem is a combination, with no indistinguishable objects and no repetitions. Hence, using Formula 3, $_nC_r$ yields

$$_3C_2 = \frac{n!}{r!(n-r)!} =$$

$$\frac{3!}{2!(3-2)!} =$$

$$\frac{3!}{2!\cdot 1!} =$$

$$\frac{3\cdot 2\cdot 1}{(2\cdot 1)\cdot 1} =$$

$$3$$

The answer is (B).

6.   In how many ways can 2 doors be selected from 3 doors for entering and leaving a room?

   (A)   1
   (B)   3
   (C)   6
   (D)   9
   (E)   12

The problem statement almost ended at "3 doors." The remaining part "entering and leaving" only explains the reason for the selection. Hence, this does not define the slots. So, this is a combination problem. Moreover, we are asked to *select*, not to *arrange*. Hence, the problem is a combination, with no indistinguishable objects and no repetitions allowed. Using Formula 3, the number of ways the room can be entered and left is

$$_nC_r = {_3C_2} = \frac{n!}{r!(n-r)!} =$$

$$\frac{3!}{2!(3-2)!} =$$

$$\frac{3!}{2!\cdot 1!} =$$

$$\frac{3\cdot 2\cdot 1}{(2\cdot 1)\cdot 1} =$$

$$3$$

The answer is (B).

7.   In how many ways can a room be entered and exited from the 3 doors to the room?

(A)   1
(B)   3
(C)   6
(D)   9
(E)   12

There is specific stress on "entered" and "exited" doors. Hence, the problem is not combinational; it is a permutation (order/positioning is important).

The problem type is "no indistinguishable objects and repetitions allowed". Hence, by Formula 1, the number of ways the room can be entered and exited is $n^r = 3^2 = 9$. The answer is (C).

8.   There are 5 doors to a lecture room. Two are red and the others are green. In how many ways can a lecturer enter the room and leave the room from different colored doors?

(A)   1
(B)   3
(C)   6
(D)   9
(E)   12

There are 2 red and 3 green doors. We have two cases:

The room can be entered from a red door (2 red doors, so 2 ways) and can be left from a green door (3 green doors, so 3 ways): $2 \cdot 3 = 6$.

The room can be entered from a green door (3 green doors, so 3 ways) and can be left from a red door (2 red doors, so 2 ways): $3 \cdot 2 = 6$.

Hence, the total number of ways is

$$2 \cdot 3 + 3 \cdot 2 = 6 + 6 = 12$$

The answer is (E).

9.   Four pool balls—A, B, C, D—are randomly arranged in a straight line. What is the probability that the order will actually be A, B, C, D ?

(A)   1/4
(B) $\dfrac{1}{_4C_4}$
(C) $\dfrac{1}{_4P_4}$
(D)   1/2!
(E)   1/3!

This is a permutation problem (order is important).

A ball cannot exist in two slots, so repetition is not allowed.

Each ball is given a different identity A, B, C, and D, so there are no indistinguishable objects.

Here, $n = 4$ (number of balls to arrange) in $r = 4$ (positions). We know the problem type, and the formula to use. Hence, by Formula 2, the number of arrangements possible is $_4P_4$, and {A, B, C, D} is just one of the arrangements. Hence, the probability is 1 in $_4P_4$, or $\dfrac{1}{_4P_4}$. The answer is (C).

10. A basketball team has 11 players on its roster. Only 5 players can be on the court at one time. How many different groups of 5 players can the team put on the floor?

  (A) 5^{11}
  (B) $_{11}C_5$
  (C) $_{11}P_5$
  (D) 11^5
  (E) $11! \cdot 5!$

The task is only to select a group of 5, not to order them. Hence, this is a combination problem. There are 11 players; repetition is not possible among them (one player cannot be counted more than once); and they are not given the same identity. Hence, there are no indistinguishable objects. Using Formula 3, groups of 5 can be chosen from 11 players in $_{11}C_5$ ways. The answer is (B).

11. How many different 5-letter words can be formed from the word ORANGE using each letter only once?

  (A) $_6P_3$
  (B) 36
  (C) $_6C_6$
  (D) 6^6
  (E) $_6P_5$

In the problem, order is important because ORGAN is a word formed from ORANGE and ORNAG is a word formed from ORANGE, but they are not the same word. Repetition is not allowed, since each letter in the original word is used only once.

The problem does not have indistinguishable objects because no two letters of the word ORANGE are the same. Hence, by Formula 2, $_nP_r$, the answer is $_6P_5$, which is choice (E).

12. How many unequal 5-digit numbers can be formed using each digit of the number 11235 only once?

  (A) $5!$
  (B) $_5P_3$
  (C) $\dfrac{_5C_5}{2!}$
  (D) $\dfrac{_5P_5}{2! \cdot 3!}$
  (E) $\dfrac{_5C_5}{2! \cdot 3!}$

The word "unequal" indicates that this is a permutation problem, because 11532 is the same combination as 11235, but they are not equal. Hence, they are permutations, different arrangements in a combination.

The indistinguishable objects in the base set $\{1, 1, 2, 3, 5\}$ are the two 1's.

Since each digit of the number 11235 (objects in the base set) is used only once, repetitions are not allowed.

Hence, by Formula 4, the number of unequal 5-digit numbers that can be formed is

$$\frac{_5P_5}{2!} =$$

$$\frac{\dfrac{5!}{0! \cdot 5!}}{2!} =$$

$$\frac{_5P_0}{2!}$$

The answer is (B).

13. How many different six-digit numbers can be formed using all of the following digits:

3, 3, 4, 4, 4, 5

(A)   10
(B)   20
(C)   30
(D)   36
(E)   60

Forming a six-digit number is a permutation because the value of the number changes with the different arrangements.

Since we have indistinguishable numbers in the base set, the regular permutations generate repeating numbers. But we are asked for only different six-digit numbers. So, we count only 1 for each similar permutation.

There are two sets of indistinguishable objects in the base set: two 3's and three 4's.

No repetitions are allowed since all elements in the base set are to be used in each number.

Hence, by Formula 4, the formula for permutations with no repetitions and with distinguishable objects, the number of six-digit numbers that can be formed is

$$\frac{_6P_6}{2! \cdot 3!} = \frac{6!}{2! \cdot 3!} = 60$$

The answer is (E).

14. This is how Edward's Lotteries work. First, 9 different numbers are selected. Tickets with exactly 6 of the 9 numbers randomly selected are printed such that no two tickets have the same set of numbers. Finally, the winning ticket is the one containing the 6 numbers drawn from the 9 randomly. There is exactly one winning ticket in the lottery system. How many tickets can the lottery system print?

(A) $_9P_6$
(B) $_9P_3$
(C) $_9C_9$
(D) $_9C_6$
(E) 6^9

The only condition is that the winning ticket has the same set of numbers as the drawn numbers (in whatever order). Hence, order is not important. Now, count the combinations.

Since the numbers in the base set (9 numbers) are different, the base set does not have indistinguishable objects.

Six of the 9 different numbers are selected by the lottery system, so no repetitions are allowed.

By Formula 3, the formula for combinations with no repetitions and no indistinguishable objects, the number of possible selections by the lottery system is $_9C_6$.

Since only one winning ticket (winning combination) exists per lottery system, there is of $_9C_6$ tickets per lottery system. The answer is (D).

15. How many different strings of letters can be made by reordering the letters of the word SUCCESS?

    (A)   20
    (B)   30
    (C)   40
    (D)   60
    (E)   420

The word SUCCESS is a different word from SUSSECC, while they are the same combination. Hence, this is a permutation problem, not a combination problem.

There are two sets of indistinguishable objects in the base set: 2 C's and 3 S's.

Each letter is used only once in each reordering (so do not allow repetition).

Hence, we have a permutation problem, with indistinguishable objects and no repetitions. Using Formula 4, the formula for permutations with no repetitions but with distinguishable objects in the Formula section, yields $n = 7$ (base word has 7 letters), and $r = 7$ (each new word will have 7 letters). The repetitions are 2 C's and 3 S's. Hence, the total number of permutations is

$$\frac{_7P_7}{2! \cdot 3!} =$$
$$\frac{7 \cdot 6 \cdot 5 \cdot 4 \cdot 3 \cdot 2 \cdot 1}{2 \cdot 6} =$$
$$7 \cdot 5 \cdot 4 \cdot 3 =$$
$$420$$

The answer is (E).

16. A company produces 8 different types of candies, and sells the candies in gift packs. How many different gift packs containing exactly 3 different candy types can the company put on the market?

    (A) $_8C_2$
    (B) $_8C_3$
    (C) $_8P_2$
    (D) $_8P_3$
    (E) $\dfrac{_8P_3}{2!}$

The phrase "8 different candies" indicates the base set does not have indistinguishable objects.

Since no placement slots are defined, this is a combination problem. We need only to choose 3 of 8 candies; we do not need to order them.

Repetitions are not allowed in the sets formed.

By Formula 3, the formula for permutations with no repetitions but with distinguishable objects yields $_8C_3$, which is Choice (B).

17.   Fritz is taking an examination that consists of two parts, A and B, with the following instructions:

   Part A contains three questions, and a student must answer two.
   Part B contains four questions, and a student must answer two.
   Part A must be completed before starting Part B.

   In how many ways can the test be completed?

   (A)   12
   (B)   15
   (C)   36
   (D)   72
   (E)   90

The problem has two parts.

Each part is a permutation problem with no indistinguishable objects (no 2 questions are the same in either part), and repetitions are not allowed (the same question is not answered twice).

Hence, the number of ways of answering the first part is $_3P_2$ (2 questions to answer from 3), and the number of ways of answering the second part is $_4P_2$ (2 questions to answer from 4).

By the Fundamental Principle of Counting, the two parts can be done in

$$_3P_2 \cdot {_4P_2} = 6 \cdot 12 = 72 \text{ ways}$$

The answer is (D).

Method II [Model 2]:

The first question in Part A can be chosen to be one of the 3 questions in Part A.

The second question in Part A can be chosen to be one of the remaining 2 questions in Part A.

The first question in Part B can be chosen to be one of the 4 questions in Part B.

The second question in Part B can be chosen to be one of the remaining 3 questions in Part B.

Hence, the number of choices is

$$3 \cdot 2 \cdot 4 \cdot 3 = 72$$

The answer is (D).

Method III [Fundamental Principle of Counting combined with Model 2]:

The first question in part A can be chosen to be one of the 3 questions in Part A.

The second question in part A can be chosen to be one of the 3 questions in Part A allowing the repetitions. Hence, number of permutations is $3 \cdot 3 = 9$. There are 3 repetitions [Q1 & Q1, Q2 & Q2, Q3 & Q3]. The main question does not allow repetitions since you would not answer the same question again. Deleting them, we have $9 - 3 = 6$ ways for Part A.

The first question in Part B can be chosen to be one of the 4 questions in Part B.

The second question in Part B can be chosen to be one of 4 questions in Part B. Hence, the number of permutations is $4 \cdot 4 = 16$. There are 4 repetitions [Q1 & Q1, Q2 & Q2, Q3 & Q3, Q4 & Q4]. The main question does not allow repetitions since you would not answer the same question again. Deleting them, we have $16 - 4 = 12$ ways for Part A.

Hence, the number of choices is

$$6 \cdot 12 = 72$$

The answer is (D).

18.   A menu offers 2 entrees, 3 main courses, and 3 desserts. How many different combinations of dinner can be made? (A dinner must contain an entrée, a main course, and a dessert.)

(A)   12
(B)   15
(C)   18
(D)   21
(E)   24

The problem is a mix of 3 combinational problems. The goal is to choose 1 of 2 entrees, then 1 of 3 main courses, then 1 of 3 desserts. The choices can be made in 2, 3, and 3 ways, respectively. Hence, the total number of ways of selecting the combinations is $2 \cdot 3 \cdot 3 = 18$. The answer is (C).

We can also count the combinations by the Fundamental Principle of Counting:

		Dessert 1
	Main Course 1	Dessert 2
		Dessert 3
		Dessert 1
Entrée 1	Main Course 2	Dessert 2
		Dessert 3
		Dessert 1
	Main Course 3	Dessert 2
		Dessert 3
		Dessert 1
	Main Course 1	Dessert 2
		Dessert 3
		Dessert 1
Entrée 2	Main Course 2	Dessert 2
		Dessert 3
		Dessert 1
	Main Course 3	Dessert 2
		Dessert 3
		Total 18

The Fundamental Principle of Counting states:

The total number of possible outcomes of a series of decisions, making selections from various categories, is found by multiplying the number of choices for each decision.

Counting the number of choices in the final column above yields 18.

19.   In how many ways can 3 red marbles, 2 blue marbles, and 5 yellow marbles be placed in a row?

(A) $3! \cdot 2! \cdot 5!$

(B) $\dfrac{12!}{10!}$

(C) $\dfrac{10!}{3!} \cdot \dfrac{10!}{2!} \cdot \dfrac{10!}{5!}$

(D) $\dfrac{10!}{3! \cdot 2! \cdot 5!}$

(E) $\dfrac{10!}{\left(3! \cdot 2! \cdot 5!\right)^2}$

Since the question is asking for the number of ways the marbles can be placed adjacent to each other, this is a permutation problem.

The base set has 3 red marbles (indistinguishable objects), 2 blue marbles (indistinguishable objects) and 5 yellow marbles (indistinguishable objects). The possible arrangements are $3 + 2 + 5 = 10$ positions.

The same marble cannot be used twice, so no repetitions are allowed. Formula 4, $_nP_r$, and the method for indistinguishable objects (that is, divide the number of permutations, $_nP_r$, by the factorial count of each indistinguishable object [see Formulas section]) yield the number of permutations:

$$\frac{_{10}P_{10}}{3! \cdot 2! \cdot 5!} = \frac{10!}{3! \cdot 2! \cdot 5!}$$

The answer is (D).

20.   The retirement plan for a company allows employees to invest in 10 different mutual funds. Six of the 10 funds grew by at least 10% over the last year. If Sam randomly selected 4 of the 10 funds, what is the probability that 3 of Sam's 4 funds grew by at least 10% over last year?

(A) $\dfrac{_6C_3}{_{10}C_4}$

(B) $\dfrac{_6C_3 \cdot {_4}C_1}{_{10}C_4}$

(C) $\dfrac{_6C_3 \cdot {_4}C_1}{_{10}P_4}$

(D) $\dfrac{_6P_3 \cdot {_4}P_1}{_{10}C_4}$

(E) $\dfrac{_6P_3 \cdot {_4}P_1}{_{10}P_4}$

There are 6 winning funds that grew more than 10%, and 4 losing funds that grew less than 10%.

The problem can be split into 3 sub-problems:

We have the specific case where Sam must choose 4 funds, 3 of which are winning, so the remaining fund must be losing. Let's evaluate the number of ways this can be done. [Note: The order in which the funds are chosen is not important because whether the first 3 funds are winning and the 4th one is losing, or the first fund is losing and the last 3 are winning; only 3 of 4 funds will be winning ones. Hence, this is a combination problem.] The problem has 2 sub-problems:

1.   Sam must choose 3 of the 6 winning funds. This can be done in $_6C_3$ ways.

2.   Sam must choose one losing fund (say the 4th fund). There are $10 - 6 = 4$ losing funds. Hence, the 4th fund can be any one of the 4 losing funds. The selection can be done in $_4C_1$ ways.

Hence, the total number of ways of choosing 3 winning funds and 1 losing one is $_6C_3 \cdot {}_4C_1$.

   3.   Sam could have chosen 4 funds in $_{10}C_4$ ways.

Hence, the probability that 3 of Sam's 4 funds grew by at least 10% over last year is

$$\frac{_6C_3 \cdot {}_4C_1}{_{10}C_4} = \frac{20 \cdot 4}{210} = \frac{8}{21}$$

The answer is (B).

21.   The retirement plan for a company allows employees to invest in 10 different mutual funds. Six of the 10 funds grew by at least 10% over the last year. If Sam randomly selected 4 of the 10 funds, what is the probability that *at least* 3 of Sam's 4 funds grew by at least 10% over the last year?

(A) $\dfrac{_6C_3}{_{10}C_4}$

(B) $\dfrac{_6C_3 \cdot {}_4C_1}{_{10}C_4}$

(C) $\dfrac{_6C_3 \cdot {}_4C_1 + {}_6C_4}{_{10}P_4}$

(D) $\dfrac{_6P_3 \cdot {}_4P_1}{_{10}C_4}$

(E) $\dfrac{_6C_3 \cdot {}_4C_1 + {}_6C_4}{_{10}C_4}$

There are 6 winning funds that grew more than 10%, and 4 losing funds that grew less than 10%.

The problem can be split into 3 sub-problems:

   1)   Sam has to choose 3 winning funds. This can be done in $_6C_3$ ways.
   2)   Sam has to choose 1 losing fund. This can be done in $_4C_1$ ways.

Or

   3)   Sam has to choose all 4 funds to be winning funds. This can be done in $_6C_4$ ways.

This is how Sam chooses at least 3 winning funds.

Hence, the total number of ways of choosing *at least* 3 winning funds is $_6C_3 \cdot {}_4C_1 + {}_6C_4$.

If there were no restrictions (such as choosing at least 3 winning funds), Sam would have chosen funds in $_{10}C_4$ ways.

Hence, the probability that *at least* 3 of Sam's 4 funds grew by at least 10% over the last year is

$$\frac{_6C_3 \cdot {}_4C_1 + {}_6C_4}{_{10}C_4}$$

The answer is (E).

22.   In how many ways can the letters of the word ACUMEN be rearranged such that the vowels always appear together?

   (A) $3!\cdot 3!$

   (B) $\dfrac{6!}{2!}$

   (C) $\dfrac{4!\cdot 3!}{2!}$

   (D) $4!\cdot 3!$

   (E) $\dfrac{3!\cdot 3!}{2!}$

The word "rearranged" indicates that this is a permutation problem.

The base set {A, C, U, M, E, N} has no indistinguishable objects.

Repetition is not allowed.

Since the 3 vowels must appear together, treat the three as an inseparable unit. Hence, reduce the base set to {{A, U, E}, C, M, N}. Now, there are 4 different units in the base set, and they can be arranged in $_4P_4 = 4!$ ways. The unit {A, U, E} can itself be internally arranged in $_3P_3 = 3!$ ways. Hence, by The Fundamental Principle of Counting, the total number of ways of arranging the word is $4!\cdot 3!$. The answer is (D).

23.   In how many ways can the letters of the word ACCLAIM be rearranged such that the vowels always appear together?

   (A) $\dfrac{7!}{2!\cdot 2!}$

   (B) $\dfrac{4!\cdot 3!}{2!\cdot 2!}$

   (C) $\dfrac{4!\cdot 3!}{2!}$

   (D) $\dfrac{5!}{2!\cdot 2!}$

   (E) $\dfrac{5!}{2!}\cdot\dfrac{3!}{2!}$

The word "rearranged" indicates that this is a permutation problem.

Since the 3 vowels A, A, and I must appear together, treat the three as an inseparable unit. Hence, reduce the base set to {{A, A, I}, C, C, L, M}.

The set has two indistinguishable objects, C's.

Also, repetitions are not allowed since we rearrange the word.

Hence, the number of permutations that can be created with units of the set is $\dfrac{_5P_5}{2!} = \dfrac{5!}{2!}$.

Now, let's see how many permutations we can create with the unit {A, A, I}.

The unit {A, A, I} has two indistinguishable objects, A's.

Also, repetitions are not allowed.

Hence, by Formula 4, the number of ways of permuting it is $\dfrac{_3P_3}{2!} = \dfrac{3!}{2!}$.

Hence, by The Fundamental Principle of Counting, the total number of ways of rearranging the letters is

$$\frac{5!}{2!} \cdot \frac{3!}{2!}$$

The answer is (E).

24. In how many ways can the letters of the word GARGANTUNG be rearranged such that all the G's appear together?

(A) $\dfrac{8!}{3! \cdot 2! \cdot 2!}$

(B) $\dfrac{8!}{2! \cdot 2!}$

(C) $\dfrac{8! \cdot 3!}{2! \cdot 2!}$

(D) $\dfrac{8!}{2! \cdot 3!}$

(E) $\dfrac{10!}{3! \cdot 2! \cdot 2!}$

The word "rearranged" indicates that this is a permutation problem.

Since all 3 G's are together, treat them a single inseparable unit. Hence, the base set reduces to {{G, G, G}, A, R, A, N, T, U, N}. There are 8 independent units, 2 A's (indistinguishable), and two N's (indistinguishable). No unit is used twice, so there are no repetitions. Hence, by Formula 4, the number of arrangements is $\dfrac{{}_8P_8}{2! \cdot 2!} = \dfrac{8!}{2! \cdot 2!}$.

The 3 G's can be rearranged amongst themselves in $\dfrac{{}_3P_3}{3!} = \dfrac{3!}{3!} = 1$ way. Hence, the total number of ways the letters can be rearranged is

$$\frac{8!}{2! \cdot 2!} \cdot 1 = \frac{8!}{2! \cdot 2!}$$

The answer is (B).

25. In how many ways can the letters of the word GOSSAMERE be rearranged such that all S's and M's appear in the middle?

(A) $\dfrac{9!}{2! \cdot 2!}$

(B) $\dfrac{{}_7P_6}{2! \cdot 2!}$

(C) $\dfrac{{}_7P_6}{2!} \cdot \dfrac{{}_3P_3}{2!}$

(D) $\dfrac{{}_6P_6}{2!} \cdot \dfrac{{}_3P_3}{2!}$

(E) $\dfrac{{}_{10}P_6}{2!} \cdot \dfrac{{}_3P_3}{2!}$

The word "rearranged" indicates that this is a permutation problem.

Since S and M must appear in the middle, treat them as an inseparable unit and reserve the middle seat for them. Correspondingly, bracket them in the base set. The new base set becomes {{S, S, M}, G, O, A, E, R, E}. Hence, we have the following arrangement:

362   ACT Math Prep Course

$$\underline{\quad} \;\; \underline{\quad} \;\; \underline{\quad} \;\; \underline{\text{\{S, S, M\}}} \;\; \underline{\quad} \;\; \underline{\quad} \;\; \underline{\quad}$$

Now, the remaining 6 units G, O, A, E, R, and E can be arranged in the 6 blank slots; and for each arrangement, every permutation inside the unit {S, S, M} is allowed.

Hence, the blank slots can be filled in $\dfrac{_6P_6}{2!}$ (E repeats twice) ways.

And the unit {S, S, M} can be internally arranged in $\dfrac{_3P_3}{2!}$ ways.

Hence, by Model 2, the total number of ways the letters can be rearranged is

$$\frac{_6P_6}{2!} \cdot \frac{_3P_3}{2!}$$

The answer is (D).

26. How many different four-letter words can be formed (the words need not be meaningful) using the letters of the word GREGARIOUS such that each word starts with G and ends with R?

   (A) $_8P_2$

   (B) $\dfrac{_8P_2}{2!\cdot 2!}$

   (C) $_8P_4$

   (D) $\dfrac{_8P_4}{2!\cdot 2!}$

   (E) $\dfrac{_{10}P_2}{2!\cdot 2!}$

Place one G in the first slot and one R in the last slot:

$$\text{G \_\_ \_\_ R}$$

The remaining letters, {G, R, E, A, I, O, U, S}, can be arranged in the remaining 2 slots in $_8P_2$ (no indistinguishable objects nor repetition). The answer is (A).

Note: Since the two G's in the base word are indistinguishable, the word G_1G_2AR is the same as G_2G_1AR. Hence, the internal arrangement of the G's or, for the same reason, the R's is not important.

27. A coin is tossed five times. What is the probability that the fourth toss would turn a head?

   (A) $\dfrac{1}{_5P_3}$

   (B) $\dfrac{1}{_5P_9}$

   (C) $\dfrac{1}{2}$

   (D) $\dfrac{1}{2!}$

   (E) $\dfrac{1}{2^3}$

The fourth toss is independent of any other toss. The probability of a toss turning heads is 1 in 2, or simply 1/2. Hence, the probability of the fourth toss being a head is 1/2. The answer is (C).

Method II:
Each toss has 2 outcomes. Hence, 5 tosses have $2 \cdot 2 \cdot 2 \cdot \ldots 2$ (5 times) $= 2^5$ outcomes (permutation with repetition over $r = 2$ and $n = 5$ [repetitions allowed: the second and the fourth toss may both yield heads or tails]).

Reserve the third toss for a head. Now, the number of ways the remaining 4 tosses can be tossed is 2^4 (repetitions allowed). The probability is $\frac{2^4}{2^5} = \frac{1}{2}$. The answer is (C).

28.   In how many of ways can 5 balls be placed in 4 tins if any number of balls can be placed in any tin?

   (A) $_5C_4$
   (B) $_5P_4$
   (C) 5^4
   (D) 4^5
   (E) 5^5

The first ball can be placed in any one of the four tins.

Similarly, the second, the third, the fourth, and the fifth balls can be placed in any one of the 4 tins.

Hence, the number of ways of placing the balls is $4 \cdot 4 \cdot 4 \cdot 4 \cdot 4 = 4^5$. The answer is (D).

Note: We used Model 2 here.

29.   On average, a sharpshooter hits the target once every 3 shots. What is the probability that he will hit the target in 4 shots?

   (A)   1
   (B)   1/81
   (C)   1/3
   (D)   65/81
   (E)   71/81

The sharpshooter hits the target once in 3 shots. Hence, the probability of hitting the target is 1/3. The probability of not hitting the target is $1 - 1/3 = 2/3$.

Now, (the probability of not hitting the target even once in 4 shots) + (the probability of hitting at least once in 4 shots) equals 1, because these are the only possible cases.

Hence, the probability of hitting the target at least once in 4 shots is

$$1 - (\text{the probability of not hitting even once in 4 shots})$$

The probability of not hitting in the 4 chances is $\frac{2}{3} \cdot \frac{2}{3} \cdot \frac{2}{3} \cdot \frac{2}{3} = \frac{16}{81}$. Now, $1 - 16/81 = 65/81$. The answer is (D).

This methodology is similar to Model 2. You might try analyzing why. Clue: The numerators of $\frac{2}{3} \cdot \frac{2}{3} \cdot \frac{2}{3} \cdot \frac{2}{3} = \frac{16}{81}$ are the number of ways of doing the specific jobs, and the denominators are the number of ways of doing all possible jobs.

30. On average, a sharpshooter hits the target once in every 3 shots. What is the probability that he will not hit the target until the 4th shot?

    (A)   1
    (B)   8/81
    (C)   16/81
    (D)   65/81
    (E)   71/81

The sharpshooter hits the target once in every 3 shots. Hence, the probability of hitting the target is 1/3. The probability of not hitting the target is $1 - 1/3 = 2/3$.

He will not hit the target on the first, second, and third shots, but he will hit it on the fourth shot. The probability of this is

$$\frac{2}{3} \cdot \frac{2}{3} \cdot \frac{2}{3} \cdot \frac{1}{3} = \frac{8}{81}$$

The answer is (B).

This methodology is similar to Model 2. You might try analyzing why. Clue: The numerators of $\frac{2}{3} \cdot \frac{2}{3} \cdot \frac{2}{3} \cdot \frac{2}{3} = \frac{16}{81}$ are the number of ways of doing the specific jobs, and the denominators are the number of ways of doing all possible jobs.

31. A new word is to be formed by randomly rearranging the letters of the word ALGEBRA. What is the probability that the new word has consonants occupying only the positions currently occupied by consonants in the word ALGEBRA?

    (A)   2/120
    (B)   1/24
    (C)   1/6
    (D)   2/105
    (E)   1/35

If we do not put restrictions on the arrangements of the consonants, then by Formula 4 the number of words that can be formed from the word ALGEBRA is $\frac{7!}{2!}$ (A repeats).

If we constrain that the positions of consonants is reserved only for consonants, then the format of the new arrangement should look like this

$$A, L, G, E, B, R, A$$

$$V, C, C, V, C, C, V$$

V for vowels, C for consonants.

The 4 slots for consonants can be filled in $_4P_4 = 4!$ ways, and the 3 slots for vowels can be filled in $\frac{3!}{2!}$ (A repeats) ways. Hence, by Formula 2, the total number of arrangements in the format is $4!\left(\frac{3!}{2!}\right)$.

Hence, the probability is

$$\frac{4!\left(\dfrac{3!}{2!}\right)}{\dfrac{7!}{2!}} = \frac{1}{35}$$

The answer is (E).

32. Chelsea has 5 roses and 2 jasmines. A bouquet of 3 flowers is to be formed. In how many ways can it be formed if at least one jasmine must be in the bouquet?

   (A) 5
   (B) 20
   (C) 25
   (D) 35
   (E) 40

This is a selection problem because whether you choose a jasmine first or a rose first does not matter.

The 3 flowers in the bouquet can be either 1 jasmine and 2 roses or 2 jasmines and 1 rose.

1 of 2 jasmines can be selected in $_2C_1$ ways.

2 of 5 roses can be selected in $_5C_2$ ways.

The subtotal is $_2C_1 \cdot {_5C_2} = \dfrac{2!}{1! \cdot 1!} \cdot \dfrac{5!}{3! \cdot 2!} = 2 \cdot 10 = 20$.

2 of 2 jasmines can be selected in $_2C_2$ ways.

1 of 5 roses can be selected in $_5C_1$ ways.

The subtotal is $_2C_2 \cdot {_5C_1} = \dfrac{2!}{2! \cdot 0!} \cdot \dfrac{5!}{4! \cdot 1!} = 1 \cdot 5 = 5$.

The grand total is $20 + 5 = 25$ ways. The answer is (C).

33. In how many ways can 3 boys and 2 girls be selected from a group of 6 boys and 5 girls?

   (A) 10
   (B) 20
   (C) 50
   (D) 100
   (E) 200

We have two independent actions to do:

   1) Select 3 boys from 6 boys.
   2) Select 2 girls from 5 girls.

Selection is a combination problem since selection does not include ordering. Hence, by Model 2, the number of ways is

$$(_6C_3 \text{ ways for boys}) \cdot (_5C_2 \text{ ways for girls}) =$$
$$\left(\dfrac{6!}{3! \cdot 3!} \right) \cdot \left(\dfrac{5!}{2! \cdot 3!} \right) =$$
$$20 \cdot 10 =$$
$$200$$

The answer is (E).

34.   In how many ways can a committee of 5 members be formed from 4 women and 6 men such that at least 1 woman is a member of the committee?

(A)   112
(B)   156
(C)   208
(D)   246
(E)   252

Forming members of committee is a selection action and therefore this is a combination problem. Whether you select A first and B next or vice versa, it will only be said that A and B are members of the committee.

The number of ways of forming the committee of 5 from $4 + 6 = 10$ people is $_{10}C_5$. The number of ways of forming a committee with no women (5 members to choose from 6 men) is $_6C_5$. Hence, the number of ways of forming the combinations is

$$_{10}C_5 - {_6}C_5 =$$
$$\frac{10!}{5! \cdot 5!} - \frac{6!}{5!} =$$
$$252 - 6 =$$
$$246$$

The answer is (D).

35.   In how many ways can 5 boys and 4 girls be arranged in a line so that there will be a boy at the beginning and at the end?

(A) $\frac{3!}{5!} \cdot 7!$

(B) $\frac{5!}{6!} \cdot 7!$

(C) $\frac{5!}{3!} \cdot 7!$

(D) $\frac{3!}{5!} \cdot 7!$

(E) $\frac{5!}{7!} \cdot 7!$

The arrangement is a permutation, and there are no indistinguishable objects because no two boys or girls are identical. The first and the last slots hold two of the 5 boys, and the remaining slots are occupied by the 4 girls and the 3 remaining boys.

The first and the last slots can hold 2 of the 5 boys in $_5P_2$ ways, and the 3 boys and the 4 girls position themselves in the middle slots in $_7P_7$ ways. Hence, there are $\frac{5!}{3!} \cdot 7!$ possible arrangements. The answer is (C).

36. In how many ways can the letters of the word MAXIMA be arranged such that all vowels are together?

    (A)   12
    (B)   18
    (C)   30
    (D)   36
    (E)   72

The base set can be formed as {{A, I, A}, M, X, M}. The unit {A, I, A} arranges itself in $\frac{_3P_3}{2!}$ ways. The 4 units in the base set can be arranged in $_4P_4/2!$ ways. Hence, the total number of ways of arranging the letters is

$$\frac{_3P_3}{2!} \cdot \frac{_4P_4}{2!} = \frac{3!}{2!} \cdot \frac{4!}{2!} = 3 \cdot 12 = 36$$

The answer is (D).

37. In how many ways can the letters of the word MAXIMA be arranged such that all vowels are together and all consonants are together?

    (A)   12
    (B)   18
    (C)   30
    (D)   36
    (E)   42

Since vowels are together and consonants are together, arrange the base set as {{A, I, A}, {M, X, M}}. Here, {A, I, A} and {M, X, M} are two inseparable units.

The two units can be mutually arranged in $_2P_2$ ways.

Each unit has 3 objects, 2 of which are indistinguishable.

Hence, the number of permutations of each is $\frac{_3P_2}{2!}$.

Hence, the total number of arrangements possible is

$$\left(_2P_2\right)\left(\frac{_3P_2}{2!}\right)\left(\frac{_3P_2}{2!}\right) =$$
$$(2)(3)(3) =$$
$$18$$

The answer is (B).

38.   In how many ways can 4 boys and 4 girls be arranged in a row such that no two boys and no two girls are next to each other?

   (A)   1032
   (B)   1152
   (C)   1254
   (D)   1432
   (E)   1564

Form the base set as {{B1, B2, B3, B4}, {G1, G2, G3, G4}}; Looking at the problem, either B's or G's occupy the odd slots and the other one occupies the even slots. Choosing one to occupy an odd slot set can be done in $_2P_1$ ways, and the other one is automatically filled by the other group.

Now, fill B's in odd slots (the number of ways is $_4P_4$), and fill G's in even slots (the number of ways is $_4P_4$ ways). The total number of ways of doing this is $_4P_4 \cdot {_4P_4}$.

The number of ways of doing all of this is $2! \cdot {_4P_4} \cdot {_4P_4} = 2 \cdot 24 \cdot 24 = 1152$. The answer is (B).

39.   In how many ways can 4 boys and 4 girls be arranged in a row such that boys and girls alternate their positions (that is, boy girl)?

   (A)   576
   (B)   1152
   (C)   1254
   (D)   1432
   (E)   1564

Form the base set as {{B1, B2, B3, B4}, {G1, G2, G3, G4}}; the set {B1, B2, B3, B4} occupies alternate positions, as does the set {G1, G2, G3, G4}.

Now there are odd slots and even slots. Each odd slot alternates, and each even slot alternates. Therefore, we have two major slots: *even* and *odd* and two units to occupy them: {B1, B2, B3, B4} and {G1, G2, G3, G4}. This can be done in $_2P_1$ ways.

An alternate explanation for this is: The person starting the row can be chosen in 2 ways (i.e., either boys start the first position and arrange alternately or girls start and do the same), either B starts first or G starts first.

Either way, the positions {1, 3, 5, 7} are reserved for one of the two groups B or G, and the positions {2, 4, 6, 8} are reserved for the other group. Arrangements in each position set can be done in $_4P_4$ ways.

Hence, the total number of arrangements is $2! \cdot {_4P_4} \cdot {_4P_4} = 2 \cdot 24 \cdot 24 = 1152$. The answer is (B).

Mathematically, this problem is the same as the previous one. Just the expression (wording) of the problem is different.

40.   The University of Maryland, University of Vermont, and Emory University have each 4 soccer players. If a team of 9 is to be formed with an equal number of players from each university, how many number of ways can the selections be done?

   (A)   3
   (B)   4
   (C)   12
   (D)   16
   (E)   25

Selecting 3 of 4 players can be done in $_4C_3 = \dfrac{4!}{3! \cdot 1!} = 4$ ways.

The selection from the 3 universities can be done in $3 \cdot 4 = 12$ ways.

The answer is (C).

41.   In how many ways can 5 persons be seated around a circular table?

   (A)   5
   (B)   24
   (C)   25
   (D)   30
   (E)   120

For a circular table, we use cyclical permutations, not linear permutations. Hence, 1 in every r linear permutations (here $n = 5$ and $r = 5$) is a circular permutation. There are $_5P_5$ linear permutations. Hence,

$$\frac{_5P_5}{5} = \frac{5!}{5} = 4 \cdot 3 \cdot 2 \cdot 1 = 24 \text{ permutations}$$

The answer is (B).

42.   In how many ways can 5 people from a group of 6 people be seated around a circular table?

   (A)   56
   (B)   80
   (C)   100
   (D)   120
   (E)   144

For a circular table, we use cyclical permutations, not linear permutations. Hence, 1 in every r linear permutations (here $r = 5$) is a circular permutation. There are $_6P_5$ linear permutations and therefore $\frac{_6P_5}{5}$ circular permutations. Now,

$$\frac{_6P_5}{5} = \frac{6!}{5} = 1 \cdot 2 \cdot 3 \cdot 4 \cdot 6 = 144 \text{ permutations}$$

The answer is (E).

43.   What is the probability that a word formed by randomly rearranging the letters of the word ALGAE is the word ALGAE itself?

   (A)   1/120
   (B)   1/60
   (C)   2/7
   (D)   2/5
   (E)   1/30

The number of words that can be formed from the word ALGAE is $\frac{5!}{2!}$ (A repeats). ALGAE is just one of the words. Hence, the probability is $\dfrac{1}{\frac{5!}{2!}} = \dfrac{2!}{5!} = \dfrac{2}{120} = \dfrac{1}{60}$. The answer is (B).

Miscellaneous Problems

Example 1: The language Q has the following properties:

    (1)   ABC is the base word.
    (2)   If C immediately follows B, then C can be moved to the front of the code word to generate another word.

    Which one of the following is a code word in language Q?

    (A) CAB   (B) BCA   (C) AAA   (D) ABA   (E) CCC

From (1), ABC is a code word.

From (2), the C in the code word ABC can be moved to the front of the word: CAB.

Hence, CAB is a code word and the answer is (A).

Example 2: Bowl S contains only marbles. If 1/4 of the marbles were removed, the bowl would be filled to 1/2 of its capacity. If 100 marbles were added, the bowl would be full. How many marbles are in bowl S?

    (A) 100   (B) 200   (C) 250   (D) 300   (E) 400

Let n be the number of marbles in the bowl, and let c be the capacity of the bowl. Then translating *"if 1/4 of the marbles were removed, the bowl would be filled to 1/2 of its capacity"* into an equation yields

$$n - n/4 = c/2, \text{ or } 3n/2 = c$$

Next, translating *"if 100 marbles were added, the bowl would be full"* into an equation yields

$$100 + n = c$$

Hence, we have the system:

$$3n/2 = c$$
$$100 + n = c$$

Combining the two above equations yields

$$3n/2 = 100 + n$$
$$3n = 200 + 2n$$
$$n = 200$$

The answer is (B).

Method II (Plugging in):

Suppose there are 100 marbles in the bowl—choice (A). Removing 1/4 of them would leave 75 marbles in the bowl. Since this is 1/2 the capacity of the bowl, the capacity of the bowl is 150. But if we add 100 marbles to the original 100, we get 200 marbles, not 150. This eliminates (A).

Next, suppose there are 200 marbles in the bowl—choice (B). Removing 1/4 of them would leave 150 marbles in the bowl. Since this is 1/2 the capacity of the bowl, the capacity of the bowl is 300. Now, if we add 100 marbles to the original 200, we get 300 marbles—the capacity of the bowl. The answer is (B).

Problem Set DD:

1. A certain brand of computer can be bought with or without a hard drive. The computer with the hard drive costs 2,900 dollars. The computer without the hard drive costs 1,950 dollars more than the hard drive alone. What is the cost of the hard drive?

    (A) 400   (B) 450   (C) 475   (D) 500   (E) 525

2. At Peabody Tech, 72 students are enrolled in History, and 40 students are enrolled in both History and Math. How many students are enrolled in Math, but not History?

    (A) 30   (B) 31   (C) 32   (D) 33   (E) not enough information to decide

3. Half of the people who take the ACT score above 21 on the math section and half of the people score below 21. What is the average (arithmetic mean) score on the math section of the ACT?

    (A) 20   (B) 21   (C) 22   (D) 23   (E) not enough information to decide

4. The buyer of a particular car must choose 2 of 3 optional colors and 3 of 4 optional luxury features. In how many different ways can the buyer select the colors and luxury features?

    (A) 3   (B) 6   (C) 9   (D) 12   (E) 20

5. A bowl contains 500 marbles. There are x red marbles and y blue marbles in the bowl. Which one of the following expresses the number marbles in the bowl that are neither red nor blue?

    (A) $500 + x - y$
    (B) $500 - x + y$
    (C) $500 - x - y$
    (D) $500 + x + y$
    (E) $500 - x - y/2$

6. What is 0.12345 rounded to the nearest thousandth?

    (A) 0.12   (B) 0.123   (C) 0.1235   (D) 0.1234   (E) 0.12346

$$\frac{v+w}{x/yz}$$

7. To halve the value of the expression above by doubling exactly one of the variables, one must double which one of the following variables?

    (A) v (B) w (C) x (D) y (E) z

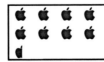

8. The picture above represents 4,250 apples. How many apples does each stand for?

    (A) 400   (B) 450   (C) 500   (D) 625   (E) 710

Answers and Solutions to Problem Set DD

1.   Let C be the cost of the computer without the hard drive, and let H be the cost of the hard drive. Then translating *"The computer with the hard drive costs 2,900 dollars"* into an equation yields

$$C + H = 2,900$$

Next, translating *"The computer without the hard drive costs 1,950 dollars more than the hard drive alone"* into an equation yields

$$C = H + 1,950$$

Combining these equations, we get the system:

$$C + H = 2,900$$
$$C = H + 1,950$$

Solving this system for H, yields $H = 475$. The answer is (C).

2.   The given information does tell us the number of History students who are <u>not</u> taking Math—32; however, the statements do not tell us the number of students enrolled in Math. The following Venn diagrams show two scenarios that satisfy the given information. Yet in the first case, less than 32 students are enrolled in Math; and in the second case, more than 32 students enrolled in Math:

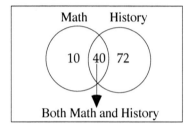

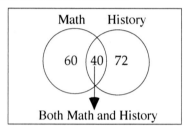

The answer is (E).

3.   Many students mistakenly think that the given information implies the average is 21. Suppose just 2 people take the test and one scores 23 (above 21) and the other scores 20 (below 21). Clearly, the average score for the two test-takers is not 21. The answer is (E).

4.   Let A, B, C stand for the three colors, and let W, X, Y, Z stand for the four luxury features. There are three ways of selecting the colors:

| A | B | | A | C | | B | C |

There are four ways of selecting the luxury features:

| W | X | Y | | W | Y | Z | | W | X | Z | | X | Y | Z |

Hence, there are $3 \times 4 = 12$ ways of selecting all the features. The answer is (D).

5.   There are $x + y$ red and blue marbles in the bowl. Subtracting this from the total of 500 marbles yields the number of marbles that are neither red nor blue:

$$500 - (x + y) = 500 - x - y$$

Hence, the answer is (C).

6.   The convention used for rounding numbers is _"if the following digit is less than five, then the preceding digit is not changed. But if the following digit is greater than or equal to five, then the preceding digit is increased by one."_

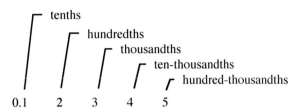

Since 3 is in the thousands position and the following digit, 4, is less than 5, the digit 3 is not changed. Hence, rounded to the nearest thousandth 0.12345, is 0.123. The answer is (B).

7.   Doubling the x in the expression yields $\dfrac{v+w}{2x/yz} = \dfrac{1}{2}\left(\dfrac{v+w}{x/yz}\right)$. Since we have written the expression as 1/2 times the original expression, doubling the x halved the original expression. The answer is (C).

8.   There are 8.5 apples in the picture. Dividing the total number of apples by 8.5 yields $\dfrac{4,250}{8.5} = 500$.

Part Two

Summary of Math Properties

Arithmetic

1. A *prime number* is an integer that is divisible only by itself and 1.
2. An even number is divisible by 2, and can be written as $2x$.
3. An odd number is not divisible by 2, and can be written as $2x + 1$.
4. Division by zero is undefined.
5. Perfect squares: $1, 4, 9, 16, 25, 36, 49, 64, 81 \ldots$
6. Perfect cubes: $1, 8, 27, 64, 125 \ldots$
7. If the last digit of a integer is 0, 2, 4, 6, or 8, then it is divisible by 2.
8. An integer is divisible by 3 if the sum of its digits is divisible by 3.
9. If the last digit of a integer is 0 or 5, then it is divisible by 5.
10. Miscellaneous Properties of Positive and Negative Numbers:

    A. The product (quotient) of positive numbers is positive.
    B. The product (quotient) of a positive number and a negative number is negative.
    C. The product (quotient) of an even number of negative numbers is positive.
    D. The product (quotient) of an odd number of negative numbers is negative.
    E. The sum of negative numbers is negative.
    F. A number raised to an even exponent is greater than or equal to zero.

$$even \times even = even$$
$$odd \times odd = odd$$
$$even \times odd = even$$

$$even + even = even$$
$$odd + odd = even$$
$$even + odd = odd$$

11. Consecutive integers are written as $x, x + 1, x + 2, \ldots$
12. Consecutive even or odd integers are written as $x, x + 2, x + 4, \ldots$
13. The integer zero is neither positive nor negative, but it is even: $0 = 2 \cdot 0$.
14. Commutative property: $x + y = y + x$. Example: $5 + 4 = 4 + 5$.
15. Associative property: $(x + y) + z = x + (y + z)$. Example: $(1 + 2) + 3 = 1 + (2 + 3)$.
16. Order of operations: Parentheses, Exponents, Multiplication, Division, Addition, Subtraction.
17. $-\dfrac{x}{y} = \dfrac{-x}{y} = \dfrac{x}{-y}$. Example: $-\dfrac{2}{3} = \dfrac{-2}{3} = \dfrac{2}{-3}$
18.
$$33\tfrac{1}{3}\% = \tfrac{1}{3} \qquad 20\% = \tfrac{1}{5}$$
$$66\tfrac{2}{3}\% = \tfrac{2}{3} \qquad 40\% = \tfrac{2}{5}$$
$$25\% = \tfrac{1}{4} \qquad 60\% = \tfrac{3}{5}$$
$$50\% = \tfrac{1}{2} \qquad 80\% = \tfrac{4}{5}$$

19.

$$\frac{1}{100} = .01 \qquad \frac{1}{10} = .1 \qquad \frac{2}{5} = .4$$

$$\frac{1}{50} = .02 \qquad \frac{1}{5} = .2 \qquad \frac{1}{2} = .5$$

$$\frac{1}{25} = .04 \qquad \frac{1}{4} = .25 \qquad \frac{2}{3} = .666...$$

$$\frac{1}{20} = .05 \qquad \frac{1}{3} = .333... \qquad \frac{3}{4} = .75$$

20.   Common measurements:
      1 foot = 12 inches
      1 yard = 3 feet
      1 quart = 2 pints
      1 gallon = 4 quarts
      1 pound = 16 ounces

21.   Important approximations: $\sqrt{2} \approx 1.4 \qquad \sqrt{3} \approx 1.7 \qquad \pi \approx 3.14$

22.   *"The remainder is r when p is divided by q"* means $p = qz + r$; the integer z is called the quotient. For instance, *"The remainder is 1 when 7 is divided by 3"* means $7 = 3 \cdot 2 + 1$.

23. $Probability = \dfrac{number\ of\ outcomes}{total\ number\ of\ possible\ outcomes}$

Algebra

24.   Multiplying or dividing both sides of an inequality by a negative number reverses the inequality. That is, if $x > y$ and $c < 0$, then $cx < cy$.

25.   Transitive Property: If $x < y$ and $y < z$, then $x < z$.

26.   Like Inequalities Can Be Added: If $x < y$ and $w < z$, then $x + w < y + z$.

27.   Rules for exponents:

$$x^a \cdot x^b = x^{a+b} \qquad \text{Caution, } x^a + x^b \neq x^{a+b}$$

$$\left(x^a\right)^b = x^{ab}$$

$$\left(xy\right)^a = x^a \cdot y^a$$

$$\left(\frac{x}{y}\right)^a = \frac{x^a}{y^a}$$

$$\frac{x^a}{x^b} = x^{a-b}, \text{if } a > b. \qquad \frac{x^a}{x^b} = \frac{1}{x^{b-a}}, \text{if } b > a.$$

$$x^0 = 1$$

28.   Rules for roots:

$$\sqrt[n]{xy} = \sqrt[n]{x}\sqrt[n]{y} \qquad\qquad \text{For example, } \sqrt{3x} = \sqrt{3}\sqrt{x}.$$

$$\sqrt[n]{\frac{x}{y}} = \frac{\sqrt[n]{x}}{\sqrt[n]{y}} \qquad\qquad \text{For example, } \sqrt[3]{\frac{x}{8}} = \frac{\sqrt[3]{x}}{\sqrt[3]{8}} = \frac{\sqrt[3]{x}}{2}.$$

$$\text{Caution: } \sqrt[n]{x+y} \neq \sqrt[n]{x} + \sqrt[n]{y}.$$

29. Factoring formulas:

$$x(y + z) = xy + xz$$
$$x^2 - y^2 = (x + y)(x - y)$$
$$(x - y)^2 = x^2 - 2xy + y^2$$
$$(x + y)^2 = x^2 + 2xy + y^2$$
$$-(x - y) = y - x$$

30. Adding, multiplying, and dividing fractions:

$$\frac{x}{y} + \frac{z}{y} = \frac{x + z}{y} \quad \text{and} \quad \frac{x}{y} - \frac{z}{y} = \frac{x - z}{y}$$
   Example: $\frac{2}{4} + \frac{3}{4} = \frac{2 + 3}{4} = \frac{5}{4}$.

$$\frac{w}{x} \cdot \frac{y}{z} = \frac{wy}{xz}$$
   Example: $\frac{1}{2} \cdot \frac{3}{4} = \frac{1 \cdot 3}{2 \cdot 4} = \frac{3}{8}$.

$$\frac{w}{x} \div \frac{y}{z} = \frac{w}{x} \cdot \frac{z}{y}$$
   Example: $\frac{1}{2} \div \frac{3}{4} = \frac{1}{2} \cdot \frac{4}{3} = \frac{4}{6} = \frac{2}{3}$.

31. $x\% = \dfrac{x}{100}$

32. Quadratic Formula: $x = \dfrac{-b \pm \sqrt{b^2 - 4ac}}{2a}$ are the solutions of the equation $ax^2 + bx + c = 0$.

Geometry

33. There are four major types of angle measures:

An **acute angle** has measure less than 90°:

A **right angle** has measure 90°:

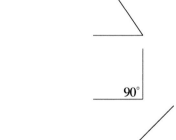

$90°$

An **obtuse angle** has measure greater than 90°:

A **straight angle** has measure 180°:

$y°$ $x°$ $x + y = 180°$

34. Two angles are supplementary if their angle sum is 180°:

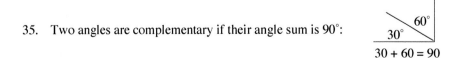

$45°$ $135°$

$45 + 135 = 180$

35. Two angles are complementary if their angle sum is 90°:

$60°$
$30°$

$30 + 60 = 90$

36.   Perpendicular lines meet at right angles:

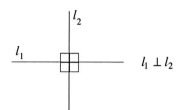

$l_1 \perp l_2$

37.   When two straight lines meet at a point, they form four angles. The angles opposite each other are called vertical angles, and they are congruent (equal). In the figure to the right, $a = b$, and $c = d$.

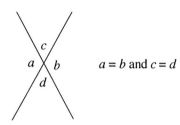

$a = b$ and $c = d$

38.   When parallel lines are cut by a transversal, three important angle relationships exist:

Alternate interior angles are equal.

Corresponding angles are equal.

Interior angles on the same side of the transversal are supplementary.

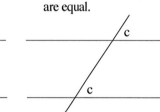

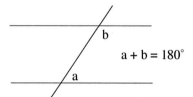

$a + b = 180°$

39.   The shortest distance from a point not on a line to the line is along a perpendicular line.

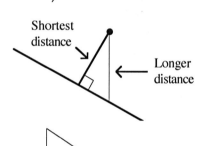

Shortest distance

Longer distance

40.   A triangle containing a right angle is called a *right triangle*. The right angle is denoted by a small square:

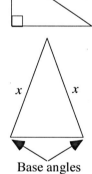

41.   A triangle with two equal sides is called isosceles. The angles opposite the equal sides are called the base angles:

x x

Base angles

42.   In an equilateral triangle, all three sides are equal and each angle is 60°:

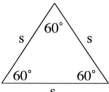

43. The altitude to the base of an isosceles or equilateral triangle bisects the base and bisects the vertex angle:

Isosceles: 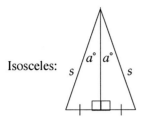   Equilateral: $h = \dfrac{s\sqrt{3}}{2}$

44. The angle sum of a triangle is 180°:

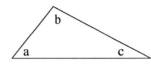 $a + b + c = 180°$

45. The area of a triangle is $\dfrac{1}{2}bh$, where b is the base and h is the height.

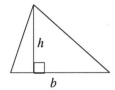   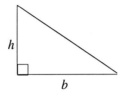   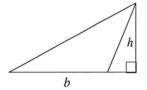 $A = \dfrac{1}{2}bh$

46. In a triangle, the longer side is opposite the larger angle, and vice versa:

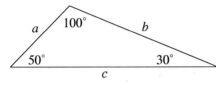   50° is larger than 30°, so side b is longer than side a.

47. Pythagorean Theorem (right triangles only): The square of the hypotenuse is equal to the sum of the squares of the legs.

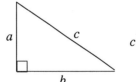 $c^2 = a^2 + b^2$

48. A Pythagorean triple: the numbers 3, 4, and 5 can always represent the sides of a right triangle and they appear very often: $5^2 = 3^2 + 4^2$.

49. Two triangles are similar (same shape and usually different size) if their corresponding angles are equal. If two triangles are similar, their corresponding sides are proportional:

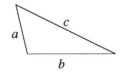   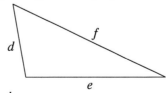

$$\frac{a}{d} = \frac{b}{e} = \frac{c}{f}$$

50. If two angles of a triangle are congruent to two angles of another triangle, the triangles are similar.

In the figure to the right, the large and small triangles are similar because both contain a right angle and they share $\angle A$.

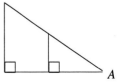

51. Two triangles are congruent (identical) if they have the same size and shape.

52. In a triangle, an exterior angle is equal to the sum of its remote interior angles and is therefore greater than either of them:

$$e = a + b \text{ and } e > a \text{ and } e > b$$

53. In a triangle, the sum of the lengths of any two sides is greater than the length of the remaining side:

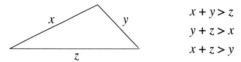

$$x + y > z$$
$$y + z > x$$
$$x + z > y$$

54. In a 30°–60°–90° triangle, the sides have the following relationships:

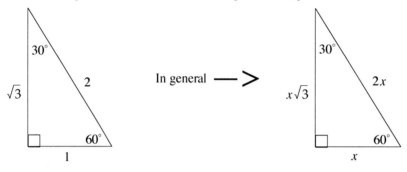

In general ——>

55. In a 45°–45°–90° triangle, the sides have the following relationships:

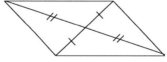

56. Opposite sides of a parallelogram are both parallel and congruent:

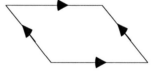

57. The diagonals of a parallelogram bisect each other:

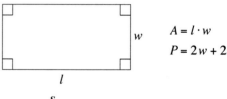

58. A parallelogram with four right angles is a *rectangle*. If w is the width and l is the length of a rectangle, then its area is $A = lw$ and its perimeter is $P = 2w + 2l$:

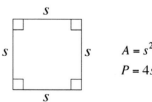

$$A = l \cdot w$$
$$P = 2w + 2l$$

59. If the opposite sides of a rectangle are equal, it is a square and its area is $A = s^2$ and its perimeter is $P = 4s$, where s is the length of a side:

$$A = s^2$$
$$P = 4s$$

60. The diagonals of a square bisect each other and are perpendicular to each other:

61. A quadrilateral with only one pair of parallel sides is a *trapezoid*. The parallel sides are called *bases*, and the non-parallel sides are called *legs*:

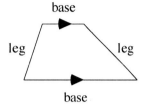

62. The area of a trapezoid is the average of the bases times the height:

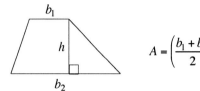

$$A = \left(\frac{b_1 + b_2}{2}\right)h$$

63. The volume of a rectangular solid (a box) is the product of the length, width, and height. The surface area is the sum of the area of the six faces:

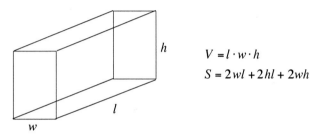

$$V = l \cdot w \cdot h$$
$$S = 2wl + 2hl + 2wh$$

64. If the length, width, and height of a rectangular solid (a box) are the same, it is a cube. Its volume is the cube of one of its sides, and its surface area is the sum of the areas of the six faces:

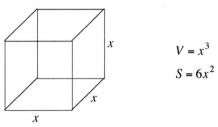

$$V = x^3$$
$$S = 6x^2$$

65. The volume of a cylinder is $V = \pi r^2 h$, and the lateral surface (excluding the top and bottom) is $S = 2\pi rh$, where r is the radius and h is the height:

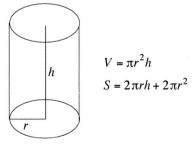

$$V = \pi r^2 h$$
$$S = 2\pi rh + 2\pi r^2$$

66. A line segment form the circle to its center is a *radius*.
    A line segment with both end points on a circle is a *chord*.
    A chord passing though the center of a circle is a *diameter*.
    A diameter can be viewed as two radii, and hence a diameter's
    length is twice that of a radius.
    A line passing through two points on a circle is a *secant*.
    A piece of the circumference is an *arc*.
    The area bounded by the circumference and an angle with vertex
    at the center of the circle is a *sector*.

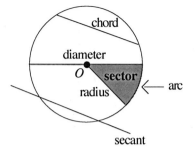

67. A tangent line to a circle intersects the circle at only one point.
    The radius of the circle is perpendicular to the tangent line at the
    point of tangency:

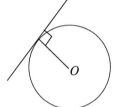

68. Two tangents to a circle from a common
    exterior point of the circle are congruent:

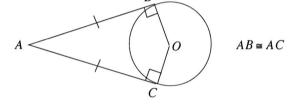

$AB \cong AC$

69. An angle inscribed in a semicircle is a right angle:

70. A central angle has by definition the same measure as its intercepted arc.

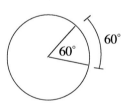

71. An inscribed angle has one-half the measure of its intercepted arc.

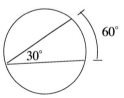

72. The area of a circle is πr^2, and its circumference
    (perimeter) is $2\pi r$, where r is the radius:

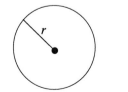

$A = \pi r^2$

$C = 2\pi r$

73. To find the area of the shaded region of a figure, subtract the area of the unshaded region from the
    area of the entire figure.

74. When drawing geometric figures, don't forget extreme cases.

Trigonometry

75. Trigonometric functions and formulas that you must know:

$$\sin\theta = \frac{opp}{hyp} = \frac{y}{r} \qquad\qquad \csc\theta = \frac{hyp}{opp} = \frac{r}{y} = \frac{1}{\sin\theta}$$

$$\cos\theta = \frac{adj}{hyp} = \frac{x}{r} \qquad\qquad \sec\theta = \frac{hyp}{adj} = \frac{r}{x} = \frac{1}{\cos\theta}$$

$$\tan\theta = \frac{opp}{adj} = \frac{y}{x} = \frac{\sin\theta}{\cos\theta} \qquad\qquad \cot\theta = \frac{adj}{hyp} = \frac{x}{y} = \frac{1}{\tan\theta}$$

76. Trigonometric identities that you should be familiar with, but probably do not need to memorize:

Sum or Difference formulas:

$$\sin(x \pm y) = \sin x \cos y \pm \cos x \sin y$$

$$\cos(x \pm y) = \cos x \cos y \mp \sin x \sin y$$

$$\tan(x \pm y) = \frac{\tan x \pm \tan y}{1 \mp \tan x \tan y}$$

Double Angle formulas:

$$\sin 2\theta = 2\sin\theta\cos\theta$$

$$\cos 2\theta = 1 - 2\sin^2\theta$$

$$= 2\cos^2\theta - 1$$

$$= \cos^2\theta - \sin^2\theta$$

$$\tan 2\theta = \frac{2\tan\theta}{1 - \tan^2\theta}$$

Pythagorean formulas:

$$\sin^2\theta + \cos^2\theta = 1$$

$$\tan^2\theta + 1 = \sec^2\theta$$

$$\cot^2\theta + 1 = \csc^2\theta$$

Half Angle formulas:

$$\sin^2\theta = \frac{1}{2}(1 - \cos 2\theta)$$

$$\cos^2\theta = \frac{1}{2}(1 + \cos 2\theta)$$

$$\sin\frac{\theta}{2} = \pm\sqrt{\frac{1 - \cos\theta}{2}}$$

$$\cos\frac{\theta}{2} = \pm\sqrt{\frac{1 + \cos\theta}{2}}$$

$$\tan\frac{\theta}{2} = \frac{\sin\theta}{1 + \cos\theta} = \frac{1 - \cos\theta}{\sin\theta}$$

Sum and Product formulas:

$$\sin x \cos y = \frac{1}{2}[\sin(x+y) + \sin(x-y)]$$

$$\cos x \sin y = \frac{1}{2}[\sin(x+y) - \sin(x-y)]$$

$$\cos x \cos y = \frac{1}{2}[\cos(x+y) + \cos(x-y)]$$

$$\sin x \sin y = \frac{1}{2}[\cos(x-y) - \cos(x+y)]$$

$$\sin x + \sin y = 2\sin\left(\frac{x+y}{2}\right)\cos\left(\frac{x-y}{2}\right)$$

$$\sin x - \sin y = 2\cos\left(\frac{x+y}{2}\right)\sin\left(\frac{x-y}{2}\right)$$

$$\cos x + \cos y = 2\cos\left(\frac{x+y}{2}\right)\cos\left(\frac{x-y}{2}\right)$$

$$\cos x - \cos y = -2\sin\left(\frac{x+y}{2}\right)\sin\left(\frac{x-y}{2}\right)$$

Law of Cosines:

$$c^2 = a^2 + b^2 - 2ab\cos\theta \qquad \text{where } \theta \text{ is the angle opposite side } c$$

Law of Sines:

$$\frac{\sin A}{a} = \frac{\sin B}{b} = \frac{\sin C}{c} \qquad \text{where angle } A \text{ is oppsite side } a, \text{ etc.}$$

Conversion factors:

$$1° = \frac{\pi}{180} \text{ radians}$$

$$1 \text{ radian} = \frac{180°}{\pi}$$

Reduction formulas:

$$\sin(-\theta) = -\sin\theta$$
$$\cos(-\theta) = \cos\theta$$
$$\sin\theta = -\sin(\theta - \pi)$$
$$\cos\theta = -\cos(\theta - \pi)$$

Trigonometric values for special angles:

Angle	$\sin\theta$	$\cos\theta$	$\tan\theta$	$\cot\theta$	$\sec\theta$	$\csc\theta$
0 or 0°	0	1	0	Undefined	1	Undefined
$\pi/6$ or 30°	1/2	$\sqrt{3}/2$	$\sqrt{3}/3$	$\sqrt{3}$	$2\sqrt{3}/3$	2
$\pi/4$ or 45°	$\sqrt{2}/2$	$\sqrt{2}/2$	1	1	$\sqrt{2}$	$\sqrt{2}$
$\pi/3$ or 60°	$\sqrt{3}/2$	1/2	$\sqrt{3}$	$\sqrt{3}/3$	2	$2\sqrt{3}/3$

Logarithms

Definition:

$$\log_b x = y \quad \text{if and only if} \quad b^y = x$$

Properties:

1) $\log_b xy = \log_b x + \log_b y$ Caution: $\log_b (x + y) \neq \log_b x + \log_b y$

2) $\log_b \dfrac{x}{y} = \log_b x - \log_b y$ Caution: $\log_b (x - y) \neq \log_b x - \log_b y$

3) $\log_b x^a = a \log_b x$ The "leap frog" rule

4) $\log_b b^a = a$

5) $\log_b 1 = 0$ This follows from the fact that $b^0 = 1$.

6) $\log_b b = 1$ This follows from the fact that $b^1 = b$.

Complex Numbers

Definition:

$$i^2 = -1 \quad \text{or} \quad i = \sqrt{-1}$$

The conjugate of the complex number $a + bi$ is $a - bi$.

The absolute value of the complex number $a + bi$ is $|a + bi| = \sqrt{a^2 + b^2}$.

For complex numbers, $\sqrt{x}\sqrt{y} \neq \sqrt{xy}$. To avoid this error, and others like it, always replace $\sqrt{-1}$ with i before performing any algebraic operations.

Matrices

To add two matrices, just add their corresponding elements:

$$\begin{bmatrix} a & b \\ c & d \end{bmatrix} + \begin{bmatrix} e & f \\ g & h \end{bmatrix} = \begin{bmatrix} a+e & b+f \\ c+g & d+h \end{bmatrix}$$

To subtract two matrices, just subtract their corresponding elements:

$$\begin{bmatrix} a & b \\ c & d \end{bmatrix} - \begin{bmatrix} e & f \\ g & h \end{bmatrix} = \begin{bmatrix} a-e & b-f \\ c-g & d-h \end{bmatrix}$$

The *zero matrix*, appropriately enough, has zeros for all its entries:

$$\begin{bmatrix} 0 & 0 & 0 \end{bmatrix} \qquad \begin{bmatrix} 0 & 0 \\ 0 & 0 \end{bmatrix} \qquad \begin{bmatrix} 0 & 0 & 0 \\ 0 & 0 & 0 \\ 0 & 0 & 0 \end{bmatrix}$$

To multiply a matrix by a number, just multiply each element of the matrix by the number:

$$2\begin{bmatrix} 1 & 0 \\ 3 & \pi \end{bmatrix} = \begin{bmatrix} 2 \cdot 1 & 2 \cdot 0 \\ 2 \cdot 3 & 2 \cdot \pi \end{bmatrix} = \begin{bmatrix} 2 & 0 \\ 6 & 2\pi \end{bmatrix}$$

To multiply two matrices, multiply the elements in each row of the first matrix by the corresponding elements in each column of the second matrix.

$$\begin{bmatrix} a & b \\ c & d \end{bmatrix}\begin{bmatrix} e & f \\ g & h \end{bmatrix} = \begin{bmatrix} ae+bg & af+bh \\ ce+dg & cf+dh \end{bmatrix}$$

Miscellaneous

77. To compare two fractions, cross-multiply. The larger product will be on the same side as the larger fraction.

78. Taking the square root of a fraction between 0 and 1 makes it larger.

     Caution: This is not true for fractions greater than 1. For example, $\sqrt{\dfrac{9}{4}} = \dfrac{3}{2}$. But $\dfrac{3}{2} < \dfrac{9}{4}$.

79. Squaring a fraction between 0 and 1 makes it smaller.

80. $ax^2 \neq (ax)^2$. In fact, $a^2x^2 = (ax)^2$.

81. $\dfrac{1/a}{b} \neq \dfrac{1}{a/b}$. In fact, $\dfrac{1/a}{b} = \dfrac{1}{ab}$ and $\dfrac{1}{a/b} = \dfrac{b}{a}$.

82. $-(a + b) \neq -a + b$. In fact, $-(a + b) = -a - b$.

83. $percentage\ increase = \dfrac{increase}{original\ amount}$

84. Systems of simultaneous equations can most be solved by merely adding or subtracting the equations.

85. When counting elements that are in overlapping sets, the total number will equal the number in one group plus the number in the other group minus the number common to both groups.

86. The number of integers between two integers <u>inclusive</u> is one more than their difference.

87. Elimination strategies:
     A. On hard problems, if you are asked to find the least (or greatest) number, then eliminate the least (or greatest) answer-choice.
     B. On hard problems, eliminate the answer-choice "not enough information."
     C. On hard problems, eliminate answer-choices that <u>merely</u> repeat numbers from the problem.
     D. On hard problems, eliminate answer-choices that can be derived from elementary operations.
     E. After you have eliminated as many answer-choices as you can, choose from the more complicated or more unusual answer-choices remaining.

88. To solve a fractional equation, multiply both sides by the LCD (lowest common denominator) to clear fractions.

89. You can cancel only over multiplication, not over addition or subtraction. For example, the c's in the expression $\dfrac{c + x}{c}$ cannot be canceled.

90. The average of N numbers is their sum divided by N, that is, $average = \dfrac{sum}{N}$.

91.   *Weighted average:* The average between two sets of numbers is closer to the set with more numbers.

92.   *Average Speed* = $\dfrac{Total\ Distance}{Total\ Time}$

93.   *Distance = Rate × Time*

94.   *Work = Rate × Time*, or $W = R \times T$. The amount of work done is usually 1 unit. Hence, the formula becomes $1 = R \times T$. Solving this for R gives $R = \dfrac{1}{T}$.

95.   *Interest = Amount × Time × Rate*

Part Three

Diagnostic/Review Test

This diagnostic test appears at the end of the book because it is probably best for you to use it as a review test. Unless your math skills are very strong, you should thoroughly study every chapter of the book. Afterwards, you can use this diagnostic/review test to determine which chapters you need to work on more. If you do not have much time to study, this test can also be used to concentrate your studies on your weakest areas.

1. If $3x + 9 = 15$, then $x + 2 =$

    (A) 2
    (B) 3
    (C) 4
    (D) 5
    (E) 6

2. If $a = 3b$, $b^2 = 2c$, $9c = d$, then $\dfrac{a^2}{d} =$

    (A) 1/2
    (B) 2
    (C) 10/3
    (D) 5
    (E) 6

$$a + b + c/2 = 60$$
$$-a - b + c/2 = -10$$

3. In the system of equations above, what is the value of b ?

    (A) 8
    (B) 20
    (C) 35
    (D) 50
    (E) Not enough information to decide.

4. $3 - (2^3 - 2[3 - 16 \div 2]) =$

    (A) −15
    (B) −5
    (C) 1
    (D) 2
    (E) 30

5. $(x - 2)(x + 4) - (x - 3)(x - 1) = 0$

    (A) −5
    (B) −1
    (C) 0
    (D) 1/2
    (E) 11/6

6. $-2^4 - \left(x^2 - 1\right)^2 =$

    (A) $-x^4 + 2x^2 + 15$
    (B) $-x^4 - 2x^2 + 17$
    (C) $-x^4 + 2x^2 - 17$
    (D) $-x^4 + 2x^2 - 15$
    (E) $-x^4 + 2x^2 + 17$

7. The smallest prime number greater than 48 is

    (A) 49
    (B) 50
    (C) 51
    (D) 52
    (E) 53

8. If a, b, and c are consecutive integers and $a < b < c$, which of the following must be true?

    (A) b^2 is a prime number
    (B) $\dfrac{a + c}{2} = b$
    (C) $a + b$ is even
    (D) $\dfrac{ab}{3}$ is an integer
    (E) $c - a = b$

9. $\sqrt{(42 - 6)(20 + 16)} =$

    (A) 2
    (B) 20
    (C) 28
    (D) 30
    (E) 36

10. $\left(4^x\right)^2 =$

    (A) 2^{4x}
    (B) 4^{x+2}
    (C) 2^{2x+2}
    (D) 4^{x^2}
    (E) 2^{2x^2}

11. If $8^{13} = 2^z$, then $z =$

    (A) 10
    (B) 13
    (C) 19
    (D) 26
    (E) 39

12. 1/2 of 0.2 percent equals

    (A) 1
    (B) 0.1
    (C) 0.01
    (D) 0.001
    (E) 0.0001

13. $\dfrac{4}{\frac{1}{3} + 1} =$

    (A) 1
    (B) 1/2
    (C) 2
    (D) 3
    (E) 4

14. If $x + y = k$, then $3x^2 + 6xy + 3y^2 =$

    (A) k
    (B) $3k$
    (C) $6k$
    (D) k^2
    (E) $3k^2$

15. $8x^2 - 18 =$

    (A) $8(x^2 - 2)$
    (B) $2(2x + 3)(2x - 3)$
    (C) $2(4x + 3)(4x - 3)$
    (D) $2(2x + 9)(2x - 9)$
    (E) $2(4x + 3)(x - 3)$

16. For which values of x is the following inequality true: $x^2 < 2x$.

    (A) $x < 0$
    (B) $0 < x < 2$
    (C) $-2 < x < 2$
    (D) $x < 2$
    (E) $x > 2$

17. If x is an integer and $y = -3x + 7$, what is the least value of x for which y is less than 1?

    (A) 1
    (B) 2
    (C) 3
    (D) 4
    (E) 5

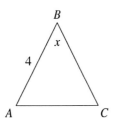

Note, figure not drawn to scale

18. In the figure above, triangle ABC is isosceles with base AC. If $x = 60°$, then $AC =$

    (A) 2
    (B) 3
    (C) 4
    (D) 14/3
    (E) $\sqrt{30}$

19. A unit square is circumscribed about a circle. If the circumference of the circle is $q\pi$, what is the value of q?

    (A) 1
    (B) 2
    (C) π
    (D) 2π
    (E) 5π

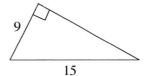

20. What is the area of the triangle above?

    (A) 20
    (B) 24
    (C) 30
    (D) 54
    (E) 64

21. If the average of $2x$ and $4x$ is 12, then $x =$

    (A) 1
    (B) 2
    (C) 3
    (D) 4
    (E) 24

22. The average of x, y, and z is 8 and the average of y and z is 4. What is the value of x?

    (A) 4
    (B) 9
    (C) 16
    (D) 20
    (E) 24

23. If the ratio of two numbers is 6 and their sum is 21, what is the value of the larger number?

    (A) 1
    (B) 5
    (C) 12
    (D) 17
    (E) 18

24. What percent of $3x$ is $6y$ if $x = 4y$?

    (A) 50%
    (B) 40%
    (C) 30%
    (D) 20%
    (E) 18%

25. If $y = 3x$, then the value of 10% of y is

    (A) .003x
    (B) .3x
    (C) 3x
    (D) 30x
    (E) 300x

26. How many ounces of water must be added to a 30-ounce solution that is 40 percent alcohol to dilute the solution to 25 percent alcohol?

    (A) 9
    (B) 10
    (C) 15
    (D) 16
    (E) 18

27. What is the value of the 201st term of a sequence if the first term of the sequence is 2 and each successive term is 4 more than the term immediately preceding it?

    (A) 798
    (B) 800
    (C) 802
    (D) 804
    (E) 806

28. A particular carmaker sells four models of cars, and each model comes with 5 options. How many different types of cars does the carmaker sell?

    (A) 15
    (B) 16
    (C) 17
    (D) 18
    (E) 20

29. If $f(x) = x^3 - 1$ and $g(x) = \sqrt[3]{x}$, then $\dfrac{f(2)}{g(1)} =$

    (A) 0
    (B) 2
    (C) 7/3
    (D) 7
    (E) 9

30. Let $f(x) = 1 - x$, for all non-negative x. If $f(f(1-x)) = f(1-x)$, then $x =$

    (A) 1/2
    (B) 3/4
    (C) 1
    (D) 2
    (E) 3

1. Dividing both sides of the equation by 3 yields

$$x + 3 = 5$$

Subtracting 1 from both sides of this equation (because we are looking for $x + 2$) yields

$$x + 2 = 4$$

The answer is (C).

2.

$$\frac{a^2}{d} =$$

$$\frac{(3b)^2}{9c} = \qquad \text{since } a = 3b \text{ and } 9c = d$$

$$\frac{9b^2}{9c} =$$

$$\frac{b^2}{c} =$$

$$\frac{2c}{c} = \qquad \text{since } b^2 = 2c$$

$$2$$

The answer is (B).

3. Merely adding the two equations yields

$$c = 50$$

Next, multiplying the bottom equation by -1 and then adding the equations yields

$$a + b + c/2 = 60$$
$$\underline{(+) \qquad a + b - c/2 = 10}$$
$$2a + 2b = 70$$

Dividing this equation by 2 yields

$$a + b = 35$$

This equation does not allow us to determine the value of b. For example, if $a = 0$, then $b = 35$. Now suppose, is $a = -15$, then $b = 50$. This is a double case and therefore the answer is (E), not enough information to decide.

4.

$$3 - (2^3 - 2[3 - 16 \div 2]) = \qquad \text{Within the innermost parentheses, division is performed before subtraction:}$$

$$3 - (2^3 - 2[3 - 8]) =$$

$$3 - (2^3 - 2[-5]) =$$

$$3 - (8 - 2[-5]) =$$

$$3 - (8 + 10) =$$

$$3 - 18 =$$

$$-15$$

The answer is (A).

5. Multiplying (using foil multiplication) both terms in the expression yields

$$x^2 + 4x - 2x - 8 - (x^2 - x - 3x + 3) = 0$$

(Notice that parentheses are used in the second expansion but not in the first. Parentheses must be used in the second expansion because the negative sign must be distributed to *every* term within the parentheses.)

Combining like terms yields

$$x^2 + 2x - 8 - (x^2 - 4x + 3) = 0$$

Distributing the negative sign to every term within the parentheses yields

$$x^2 + 2x - 8 - x^2 + 4x - 3 = 0$$

(Note, although distributing the negative sign over the parentheses is an elementary operation, many, if not most, students will apply the negative sign to only the first term:

$$-x^2 - 4x + 3$$

The writers of the test are aware of this common mistake and structure the test so that there are many opportunities to make this mistake.)

Grouping like terms together yields

$$(x^2 - x^2) + (2x + 4x) + (-8 - 3) = 0$$

Combining the like terms yields

$$6x - 11 = 0$$
$$6x = 11$$
$$x = 11/6$$

The answer is (E).

6.
$$-2^4 - (x^2 - 1)^2 =$$
$$-16 - [(x^2)^2 - 2x^2 + 1] =$$
$$-16 - [x^4 - 2x^2 + 1] =$$
$$-16 - x^4 + 2x^2 - 1 =$$
$$-x^4 + 2x^2 - 17$$

The answer is (C).

Notice that $-2^4 = -16$, not 16. This is one of the most common mistakes on the test. To see why $-2^4 = -16$ more clearly, rewrite -2^4 as follows:

$$-2^4 = (-1)2^4$$

In this form, it is clearer that the exponent, 4, applies only to the number 2, not to the number -1. So $-2^4 = (-1)2^4 = (-1)16 = -16$.

To make the answer positive 16, the -2 could be placed in parentheses:

$$(-2)^4 = [(-1)2]^4 = (-1)^4 \, 2^4 = (+1)16 = 16$$

7. Since the question asks for the *smallest* prime greater then 48, we start with the smallest answer-choice. Now, 49 is not prime since $49 = 7 \cdot 7$. Next, 50 is not prime since $50 = 5 \cdot 10$. Next, 51 is not prime since $51 = 3 \cdot 17$. Next, 52 is not prime since $52 = 2 \cdot 26$. Finally, 53 *is* prime since it is divisible by only itself and 1. The answer is (E).

Note, an integer is prime if it greater than 1 and divisible by only itself and 1. The number 2 is the smallest prime (and the only even prime) because the only integers that divide into it evenly are 1 and 2. The number 3 is the next larger prime. The number 4 is not prime because $4 = 2 \cdot 2$. Following is a partial list of the prime numbers. You should memorize it.

$$2, 3, 5, 7, 11, 13, 17, 19, 23, 29, 31, \ldots$$

8. Recall that an integer is prime if it is divisible by only itself and 1. In other words, an integer is prime if it cannot be written as a product of two other integers, other than itself and 1. Now, $b^2 = bb$. Since b^2 can be written as a product of b and b, it is not prime. Statement (A) is false.

Turning to Choice (B), since a, b, and c are consecutive integers, in that order, b is one unit larger than a: $b = a + 1$, and c is one unit larger than b: $c = b + 1 = (a + 1) + 1 = a + 2$. Now, plugging this information into the expression $\dfrac{a+c}{2}$ yields

$$\frac{a+c}{2} =$$
$$\frac{a+(a+2)}{2} =$$
$$\frac{2a+2}{2} =$$
$$\frac{2a}{2} + \frac{2}{2} =$$
$$a + 1 =$$
$$b$$

The answer is (B).

Regarding the other answer-choices, Choice (C) is true in some cases and false in others. To show that it can be false, let's plug in some numbers satisfying the given conditions. How about $a = 1$ and $b = 2$. In this case, $a + b = 1 + 2 = 3$, which is odd, not even. This eliminates Choice (C). Notice that to show a statement is false, we need only find one exception. However, to show a statement is true by plugging in numbers, you usually have to plug in more than one set of numbers because the statement may be true for one set of numbers but not for another set. We'll discuss in detail later the conditions under which you can say that a statement is true by plugging in numbers.

Choice (D) is not necessarily true. For instance, let $a = 1$ and $b = 2$. Then $\dfrac{ab}{3} = \dfrac{1 \cdot 2}{3} = \dfrac{2}{3}$, which is not an integer. This eliminates Choice (D).

Finally, $c - a = b$ is not necessarily true. For instance, let $a = 2$, $b = 3$, and $c = 4$. Then $c - a = 4 - 2 = 2 \neq 3$. This eliminates Choice (E).

9.

$$\sqrt{(42-6)(20+16)} =$$
$$\sqrt{(36)(36)} =$$
$$\sqrt{36}\sqrt{36} = \qquad \text{from the rule } \sqrt{xy} = \sqrt{x}\sqrt{y}$$
$$6 \cdot 6 =$$
$$36$$

The answer is (E).

10.

$$\left(4^x\right)^2 =$$
$$4^{2x} = \qquad \text{by the rule } \left(x^a\right)^b = x^{ab}$$
$$\left(2^2\right)^{2x} = \qquad \text{by replacing 4 with } 2^2$$
$$(2)^{4x} \qquad \text{by the rule } \left(x^a\right)^b = x^{ab}$$

The answer is (A). Note, this is considered to be a hard problem.

As to the other answer-choices, Choice (B) wrongly adds the exponents x and 2. The exponents are added when the same bases are multiplied:

$$a^x a^y = a^{x+y}$$

For example: $2^3 2^2 = 2^{3+2} = 2^5 = 32$. Be careful not to multiply unlike bases. For example, do not add exponents in the following expression: $2^3 4^2$. The exponents cannot be added here because the bases, 2 and 4, are not the same.

Choice (C), first changes 4 into 2^2, and then correctly multiplies 2 and x: $\left(2^2\right)^x = 2^{2x}$. However, it then errs in adding $2x$ and 2: $\left(2^{2x}\right)^2 \neq 2^{2x+2}$.

Choice (D) wrongly squares the x. When a power is raised to another power, the powers are multiplied:

$$\left(x^a\right)^b = x^{ab}$$

So $\left(4^x\right)^2 = 4^{2x}$.

Choice (E) makes the same mistake as in Choice (D).

11. The number 8 can be written as 2^3. Plugging this into the equation $8^{13} = 2^z$ yields

$$\left(2^3\right)^{13} = 2^z$$

Applying the rule $\left(x^a\right)^b = x^{ab}$ yields

$$2^{39} = 2^z$$

Since the bases are the same, the exponents must be the same. Hence, $z = 39$, and the answer is (E).

12. Recall that percent means to divide by 100. So .2 percent equals .2/100 = .002. (Recall that the decimal point is moved to the left one space for each zero in the denominator.) Now, as a decimal 1/2 = .5.

In percent problems, "of" means multiplication. So multiplying .5 and .002 yields

$$\begin{array}{r} .002 \\ \times\ \ \ .5 \\ \hline .001 \end{array}$$

Hence, the answer is (D).

13.

$$\frac{4}{\dfrac{1}{3} + 1} =$$

$$\frac{4}{\dfrac{1}{3} + \dfrac{3}{3}} = \qquad \text{by creating a common denominator of 3}$$

$$\frac{4}{\dfrac{1+3}{3}} =$$

$$\frac{4}{\dfrac{4}{3}} =$$

$$4 \cdot \frac{3}{4} = \qquad \text{Recall: ``to divide'' means to invert and multiply}$$

$$3 \qquad\qquad \text{by canceling the 4's}$$

Hence, the answer is (D).

14. $3x^2 + 6xy + 3y^2 =$

$3(x^2 + 2xy + y^2) = \qquad$ by factoring out the common factor 3

$3(x+y)^2 = \qquad$ by the perfect square trinomial formula $x^2 + 2xy + y^2 = (x+y)^2$

$3k^2$

Hence, the answer is (E).

15. $8x^2 - 18 =$

　　$2(4x^2 - 9) =$　　　　　　　　by the distributive property $ax + ay = a(x + y)$

　　$2(2^2 x^2 - 3^2) =$

　　$2([2x]^2 - 3^2) =$

　　$2(2x + 3)(2x - 3)$　　　　　by the difference of squares formula $x^2 - y^2 = (x + y)(x - y)$

The answer is (B).

It is common for students to wrongly apply the Difference of Squares formula to a perfect square:

$$(x - y)^2 \neq (x + y)(x - y)$$

The correct formulas follow. Notice that the first formula is the square of a difference, and the second formula is the difference of two squares.

Perfect square trinomial:　　　　$(x - y)^2 = x^2 - 2xy + y^2$

Difference of squares:　　　　$x^2 - y^2 = (x + y)(x - y)$

It is also common for students to wrongly distribute the 2 in a perfect square:

$$(x - y)^2 \neq x^2 - y^2$$

Note, there is no factoring formula for a sum of squares: $x^2 + y^2$. It cannot be factored.

16. First, replace the inequality symbol with an equal symbol:　　　　　　$x^2 = 2x$

Subtracting $2x$ from both sides yields　　　　　　　　　　　　　　　$x^2 - 2x = 0$

Factoring by the distributive rule yields　　　　　　　　　　　　　　$x(x - 2) = 0$

Setting each factor to 0 yields　　　　　　　　　　　　　　$x = 0$ and $x - 2 = 0$

Or　　　　　　　　　　　　　　　　　　　　　　　　　　$x = 0$ and $x = 2$

Now, the only numbers at which the expression can change sign are 0 and 2. So, 0 and 2 divide the number line into three intervals. Let's set up a number line and choose test points in each interval:

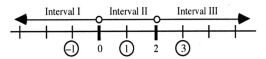

When $x = -1$, $x^2 < 2x$ becomes $1 < -2$. This is false. Hence, no numbers in Interval I satisfy the inequality. When $x = 1$, $x^2 < 2x$ becomes $1 < 2$. This is true. Hence, all numbers in Interval II satisfy the inequality. That is, $0 < x < 2$. When $x = 3$, $x^2 < 2x$ becomes $9 < 6$. This is false. Hence, no numbers in Interval III satisfy the inequality. The answer is (B). The graph of the solution follows:

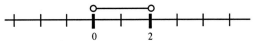

17. Since y is to be less than 1 and $y = -3x + 7$, we get

　　$-3x + 7 < 1$

　　$-3x < -6$　　　　by subtracting 7 from both sides of the inequality

　　$x > 2$　　　　by dividing both sides of the inequality by -3

(Note that the inequality changes direction when we divide both sides by a negative number. This is also the case if you multiply both sides of an inequality by a negative number.)

Since x is an integer and is to be as small as possible, $x = 3$. The answer is (C).

18. Since the triangle is isosceles, with base AC, the base angles are congruent (equal). That is, $A = C$. Since the angle sum of a triangle is 180, we get

$$A + C + x = 180$$

Replacing C with A and x with 60 gives

$$A + A + 60 = 180$$
$$A + A + 60 = 180$$
$$2A + 60 = 180$$
$$2A = 120$$
$$A = 60$$

Hence, the triangle is equilateral (all three sides are congruent). Since we are given that side AB has length 4, side AC also has length 4. The answer is (C).

19. Since the unit square is circumscribed about the circle, the diameter of the circle is 1 and the radius of the circle is $r = d/2 = 1/2$. This is illustrated in the following figure:

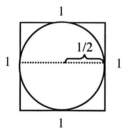

Now, the circumference of a circle is given by the formula $2\pi r$. For this circle the formula becomes $2\pi r = 2\pi(1/2) = \pi$. We are told that the circumference of the circle is $q\pi$. Setting these two expressions equal yields

$$\pi = q\pi$$

Dividing both sides of this equation by π yields

$$1 = q$$

The answer is (A).

20. Let x be the unknown side of the triangle. Applying The Pythagorean Theorem yields

$$9^2 + x^2 = 15^2$$
$$81 + x^2 = 225 \qquad \text{by squaring the terms}$$
$$x^2 = 144 \qquad \text{by subtracting 81 from both sides of the equation}$$
$$x = \pm\sqrt{144} \qquad \text{by taking the square root of both sides of the equation}$$
$$x = 12 \qquad \text{since we are looking for a length, we take the positive root}$$

In a right triangle, the legs are the base and the height of the triangle. Hence, $A = \dfrac{1}{2}bh = \dfrac{1}{2}\cdot 9 \cdot 12 = 54$. The answer is (D).

21. Since the average of $2x$ and $4x$ is 12, we get

$$\frac{2x + 4x}{2} = 12$$
$$\frac{6x}{2} = 12$$
$$3x = 12$$
$$x = 4$$

The answer is (D).

22. Recall that the average of N numbers is their sum divided by N. That is, average = sum/N. Since the average of x, y, and z is 8 and the average of y and z is 4, this formula yields

$$\frac{x+y+z}{3} = 8$$

$$\frac{y+z}{2} = 4$$

Solving the bottom equation for $y + z$ yields $y + z = 8$. Plugging this into the top equation gives

$$\frac{x+8}{3} = 8$$

$$x + 8 = 24$$

$$x = 16$$

The answer is (C).

23. Let the two numbers be x and y. Now, a ratio is simply a fraction. Forming the fraction yields $x/y = 6$, and forming the sum yields $x + y = 21$. Solving the first equation for x yields $x = 6y$. Plugging this into the second equation yields

$$6y + y = 21$$
$$7y = 21$$
$$y = 3$$

Plugging this into the equation $x = 6y$ yields

$$x = 6(3) = 18$$

The answer is (E).

24. Let $z\%$ represent the unknown percent. Now, when solving percent problems, "of" means times. Translating the statement "What percent of $3x$ is $6y$" into an equation yields

$$z\%(3x) = 6y$$

Substituting $x = 4y$ into this equation yields

$$z\%(3 \cdot 4y) = 6y$$

$$z\%(12y) = 6y$$

$$z\% = \frac{6y}{12y}$$

$$z\% = 1/2 = .50 = 50\%$$

The answer is (A).

25. The percent symbol, %, means to divide by 100. So $10\% = 10/100 = .10$. Hence, the expression 10% of y tranlsates into $.10y$. Since $y = 3x$, this becomes $.10y = .10(3x) = .30x$. The answer is (B).

26. Let x be the amount of water added. Since there is no alcohol in the water, the percent of alcohol in the water is $0\%x$. The amount of alcohol in the original solution is $40\%(30)$, and the amount of alcohol in the final solution will be $25\%(30 + x)$. Now, the concentration of alcohol in the original solution plus the concentration of alcohol in the added solution (water) must equal the concentration of alcohol in the resulting solution:

$$40\%(30) + 0\%x = 25\%(30 + x)$$

Multiplying this equation by 100 to clear the percent symbol yields

$$40(30) + 0 = 25(30 + x)$$
$$1200 = 750 + 25x$$
$$450 = 25x$$
$$18 = x$$

The answer is (E).

27. Except for the first term, each term of the sequence is found by adding 4 to the term immediately preceding it. In other words, we are simply adding 4 to the sequence 200 times. This yields

$$4 \cdot 200 = 800$$

Adding the 2 in the first term gives $800 + 2 = 802$. The answer is (C).

We can also solve this problem formally. The first term of the sequence is 2, and since each successive term is 4 more than the term immediately preceding it, the second term is $2 + 4$, and the third term is $(2 + 4) + 4$, and the fourth term is $[(2 + 4) + 4] + 4$, etc. Regrouping yields (note that we rewrite the first term as $2 + 4(0)$. You'll see why in a moment.)

$$2 + 4(0), 2 + 4(1), 2 + 4(2), 2 + 4(3), \ldots$$

Notice that the number within each pair of parentheses is 1 less than the numerical order of the term. For instance, the *first* term has a 0 within the parentheses, the *second* term has a 1 within the parentheses, etc. Hence, the nth term of the sequence is

$$2 + 4(n - 1)$$

Using this formula, the 201st term is $2 + 4(201 - 1) = 2 + 4(200) = 2 + 800 = 802$.

28. For the first model, there are 5 options. So there are 5 different types of cars in this model. For the second model, there are the same number of different types of cars. Likewise, for the other two types of models. Hence, there are $5 + 5 + 5 + 5 = 20$ different types of cars. The answer is (E).

This problem illustrates the *Fundamental Principle of Counting*:

> If an event occurs m times, and each of the m events is followed by a second event which occurs k times, then the first event follows the second event $m \cdot k$ times.

29. $\dfrac{f(2)}{g(1)} = \dfrac{2^3 - 1}{\sqrt[3]{1}} = \dfrac{8 - 1}{1} = 7$. The answer is (D).

30.
$$f(f(1 - x)) = f(1 - x)$$
$$f(1 - (1 - x)) = f(1 - x)$$
$$f(1 - 1 + x) = f(1 - x)$$
$$f(0 + x) = f(1 - x)$$
$$f(x) = f(1 - x)$$
$$1 - x = 1 - (1 - x)$$
$$1 - x = 1 - 1 + x$$
$$1 - x = x$$
$$1 = 2x$$
$$\frac{1}{2} = x$$

The answer is (A).

Study Plan

Use the list below to review the appropriate chapters for any questions you missed.

Equations: Page 155
Questions: 1, 2, 3
Algebraic Expressions: Page 196
Questions: 4, 5, 6
Number Theory: Page 29
Questions: 7, 8
Exponents & Roots: Page 178
Questions: 9, 10, 11
Fractions & Decimals: Page 144
Questions: 12, 13

Factoring: Page 187
Questions: 14, 15
Inequalities: Page 130
Questions: 16, 17
Geometry: Page 45
Questions: 18, 19, 20
Averages: Page 166
Questions: 21, 22
Ratio & Proportion: Page 172
Question: 23

Percents: Page 204
Questions: 24, 25
Word Problems: Page 228
Question: 26
Sequences & Series: Page 244
Question: 27
Counting: Page 250
Question: 28
Functions: Page 261
Questions: 29, 30

Index

LaVergne, TN USA
15 July 2010
189673LV00001B/13/P